TANKER CHARTERING

OUR WORD OUR BOND

TutorShip

Distance Learning Programme
of
The Institute of Chartered Shipbrokers

WITHERBY **Shipping**
BUSINESS

Witherby Shipping Business
A Division of Witherby Publishing Group Ltd
4 Dunlop Square, Livingston, Edinburgh, EH54 8SB, Scotland, UK
Tel No: +44(0)1506 463 227 - Fax No: +44(0)1506 468 999
Email: info@emailws.com - Web: www.witherbys.com

Published for the Institute of Chartered Shipbrokers

2011/2012 Centenary Edition

ISBN 978 1 85609 467 2

© Institute of Chartered Shipbrokers

British Library Cataloguing in Publication Data
A catalogue record for this book is available from the British Library.

Printed and bound in Great Britain by Bell & Bain Ltd, Glasgow

Published by

Witherby Publishing Group Ltd
4 Dunlop Square, Livingston,
Edinburgh, EH54 8SB,
Scotland, UK

Tel No: +44(0)1506 463 227
Fax No: +44(0)1506 468 999

Email: info@emailws.com
Web: www.witherbys.com

TUTORSHIP COURSE BOOKS

PREFACE

Gain a professional qualification and the knowledge to develop your career in the shipping industry by embarking on a TutorShip course of the Institute of Chartered Shipbrokers (ICS).

The Institute of Chartered Shipbrokers (ICS) is the professional body to commercial shipping worldwide. The ICS syllabus reflects the breadth and complexity of all the shipping sectors. The syllabus aims to be Relevant to and Respected by the shipping industry whilst being a Robust challenge to those candidates embarking on a career in shipping.

The TutorShip series of course books are aimed at preparing students for ICS examinations through a distance learning programme. Each course has a combination of self assessment questions and a tutor marked assignment at the end of each chapter. Additionally students are encouraged to submit a mock examination for marking. On enrolment of a TutorShip programme a student is allocated a tutor – an experienced practitioner in their sector – who will guide a student through the course by marking and providing feedback on the assignments submitted.

Although the TutorShip course books are an invaluable reference to any shipping company library their true value can only be realised by enrolling on a TutorShip distance learning programme supported by the expert knowledge of the approved tutors.

For further details on TutorShip courses please contact **tutorship@ics.org.uk** or visit **www.ics.org.uk**

TANKER CHARTERING SYLLABUS

N.B. Students will be expected to be able to draw simple plans of main vessel types and identify main characteristics and dimensions.

SHIPS AND CARGOES

Understand the basic procedures involved in the extraction of crude oil, of oil refining and its products and by products, Be aware of a simple refining model showing the differences between crude oils and products.

Thoroughly understand the basic constructional details and approximate tonnages and dimensions of vessels employed in the tanker trades.

Thoroughly understand the terminology of measuring ships including dimensions, actual tonnages – deadweight (dwat & dwcc), displacement (total & light); pseudo tonnages – NT & GT

Understand the information that is contained in Capacity and General Arrangement plans.

Understand vessel systems: Pumps, Pipelines, Manifolds, Cargo Heating (coils/heat exchangers), Crude Oil Washing (COW), Inert Gas Systems (IGS), Segregated Ballast Tanks (SBT), Double Hulls.

Thoroughly understand the nature of crude oil, its characteristics and the vessels used for its carriage – VLCC, ULCC, OBO, O/O, Suezmax, Aframax and their pumping systems.

Thoroughly understand the nature of the main petroleum products and their characteristics and the use of product carriers. Be aware of special requirements for dirty cargoes (heating) and light clean cargoes (high standards of cleanliness in tanks and pipes). Understand the nature of chemical cargoes and special vessel requirements including tank coatings and IMO Certification. Be aware of the problems of compatibility of grades and coatings.

Understand the commercial requirement for parcel cargoes and specialist role of parcel carriers.

Thoroughly understand the difference between liquid natural gas (LNG) and liquid petroleum gas (LPG). Be aware of vessels used, cargo tank types; pressure, semi-refrigerated and refrigerated and typical size ranges.

Understand the requirements for the carriage of vegetable oils and juice, and wine and the vessels used.

Thoroughly understand the critical importance of ship classification; the importance of oil company vetting inspections, questionnaires and oil company acceptability.

THE TRADES

Thoroughly understand the essential geography of the tanker trades and the cyclical nature of the oil markets.

Understand the impact of seasonal climate, weather and physical restrictions.

Understand where the main oil producing areas are located their comparative importance and the main routes for crude oil.

Understand the location of production areas, refineries, pipelines and oil terminals and the routes used for the movement of products, chemicals and gas cargoes.

Understand the structure of and typical locations of off abbreviations (SBM, SPM, FSO, FPSO).

Thoroughly understand the implications for the tanker trades and the practical effects of environmental protection and pollution liability legislation including MARPOL, USA OPA and EU legislation.

FREIGHT MARKETS

Thoroughly understand the role of the different market practitioners; Charterers, Shipowners, Operators, Oil Companies, State Companies and Trading Companies.

Understand the structure of the International Tanker Chartering Market and the relative importance of the major market centres.

Thoroughly understand the role of the Broker and its relationship to the principals as an agent.

Be aware of the tendency for only one Broker to be involved in tanker chartering.

Understand the advantages and disadvantages of different methods of communications.

Understand the structure and content of market reports and market indices.

Thoroughly understand the nature and impact of external factors affecting the market including natural catastrophes, environmental, aid programmes, political crises and the role of OPEC.

Understand the role and function of international organisations relevant to the tanker trades especially International Maritime Organization (IMO), Worldscale, Oil Companies International Maritime Forum (OCIMF), Intertanko, International Tanker Operators Pollution Fund (ITOPF).

Thoroughly understand the impact of e-commerce on market practice, its advantages and disadvantages. Be aware of the main alternative electronic solutions available to brokers.

CONTRACTS

Thoroughly understand the basic format and purpose and content of those main clauses common to all Charter Party forms.

Thoroughly understand the differences between the structure and purpose of voyage and time charters.

Understand the reasons for the use of standards forms of voyage and time charter parties and their suitability to different trades including a working knowledge of the content of commonly used standard forms including: voyage charters – ASBATANKVOY, SHELLVOY 6 and Time Charters – SHELLTIME 4, ASBATIME.

Thoroughly understand the importance and proper use of additional clauses and addenda and be able to draft simple specimen clauses. Be aware of the common standard oil company additional clauses.

Understand the individual rights responsibilities and liabilities of Owners, Charterers and Brokers which arise under the charter party.

Understand the use of consecutive voyage contracts and contracts of affreightment and be aware of the particular terminology required.

Understand the concept of Bareboat chartering and be aware of the main charter party terms.

BILL OF LADING

Thoroughly understand the role of the bill of lading in charter parties and in particular the liabilities of the shipowner to the bill of lading holder.

Thoroughly understand the requirements regarding delivery of cargo against bills of lading.

Understand the problems arising from the non-production of originals at discharge ports and practical solutions including the use of letters of indemnity,

Understand the particular problems for owners arising from bills of lading under time charters and the potential special problems of freight prepaid bills.

CHARTERING MARKET PRACTICE

Thoroughly understand the details required to quote a new order and the procedure of negotiations.

Understand all the customary abbreviations used during negotiation.

Understand the process of offer, rejection and new offer (counter offer, accept/except) and acceptance.

Thoroughly understand the details to be included in offers for both voyage and time charters and be able to draft a firm offer

Understand what "subjects" are, be able to identify some common examples of subjects and explain how they are lifted. Understand at which point the ship and cargo are "fully fixed".

Understand the role of the post fixture department and be able to identify and explain its functions.

Thoroughly understand the legal, tactical and ethical requirements of the market and the avoidance of conflicts between them.

Thoroughly understand the Brokers responsibility to the principal and the circumstances under which breach of warranty of authority (with and without negligence) might arise. Be aware of the consequent penalties.

Understand the importance of professional negligence and indemnity insurance for Brokers and be aware of the cover provided.

Be aware of the remedies available to the broker in the event of the principal defaulting on its obligations.

THE FINANCIAL ELEMENTS OF CHARTER PARTIES

Thoroughly understand the various ways in which freight and hire calculations (rate per day or per dwt/month) are made and the time when payment is due. Thoroughly understand that reasons for and calculation of additional payments due under charter parties and the appropriate clauses: for Voyage Charters – deadfreight, demurrage, damages for detention and freight taxes; for Time charters – payment for bunkers, ballast bonuses.

Understand the importance of clauses in time charters relating to late hire payment and the remedies available to the owner.

Understand the importance in time charters of performance claims and the nature of off-hire events.

Understand the arrangements for and relevant clauses regarding delivery, final voyage and re-delivery.

Thoroughly understand how commissions and brokerage are calculated and who is responsible for payment.

Understand the use of freight market derivatives as a hedging tool and be aware of the operation of the derivatives market.

LAYTIME

Thoroughly understand the importance of the clarity of notice of readiness clauses and be able to draft a concise clause.

Understand the procedure for tendering a valid NOR and common problems relating to acceptance.

Understand the point at which laytime commences and the circumstances under which laytime may be interrupted; understand what time is excluded from laytime.

Understand the application of the pumping warranty.

Thoroughly understand the extent and nature of the information contained in the Statement of Facts and how the Laytime Statement is prepared. Be able to calculate the laytime used and demurrage earned from appropriate data.

Thoroughly understand the principle of "once on demurrage always in demurrage" and the rare exceptions.

Be aware of the strict time-bar exercised in tanker demurrage claims.

CALCULATIONS

Thoroughly understand the structure of Worldscale and be conversant with its main features and use in calculating freight.

Be aware of the Owners and Disponent Owners cost base.

Thoroughly understand the essential procedures used to create a voyage estimate and be able to make complete calculations from given data using Worldscale and money rates.

Be aware of the main variables including change of loadline zones, fresh water allowances, draft limitations (including draft calculation – tpi/tpcm).

Understand the techniques used and be able to make the calculations to compare alternative routes, alternative voyages, compare voyage with time charter, compare Worldscale, $/tonne with lump sum rates and $/day with DWT/month.

Understand the reason for and means of calculation of Ballast Bonus in time charters.

GENERAL

Thoroughly understand the charter party clauses for the resolution of disputes including the application of arbitration and jurisdiction clauses. Be aware of the BIMCO Arbitration Clause.

Understand the roles of the commercial courts, arbitration and Alternative Dispute Resolution (ADR) in settling disputes and be aware of the differing procedures.

Understand the importance of Ship Owners' P&I Associations and their role in the context of cargo claims, be aware of the other sectors of owners P&I cover.

Understand the role of Intermediaries P&I Associations and, the classes of cover offered to Brokers and Agents.

Be aware of the importance of keeping full and proper records to assist in dispute resolution.

CONTENTS

3 THE MARKET STRUCTURE (continued)

4 VOYAGE ESTIMATING   69

5 CHARTERING MARKET PRACTICE   79

7 TANKER TIME CHARTERS (continued)

8 TANKER LAYTIME 125

9 FINANCIAL ELEMENTS OF TANKER CHARTER PARTIES 135

Chapter 1

HISTORY AND DEVELOPMENT

1.1   BRIEF HISTORY OF TANKER TRADES

Crude oil was first produced commercially in 1859 when 'Colonel' Edwin Drake struck oil at a depth of 60 ft. at Titusville, Pennsylvania, U.S.A. The discovery led to the building of refineries nearby with the major product, kerosene used for heating and lighting. The heavier oils were used for lubrication.

The first ship to carry oil was the 'Elisabeth Watts' in 1861, she carried 900 wooden barrels from Delaware to London. This trade increased and by 1864 about a quarter of US kerosene production, some 7 million gallons per year, was being shipped to Europe. The carriage of oil in barrels was less than satisfactory because the empty barrels had to be scrapped, it not being economic to carry the empties back for reloading. Although the barrels themselves have long been replaced we still use the expression 'Barrel' as a common unit of measurement of liquids in the petroleum industry; it equals 42 US Standard gallons or 35 Imperial gallons. In 1859 the 'Charles' was fitted with tanks to carry the liquid in bulk, but inefficient joints, leakage of cargo and gas, caused a fire hazard and she survived only 3 years before burning to the waterline. 1866 may be considered the start of the tanker industry when the German owned vessel 'Glukauf' was launched in Newcastle, England. She was a purpose-built petroleum carrier with eight sets of tanks running the full width of the ship and was a coal fired steamer with engine aft, a configuration which has stayed with tankers ever since.

Over the next twenty years shipyards in the north east of England built 200 tankers. The dominant tanker trades in this period were USA to Europe and Baku oil fields through Batumi in the Russian Black Sea to Europe.

The oil industry was developing in three areas. In America, John D. Rockefeller set up the Standard Oil Trust in America, whilst the Nobel brothers owned the Baku concession. In London, a trader named Marcus Samuel, whose business included importing ornamental shells from the Far East, ordered a fleet of tankers in 1893 naming them after shells. This was the start of the Shell International Company.

As the automobile industry grew so did the demand for gasoline. Coal fired boilers were adapted to burn the easier to handle fuel oil. In the early 1900s oil was being produced in the Caribbean Basin, principally Mexico and Venezuela. By 1908 oil was discovered in the southern part of Persia by an Englishman, William Knox D'Arcy and the Anglo-Persian Oil Company, the forerunner of British Petroleum, was established.

In 1913 the first Middle East refinery was built at Abadan, shortly followed by the export of refined products.

As world oil production rose so did the demand for tankers. The majority of tankers were owned directly by the oil companies, but the profits to be earned in this market soon attracted independent Owners. There was a shipping boom in 1911/12 when tanker rates for USA to Europe voyages rose from ten shillings per ton to seventeen shillings per ton. In the following year rates dropped to original levels and such cycles are regularly seen in the shipping market.

The size of tankers increased so that by 1920 vessels of 10,000 deadweight were being built. Over the next few years the tanker did not become much bigger, 12,000 deadweight being typical in the 1940s.

The 1930s are renowned for the depressed economic conditions and as with other trades the shipowners suffered with poor returns. In 1935/36 a scrap and build scheme was operated by the British Government offering 12 year finance at 3% interest for British shipowners. This period saw the formation of the International Tanker Owners' Association – the forerunner of Intertanko – which operated a lay-up scheme where tankers that were laid up were subsidised by the contributions from the vessels that were still trading. Known as the Schierwater Plan, it was considered to be reasonably successful in raising tanker freights, but at the start of World War II in 1939 this scheme was dropped.

By 1938 the world tanker fleet stood at 16.6 million tons. According to UN statistics, seaborne movement of oil reached 99 million tons in 1937 (470 million tons in 1960/1.8 billion tons in 1973 and 2.4 billion tons in 2005) making it the largest single influence on bulk shipping. Over three-quarters of the trade was in the form of refined products because refineries were built near the oil producing locations. The development of the crude oil carrier occurred after World War II. From the mid-1940s the world economy began a recovery which led to increased demand for oil and with it tankers. During the war the United States created welded prefabrication of a tanker the T.2 – a turbo-electric steam tanker of over 15,000 tons capacity and a speed of about 14.5 knots – many of these were sold to independent owners after the war and proved highly profitable during the first tanker boom in the 1950s.

By the late 1940s large oil finds were made in Saudi Arabia and other Gulf States and these were developed. The refineries were now being built in the consuming areas and the crude oil carrier was needed. By 1950 the largest tanker was 40,000 deadweight and the pattern of increasing size continued so that in 1979 the largest tanker (and incidentally the largest ship) the 564,843 dwt 'Seawise Giant', was launched (termed an Ultra Large Crude Carrier - ULCC).

In January 1988 she suffered very bad fire damage following a bombing raid on vessels anchored at Larak island. Subsequently, she was sold to Norwegian investors and underwent repairs at Singapore, resuming trading as the 'Jahre Viking'. As the single hull phase began to take effect she was sold to perform storage duties in the Arabian Gulf as the 'Knock Nevis'. Vessels of such a size are inflexible due to the few terminals (and charterers) that can handle the very large physical dimensions with large quantities of oil and have to be committed to major producers and refiners.

The growth in ship size was assisted by advances in shipbuilding and ship design techniques. The use of computers in design and building, together with improved steel quality meant that by the mid 1960s the first VLCCs 'very large crude carriers', vessels over 200,000 deadweight, were ordered by Shell Tankers. Initially the major oil companies maintained that such large tankers requiring a committed crude oil trade should be built only by the oil companies, but use of outside finance by independent Owners changed the policy and released capital for oil company investment in oil production and research. Also with nationalisation of production in several countries the vertical monopoly envisaged by major oil companies was destroyed and a degree of fragmentation of the industry occurred making it more difficult to programme ships above the VLCC size. These vessels came into their own with the closing of the Suez Canal in 1967 as a result of the Six Day War between Israel and Egypt calling for routing to Europe via Cape of Good Hope for any size of tanker.

Outline of a typical VLCC

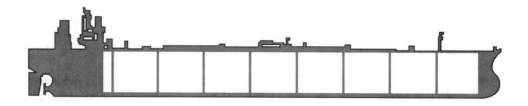

305,000 dwt - 24,000 hp

Midship Section - Single Hull Tanker

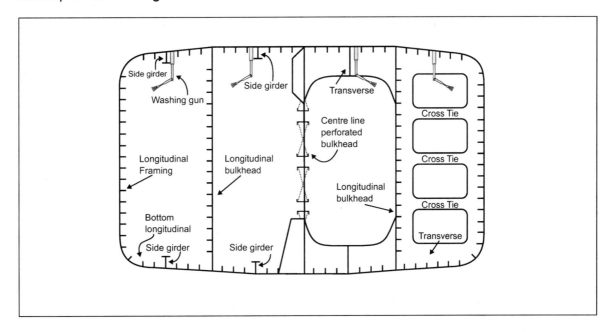

Midship Section - Double Hull Tanker

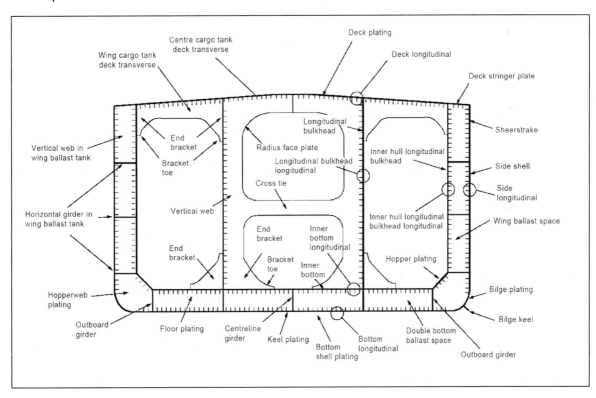

The demand for tankers, as for all vessels, is measured in ton miles. Thus, if route distance is increased, say due to political factors such as the closure of the Suez Canal, or economic factors such as the discovery of a raw material further from the consumer, so the demand for tankers is thereby increased. These factors led to continuing increase in demand until 1973. The thirty years between 1939 and 1969 saw a six-fold increase in consumption of oil from 10 million barrels per day to 64 million barrels per day. The tanker market suffered a very serious setback in 1973 when oil demand was curtailed by the imposition of an oil price rise by the OPEC producers taking the price of oil from $2.75 a barrel in July 1973 to $10.84 per barrel by January 1974, virtually a fourfold increase.

At this time the tanker order books stood at almost the same level as tonnage operating implying that if the newbuildings had been delivered the tanker fleet would have doubled, whereas the rate of increase in consumption of oil never called for an increase in ton/miles above around 12.5% making over-tonnaging a certainty. 1979 saw another steep rise in prices imposed taking the price very quickly up to $28 per barrel, the posted price eventually peaking at $34 by January 1982. The price is still volatile, dropping to below $10 in July 1986 and prior to the Iraqi invasion of Kuwait in August 1990 was oscillating at between $15 and $20 per barrel.

Question: "What is the current price per barrel?-"

Question: "'What was the highest price reached per barrel and when was that?"

All readers of this text should know the answer on a daily basis!

It is worth mentioning that such a rise in price and supply uncertainty made the search for alternative oil reserves in inhospitable areas such as the North Sea and Alaska an economic proposition and oil finds in these areas have affected the structure of the tanker market and as long as such supplies last have partly reduced the number of ton/miles needed to move crude oil to consuming areas.

The tankers delivered in 1973/74 came into a market that had no need for them, leading to a swift decline in tanker freight rates, vessels proceeding directly to lay up from newbuilding yards and eventually an increase in the number of vessels being scrapped. A depression that lasted almost a decade.

To sum up the oil market and thus the tanker market operates within a framework formed by the location of crude oil reserves in relation to the major consumers in the USA, Europe, Japan, China, Korea and developing countries.

1.2   TANKERS – THEIR CARGOES AND EQUIPMENT

1.2.1   Measurements

The most common measurements we come across in Tanker chartering are as follows:

Length Overall (LOA), extreme length of vessel.

Length Between Perpendiculars (LBP), length between the forward and after perpendiculars measured along the summer loadline.

Breadth Moulded, width measured inside the shell plating.

Beam, extreme width of vessel.

Draft (draught), the depth of the lowest point of the vessel below the waterline.

Depth, distance from the upper deck to the lowest point of keel measured at the ship's side.

Capacity is measured in barrels, or cubic metres and refers to the cargo carrying volume. The capacity for the carriage of oil is 98% of the total volume of the vessel, basically to allow for possible expansion with temperature changes.

Bow to Centre of Manifolds (BCM). Used to assess the position of the loading arm carrying the shore pipeline to the ship on an assigned berth.

Air Draft, distance from waterline to the highest point on the uppermost mast, or other structure (some masts can be stepped – i.e. the top can be lowered).

Keel to Top of Mast (KTM), distance from the keel to the highest place on the uppermost mast.

1.2.2 Tonnages

Lightweight (Lightship weight, light displacement tonnage), the weight of the vessel as built, including engines, boiler water, lubricating oil and cooling water system. It is this figure that is used when negotiating the sale of a ship for demolition.

Deadweight (DWT), the difference between the lightweight and loaded displacement, i.e. weight of cargo plus fuel, stores, water ballast, freshwater, crew and passengers. The deadweight of a ship varies with each draft. When describing a ship it is usual to use the vessel's Summer Deadweight (SDWT). Sometimes the vessel's deadweight is referred to as the Deadweight All Told (DWAT).

Displacement (Displ) at any given time this is the lightship plus deadweight of the vessel and is the total weight of water displaced by the vessel at the draft applicable (summer or winter or other).

Deadweight Cargo Capacity (DWCC), deadweight tonnage, less bunkers, water and constant weights, i.e. the cargo capacity of the vessel at any particular time at a given draft.

1.3 CRUDE OIL

When it comes out of the ground the oil is known as 'crude oil' and is a mixture of many different components. So that it can be used it must first be separated into the different products. This process is known as refining. The first stage is carried out at the oilfields where the gas, which is mixed with the crude oil in its natural state has to be extracted in order to make it safer for transport. The original method was to 'flare off' or burn the gas. Clearly this process was wasteful – to say nothing of damaging the environment by adding to greenhouse gas emissions – as much of the gas is a valuable raw material, so wherever the economics allow, the gas will be retained for further use including export. The problem with the particular gas which can be seen being flared off at refineries as well as at the oil wells is that it cannot be stored economically and used for other purposes. In refineries the gas can be used for heating at various stages in the refining process. Even so there may still be a surplus that has to be wasted, depending on refinery throughput, but if possible it is kept to a minimum.

One use of waste gases developed in Bahrain and Dubai was the generation of electric power that could be used for aluminium production in competition with producers using hydro-electricity. This process competes with production from hydro-electric sites.

The more crude oil that is produced, the more likelihood that dissolved gas will be available. This gas is known as Liquid Petroleum Gas (LPG), typically butane or propane.

1.3.1 Crude Oil Tankers, Crude Carriers

Crude oil cargoes are frequently homogeneous, and even when different crudes are carried in the same ship there is little need to worry about contamination because the oil will be refined before sale to the customer. Existing crude carriers, therefore, are relatively straightforward to build and operate. Crude carriers are used for the deep sea transportation of unrefined oil from producing countries to refineries. Typically they range in size from 50,000 deadweight to over 400,000 deadweight. These ships can usually carry one or two grades of cargo and have relatively straightforward pumping and pipeline systems for loading and discharging. In sizes below about 150,000 deadweight the ships are frequently capable of heating the cargo, when required, to maintain its pumpability. Before 1996, when all newbuilding tankers had to be double hull design, the single tankers had to be fitted in compliance with marine pollution prevention (MARPOL) requirement. For a crude oil carrier that meant the vessel must be fitted with a Crude Oil Washing (COW,) an Inert Gas System (IGS) and with Segregated Ballast Tanks (SBT). As these requirements were introduced they made older tonnage obsolete so that a number of ships were scrapped that had no economic means of segregating ballast without considerable loss of cargo capacity.

The single hull tanker is being phased out, with a deadline of 2010, although there are still some trading in 2011. In certain areas they may continue until 2015 or their 25th Anniversary, whichever comes sooner. This apparent contradiction relies on trades being available between countries that have not ratified the MARPOL regulations.

1.3.2 COW

When crude oil is discharged from a tank there is a certain amount of clingage – that is to say some oil sticks to the tank sides. At the bottom of the tank there will be residue such as sands or waxy deposits, therefore there is a cargo loss through this retention. To reduce this loss a system of tank cleaning guns is fitted within the tanks, during discharge approximately 10% of the cargo is re-circulated through the guns that are rotating. As the jet hits the tank sides some of the clingage is washed down. By the time pumping is complete very little residue is left and is easily removed by the usual cleaning processes. Once such tanks are empty, water ballast can be pumped in. When a tanker is not loaded with cargo, to proceed to sea in a safe condition, she must have the equivalent of about one-third of her deadweight on board as ballast. Prior to loading she would need to discharge such ballast and unless the tanks were clean before ballasting, this would be 'dirty ballast' which must not be discharged in port or historically within 50 miles of land but now restrictions are far wider including the Mediterranean, Red Sea, Baltic and North Europe, thus dirty ballast reception facilities would be required at the load ports. Since crude oil is a volatile and a gaseous cargo, the COW system causes a lot of flammable vapours to be released. In the early days of cleaning these large ships there were a number of disastrous explosions on tankers and as a safety measure tankers operating COW were required to inert the tank spaces, that is, to keep the oxygen content below 5% from the plant and 8% in the tanks.

1.3.3 IGS

This keeps the tank under pressure with inert gas produced by an Inert Gas generator or exhaust gases from the main engine and auxiliaries so that air cannot enter. These gases are scrubbed and cooled before being injected into the tanks. As the cargo level declines the inert gas is pumped in, thereby preventing the cargoes' gases vaporising and air entering causing an explosive mixture.

Before a fire or explosion can occur three factors must be present, i) fuel, ii) ignition, iii) oxygen. Hydrocarbons will not burn in air unless they are mixed in the correct proportions; the dangerous limits are between 1% and 10% hydrocarbons in air. These are known as the upper and lower explosive limits respectively. As far as a tanker is concerned it is not possible to remove the 'fuel' as long as the ship carries cargo. Despite strenuous efforts over a long period of time it is not possible to eliminate any source of ignition such sources are still possible. This leaves the oxygen as the only part, which can be eliminated in normal operations, provided the proper procedures are carried out.

Air consists of 21% oxygen and 79% nitrogen with traces of other gases. There must be a minimum of 11% oxygen present before combustion can take place. Hence IMO requirements are for a maximum of 8% oxygen by volume in the atmosphere of a ship's cargo tanks after they have been inerted.

Since inert gas such as carbon dioxide is obtained from the exhaust gases from the main engines and auxiliaries, a steamship has a constant supply of this because her boilers are always alight to provide steam for pumping or for the main turbine. On the majority of ships, which are diesel engined, an auxiliary boiler may have to be used or a special inert gas generator fitted in order to produce carbon dioxide or nitrogen, both being explosively inert.

1.4 PUMPS AND PIPELINE SYSTEMS

Cargo pumps are placed at the bottom of a ship, the height that a pump can push a liquid being limited only by the power in the pump. However, a pump can only suck a liquid to a height of about 10 metres. For ease of maintenance they are housed in special 'pump rooms'. There is a danger that gas can escape in a pump from the seals of the pumps so the pump room is kept separate from the rest of the ship and are usually situated forward of the engine room and aft of the cargo tanks. A tanker uses her own pumps for discharging cargo and loading and discharging ballast whilst loading is carried out using shore pumps. In the largest ships the most common form of pump is the centrifugal pump which is capable of a high discharge rate. In order to deliver the power necessary with a reasonable size and economy these pumps are driven by steam, diesel power or electric power. As none of these power sources would be safe in a pump room the pump is driven by means of a shaft passing through the engine room bulkhead and sealed in a gas-tight gland to prevent gas from entering the engine room. The centrifugal pump is limited to the range of products it can handle easily. It is not efficient with highly viscous liquids and on its own it is not able to drain the last metre or so of cargo in a tank.

Centrifugal cargo pumps

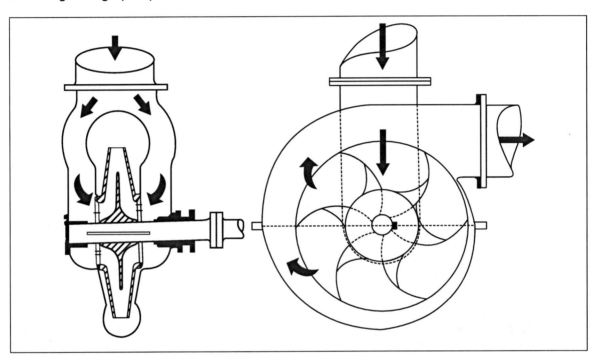

Reciprocating cargo pumps

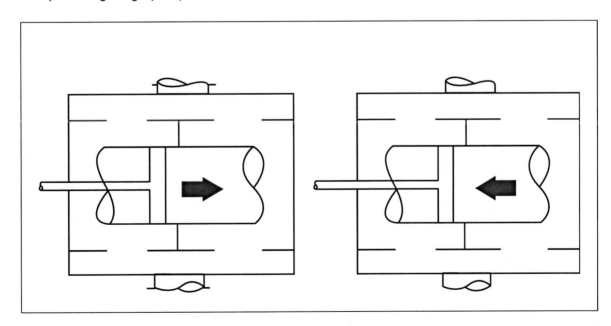

Some tankers are fitted with the reciprocating pump which is a double acting steam pump, the piston is driven by steam and it will pump liquid at each stroke. It is not a very powerful pump but it can handle a wide range of products and as long as liquid flows into the chambers it can be pumped. It has a high reliability but is not capable of a high discharge rate so it is found on smaller tankers. The pump is driven by saturated steam, that is steam and water vapour at comparatively low temperatures, the steam is required to lubricate the pump. The modest steam requirements mean that this pump can be sited anywhere in the ship and it is common to find pump rooms among the cargo tanks associated with a ring main.

Ships fitted with centrifugal pumps must also be fitted with stripping pumps. They are normally small capacity reciprocating pumps used to drain the last metre of cargo from the tank which the larger centrifugal pump is unable to handle being effectively a turbine liable to draw in air as compared with a piston that tends not to do so.

Some vessels are fitted with Vac-strip which is the trade name for a system which allows the large centrifugal pump to drain a cargo tank completely operating by using a smaller vacuum pump to maintain suction on the larger pump.

1.4.1 Eductor

When a liquid is forced through a constriction there is a drop in pressure just beyond the constriction, this low-pressure area can be used to draw up a liquid. This is used more commonly for tank cleaning because a high capacity pump is used to discharge a tank, and an economical pump for draining.

1.4.2 Screw Pump

Used more for chemical and vegetable oil tankers a low capacity pump that uses the action of two gears in mesh to drive the liquid. It is a positive displacement pump that can handle a wide range of liquids.

1.4.3 Deep Well Pump

Found on chemical and gas tankers as well as some modern product carriers, a deep well pump is situated in the bottom of each tank and thus eliminates the need for a pump room. Useful for chemical cargoes where each tank has its own pipeline leading to the ship's manifold. This is for ships where a very high standard of segregation is required and avoids the problems arising from trying to suck out a tank from deck level.

Pipeline System 25,000 DWT

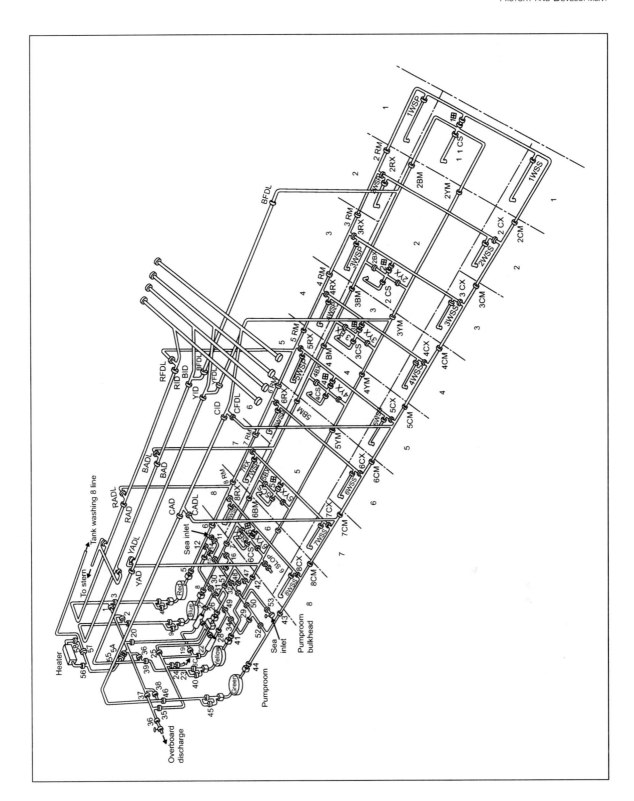

1.4.4 Pipelines

The type of pipeline system fitted is crucial to the operation of the tanker. The cargo has to be loaded and discharged through these lines and therefore the types and grades of cargo the ship can carry are determined by the type of pipeline system fitted. The main considerations that determine the choice of pipeline are:

Protection of the cargo. Must be possible to load and discharge the cargo without contamination from any other grade of oil or seawater ballast that may be in the ship. With a crude oil tanker this presents little problem, as these ships are seldom required to carry many different grades. Two or three grades of crude oil at the most and then because the

9

crude oil will be refined before it is sold to the customer a degree of contamination can be tolerated. Contamination is a vital consideration for product tankers because the cargo has to be delivered directly to the customer and a small amount of contamination can make the product unusable or even unsafe. Thus the product tanker has a more complicated and sophisticated pipeline system than the crude oil carrier.

With all tankers, if they are to take advantage of a segregated ballast system and load or discharge ballast concurrently with cargo handling, the port authorities' approval must be first obtained and their pipeline system must be such that there is no danger of oil coming into contact with the ballast water.

Speed of discharge. It is important that a tanker spends as short a time as possible in port handling cargo. Many terminals have limited jetty capacity and they therefore require a tanker to vacate a jetty as soon as possible. In the crude and product trades the majority of charter parties require a tanker to discharge her entire cargo within twenty-four hours. The restrictions on the speed that a liquid can be pumped through a pipe are the viscosity of the cargo, the diameter of the pipe, the number of bends in the pipe and the height of the receiving tanks, all of which will affect the 'back pressure', thus for fast cargo handling large diameter straight pipelines are preferred, with tanks at no great distance from the ship.

Pipelines are costly to install and maintain so an Owner will fit the simplest pipeline system that is required for the intended trade.

Pipelines are mostly made of mild steel and they suffer from corrosion, particularly in the ballast system that contains a mixture of air and salt water, ideal conditions for corrosion. In addition, the movement of the ship causes water to run backwards and forwards along the pipeline, which erodes as well as corrodes the steel. To prevent this each section of pipeline should be turned at intervals but this is an awkward and time-consuming operation and is frequently neglected. Many cases of cargo contamination occur because a pipeline passing through a tank becomes corroded and the oil passes through holes in the pipeline into the tank.

A new development is Glass Reinforced Plastic (GRP) pipes, which are being fitted to some ships for both cargo and ballast lines. These will not corrode and so should last longer than conventional mild steel pipes.

1.4.5   Pipeline systems.

There are a number of different pipeline systems fitted to tankers but in general they are all based on a combination of one or more of the following three main types:

1.   Ring Main

The pipes run round the bottom of the ship like a ladder. The main advantage is that there are always at least two lines running the full length of the ship so there are alternative routes for loading and discharging cargo. To make the system more flexible some ships are fitted with two ring mains giving four lines running the length of the ship. The ring main is more expensive than other systems but is the most flexible system of cargo handling. Crossover pipelines can connect the port and starboard mains, but care is needed to prevent the risk of contamination.

Ring Main

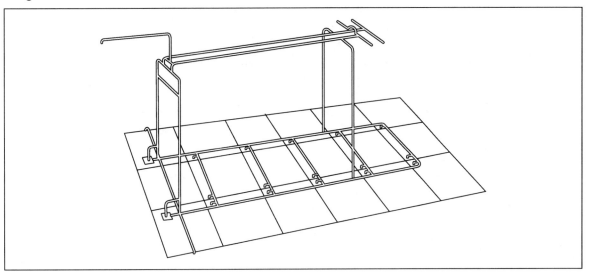

2. Block System

In this system only one pipeline runs the full length with the others running about two-thirds and one-third of the ship's length from aft. The system is less flexible because the forward section can only be reached through one line but it is a popular system for both crude and product tankers because it is simpler than the ring main and is ideal for ships fitted with three cargo pumps. There is no choice of the pipeline for the forward section of tanks.

Block System

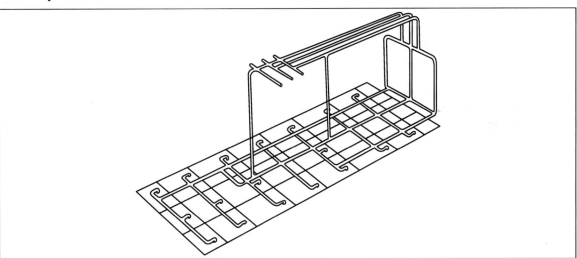

3. Free Flow

This largely eliminates the use of pipelines. Instead large valves in the bulkheads control the flow of oil between the cargo tanks. Only a very limited segregation, between centre and wing tanks, is possible and so this system would only be found on crude oil tankers. It is rare to find a completely free flow ship. This system is usually combined with another pipeline system, but it effectively commits the ship to one grade of crude oil.

4. Stripping Lines

The larger cargo pumps are not suitable for draining the last dregs of liquid from a cargo tank so the ship is fitted with small pumps known as 'stripping pumps'. These pumps are fitted with their own pipeline system known as stripping lines. Stripping lines are very much smaller than the main cargo lines because the quantities of oil to be moved are much smaller and therefore pumping rates are slower. It is important when segregation of grades of cargo is considered that the stripping lines are taken into account. A large pump would tend to suck air with oil and become ineffective.

5. Ballast Line – Segregated Ballast Tanks (SBT)

These are special pipelines used in conjunction with a dedicated ballast pump for loading or discharging clean ballast into segregated tanks.

There are no connections between the cargo and ballast lines so it is possible to load and discharge ballast at the same time as the cargo without any fear of pollution.

There may also be a separate stripping line for the ballast tanks. Where ballast lines pass through cargo tanks and wee *versa* there is always the possibility of pollution or contamination if the pipelines have been allowed to corrode to the extent that leaks are possible.

6. Decklines

The point where the ship's pipelines connect with the shorelines is the manifold, a section of pipes running across the deck somewhere about the mid length of the ship. The lines end with flanges to enable the shorelines to be bolted on. There is a range of different sizes of pipeline in use both on ships and in the different terminals at which the ship will call so short sections of pipeline known as reducers are carried. The ship will be supplied with a set of reducers so that the manifold can connect to all common pipeline sizes found at the different terminals.

7. Direct Loading Lines

These are loading lines that lead directly into certain tanks or into the pipeline system without passing through the pump room.

These are useful for segregating different grades of cargo but with some ships it is possible to load a complete cargo without any liquid passing through the pump, so that segregation is virtually guaranteed.

8. Stern Discharge Line

This is a pipeline with a loading connection at the stern of the tanker, used in some ports where the ship berths stern to the jetty. It is not popular because with only one line connected to the ship, loading and discharging rates are very slow.

9. Pump Room Lines

The most complicated pipeline system on a tanker will be in the pump room. The pipelines must allow any pump to be connected to any of the pipelines. Each cargo pump will be directly in line with one of the ships fore and aft pipelines, but ahead of the pumps there is a line reaching right across the ship. This is the bottom crossover and it makes it possible to connect any cargo pump to any of the main pipelines, or the sea suctions. There is also a top crossover, which allows each pump to be connected to any of the discharge lines. Connecting the discharge lines are the pump room drop lines. There is a bypass line for each cargo pump so that it can be isolated while loading.

10. Gas Lines

As well as allowing cargo into the ship it is important to allow for the air and gas displaced during loading to escape and to allow air or inert gas to be drawn into the tanks when discharging. While the ship is on passage solar heating during the day will cause evaporation of the cargo and the gas so produced must be allowed to escape before a dangerous pressure builds. During the night cooling will cause a contraction of the cargo and air or inert gas will be allowed to enter the tanks. In either case, unless steps are taken to relieve the pressure differential the ship's structure could be put under severe pressure with a possible fracture occurring.

During loading a gas mixture is naturally forced out of the tank into the air and rather than allow such an explosive mixture to gather at deck level it can be vented via gas lines up the mast.

It is now common to have a Closed Loading System (CLS) to avoid gas release.

Gas lines are of two main types. As a product cargo may be contaminated by gas, it is important that a gas from one grade is not allowed to enter a tank containing another grade. One method of achieving this is to use a device known as 'Martin high-jet'. This is a short gas vent attached to each tank. When loading or discharging the gas is ejected upward in a venturi effect. The other system is where gas risers are fitted on the masts and the lines from each tank run to the risers. In order to achieve segregation the gas lines may be split into two or more sections.

11. Pressure Vacuum Valves

When the ship is at sea spring loaded PV valves are used to allow the pressure difference between the tank and the outside air to be relieved. When the ship is loading or discharging these valves must be bypassed, as they do not have sufficient capacity to keep up with the ship's pumps. There must be spark-arresting gauzes in the ship's lines to prevent a flame spreading past the gauze into an explosive tank.

1.5 VALVES

Valves control the flow of oil through a pipeline. These can be hand operated by means of a spindle on the deck or power operated by remote hydraulic controls sometimes from a cargo control room adjacent to the remote tank level indicators.

The main type of valve used in tankers is the gate type, where a flange or spade is positioned in a seat to block the flow in the pipeline. A nut on the flange through which runs a screw thread from the spindle controls this. By rotating the spindle the flange is moved up and down, the spindle thus opening or closing the valve.

A tight valve seat on which the flange is located when it is closed maintains the integrity of this valve. This seat can be blocked by rust or debris and the valve will then allow oil to pass.

Thus on well-run ships there is a maintenance programme where the valves are all dismantled at intervals and any worn parts renewed.

Types of Valve found on an Oil Tanker

1. Tank Valves

These control the flow of oil into and out of a tank. They are always situated on the after end of the tank and frequently in one of the corners to aid draining the tank when discharging. From the valve a length of suction about 2 metres long terminates in an open end between 2.5 cms and 9 cms above the tank bottom (depending upon size of ships, tank, etc). This is known as the 'elephant's foot'.

2. Crossover Valves

These valves control the flow of oil in the athwart ships (side to side) direction in the pipeline system. This is used to enable two different fore and aft pipelines to handle two different grades without them becoming contaminated through the athwart ship sections of the pipeline.

3. Master Valves

Controls the flow of oil in the fore and aft direction in the pipeline. This is used to isolate a section of the cargo lines when segregating different grades.

4. Gate Valve

The valves in the ship's loading manifold where it connects to the shorelines. Drip trays must be fitted underneath because it is impossible to avoid some spills when the lines are being connected. It is important that these valves are never closed when loading cargo, otherwise the flexible lines connecting the ship to the jetty are likely to be pressurised and burst. The same applies to tank volves when switching the loading from tank to tank.

5. Bulkhead Valves

Valves found in the bulkhead between two tanks. They are used to allow liquid to flow from one tank to another. In a tanker with a free flow system this is the only way for the cargo to be transferred between different tanks.

6. Sea Valves

These are valves at the bottom of the pump room at each side of the ship, which may be connected by a pipeline. They are used during ballasting operations to allow seawater ballast into or out of the ship.

Sea valves are fitted in pairs for extra security and are sealed shut before loading or discharging is allowed to commence.

This is to ensure that the valves are not open during cargo operations to prevent the possibility of pollution following escape of oil through the sea valves. In the case of a claim against the ship for oil pollution, the integrity or otherwise of these seals is an important piece of evidence.

1.6   COMBINATION CARRIERS

These are hybrid ships known as the Ore/Oil carrier (the O/O) and even more sophisticated the Oil/Bulk/Ore (the OBO), which as the name implies is designed to carry 'oil' or 'ore' or other bulk cargo. The O/O and OBO are usually designed to carry crude oil or dirty products but the more modern vessels are designed to carry clean products and are differentiated by being called PROBOs.

Combination carriers are approximately 25%/30% more expensive to build than a single hull tanker, partly due to the extra steel required and partly due to the more complicated design and building techniques involved. The Owners buying such ships have the flexibility of using them either in the wet or dry trades as the market dictates. Alternatively it is possible to follow an oil cargo with a dry cargo, thereby reducing the ballast legs.

Typical Combination Carrier Layout

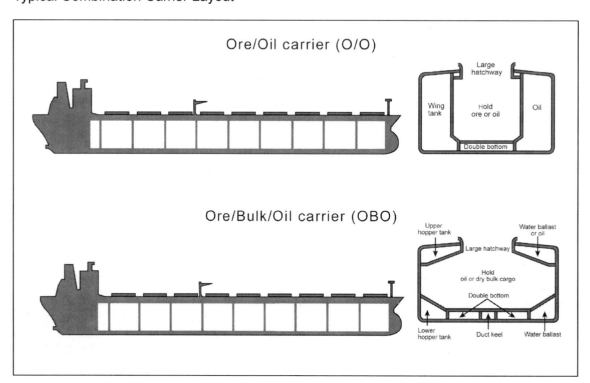

1.6.1   Product Carriers

When refined, crude oil separates into various grades or products. At the lightest end are the gasolines, kerosenes, gasoils and at the bottom the heaviest constituents known as fuel oils or residual oils. Product carriers may be divided into two types, the clean product carriers and the dirty product carriers. The clean product carrier requires a great deal of care in the cleaning of the tanks between each of the cargoes carried and to facilitate the cleaning the tanks are frequently coated with special paints which also serve to reduce the chance of corrosion within the tanks.

Dirty product carriers do not normally have such coatings but are usually fitted with heating coils to make it possible to pump the viscous high density grades of fuel oil that are being used today.

Typically dirty product carriers can be virtually any size up to about 150,000 deadweight. Clean product carriers are more usually up to about 70,000 deadweight. However, in recent years, as the oil producing countries have built refineries, the requirement for larger clean product carriers has increased so that today one finds such ships in the 115,000 deadweight range. In fact a Middle East refiner is experimenting with the carriage of Clean Petroleum Products (CPP) in vessels over 200,000 dwt (VLPC) – such vessels are dedicated to the carriage of CPP. Politics aside, is it more economic to site the refinery in the consuming area, or for the producer to invest in such a refinery.

Clean product carriers will frequently be able to carry at least four separate grades of cargo without risk of contamination. As in all tankers product carriers is that they are to be fitted with Segregated Ballast Tanks (SBT).

A Typical Product Carrier

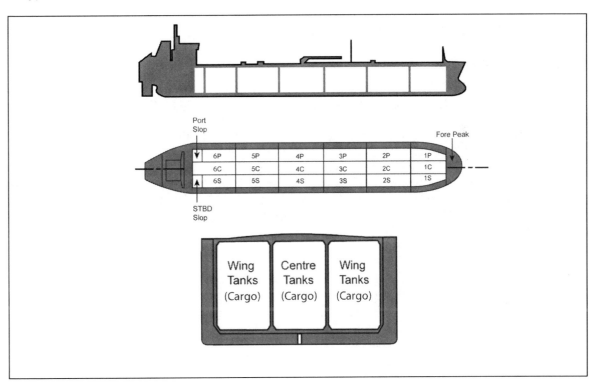

1.6.2   Chemical Carriers (Parcel Tankers)

There are two distinct trades for these ships, the bulk liquid chemical trades where a range of chemicals, many of which are extremely hazardous, are carried and the edible/vegetable oil trade. The hazards from the chemicals are not only those of fire and explosion, which are found on any tanker, but of toxicity, incompatibility and corrosion. In order to carry these cargoes in safety the parcel tanker has to be equipped to a very high standard and is, therefore, for her size a very expensive ship.

In oil trades it is possible to talk about allowable contamination but in these trades there is frequently no such thing and the tanks must be perfectly clean before a cargo can be loaded. The tanks on these ships are therefore coated with high-grade materials such as stainless steel, zinc silicate epoxy resin and polyurethane being the most popular. The purpose of these coatings is to prevent the chemical cargoes from reacting with the ship's structure and damaging the ship or cargo.

The secondary function of the coating is to make it possible to clean the tanks to the exacting standards required in the industry. The high quality of these coatings makes it possible to carry edible/vegetable oils, which share with chemicals the same exacting requirements for purity.

The high value and susceptibility to contamination of any of these cargoes means that some of the more sophisticated ships have a separate deepwell pump and pipeline system for each tank to increase the number of chemicals that can be safely carried at the same time and pipelines may be of stainless steel.

It is accepted that no amount of cleaning can remove all traces of chemicals from the tank, so in order to reduce the risk of contamination, the shipper will want to know the details of the last three cargoes carried in the tank before accepting it for a particular consignment.

Within this constraint an Owner will try to reduce ballast time to a minimum by carrying cargoes for a number of different shippers at the same time. The legislation for chemical carriers has for many years required that they should be double hulled. That is to say the bottom, sides and top of the cargo tanks have a void space between them and the ship's shell plating.

Even with product tankers the carriage of leaded gasoline will prevent the carriage subsequently of aviation turbine fuel and of course vegetable oils for human consumption as well as any other cargo liable to suffer from lead contamination.

1.6.3   Gas Carriers

Gas carriers are a highly specialised form of tanker. The two types of gas carried are known as Liquefied Natural Gas (LNG) and Liquid Petroleum Gas (LPG).

LNG – methane – is the product of a dedicated gas field and is carried in insulated tanks at minus 162°C at atmospheric pressure to keep it liquid. The first commercial LNG trade started in 1964 between Algeria and Canvey Island in the United Kingdom using two specially built ships – the *"Methane Princess"* and the *"Methane Progress"*. This was followed shortly afterwards by a major scheme for the export of LNG from Brunei to Japan. In 2005 a number of other trades to export natural gas from gas fields for example in Algeria, West Africa, Indonesia, Malaysia, Middle East and Caribbean are under way.

This diagram shows a typical Gas Carrier

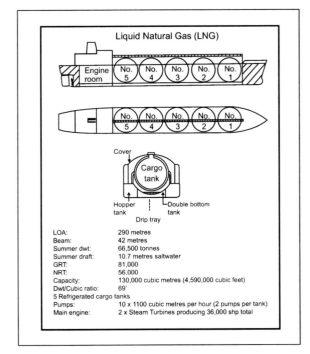
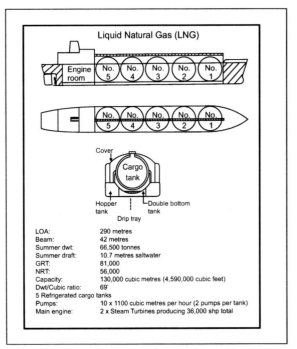

LPG – propane and butane – is the by-product of the oil producing process and is either kept under high pressure, 10-12 BAR or it is cooled to minus 50°C to keep it liquid. The LPG carriers may also be used in the carriage of chemical gas, ammonia, etc.

Commercially there is a fundamental difference between these two gases. LPG production is linked to the production of crude oil output. As a result the supplier does not directly control the quantities of LPG reaching the export market. Gas carriers are the most expensive cargo ships requiring a high degree of sophistication, not only in the building and running but also from the personnel employed ashore and afloat. The LNG carriers are usually built for certain projects and as such are not often seen in the chartering market. They require a dedicated supplier and receiver and fast transport with no delays due to the nature of the cargo.

1.7   SELF-ASSESSMENT AND TEST QUESTIONS

Attempt the following and check your answers from the text:

1.   What is the common unit of measurement in the oil industry and what is its quantity?

2.   How large was the biggest tanker ever to trade?

3.   Where can you look up the current price of oil and what is it?

4.   What system is used to avoid explosive gas accumulating in a ship's tanks?

5.   What is the most usual way for a VLCC to clean her tanks after discharge?

6.   Why are a tanker's cargo pumps placed as low as possible in the ship?

7.   What are the differences between LNG and LPG?

Having completed Chapter One attempt the following and submit your essay to your Tutor. Discuss the factors which led to the increase in tanker sizes and why this progress eventually halted.

Chapter 2

GEOGRAPHY FOR TANKER CHARTERING

It is assumed you have a good understanding of the basics of geography. That is to say, you know the location and names of the major oceans, the meaning of latitude and longitude, the purpose of charts, the wind patterns, the causes and effects of tides, currents, time zones and general distances.

In this Chapter we distil a lot of the foregoing information down to its relevance for tanker trades and expand on the various points where necessary.

2.1   CRUDE OIL

There seems to be little doubt among petroleum geologists that crude oil originates from organic matter of animal and plant origin which has accumulated in fine grained sediment in quiet conditions deficient in oxygen. The majority of crude oil found in commercial quantities has been in sedimentary basins. Crude oils are mixtures of hydrocarbons and carbons with as much variation between crudes in rocks of the same age as between crudes of different ages.

The sediment has been under pressure for millions of years with mud forming an impermeable layer that caps the oil. Sands tend to have porosity so that gas, oil and water (usually salt water or brine) fill the spaces in the sandstone forming a reservoir. Within the reservoir oil lies on the water and in certain cases there will be a gas cap. Crude oil under pressure will contain a significant quantity of dissolved gas – the amount being dependant upon the temperature and pressure of the reservoir. The reservoir of crude could be very heavy, viscous (i.e. thick) oil containing little or no gas to an extremely light, less viscous (i.e. thinner), straw-coloured oil containing a large amount of dissolved gas.

Cross Section Through an Oil Reservoir

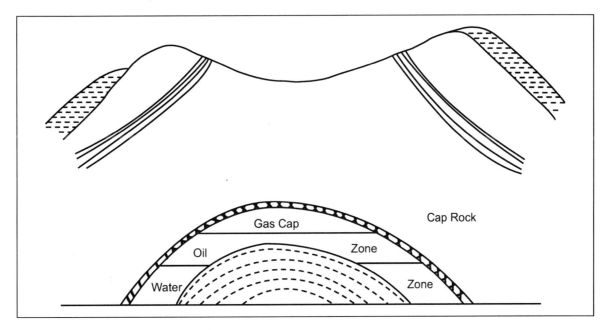

2.2   TRADES

There are 68 countries listed as oil producers in the International Petroleum Encyclopaedia. Virtually all producers will be consumers and therefore may not be exporters of crude or products. Note that although by law the United States did not export crude oil some Alaskan crude is now exported they have exported products; the U.S. is the largest importer of crude.

In this Chapter we examine the trade routes and terminals in the tanker industry. By looking at ports, canals and current usage of tankers, we can put into focus the sizes and utilisation of ships in the various routes thereby highlighting the fundamental geography for oil transport. It is important to keep in mind that we are considering seaborne movements as opposed to international movements since the latter will include pipeline and land vehicle transport (i.e. road and rail).

We will see later in the Chapter that pipelines, particularly in the Middle East, have affected the structure of seaborne trade. However, from the simplified map oppsite you will see that the Middle East dominates exports by sea.

Main Oil Movements by Sea

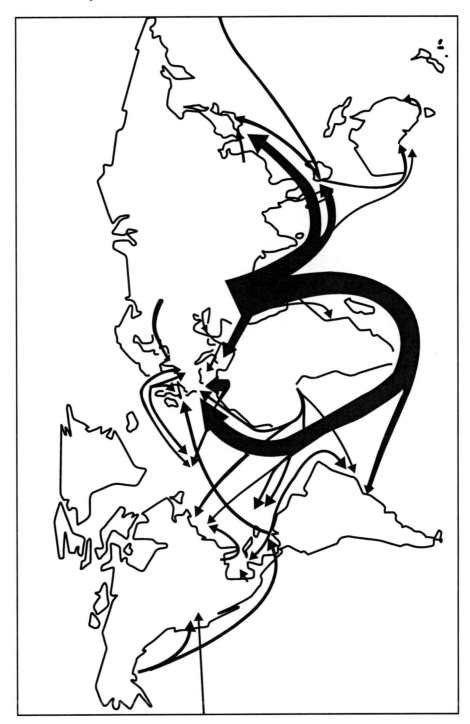

The first item to look at is the producing and consuming areas. For our purposes probably the most useful source for this information is the *BP Statistical Review of World Energy* which is published annually, usually in June and available on the internet.

To put the oil movements into focus the Inter-Area Movements together with imports and exports figures 2008 are given as follows:

Inter-area movements 2009

Million tonnes

From	US	Canada	Mexico	S. & Cent. America	Europe	Africa	Austral-asia	China	India	Japan	Singapore	Other Asia Pacific	Rest of World	Total
US	–	7.2	15.4	27.9	20.3	2.9	0.7	2.8	1.5	3.7	6.9	0.7	1.7	**91.7**
Canada	121.7	–	0.1	0.1	0.3	–	–	†	–	†	–	–	†	**122.2**
Mexico	61.2	1.1	–	1.6	5.6	–	–	†	1.9	0.1	0.3	†	†	**71.9**
S. & Cent. America	115.7	5.3	0.8	–	21.0	1.1	–	17.7	9.9	0.3	10.5	0.9	0.1	**183.3**
Europe	36.2	13.8	3.9	3.9	–	18.7	0.1	0.6	0.3	0.6	6.1	1.9	9.8	**96.0**
Former Soviet Union	28.7	4.0	0.1	0.2	347.8	1.4	0.9	26.6	1.0	8.9	6.9	13.4	7.1	**447.1**
Middle East	86.9	5.0	0.6	5.4	105.9	33.5	5.8	103.2	110.1	179.4	48.0	230.0	†	**913.8**
North Africa	28.2	5.1	†	4.3	81.0	–	0.3	8.9	4.5	0.3	0.2	3.3	0.1	**136.4**
West Africa	79.2	3.9	0.2	14.8	48.3	3.9	0.5	41.7	17.4	†	†	7.4	0.1	**217.6**
East & Southern Africa	0.8	–	–	†	0.1	†	†	12.2	0.9	0.1	–	1.7	†	**15.1**
Australasia	0.5	0.1	–	4.0	1.8	0.7	0.4	1.6	0.1	2.9	3.4	5.9	†	**14.8**
China	0.7	–	0.1	1.0	3.5	0.4	†	–	0.6	1.5	4.7	18.8	0.9	**34.1**
India	–	0.1	0.1	0.3	1.1	–	2.4	0.2	–	1.7	5.5	21.7	0.9	**35.5**
Japan	–	–	–	–	–	–	–	3.6	–	–	6.5	2.6	†	**16.5**
Singapore	–	0.1	0.1	0.3	1.9	2.5	10.9	6.6	2.5	0.9	–	47.8	0.8	**74.4**
Other Asia Pacific	5.1	0.2	0.2	2.8	4.4	0.4	16.6	27.5	5.4	10.0	26.8	–	0.7	**100.1**
Unidentified*	–	8.7	–	†	22.1	2.8	1.4	–	–	1.1	–	–	–	**36.0**
Total imports	564.9	54.4	21.5	66.4	665.3	68.1	40.0	253.3	156.2	211.8	126.1	356.2	22.5	**2606.4**

Thousand barrels daily

From	US	Canada	Mexico	S. & Cent. America	Europe	Africa	Austral-asia	China	India	Japan	Singapore	Other Asia Pacific	Rest of World	Total
US	–	150	322	563	424	60	15	58	30	78	145	15	37	**1916**
Canada	2464	–	2	2	7	–	–	‡	–	–	–	1	‡	**2476**
Mexico	1234	22	–	33	113	–	–	‡	37	3	6	‡	1	**1450**
S. & Cent. America	2345	108	16	–	428	22	‡	360	200	6	219	19	3	**3725**
Europe	750	280	82	82	–	390	2	13	6	12	128	38	204	**1987**
Former Soviet Union	591	81	2	5	7043	28	18	539	21	179	143	271	144	**9065**
Middle East	1747	100	12	108	2135	674	116	2078	2215	3619	974	4647	‡	**18426**
North Africa	576	103	1	88	1636	–	6	180	90	7	5	66	3	**2760**
West Africa	1593	78	3	298	970	77	9	837	350	7	1	148	3	**4373**
East & Southern Africa	15	–	–	‡	3	‡	‡	245	18	–	3	34	1	**303**
Australasia	10	1	–	63	38	15	8	33	3	60	69	119	‡	**300**
China	14	–	1	20	74	8	‡	–	13	31	99	392	19	**709**
India	–	–	–	1	23	–	49	4	–	35	115	453	18	**742**
Japan	–	–	–	–	–	–	–	76	1	–	136	55	1	**345**
Singapore	–	3	2	6	39	51	227	138	52	19	–	1000	17	**1552**
Other Asia Pacific	105	4	5	58	92	9	336	567	110	204	556	–	14	**2059**
Unidentified*	–	174	–	‡	458	57	30	–	–	22	–	–	–	**741**
Total imports	11444	1105	448	1366	13485	1391	817	5127	3145	4283	2598	7258	464	**52930**

*Includes changes in the quantity of oil in transit, movements not otherwise shown, unidentified military use, etc.
†Less than 0.05.
‡Less than 0.5.

Courtesy of BP

Imports and exports 2009

	Million tonnes				Thousand barrels daily			
	Crude imports	Product imports	Crude exports	Product exports	Crude imports	Product imports	Crude exports	Product exports
US	442.8	122.0	2.2	89.5	8993	2550	44	1671
Canada	39.1	15.3	96.5	25.7	785	320	1938	538
Mexico	0.5	21.0	63.8	8.0	9	439	1282	168
S. & Cent. America	25.1	41.3	128.9	54.4	504	863	2588	1137
Europe	513.3	152.0	23.1	72.9	10308	3177	464	1523
Former Soviet Union	0.9	3.2	342.0	105.1	18	67	6868	2197
Middle East	7.0	10.5	822.1	91.6	140	219	16510	1916
North Africa	18.4	10.0	111.1	25.3	369	209	2232	528
West Africa	†	12.1	212.3	5.3	1	254	4263	110
East & Southern Africa	21.9	5.7	14.8	0.3	439	119	297	6
Australasia	22.8	17.1	12.8	2.0	458	358	258	42
China	203.5	49.8	4.7	29.4	4086	1041	94	614
India	145.8	10.4	0.1	35.4	2928	217	19	740
Japan	176.5	35.3	–	16.5	3545	738	–	345
Singapore	46.3	79.8	2.3	72.0	930	1668	47	1505
Other Asia Pacific	228.6	127.6	40.2	59.9	4590	2667	907	1252
Unidentified*	–	0.9	15.5	20.6	–	18	311	430
Total World	1892.5	714.0	1892.5	714.0	38005	14925	38005	14925

*Includes changes in the quantity of oil in transit, movements not otherwise shown, unidentified military use, etc

†Less than 0.05.

Note: Bunkers are not included as exports. Intra-area movements (for example, between countries in Europe) are excluded

Courtesy of BP

In the context of this section it is also worthwhile to look at the Reserve Production Ratios (R/P) for the main producing areas. The R/P ratio is arrived at simply by dividing known reserves by the current year's production figure. For example, say reserves are 100 and current annual production is 10, the R/P ratio would be ten (or ten years of reserves remain). Thus if further reserves are discovered or the production rate changed then the R/P ratio would alter, indeed you will notice that there are frequent changes in R/P ratios for many areas.

This clustered bar chart shows world oil R/P (reserve to production) ratios for the year 2008 according to geographic region. R/P ratios are measured in years.

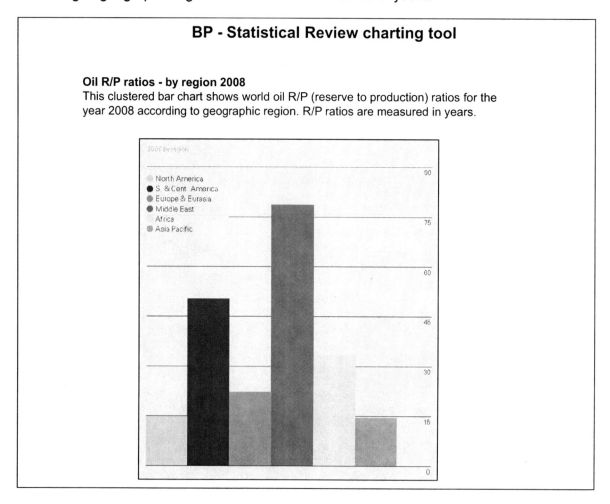

BP - Statistical Review charting tool

Oil R/P ratios - by region 2008
This clustered bar chart shows world oil R/P (reserve to production) ratios for the year 2008 according to geographic region. R/P ratios are measured in years.

From this table it can be seen that North America, the world's largest consumer, has about 12 years, Asia Pacific about 15 years, Europe and Eurasia just over 20 years, Africa about 30 years, south and central America just over 40 years but way ahead is the Middle East with more than 80 years reserves.

This highlights the importance of the Middle East as the world producer of crude oil in the long run and should make the tanker industry consider how its transportation requirements will alter over the medium to long term. Remember the longer the sea route the bigger the ship required to carry the cargo economically.

2.3   MAJOR LOADING AND DISCHARGING AREAS

The previous section has laid a foundation for us to identify the regions, ports and facilities which are essential for the geography of the tanker trades. We will now look at the major loading/discharging areas, identify the most important ports, restrictions and finally consider the developments which are likely to affect seaborne oil movements.

You may be wondering why we differentiate between ports and loading areas. The reason is that the conventional meaning of the term port is a place on land that forms the interface with the seagoing craft enabling transfer of cargo and/or passengers or repairs to be carried out. This port may be on the banks of the major river or an island or in a natural bay.

The tanker ports have always been placed close to the sea. Somewhat influenced by the size of ships as well as the need to utilise a lot of acreage of land to build the refinery and its accompanying terminals and be as far away from the population as possible. Some terminals, particularly in the Middle East, are out of sight of land. Today there are a large number of off-shore loading and discharging facilities where tankers make fast to a Single Point Mooring (SPM) or possibly a Single Buoy Mooring (SBM) which connect to an oil field ashore, an undersea oil production facility or in some cases floating storage/production vessels and semi-submersible platforms connected directly to the oil field. The first SPMs were introduced in 1959 in Brunei and they have become more popular ever since. In about 1973 the first oil from the British sector of the North Sea was shipped by Hamilton Brothers from a semi-submersible connected to a SBM. Today these facilities (i.e. SBM's or SPM's) are found in many of the loading areas.

The SBM: the buoy is used to moor the loading tanker and hold the pipelines. The loading will often take place through submarine hoses which have to be picked up by the vessel's own equipment, thus derricks of minimum 15 tonnes SWL will be preferred.

The SPM facility will have a similar mooring method but will be rigidly secured to the sea bed and possibly have a storage facility included. The cargo hoses may well be buoyant.

The SPM may well be directly connected to a process storage tanker – such a vessel collects oil from a small producing field through a well head platform and SPM facility, then carries out some basic processing and stores the oil until there is sufficient cargo to be transferred to a shuttle tanker. The shuttle tankers may either come alongside the mother vessel or make fast in a similar manner to that used for SPMs. The operational safety of the two ships is somewhat complicated by the fact that as the discharging vessel pumps out she rises in the water and the shuttle tanker, of course, is deepening her draft as she loads. The vessels must therefore be fitted with suitable panama leads.

The SPM facilities are used in Louisiana, USA (L.O.O.P), Malaysia, the Indonesian Archipelago, East and West Africa, Japan, Middle East Gulf, North Africa, Mexico, North Sea, South Korea, Australia, Brazil and China.

In the tanker industry it is important to know the political boundaries and names of the countries which have oil terminal facilities because the load or discharge ranges agreed during negotiations may be described in terms of a country or countries, equally, when given a named port you should be conscious of any possible existing problems e.g. will the vessel's flag be acceptable? (Cypriot vessels are banned from Turkish ports).

For this section of the Chapter we will split the world into the major geographical regions, where applicable, and consider the physical restrictions and possible developments.

We also list some of the more important loading and discharging areas to which you should enter the applicable distances. This way they should stick in your mind more easily than just reading them off a table but you do not have to do them all, it is an exercise you can return to over a period of weeks. Make sure you apply your knowledge to estimate from a producing area to a consuming area or locally for product. You are invited to translate the distances into days because you might find it easier to remember distances in terms of steaming times.

At 14 knots 1,000 miles = 3 days

This exercise is very much student driven but everyday practitioners may find it useful to ensure they are still up to speed. You can tackle it at your own time as you progress with the rest of the Chapters.

i) Middle East Gulf/Red Sea

ii) Mediterranean/Black Sea

iii) UK, Continent and Baltic Sea

iv) West Africa

v) East Coasts of Canada and USA

vi) Gulf of Mexico/Caribbean Sea

vii) Central and South America

viii) Australia, New Zealand

ix) Far East

x) India, Pakistan, Bay of Bengal

xi) Canals

i) The Middle East Gulf/Red Sea

The most important loading area is undoubtedly 'The Gulf. Commonly known as the Arabian or Persian Gulf – however either of these labels might cause offence. Thus today, quite often it is referred to as the Middle East Gulf.

Oil cargoes are also loaded in the Gulf of Oman and in the Red Sea, it is the latter area which has seen an increase in refinery development in recent years.

On the maps of the Middle East Gulf, Red Sea and Egyptian ports underline the main terminals and on the appropriate maps insert Quoin Island, Aden and Ras Isa as well as national boundaries and names of countries.

Middle Eastern Gulf

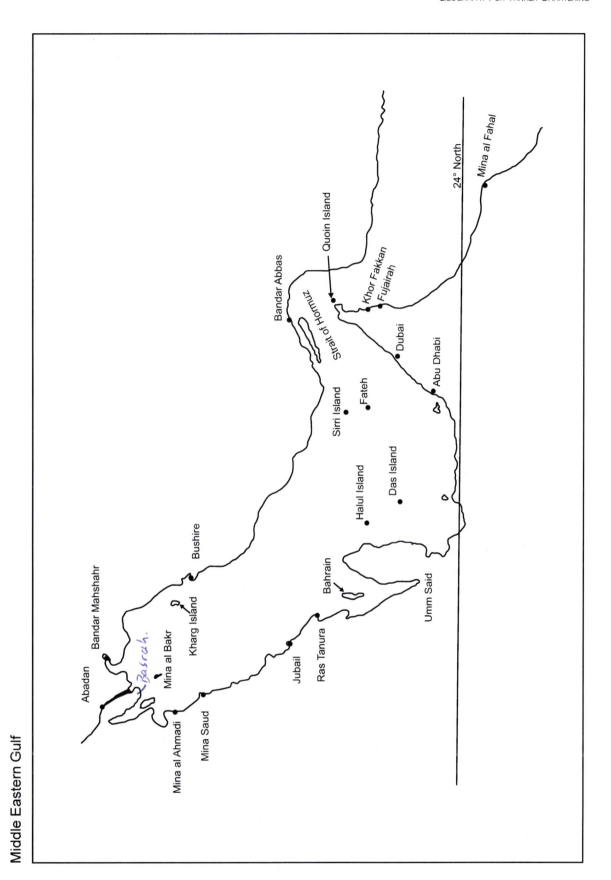

Red Sea

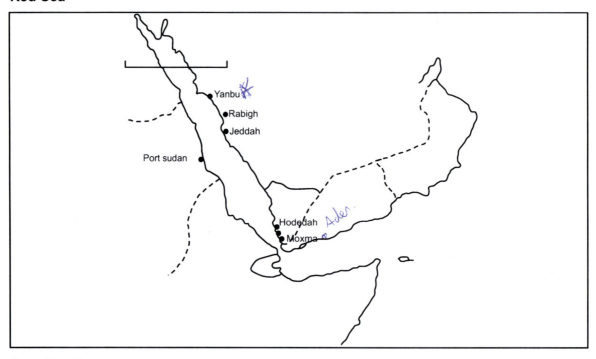

Egyptian Ports

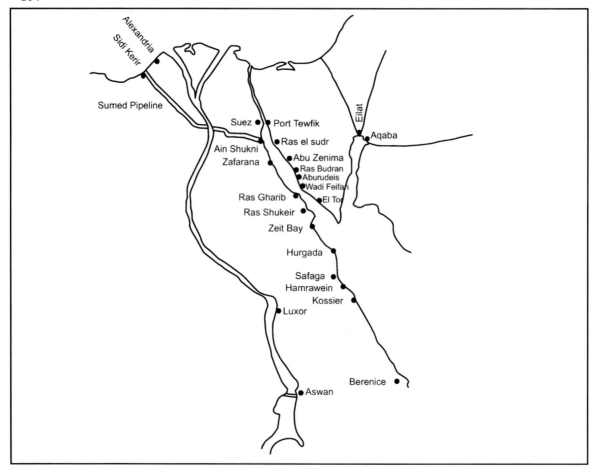

The Middle East Gulf is rather shallow, only having a depth of 70 metres at its deepest, therefore considerable use is made of natural islands and offshore loading terminals, such as Juaymah off Ras Tanura and Kharg Island.

The largest producer in Saudi Arabia (8 million Bbls/day) followed by Iran (3.7), United Arab Emirates (2.24), Kuwait (2), Iraq (0.65) under restriction and Qatar (0.48).

From the point of view of oil tanker demand measured in ton/miles Middle East Gulf is by far the most important loading area in the world.

Kuwait exports a great deal of product through Mina Al Ahmadi.

Taking the Worldscale convention using Quoin Island or other distance tables using a suitable Gulf Port base look up the following distances and enter them in the following table.

	Distance (miles)	Days at 14 KTS
Quoin Island to:		
Karachi		
Chittagong		
Singapore		
Kadhsiung		
Yosu		
Yokohama		
Sydney		
Suez		
Mombasa		
Durban		
St. Croix		
Corpus Christi		
New York		
Gibraltar (via CGH)		
Gibraltar (via Suez)		
Rotterdam (via CGH)		
Rotterdam (via Suez)		

ii)   Mediterranean/Black Sea

On the accompanying map underline the main oil terminals.

Insert the ports of Aghio Theodori and Omisalj.

In this region the major crude exporters are the former Soviet Union countries, Russia, Ukraine, Gerogia from the Black Sea, the Iraq through Ceyhan, and various Middle East charterers via the SUMED pipeline from Ain Suhkna to Sidi Kerir. Libya, Algeria and Tunisia also export crude and crude condensate.

Clean product cargoes are sourced from Italy, Spain, France and Libya.

	Distance (miles)	Days at 14 KTS
Gibraltar to:		
Port Said		
Ceyhan		
Piraeus		
Istanbul		
Novorosisk		
Odessa		
Trieste		
Augusta		
Genoa		
Essider		
Arzew		
Rotterdam		
New York		
New Orleans		
Bonny		
Quinfoqueni		

Mediterranean and Black Sea

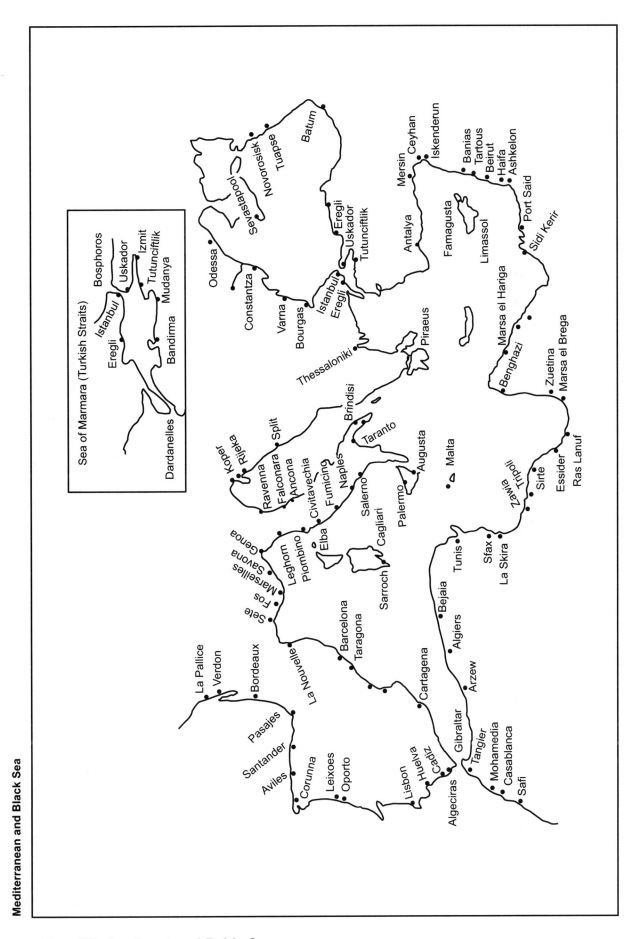

iii)   **UK, Continent and Baltic Sea**

As far as the hydrocarbon trades are concerned, the geography of north-west Europe has two major influences. The first is the oil and gas production in the inhospitable waters of the North Sea.

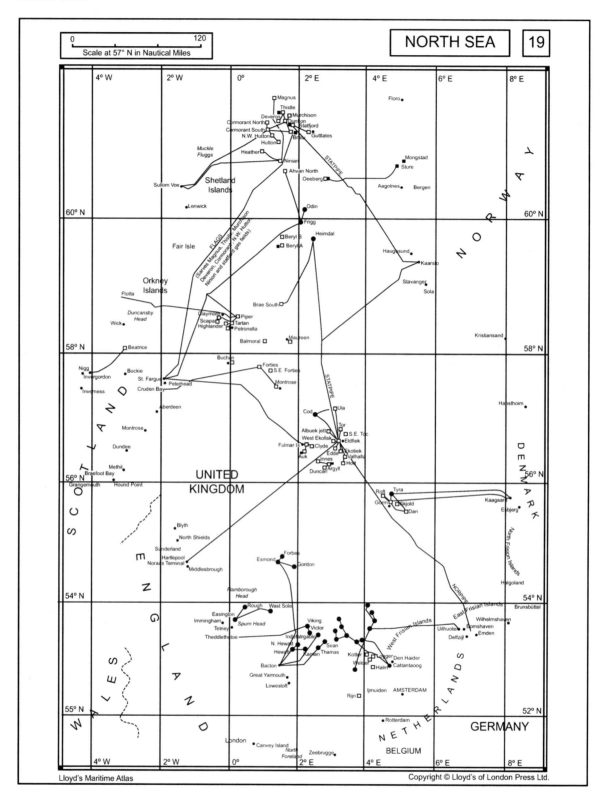

Lloyd's Maritime Atlas

Copyright © Lloyd's of London Press Ltd.

The oil is typically found in the northern sector whereas the southern sector is mainly gas fields. The oil from the major fields is pumped to shore based terminals at Sullom Voe, Flotta, Tees Port, Nigg Bay, Cruden Bay and Sture. It is worth noting that these terminals have certain preferences which discriminate against combination carriers; they would always prefer to take straight tankers. Sullom Voe will not accept a combination carrier with last cargo dry, for loading if 144 hours have not elapsed since discharging the dry cargo. Tees will not accept combination carriers unless they have discharged their previous wet cargo within the last two months. Flotta has a rule that no ballast water whatsoever will be discharged overside, either it must be pumped ashore – which is costly – or kept onboard. This is to prevent polluted ballast water affecting the local marine life.

The second influence is the distribution of crude products on the coast of the United Kingdom and to the industrialised hinterland of Continental Europe through such ports as Europoort, either via pipeline, river and coastal barges or transhipment to tankers occupied in coastal voyages to Scandinavia and the Baltic.

The Baltic has a low salinity and freezes in the winter. It can be reached via the Kiel Canal or on the large vessels via the Skagerrak anc' the Skaw. The Baltic is the main distribution medium for many commodities in this area, oil and products included, to the numerous small ports in Sweden, Finland and Denmark. Using crude oil from the North Sea, Norway has created its own oil industry from production to refining for export having terminals at Mongstad, Sture, Karstoe, Sola and Stavanger.

On the accompanying map enter the names and locations of the following ports:

Wismar, Nantes, Gulf of Bothnia, Brunsbuttel, Studstrup, Turku, Gdansk, Mongstad, Lyme Bay, Europoort, Wilhelmshaven, Tees, Tranmere, Sullom Voe, Bremerhaven, Immingham, Fawley and Le Havre.

	Distance (miles)	Days at 14 KTS
Rotterdam to:-		
Sullom Voe		
Oslo		
Leningrad		
Gdynia		
Fawley		
Montreal		
New York		
Loop		
Bonny		

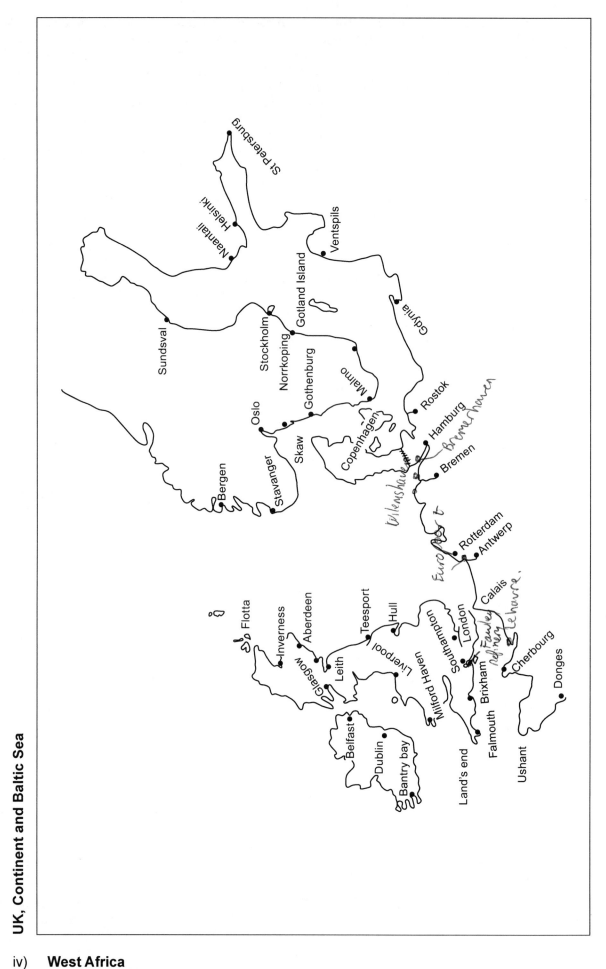

UK, Continent and Baltic Sea

iv)   **West Africa**

In this section we are concentrating on the West African ports which are principally the loading terminals from Nigeria through to Angola. West Africa is renowned for its lack of natural harbours, smooth coastline and shallow coastal shelf. Development of ports is hindered by silting. Nigeria is the Continent's single largest oil producer. Bonny terminal can take vessels up to 300,000 dwt, and Forcados up to about 250,000 dwt. Such size vessels are not often fixed from this port however. Can you think of any reason for this? To give you a clue, the larger the ship the longer the route...

Virtually all the loading facilities are off-shore terminals of one type or another

Tankers loading at Nigerian ports must load a quantity of cargo not less than 90% of their summer deadweight as recorded in Lloyds Register. Not surprisingly this is known as the 90% rule. The only exception is vessels loading at inner berth Bonny, which is draft restricted (find out what the draft restriction is and enter it here:_____) and the figure is 60% of the vessel's summer deadweight.

The two main oil ports in East Africa are Mombasa and Dar es Salaam which are used for importing crude and products. There are restrictions at these ports. What are they?

Port	DWT	LOA	Draft
Mombasa			
Dar es Salaam			

Locate the following places on the accompanying map:

Dares Salaam, Port Elizabeth, Cape Town, Walvis Bay Lagos, Accra, Port Sudan, Bashayer, Canary Islands, Cape Verde Islands, Ceuta, Mohammedia.

The main loading terminals, however, are situated between Nigeria and Angola. On the map you will see they are numbered 1-15. Using an atlas identify which port each number represents and enter its name alongside the number on the table on the map.

	Distance (miles)	Days at 14 KTS
Rotterdam to:		
Dakar		
Bonny – ING.		
Quinfuquena		
Bonny to:		
New York		
Houston		
Quoin		
Singapore		

Africa

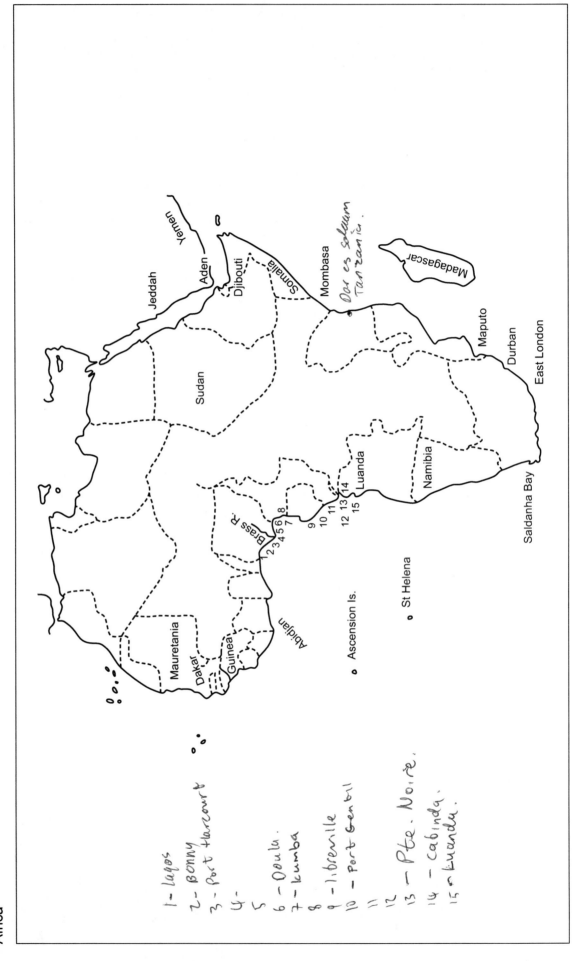

1 – Lagos
2 – Bonny
3 – Port Harcourt
4 –
5 –
6 – Doula.
7 – kumba
8 –
9 – Libreville
10 – Port Gentil
11 –
12 –
13 – Pte. Noire.
14 – Cabinda.
15 – Luanda.

v)   East Coasts of Canada and USA

The ports on the East Coast of Canada and USA are in some cases 'beam' and 'length' restricted but mainly 'draft' restricted and a certain amount of lightering has to be carried out. Boston, New York and the Delaware River have large oil refineries which receive crude oil and fuel oil and export clean products. The USA is the largest oil consuming country in the world and as domestic production declined it has become the largest importer of crude oil and its products. The crude oil supplies come mainly from the Middle East. That is a long route which is best served by the largest vessels that can be reasonably programmed for the trade in order to reduce the ton/mile cost. On the accompanying map underline the main oil terminals.

	Distance (miles)	Days at 14 KTS
New York to:		
Sullom Voe		
Rotterdam		
Gibraltar		
Bonny		
Quoin (via Suez)		
Quoin (via CGH)		
Dumai (via Suez)		
Dumai (via CGH)		
Dumai (via Cape Town)		

East Coasts – Canada and United State

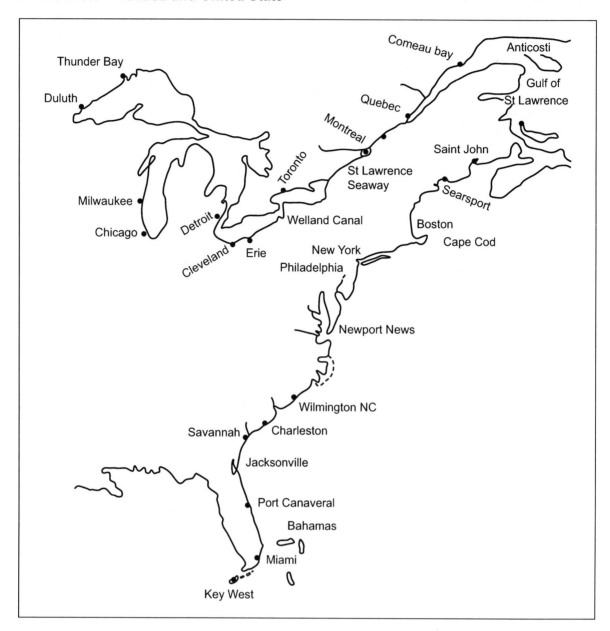

vi)   Gulf of Mexico/Caribbean Sea

The oil terminals of the US ports of the Gulf of Mexico are principally for the import of crude oil and products and the export of products. As with all the USA ports they are draft restricted with the exception of the Louisiana Offshore Oil Port (LOOP) which can take VLCCs. The crude carriers will either lighten offshore or tranship cargoes in the Caribbean. Houston is beam (115 ft) and draft restricted (39 ft).

Mexico and Venezuela are the largest oil producers in the vicinity of the USA (other than Canada) and as a result they have no difficulty in marketing oil to the largest consumer. Columbia and Trinidad are also involved to a small extent.

On the accompanying map name the countries and locate the following ports:

Loop, Dos Bocas, Cayo Areas, Aruba, Havana.

	Distance (miles)	Days at 14 KTS
Aruba to:		
Houston		
New York		
Gibraltar		
Rotterdam		
Bonny		
Quoin		
Loop to:		
Sullom Voe		
Rotterdam		
Gibraltar		
Bonny		
Quoin (via Suez)		
Quoin (via CGH)		
Dumai (via Suez)		
Dumai (via CGH)		

United States Gulf of Mexico and Caribean

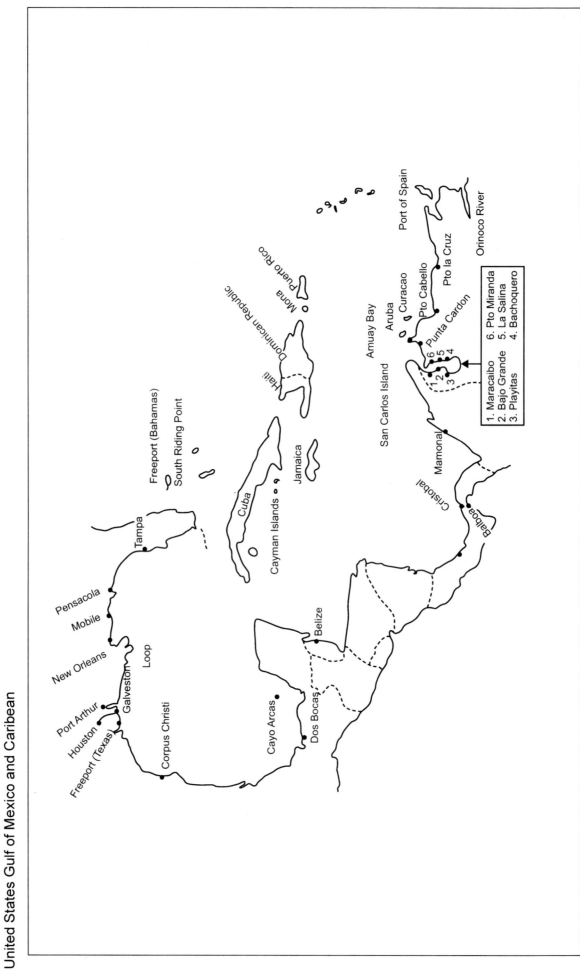

vii)   **South America**

The major exporter from South America is Venezuela which we covered under the Caribbean. Brazil is not yet self-supporting but has found large reserves offshore and has developed floating production systems to allow recovery.

Colombia exports through Covenas, Buenaventura and Cartagena, Ecuador from Esmeraldas and La Libertad, and Peru from Talara and Puerto Bayovar. Chile draws oil by pipeline from Argentina and Bolivia and has some production down south in Clarencia.

Chilean imports are affected by tender whereby they tender for CIF supplies. The possible origins of the oil include the Far East, West Africa and Middle East Gulf. Thus, when fixing ships from these destinations it is not unusual for charterers to ask for a Chile discharge option to enable them to participate in the tenders.

On the accompanying map enter the names of the countries.

Enter the following ports on the map:

   Quintero, Punta Arenas, Jose Ignacio, Antofagasta, Recife, Cartagena, Lake Maracaibo, Straight of Magellan, Aracaju, Ilo, La Pampilla, Esmeraldas.

	Distance (miles)	Days at 14 KTS
Valparaiso to:		
Capehorn		
Balbao		
Hawaii		
Yokohama		
Singapore		
Sydney		
Capehorn to:		
Houston		
Rotterdam		
Gibraltar		
Bonny		
New York		
CapeTown		
Buenos Aires to:		
Rotterdam		
Houston		
Bonny		
Gibraltar		
New York		
Capetown		
Cristobal to:		
Houston		
New York		
Rotterdam		
Gibraltar		

South America

viii) **Australia and New Zealand**

The majority of the oil trades in Australia and New Zealand are imports from Indonesia and the Middle East Gulf. Australian domestic crude production is now equal to about half that of Indonesia and gas production over a third of that of the United Kingdom.

On the accompanying map underline the oil terminals.

What restrictions are there at Kwinana?

	Distance (miles)	Days at 14 KTS
Quoin to:		
Kwinana		
Brisbane		
Whangerei		
Sydney		
Singapore to:		
Kwinana		
Brisbane		
Whangerei		
Sydney		

Australia

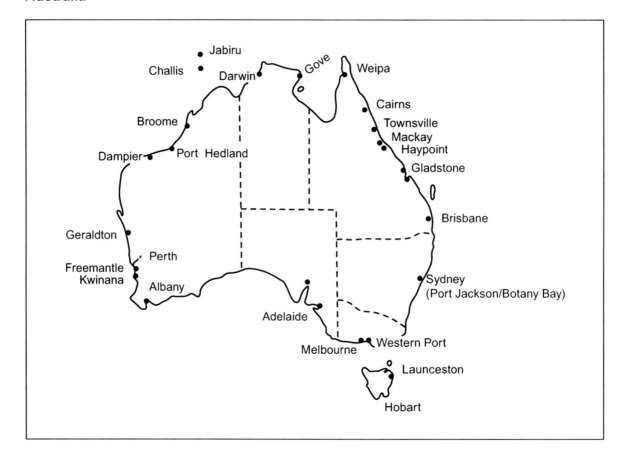

New Zealand

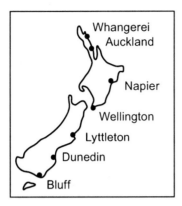

ix)   **Far East**

In this context we are covering the area from Indonesia to Japan, two areas of complete contrast. In simple terms Japan is heavily industrialised with a sophisticated and integrated economy and the Indonesian Archipelago has large reserves of raw materials, a struggling economy and very little industry. Indonesia relies heavily on the exports of crude oil and gas, much of which goes to Japan.

There are thriving economies in Singapore, Hong Kong, Taiwan and Korea, but it is only the southernmost countries which are regular exporters of oil. China is developing its oil reserves but much of the resulting increase in production is being used for domestic consumption.

For those of us involved in tanker chartering the main trades in this area are the Middle East Gulf to Singapore, Taiwan, Korea and Japan. The Japanese trades, however, are very much tied to Japanese owned tonnage and vessels with the maximum age of 12 years required. (Although officially maximum 15 years).

The current developments will lead to an increase in exports of gas and oil from Indonesia, oil from East Coast Malaysia, Vietnam and China.

Many ports are already on the accompanying map. Underline the oil terminals and locate and name the following:

Arjuna, Cinta, Blang Lancang, Port Dixon, Tapis, Santan, Labuan, Sri Racha, Tabangao, Yosu, Daesan.

	Distance (miles)	Days at 14 KTS
Quoin to:		
Yokohama		
Yosu		
Sri Racha		
Singapore to:		
Houston		
Suez		
Rotterdam (via CGA)		
Rotterdam (via Suez)		

Far East Ports

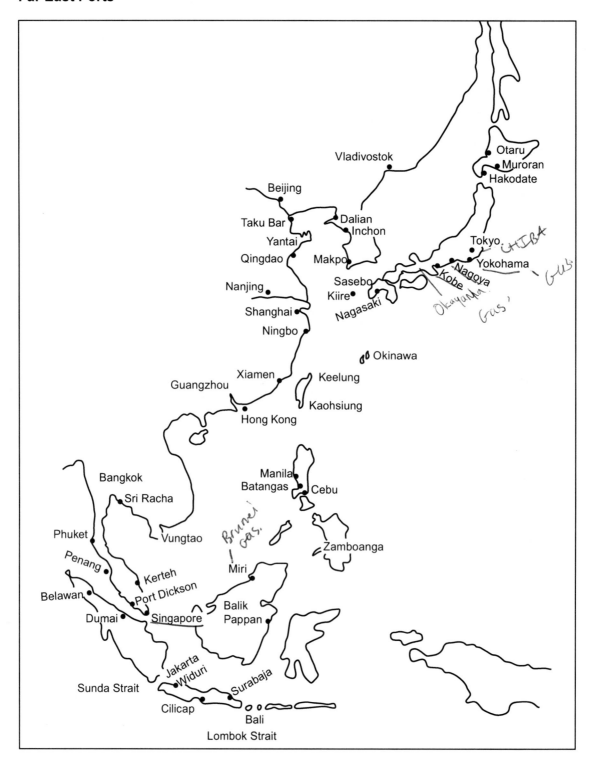

x)   India, Pakistan and Bay of Bengal

This area is a net importer of oil, although each country has exploration going on plus the benefit of domestic production. The oil is needed as fuel for primary energy generation to support a large industrialisation programme and a huge population.

The major supplier for all this area is predictably the Middle East Gulf. India has an oil field off Bombay. Pakistan may get some support from the wealthier Middle Eastern states. Product can be imported from the Middle East and also from Singapore. Bangladesh naturally can only afford a small oil consumption.

On the accompanying map identify the countries and locate and name the following terminals:

Colombo, Bhavangar, Madras, Rangoon, Chittagong, Chalna, Pardip, Vadinar, Haldia.

	Distance (miles)	Days at 14 KTS
Quoin to:		
Karachi		
Mumbai		
Madras		
Calcutta		
Chittagong		
Rangoon		

India, Pakistan and Bay of Bengal

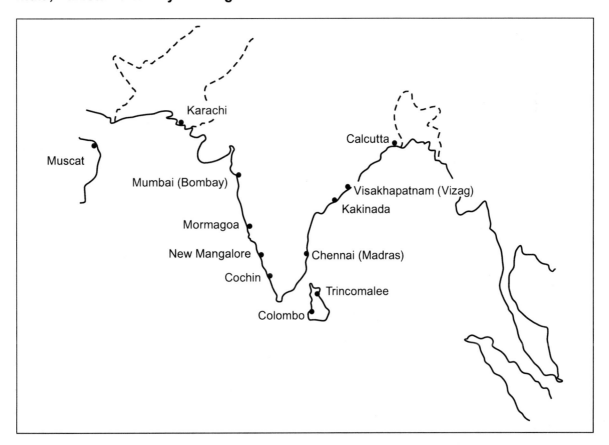

xi) Canals

The most significant canals with regard to the design and employment of tankers are the Suez and Panama Canals.

All brokers will be familiar with the term Panamax. Typically a ship of up to about 80,000 mt dwt. which has the maximum dimensions capable of transiting the Panama Canal. (900 ft. loa/106 ft. beam/37 ft freshwater draft).

In tanker chartering we also use the term Suezmax. Typically this is a ship of between 130/150,000 sdwt that can lift about 1.0 m bbls and perhaps 120/140,000 mt. of cargo through Suez northbound.

The two canals differ in one fundamental way. That is, the Panama Canal is cut out of rock and has a lock system to lift vessels over the intervening mountain range, whilst the Suez Canal is dredged out of sand. Hence the Panama Canal restrictions are rigid. The Suez Canal is continually being dredged and its maximum size for vessels can, overtime, be increased. The accompanying maps give further information.

	Distance (miles)	Days at 14 KTS
Cristobal to:		
New York		
Loop		
Rotterdam		
Gibraltar		
Balboa to:		
Los Angeles		
Yokohama		
Shanghai		
Singapore		
Suez to:		
Quoin		
Singapore		
Yokohama		
Sydney		
Port Said to:		
Gibraltar		
Rotterdam		
New York		
Loop		

Suez Canal

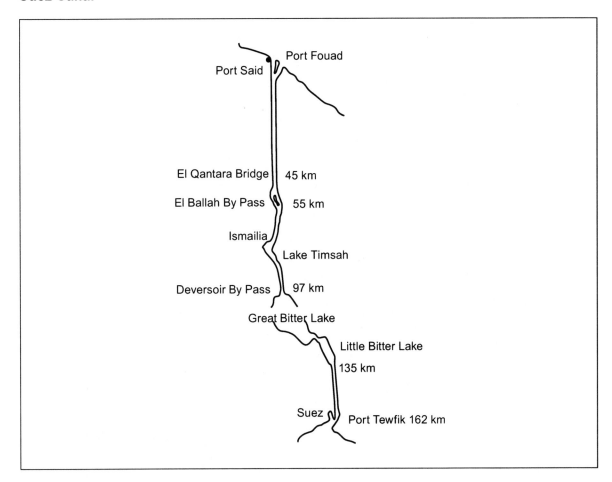

Canal length: 162 km
Max Draft: 62 ft (18.9 m) at Beam: 164 ft (50 m)
Max Beam: 254 ft 03" (77.5 m) at Draft: 40 ft (12.19 m)
Loa: No restriction
Air Draft: 223 ft (68 m)
Convoys schedule:
1st Southbound Convoy starts 01:00 hrs
2nd Southbound Convoy starts 06:00 hrs
Northbound Convoy starts 06:00 hrs
Transit time: 10-14 hours
Min transit speed
15 km/hour Tankers group
16 km/hour for other vessels group
(valid 2003)

Panama Canal

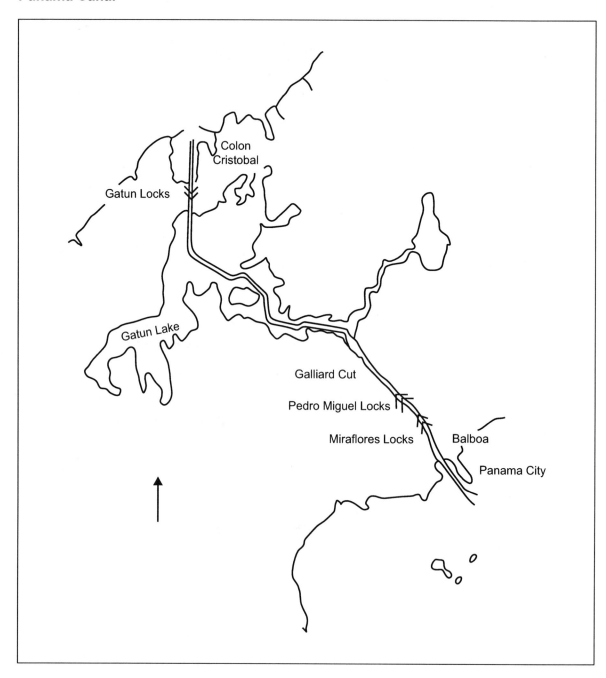

Maximum Dimensions

Maximum L.O.A.	900' (274.32 m)
Maximum Beam	106' (32.31 m)
Draft (Tropical Fresh)	37' (11.28 m)

Container vessels, passenger vessels and other light drafted vessels (up to 37' (11.28 m) TFW) are accepted up to 950' (289.55 m) L.O.A. In dry seasons – March, April, May – when the level of Gatun Lake is less than 83' (25.3 m) above sea level, draft may be restricted to 36' (10.97 m) RFW. Conversely, in the rainy season, the maximum draft may be increased to 39' 6" (12.05 m) TFW or a little more.

2.4 TEST QUESTIONS

Having completed Chapter Two, answer the following and submit your essay to your Tutor:

Your VLCC will be ready to load in the Middle East Gulf second half October. Most suitable cargoes are destined for Western options. (USAC, USG, ECCAN, UK Cont, Scand, Mediterranean). What factors would you need to take into account when deciding how much cargo you can load and which discharge ranges you are prepared to agree?

Your vessel is a modern product tanker of about 110,000 DWT, and she is ready to load on the European North Continent early December. You have the possibility of a full cargo for Singapore/Japan range. What factors would influence your plans for the voyage?

Chapter 3

THE MARKET STRUCTURE

3.1   INTRODUCTION

This Chapter sets out to explain the market structure of the tanker market and who are the practitioners. Then we look at the various trading methods that have evolved and, it is true to say, still are evolving. We will look at the factors which have influenced freight market levels and consider whether or not events and, perhaps more importantly, the effects were predictable. This could help us look for the signs in the future. We finish by considering the market reports that are available.

It is important to remember that shipping is a derived demand, that is to say it is not the ships that are in demand but rather the goods they carry. If consumers want oil, the method of transport is of very little interest to them, just so long as the commodity is delivered.

Until the early seventies the greater part of the oil business was in the hands of the major oil companies. Their involvement in the production process started with exploration carried on through discovery, production, transportation, refining, marketing and retailing. They were able to control production; distribution and price (in competition with each other), enabling them to make forward predictions with some degree of accuracy and thereby- in an ideal situation – keep costs to a minimum

Within the tanker market, the oil companies planned their transportation requirements including quantity, type of product, type of ship and managed the strategy of ships needed to fit their production and refining programmes.

It is estimated that until the early seventies the oil companies owned about 40% of their tonnage requirement, took about 45%/50% in on period time charter (say 3 up to 15 years) and the remainder was chartered in from the independent owners on the 'spot market'.

You will appreciate that oil refineries will be called on to provide a differing proportion of products throughout the year. For instance, in the USA more gasoline is required during the summer months and more heating oil in the winter months. The same pattern applies in northern Europe but not to such extremes, the reason being, in part, that the American demand for gasoline is driven (no pun intended) by the greater use of cars over longer distances, which typically have high fuel consumptions whereas in Europe the fuel consumption figure would be lower and the car smaller. This change of product mix influences the choice of crude oil required for the American refineries at different times of the year.

The vertical integration meant that the oil companies were able to stabilise costs of transport and balance their programmes according to the fluctuation in their requirements. The independent tanker owner was the source of tonnage, time chartered in by the oil companies and operating on the spot market enabling them to have a buffer to cover peak demand. It has been estimated in 1973 that 75% of the independently owned tanker fleet was engaged on period time charter. It was this ongoing period demand which enabled owners to finance and build new ships thereby keeping the average age of the fleet down.

As the market declined the oil companies gradually redelivered time charter tonnage. In some cases selling their own tonnage thereby reducing their overall controlled fleet and releasing capital for exploration and production. The reduction of demand for tankers in general and of time charter employment in particular during the late 70s and early 80s caused serious financial problems for the industry leading to a number of distressed sales of second-hand tonnage.

In the early 1970s the governments of the Organisation of Petroleum Exporting Countries (OPEC) nationalised their oil reserves and installations and therefore the oil companies could no longer control the oil production and could only control the price of crude oil through alternative suppliers and the effect of price on consumption. One of the effects was that a new player came into the market and that was the oil trader.

Traders could approach the producer direct and negotiate to buy oil at prices above or even below those of the contract prices agreed by the oil majors with the producers. The majority of oil traders use the spot market for the movements of their cargoes bought and sold 'one off'.

In times of volatile oil prices the trader's preference is to lift the crude cargoes in sizes of half a million or one million barrels, say about 65,000 or 130,000 metric tonnes giving a flexibility in cargo sale.

Therefore, we can see that the multi-user tanker market operating hand to mouth inherently has long term inefficiencies which could reduce the supply of tonnage. The factors affecting efficiency are speed of the fleet, an irregular trade pattern and waiting times between spot fixtures. The former is probably the only one over which an Owner may have any control for example, in times of high bunker prices and a low market an owner would probably want to reduce speed (thus reducing the bunker costs for the voyage).

When the market improves and rates rise, the owner would want to be available for employment again as soon as possible. Therefore, increased demand in a rising market could be met in part by increasing the operational speed of the fleet.

The three other influences on the structure of the tanker market are:

Ship Size: in simple terms, the further a cargo has to be carried, the larger the vessel that is required to carry it economically. The result is that if commodities are produced a long distance from the consuming area, then to compete with products from nearby the transport costs must be economical. Thus, larger ships tend to facilitate the carrying of goods a longer distance within the physical restraints of port restrictions i.e. draft, beam and length overall. You can see from the map of main oil movements how important is the place of the Middle East for ships, meaning VLCCs and larger.

New Producing Areas: alter the structure of trade in a most fundamental way. Take, for example, oil reserves found in the North Sea, Alaska, Indonesia or Australia. These fields may supply local consumers reducing the need for imports or possibly that area could become an exporter. For instance the crude oil produced in the North Sea is a light crude suitable for many refineries in the United States. This means that although in the late 1980s and early 1990s Britain produced enough oil to be self-sufficient, importing into the UK continued and the export of North Sea crude oil became a trade.

However, with finds in the state of Alaska, where the local market is virtually non-existent, the production is transported to the rest of the United States. For those of us involved in chartering, the Alaskan trades make very little difference to our business. When the cargo moves from Alaska the majority must be refined in the USA and as such that is a domestic movement subject to the strict Cabotage laws and the cargo can only be carried in American flag tankers.

Pipelines: particularly in the Middle East – have affected the structure of markets since the early eighties and even historically, but political differences means that the routes used can be vulnerable. A factor often overlooked is the cost of pumping oil through pipelines, requiring both the pump stations and energy used to run them.

The map on the following page shows that the pipelines give The Gulf producers an alternative to transport oil by tanker, either through the Straits of Hormuz or the Suez Canal.

In the Far East, the port of Kozmino has been built to export Russian Siberian Crude oil, pumped over 1,200 miles, for delivery by sea to their Pacific Ocean and South East Asian consumers.

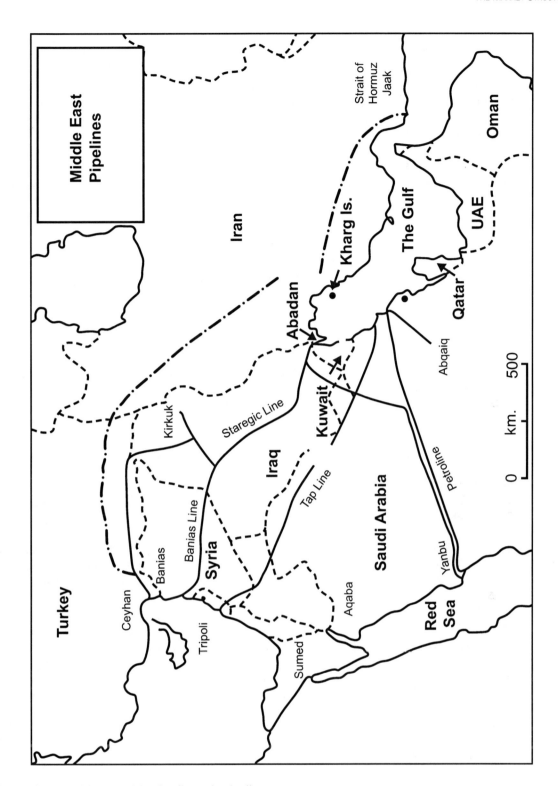

Middle East
Pipelines

There are problems with pipelines including:

(a) Vulnerability to attack.

(b) Damage at one point will affect a whole line.

(c) Increased handling of oil, e.g. pumping en route.

(d) Low capacity.

(e) The fees charged for transit.

(f) As is predictable these points tend to increase the cost of transportation

We will now look at the market as seen from the commercial standpoint. The Shipbroker's job, whether working for a Principal or Broker, or whether involved in management, chartering, agency or sale and purchase, is at the forefront of the commercial sector of the industry. In tanker chartering we can visualise three players, namely the Owners, the charterers and the Brokers. The Principals are the Owners and Charterers; in any organisation, be it a major oil company like Shell or an independent Ship Owner, you may be a Charterer and an Owner. The easiest example of this would be the oil major, at first glance apparently "the Charterer". However, they may own vessels, have some in on period and charter tonnage in for spot cargoes. It is quite usual for the company to re-let tonnage under its control, and thereby is in the position of an Owner. Similarly an independent Owner may see an opportunity, to take tonnage in on time charter for period. The Owner with a significant size fleet may well fix a contract of affreightment for a given quantity over a certain period of time. Possibly when a lifting is due a ship will be fixed in to carry the cargo. Thus the Owner is "the Charterer".

The third commercial entity in the market is the independent Broker. Success in any trading or free market environment relies heavily on information: it has been said that the right information at the right moment is essential to be successful. An Owner with a tanker open in the Mediterranean not only needs to know what cargoes are available in that area, but must consider the possibility of ballasting the ship to another loading area e.g. UK Continent, West Africa, Red Sea or The Gulf.

Thus the Owner needs to know the market rates and the tonnage that is likely to be in competition in all possible loading areas. In addition the Owner will be considering the market levels in the areas of discharge for those alternative cargoes. For an Owner or charterer with anything but the largest fleet, the majority of such information comes from the broking network. In London, for example, with a mixed fleet or cargo requirements for various trades, to gain a complete picture of a market may require talking to upwards of a dozen brokers.

It is unusual for Charterers to talk directly to Owners when quoting or negotiating business. Typicaiiy the oil majors will have a selected number of Brokers through whom they keep in contact with the market, frequently referred to as their "Panel Brokers"

It would not pay an Owner or a Charterer to maintain a team of in house Brokers capable of working world-wide 24 hours a day throughout the year. The information made available to a Principal acting as a Broker, would be limited due to the blocking of such information by the competing companies.

The world is becoming conscious of "green issues" and the oil companies are in the forefront of criticism when any incident occurs which results in pollution, the media attention given to incidents in recent years has been a salutary lesson to all oil companies. Many of them keep their own data banks with information on the vast number of tankers which they may need to charter at one time or another. The object is to minimise, if not totally eliminate, the risk of incidents, which may give rise to a pollution incident. The oil majors cannot afford to fix vessels that may be below standard and most have "vetting procedures" to enable them to decide which ships are acceptable to them. This actually reduces the number of vessels an oil company can physically fix, so the rates should, in theory, rise. Against this many Owners will prefer to fix with an oil major thereby reducing the financial risk involved in dealing with unknown Charterers. The Charterer will be most impressed with the fixture that runs so smoothly, nothing is heard about the ship from fixing until discharge when the freight invoice is payable.

The Charterer's requirement is to fix a ship that can load all his cargo on the dates stipulated by the shipper and deliver it uncontaminated at a destination, possibly unknown at the time of fixing. To do this he will first establish the readiness of his cargo – usually a two day spread – the 'window' and this will then be the laydays/cancelling. Therefore in selecting a suitable ship the dates will be important.

Next the Charterer must be careful in making sure that the vessel can load his cargo and all his grades can be loaded without contamination. This of course means that he may need to know the number of pumps and pipeline system available as well as the number of tanks where appropriate. However if an Owner has agreed to load a number of grades and after some discussion about the relative quantities that the ship can handle, it is the Owner's responsibility to carry that cargo safely. The order in which grades are loaded and discharged can also present problems with respect to strength, trim and ballasting.

Perhaps the cargo will need heating, either to be maintained at loading temperature or possibly heated to a higher temperature en route. These physical factors will all influence the decision as to which is the most suitable vessel for fixing.

The Tanker Broker's role can perhaps be summarised as providing a means of communication, which helps to achieve a free market. The Broker will need to collect and distribute information about the markets. (Some Brokers may specialise in very small sectors of the market, others aim to provide a comprehensive cover essentially as a service to a major Principal indirectly benefiting other clients, act as an intermediary for a negotiation and provide the skill and expertise to deal with the post fixture administration which is normally known as 'operations' within tanker chartering).

Working the market as an independent Tanker Broker means long hours to ensure proper cover of the market. Taking a London based broker as an example he is geographically well placed between the Far East and the United States. The Broker will need to be in the office shortly after 8 am to check what has been going on in the east overnight (often with a colleague who will have been working with Tokyo or Singapore from home since the early hours).

Then read all the overnight messages from their various contacts to establish a picture of what has been going on in the other markets. As the reports are received, fixtures may be entered in a computer database for all brokers to view at their desks, although an information board visible to everyone has its use provided it is updated.

The individuals within the broking company will usually have a list of Owners with whom they will keep in daily contact advising them of the various market information. This regular contact is important, even when the Owner does not have a ship ready for fixing – it is not good broking practice only to talk to a Principal only when there is something to say on their ship or cargo. Most individuals will also be talking to certain Charterers, perhaps who are based in certain geographical areas, say Singapore/Italy/Norway etc.

By the time the Owners and Charterers have arrived in their office and sorted through their own overnight messages, the Broker will be in a position to provide a synopsis of the markets. The Brokers need to know their Principal and in particular whether a full breakdown is required, e.g. there is not much point in giving an owner clean market information if there are only VLCC's in the fleet. Some owners just want the fixtures and new orders, others possibly a full rundown of who has been working what.

The Charterers will be similarly updated and they will be looking at whether or not they should be buying or selling cargoes and whether or not it is the right time to enter the market for a ship.

By lunch time the Broker will have updated the lists of tonnage and cargoes available and, to keep the competitive edge, they will be keeping their Principals at home and overseas up to date hoping to be seen to be doing the most business in his own area. At lunch time perhaps the Broker may have the chance of meeting a Principal over lunch to establish or maintain more than just a telephone relationship. Problems will often be smoothed out more easily if the people involved know each other.

By about 1400 hours in London the New York Brokers will be starting to call and the London Brokers will be passing their information to their American colleagues and establishing what changes have happened to the ships and cargoes on that side of the Atlantic. They need to be ready to quote American orders to their London based Owners and *vice versa.*

By about 1800 hours in London the market is virtually closed and any individuals not on late duty or involved in negotiating a ship can think about going home for the day.

With the development of modern communications efficient computerised, E-mail, Yahoo! Messaging, direct dialling, and fax machines, the broking profession operates far more quickly and consequently is far more fragmented than in the past.

Tanker chartering companies have been set up in the majority of the main maritime centres, so that today we see tanker brokers in such places as Tokyo, Beijing, Shanghai, Hong Kong, Seoul, Singapore, Australia, India, Middle East Gulf, Piraeus, Genoa, Paris, Hamburg, London, Connecticut, New York, Houston, Los Angeles...etc. The ethical standards normally associated with the shipbroking community have been subject to attack. We see Brokers trying to commit a principal to work with them for business and the less scrupulous may use some basic ploys such as working out when a Charterer's next cargo is likely to be and 'quote' it to an Owner with a vessel in position before the cargo is ready to work; using the name of a Charterer, working ships and putting them on subjects without the Principal's authority. Some Charterers have been known to put two ships on 'subject Charterer's management approval' for the same business, without the other party knowing and then lifting the subjects on the cheapest ship.

It is unlikely that we will return to the "pre 1973 days" such that when tonnage was scarce shipowners would not work business that had to be 'on subjects'. They would say 'when your business is ready to work fully firm we will give you an offer'. Today many influences – not least terminal's confirmation of their acceptability of the tanker – will be taken into account before fixing so "subjects" are here to stay.

The tanker market works quickly. Typically Charterers come into the market in the morning with their requirements and are often fixed by the end of that day's business. The Owner's Broker must therefore be ready to do his voyage calculation and possibly offer his ship for suitable business within the hour.

Commissions in the tanker trade are usually 1.25% Address plus 1.25% Brokerage and rarely in excess of 5%. Low commission levels encourage the development of independent competitive broking houses. The vast majority of the tanker negotiation will be carried out on the telephone or via instant messaging such as Yahoo! with a written confirmation, the 'recap', usually in the form of an e-mail or telex being used only at the final stage of a fixture. A modern trend is that the 'recap' will form the written contract and will contain all details of the ship, voyage as well as the charter party form. The original charter will not then be drawn up and signed by both parties unless requested by one of the principals.

Widely used standard charterparty forms such as ASBATANKVOY usually consist of two parts. The first, a series of blanks relating to the key terms of the fixture, must be agreed during negotiations, and the second part contains the detailed terms and conditions which are largely left unaltered. The majority of Charterers have their own special terms covering not only matters which are not fully specified in the standard form but impose duties and obligations on the Shipowner which may owe more to the weak bargaining position of Owners in a poor market than to the principles of a fair deal. On a stronger market Owners may attempt to introduce their own "additional" clauses.

It is usual in the tanker markets that the cargo will be sold at least once but frequently more times after loading and prior to discharge. The result is that the destination of the vessel will not be known until long after she has sailed from the load port. Taking a simple case of a vessel discharging in north-west Europe, the charterparty may allow the Charterer to choose any port between Bordeaux and Hamburg. There are a large number of ports in that range all with different costs for the same ship, and to calculate the required freight rate for all these ports would be a lengthy process and by no means quick enough.

As a result the tanker industry uses Worldscale which takes into account not only the different port costs but different steaming times to each of the ports. For a given Worldscale rate the Owners know they will earn approximately the same equivalent timecharter return whichever port of discharge is nominated in that range at the applicable Worldscale rate per tonne of cargo.

3.2   ORIGIN AND USE OF WORLDSCALE

Tanker scales were introduced during World War II by the United Kingdom and United States Governments to enable tanker voyages to be performed without calculating each individual dollar per ton or pound per ton rate for each port. They were referred to as the M.O.T and U.S.M.C. rates respectively.

These schemes developed into the present day 'New Worldwide Tanker Nominal Freight Scale' or better known as 'Worldscale'. The present method of calculation was introduced on January 1st 1989 and was known for that year, 1989, as 'New Worldscale'. The basic rate is described as the "flat" rate of W100 so that a rate of W120 is 20% more than the flat rate.

The Schedule is the printed book issued once a year on the 1st January. This Schedule is a book of A4 size about three centimetres thick listing over 60,000 voyage rates and distances, together with the applicable terms and conditions. If the voyage in question is not listed in this Schedule, subscribers can telephone or e-mail the Worldscale association who will calculate the flat rate for the voyage in question. The schedule is also available to subscribers, using a password, through the Worldscale web site and this is a very convenient way to access rates.

To calculate the flat rate in dollars per metric tonne the Worldscale Association use a standard vessel of 75,000 mt dwt, 14.5knots on 55 mt (380 cst) per day plus 100 mt per round voyage and 5 mt per port involved. Allowing port time of four days plus 12 hours for each extra port used, fixed hire rate US $12,000 per day, bunker prices (average price for the year 1st October to 31st September prior to the year in question). Port costs are assessed from information supplied by the various port authorities. Should a canal transit be involved 24 hours is allowed for the Panama Canal and 30 hours for the Suez Canal transit.

The calculation is made on a round voyage basis from the first load port to the discharge port and back to the first load port.

Worldscale flat rates are completely recalculated once every twelve months with the new rates effective for all loadings from January 1st of each year. Should there be any significant changes in port charges in the intervening period, the rates will be revised in the ports involved and the new rates promulgated in circulars published on the Worldscale website and sent to the subscribers. Remember to check the circulars when you are calculating a Worldscale rate just to see if any of the ports you intend to use have been affected.

Due to copyright laws, we have had to remove all commercial information, but you will glean a flavour for the layout of a worldscale schedule.

Look at the following parts in **Appendix 1** with extracts from:

Preamble A – Explanatry notes (pay particular attention to 4,5 and 9).

Preamble B – Terms and Conditions.

Preamble C – Demurrage Rates.

Preamble D –

- List 1 Ports in alphabetical order.
- List 2 Countries in alphabetical order with ports.
- List 3 Transhipment areas (TSA).

It is possible that other places may be designated as TSA and rates are available for such places from the Association. However where one of the places not shown is used for partial loading or discharging combined with another port or ports, such a rate will be regarded as a 'Special Rate' and its use will be dependent upon agreement between the parties.

To find the flat rate, first look for the discharge port, listed in alphabetical order at the top of each page. For example if the discharge port is London, look at the page in the Schedule showing London at the top. You will see that the flat rate and round voyage distance is printed for a number of voyages.

e.g. Under Worldscale (2010)

Montreal/London = US $11.36 pmt 6301 miles

You must remember that the rate is per 'metric tonne' (pmt).

The distance listed must be divided by 2 for each leg.

The rates listed are all Worldscale 'flat rates' i.e. Worldscale 100.

You will find that for some load ports there are two rates. For example,

Mina al Fahal/London $28.98 C   21,351 miles
(the rate and distance via Cape of Good Hope both loaded/ballast legs) and,

Mina al Fahal/London $17.94 S   11,825 miles
(the rate and round voyage distance via the Suez Canal both loaded/ballast legs)

The reason for printing two rates is that although the shortest distance would be through the Suez Canal many larger ships cannot pass the Canal when laden so would have to contact the Association for the rate around the Cape if it was not printed in the Schedule.

Remember the rate to be used for a particular voyage has to be agreed by both parties (Section 6, Route policy/Distances).

Now to find the rate from a port in the Arabian Gulf to London, let us say loading Ras Tanura – you will see that Ras Tanura is not listed under London. The reason for this is that there are thirty-seven ports listed in the Arabian Gulf. Thus for each discharge port it would be necessary to list an additional 37 separate rates for each discharge port – a lot of space would therefore be wasted so **Quoin Island** is used as a waypoint. (Rates for voyages to and from the Black Sea and Lake Maracaibo are treated in the same way, therefore for the Black Sea you would look for **Uskudar** and for Lake Maracaibo you would look for **San Carlos Island).**

The calculation is therefore in two parts, and for the following example let us assume that we need the Cape/Cape rate:

Under Worldscale 2010

1. Quoin/London $29.10 C   21,740 miles

Now turn to page 1,

Arabian Gulf rates:

Ras Tanura/Quoin $1.07   747miles

Therefore WS flat	$30.17	22,487 miles

3.2.1   Variable Differential

To see how the variable differential is applied we take the example below. At the top of the list there is "(see page D-3)" which is where the variable differential is listed. What is the flat rate for a vessel loading at Ash Shihr and discharging at Jamnagar SPM?

Ash Shihr/Jamnagar SPM	$5.05	2,530 miles
Variable diff.	$0.10	
WS100	= $5.15	
Therefore W140	$= \dfrac{140 \times 5.15}{100} = \$7.21$	

You will see that because this is a 'variable differential' the total is multiplied by the Worldscale rate as fixed.

You may wonder why it is necessary to have a variable differential. These usually apply where the port charges on a given ship will be assessed differently depending upon whether she is carrying products or crude and whether she is loading or discharging and so it is easier for these differences to be tackled just on one page of the Schedule as part of the market rate level agreed.

Fixed Differentials

Fixed differentials are applied in a different way to calculate the freight earned. The Worldscale page for discharge ports in the U.S.A. will be notated "(See page D-5)"; we will look at the calculation of the freight for a tanker loading 130,000 mt at Lucina Terminal (see page D-4)

GT 70,000 Under Worldscale 2010

Lucina/Philadelphia	= $15.56/pmt	11,010 miles
Therefore freight	= 130,000 x 15.56 =	$2,022,800

Fixed differentials.		
Philadelphia plus 0.0647x 70,000	= 4,529	
Lucina plus 1.63 X 130,000	= 211,900	
Gross freight	= $216,429	$2239,229

If the rate was W75 the calculation would be as follows:

15.56 × 0.75	= $1.67/pmt
11.67 × 130,000	= $1,517,100
plus .0647 X 70,000	= $4,529
plus 1.63 x 130,000	= $211,900
Therefore Gross Freight	= $1,733,529

N.B. A fixed rate differential does not alter with the Worldscale rate as fixed.

In general the fixed differentials apply where the port costs vary due to some levies or dues which are calculated irrespective of the amount of cargo loaded. A special case of a fixed rate differential would be the canal rate differentials.

Here is another example:

> Calculate the freight payable from Yanbu to Lavera via Suez. Loading 100,000 metric tonnes of crude oil the vessel has an SCNRT of 55,000 and a GT of 56,000 fixed at a rate of W85.

Under Worldscale 2010

Yanbu/Lavera (S)	= $8.76	4,147 miles
Worldscale flat	= $8.76	
Therefore W85	= $7.446	
Rotterdam fixed differential	= $0.27	

(Note: Use all the decimal points in these calculations as they are multiplied by a large figure)

Freight payable =$7.446 x 100,000	= $744,600
Rotterdam diff = 100,000 x .027	= $27,000
Suez diff = 55,000 x 4.49	= $246,950
plus lump sum increase	= $219,500

Vessel under 130,001 metric tones
vessel's draft less than 47 ft. so no
additional lumpsum applied)

Total payable	= $1,238,050

Worldscale is an easy reference point of market figures and you can see at a glance from market reports whether the market is rising or falling. For example VLCCs fixing AG/West WS 62.5 one week and WS 65 the next indicates a rise in the markets. Very few people know, or need to know, what this equates to in dollars per tonne. Remember, dollar per tonne fixtures in the dry cargo trades, to be equated, need to take account of laytime, distances, port costs and conditions to gain any accurate comparison between one voyage and another

Although Worldscale does supply a list of demurrage rates (liquidated damages paid by a Charterer for delaying the ship) it is common to agree a cash lumpsum per day or pro rata usually relative to the Owners anticipated income per day on the voyage plus an allowance for heating the cargo and daily port costs.

The convenience of Worldscale is that by agreeing a Worldscale rate to any one port out of a range, let us say Havre/Hamburg, the Owner knows that the additional steaming distance and differential of port charges is allowed for in the calculation of the flat rate and that his daily return will be the same or as near as makes no difference whichever port is used in that range. However extreme differences in port costs can affect income on short voyages at high or low rate levels.

It is important to remember that these calculations are all done on the Worldscale standard ship, therefore if your ship is of a different size, speed or consumption, or indeed if bunker prices have altered dramatically from those used, the returns will be vastly different from those implied by the Worldscale rate.

On the standard Worldscale a ship fixing Worldscale 100 from the Arabian Gulf to the Mediterranean will give a return of 12,000 per day. Similarly, fixing that ship from Sidi Kerir cross Med. will also give a return of 12,000 per day. You cannot do the same calculation for a VLCC. Worldscale 60 from the Arabian Gulf to Rotterdam and back will give a much better return per day than Worldscale 60 from Sidi Kerir/Genoa and back. This is because for the shorter trip the port charges on a bigger ship are out of proportion to the port charges on the standard ship, therefore when comparing rates you must always compare like with like, that is to say, one size of ship with a similar size of ship on a similar voyage length.

3.3 AVERAGE FREIGHT RATE ASSESSMENT – AFRA

Initially devised and developed by Shell and latterly BP, AFRA became accepted by various Taxation authorities as a basis for assessing transportation costs for such things as intercompany movements of oil.

AFRA is compiled by the London Tanker Brokers Panel and based on all known fixtures in the open market and information relating to transport agreements supplied by various oil companies.

Essentially AFRA provides an average (historical) freight rate for given trades over a monthly period 16th/15th of the month respectively in the given size ranges. For example when oil companies swap cargoes or the shipping departments provide ships to subsidiaries or affiliates the use of the AFRA Rate is a convenient way to agree the freight rate.

NB: these rates are only available to subscribers.

The term AFRAMAX was initially accepted to mean 79,999 but in fact there is more than one range of sizes in the scale viz:

GP	General Purpose	16,500/ 24,999 dwt
MR	Medium Range	25,000/ 44,999 dwt
LRI	Large Range 1	45,000/ 79,999 dwt
LR2	Large Range 2	80,000/159,000 dwt
VL	VLCC	160,000/319,999 dwt
UL	ULCC	320,000/549,999 dwt

3.4 FACTORS INFLUENCING THE FREIGHT MARKETS

Shipping has not been short of forecasters willing to predict future market levels. To understand forecasts we really need to look at how the market is measured on a day-to-day basis. To watch the market effectively we start by keeping a note of the fixtures for our own trades. For example those involved in the dirty trades would probably look at some if not all of the following:

VLCCs	AG/West
	AG/East
	WAF/USA
1.0 million barrels	WAF/West
	Black Sea/Med
70/80,000 dwt	AG/East
	UK/Cont
	Cross Med
50,000 dwt	Caribbean/USAC

In the clean trades:

30/70,000 dwt	AG/East
	Caribbean/up coast
	UK/Cont/Med

There will be other trades that will be fixed regularly and may give you a better reference point for your own particular market movements.

By studying the graph of the market rates you will readily appreciate that the market is volatile to say the least. We can see, with the benefit of hindsight, when it was best to fix a ship for a long-term timecharter and when it was best to fix for a short-term that is, from the Owner's point of view and always assuming a charterer could be found.

We obviously would like to make use of this knowledge and the first step is to see when the market was rising and what caused it. In fact we soon see that political events have the most significant impact on rates – usually such incidents are unpredictable (for those not directly involved) – for example wars. One time that a political event did not cause a rise in the market was in August 1990 with the occupation of Kuwait by Iraqi forces, which resulted in the effective loss of 4.0 m BBLS per day production from those two countries. A look at the pipeline map will show that the Iraqi production exported by pipeline through Ceyhan and Saudi Arabia was stopped. The exports of product and to a lesser extent crude stopped virtually overnight. Demand for oil temporarily declined and the availability of crude oil from other Middle East producers, as well as the North Sea, West Africa and Venezuela, more than made up the shortfall.

One of the factors much discussed at the time was the effect high prices could have on the search for alternative energy and gas fields close to consumers. High prices could not only cause inflation in consuming economies but also reduce throughput and reduce the income to producers, at least in the short term.

Wars in general tend to increase demand for shipping but in this case shorter alternative supply routes and reduced consumer demand caused crude oil rates for tankers to decline.

However, a side effect occurred with the war causing a shortage of clean product East of Suez. The armed forces moving into Saudi Arabia needed large quantities of jet and diesel fuel. Thus a reduced amount was available for export to their major customers – the Far East in general and Japan in particular. Substitute supplies were available in the Mediterranean, in UK Continent and Caribbean – all these areas being much further from the consumer increased the 'tonne mile' demand, so we saw clean tanker rates rise sharply. The invasion itself took the world by surprise but who could have accurately predicted the effect such an action would have on the tanker market?

From the point of view of an independent Owner think of the difficulty of making an investment decision (possibly for up to $120 million for a new double hull VLCC) with so many imponderables affecting not only the earning capacity of your investment but also its re-sale value. It is little wonder many banks, institutions and individuals find other more attractive areas of investment. Companies do, however, become involved in buying ships and there are two extremes of approach to illustrate the dilemma. Take the company ordering a new building today. Perhaps it will be two years before the vessel is delivered; who can predict what the market will be doing then? Assume a 15-year economic life, the investor, therefore, is likely to be trying to predict the market for 17 years ahead. The highest price a ship will receive will be the building price (perhaps as a re-sale). The lowest price will be her scrap value. Thus a newbuilding VLCC with a light weight of approximately 30,000 metric tons will be purchased for $100 million and sold 17 years later for scrap say, at $200 per lt weight ($6.0 m). The downside could be considered $94 million.

The second case is the purchase of a secondhand ship between 15/20 years old for, say, $17-$20 million. The Owner will probably take delivery in 2/3 months and have to forecast the market over the next 4/9 years by which time the vessel will be reaching the end of her economic life. The downside risk is much less and the secondhand price will be more closely related to market levels as dictated by sentiment, than the newbuilding price. Thus, the secondhand purchase appears to be less risky.

Freight index graphs tell us what has gone on in the past but we now have to consider how we can measure what is going on in today's market. This is where the market report comes in. Market reports are in various forms and complexity, each serving a different purpose, see **Appendix 2** for examples. Initially the brokers will pick up fixtures during the working day and collate these for circulation to their correspondents by various means. This is a daily fixture list and by its nature cannot give much of a commentary on what is happening. It should be borne in mind that a large number of fixtures are private and will not be reported – of course it is impossible to know how many private fixtures are included but as a guide it is estimated that perhaps 25% of spot fixtures are not reported.

Weekly reports usually enable the compiler to become an author and make comments on the preceding week's fixtures without necessarily being able to devote space to commentary on the longer term. These tend to be just one or two pages and easily read. However, even with available speed of e-mail communication a weekly report circulated on Friday and read on Monday tends to become a historical reference.

In-house research departments with comprehensive cover of more trades and commodities frequently write monthly reports. Greater depth of content and graphs are in evidence and the writer will be able to examine the main trends and discuss the reasons behind them. It is quite common for monthly reports to be available only to selected clients or subscribers for a small charge; nowadays these reports will often be available through the broker's website and be downloaded making the whole process much less costly in terms of distribution.

The leading six monthly report (January/June plus July/December) is the World Tanker Fleet Review once published by brokers John I Jacobs and now taken over by SS+Y, London, for which an annual charge is made. This gives a comprehensive review of the tanker market during the preceding six months and contains very good statistics.

Various journals and periodicals will publish fixture reports and market commentary. Lloyd's List, daily; Fairplay, weekly; Tradewinds, weekly. Members of the Baltic Exchange have access to the Tanker Indices.

It is important for the reader of these reports to establish the dates that are covered in the report and always to compare like with like.

One of the difficulties in assessing the oil market and the relative use of tankers is that detailed statistics often from government sources tend to be six months out of date, so that by the time a trend is indicated in "official" statistics, that trend is already apparent on the market.

A tendency for a section of the market to be stable combined with economic and even political information that indicates a chance of steady growth may be much more valuable than a "fashion". With world ability to build a ship in six months, any published suggestion that a class of ship will be needed tends to produce a flush of newbuilding orders and that section of the market is likely to be weakened before the projected growth. In shipping it is only the leaders that make money or if they are wrong lose it!

It is the same on the spot market. If one market is strong, ships will head for that area, so that as an owner facing a two-week ballast you may do better to head for a weak area as by the time you get there it will be an area that has been avoided by others so competition will be minimal.

These are tactical points that must be based on sound current market information secured as a professional service from the shipbrokers specialising in that sector.

The Shipbroker needs to assemble the facts, that is reported and unreported fixtures plus any market gossip where applicable and which have been checked or on which reservations need to be made. These should be reported in a logical order and any explanation of unusual rates given for an understanding of the market. A good report will start with a summary of the trends and follow with more detail. Perhaps the report may give an opinion of the future. As a word of warning it is not helpful to make obvious remarks, such as a shortage of ships will cause the market to get firmer! Nor expose yourself on a forecast with a few "ifs and buts"!

To look at the future trends you must take account of supply and demand of tankers as follows:-

Demand: The future demand for oil and its substitutes

The areas of production and consumption (e.g. the rate of increase in consumption in the Far East has been greater than Europe).

Supply: Future level of newbuilding activity

The technical specification of ships
Future levels of tanker scrapping
The efficiency of the existing fleet.

External   Environmental issues

Pressures   Oil companies' policies and mergers

3.5   OIL DEMAND

The effectiveness of energy conservation measures and oil substitution were undermined by the decline in oil prices between 1985/88. Oil consumption has risen since then and the developing countries have been the areas of greatest growth. Industrial countries, in particular United States of America, Japan and Europe, are the greatest users of VLCC tonnage. Some developing countries have to live with port restrictions giving the smaller vessel a trading opportunity for such destinations.

It has been estimated that a 1% growth in GDP (gross domestic product) will lead to a 0.3% rise in oil demand. This with OECD economic activity expected to rise at no more than 2% per annum a rise in oil demand should follow.

Any increased demand could be supplied from new areas of production; the closer the production is to the consumer the smaller the demand for transport. We are told that the new areas we can expect to see producing oil in the medium term are Mainland China and the new market economies of Eastern Europe, both have a high domestic need for oil, but any expanded oil market normally has a call for tankers even if it relies on the need for foreign exchange drawn from exports.

3.6   NEWBUILDING ACTIVITY

Virtually any newbuilding petrochemical tanker delivered over the last twenty-five years has not earned enough to justify construction costs but ordering continues and newbuilding prices were rising until December 1991 when tanker ordering slowed down – mainly due to low spot market rates and lack of period business, that is until 2000 when 'low' newbuilding prices and higher freight markets resulted in a surge of ordering and prices have risen continually in the past two years.

The reasons for this apparent irrational ordering include:

1. Technological progress. Newbuildings offer cargo flexibility and better efficiency due to improved engine design, hull form and propeller design. More automation allows lower manning scales thus together even in a bad market, ignoring capital repayments, a modern ship can earn a better return.

2. Attractive prices and terms. Whilst the levels of charter rates were consistently low, demand for newbuilding declined. In an effort to attract the few orders being made shipyards offered very attractive terms to keep the workforce ticking over. Prices had reached 'bargain basement' levels by 1985 coupled with the encouragement of government involved soft loans. Thus, the majority of newbuildings will usually be financed through the yard's own bank with a guarantee from the relevant government department.

   In fact one of the reasons why the tanker market is prone to overtonnaging is the bait provided to owners to build on attractive credit the latest "fashion" of tanker designed by the relative yard. If Owners were restricted on newbuilding credit by banks (as they tend to be on second hand ships) and if international agreement on such credit was more onerous, newbuilding would need to be financed by trading profit and there would be less risk of slump conditions persisting over a long period.

3.   Speculative building has seen the price of a VLCC newbuilding rise from US $50 million to over $120million.

3.7   TANKER SCRAPPING

In the last 25 years the peak year for tanker scrapping was 1985 when 26.63 million tons was broken up. Whereas in 1990 only 20 tankers of 0.75 million tons representing about 0.3% of the world tanker fleet was scrapped, the lowest proportion since 1974.

Scrap prices in early 1997 were between USD 150 and USD 175 per ldt whereas in IQ 2005 US$400 has been exceeded. Bearing in mind that a VLCC will have between 30,000 and 40,000 tons of steel she is worth between about $12.0 and $16 million dollars for scrap. The scrap price is, of course, driven by the demand for its product – billets and reinforcing bars.

The importance of the Middle East as a long-term producer can be understood mainly by looking at their estimated reserves, more than 50 years greater than their nearest rival. As European and US domestic production declines the oil from further afield will be substituted. This will be of assistance to the VLCC and ULCC owners. Although producers in the Middle East have built new refineries designed to increase the value of exported oil by offering relatively expensive petrochemicals to markets worldwide, a difficulty always exists in transportation which is much more expensive in a product tanker than a simple crude oil VLCC. This is why major oil companies built refineries close to the consumers market which they were supplying.

However, as soon as producers start to have control over a limited supply of crude oil, such product will have a readier market beyond areas that can today be economically supplied. Much depends on the internal raw material pricing policy.

To avoid transport problems, some countries, such as Kuwait, purchased downstream facilities such as oil terminals and retail petrol outlets in the main consuming areas giving them greater control of production and marketing. Long haul product routes will not be of significant help to the smaller product carrier because longer routes require larger ships and there are now product carriers on order of 120,000 dwt.

The shorter the trade route the less need for economy in size as compared with flexibility, so that pipelines terminating in the Mediterranean can call for ships of 100/150,000 dwt for the short passage particularly to the European Mediterranean. It is not always convenient for a refiner to receive a large quantity of one grade of crude oil calling for storage and interest on the capital tied up during usage

External Pressures

The oil companies have achieved cheap oil transportation for almost 30 years. The fleet is frequently criticised for being old. A newbuilding, however cannot be paid for at historic charter rates. The pressure of politicians and environmentalists after some "landmark oil spills" has lead to the introduction of legislation requiring all tankers over 5,000 tonnes to be double hull construction, by 2010. This is an upward pressure on freight rates.

The oil companies are the tanker industry's major customer. Some, e.g. Shell and BPAmoco treat their shipping as a service to their oil side – central control. Others, e.g. Exxon Mobil are decentralised, the shipping division must make a profit and compete with other divisions for investment funds. Since the *Erika* incident (Nov 2001) the latter approach will be seen as irresponsible, the choice of ship being price driven

If the proposition that "the Charterer is in control of the tanker under a voyage charter" is accepted we are likely to see effective steps taken to ensure that cargo is carried on modern well-found vessels – this implies long term charters and ordering of newbuildings by the oil companies.

3.8 SELF-ASSESSMENT AND TEST QUESTIONS

Attempt the following and check your answers from the text:

1. In what ways could the efficiency of the existing tanker fleet be improved?
2. What factors affect the structure of the tanker market?
3. What information is a broker trying to find when covering the market?
4. What are the advantages of Worldscale to the tanker industry?

Having completed Chapter Three, answer the following and submit your essay to your Tutor:

How do you see the tanker market developing over the next five years for **ONE** of the following ship types?

VL + ULCC = s; 1.0 m BBLS; Product Tankers; Gas Carriers

Chapter 4

VOYAGE ESTIMATING

4.1   INTRODUCTION

In this Chapter we examine the voyage estimate and the procedures for calculating the value of a piece of business.

It is useful to remember the following:

Owner is interested in dollars per day income.

Charterer is interested in dollars per tonne delivered.

Voyage estimating is not only an Owner's requirement; Charterers and Brokers will also need to carry out estimates. Charterers are interested in the cost per ton for the carriage of their cargo and in voyage charters this is purely a case of a dollar per ton rate. In others, such as time charters, it is necessary to calculate the costs over a given time span and quantity of cargo carried. Calculations for more than one vessel may be needed to determine the optimum choice.

Brokers should be able to use simple estimates to enable them to compare one market with another. For example, let us say a tanker is discharging in the Far East. The Owner may consider ballasting back to The Gulf for his next cargo but suppose a cargo became available in Indonesia, a shorter ballast, perhaps to discharge in Japan or the United States, how will the Broker be able to estimate the equivalent level required, probably as a lumpsum, if he does not know the going return for a Gulf loading? The Broker should be able to equate Worldscale rates to daily returns for at least a few proforma voyages in his trades – for Brokers involved in the dirty trades, the following may be considered:

VLCC	AG/East options
	AG/West options
	AG/Red Sea
120/130,000 dwt	AG/West options
	Cross Med
	WAF/West options
35/80,000 dwt	AG/East options
	UK/Cont
	UKC/USA

Perhaps you can identify others that suit your particular trades better.

Whatever the reason you may be involved in estimating there are some basic rules, which will assist you to do your estimates quickly and accurately.

1.   Use the same estimate format.

2.   Be neat so that you can check back easily.

3.   Be as accurate as possible. Check your calculations.

4.   File the estimates for future reference.

5.   Build up a file of current port costs.

To be fair, it is true to say that a simple 'spread sheet' on a computer will do all the above for the estimator provided the data inserted is accurate.

To compare the different alternatives that may be available when the ship is open an Owner has to consider many different factors: –(e.g. the length of voyage, port costs, port time, freight rate and how much cargo the vessel can lift.) These factors are taken along with the standard information for each vessel such as the speed and bunker consumption, the price and quantity of bunkers remaining on board at the commencement of the voyage and any replenishment en route. These figures combined in the estimate give the Owner the daily surplus which, for an Owner, is the yardstick for comparison of the voyages on offer.

There are four elements of an estimate:

1.	The collection of known facts common to the estimates.

2.	The introduction of information relevant only to the voyage in question.

3.	Calculation of earnings.

4.	The final analysis resulting in the daily surplus figure.

From the outset we need to understand the fundamental difference between 'voyage' and 'running' costs. Voyage costs are those applicable to the voyage in question: port charges, cost of bunkers needed to perform the voyage, special cleaning or tank preparation including ballast disposal, cost of extra insurance which may be required, such as additional war risk premium, premiums for breaking Institute Warranty Limits and over age insurance, if applicable. Running costs, on the other hand, would include crew wages and costs for such things as crew repatriation, stores, provisions, minor repairs, hull and machinery insurance premiums and possibly allowance for dry dock and special survey costs. Running costs are used in an estimate but usually as a deduction from the TCE.

Most shipping companies have an accounts department which collates the ship's running expenses from invoices paid and on a regular basis produce a daily running cost which will be the figure used by the estimator.

Obviously an Owner may have a different attitude to long term running costs (say, including docking and survey) to his view of costs on a single voyage lasting a few days, but ultimately one adds up to the other.

To carry out the estimate it is important to decide what voyage legs will be included for purposes of the calculation. If there are a number of alternatives it is best to calculate the round voyage, load/discharge/load ports (as Worldscale does). However, if only one piece of business is available we should start the voyage at the discharge port through the load port to the final discharge port, but beware of and if necessary allow for a long ballast to the next probable load port or indeed a short ballast as a benefit. When calculating the potential value of a voyage the estimator needs to have a sound understanding of the basics involved and to follow a suitable pattern. Sample estimate forms are included with this Chapter, see **Appendix 4,** (or you might like to set up a spreadsheet) and it is recommended that you use these throughout these Chapters, although in your working environment you might find other layouts more suitable to your requirements. The purpose is to have a layout with which you are familiar so that you can be sure of including all the factors involved, look for possible errors or results and find them easily.

On the first line of the form we insert the Charterer's name and the Broker's name and date. This enables us at some future time to know to whom we were talking and about which cargo. In the next section we insert the details of the vessel, the name, speed, consumptions and any other details that are relevant to this particular voyage including the consumptions at sea and in port.

## 4.2	ROUTE

Each leg of the proposed voyage is entered. For example, as suggested, from the previous discharge port to the load port followed by the loaded leg from load to discharge port and possibly some allowance for loss of or benefit of position relative to the next possible load port. The majority of tanker distances are now published in the Worldscale Schedule and is a great timesaver for all estimators. Be aware, however, that distances printed in the book are for the **'round voyage'** and so for a single leg remember to divide the printed distance by two. The fact that Worldscale rates are calculated on a round voyage from load to discharge and return to the first load port can cause wide rate differentials when the voyage concerned is partly a "backhaul", i.e. a voyage that would normally be wholly or partly a ballast leg.

For example a ship loads in Saudi Arabia, say, Ras Tanura, for Japan The rate paid allows for a ballast return to Ras Tanura.

The ship might follow with a voyage from Saudi Arabia to the US Gulf via the Cape or via Suez, if she is Suezmax size.

But a cargo comes on the market from Indonesia to US Gulf – the same ultimate discharge area.

By loading Indonesia on freight earning passage the Owner has saved his ballast expenses, say, Singapore/Ras Tanura. The distances Singapore/Cape and Ras Tanura/Cape are not all that different, but if he was going via Suez in both cases the saving in steaming time is only the deviation into the Gulf to Ras Tanura.

This situation could be one of the reasons for a lump sum rate being agreed rather than a Worldscale rate and makes approximate voyage estimating even by a Broker of great importance.

Again one could have a cargo quoted, say, from Sidi Kerir (Egyptian Med) to Bourgas (Black Sea) and if the Owner had a chance of reloading Black Sea his ballast voyage is considerably reduced. It is unlikely that he could fix both voyages at the same time, but a voyage estimate combining both voyages would be valuable in assessing the possible benefit.

Once all the distances have been obtained you should consider whether or not to make an allowance for bad weather. For instance, a vessel ballasting across the North Atlantic in the winter may be delayed by as much as three days due to bad weather. A laden VLCC going around the Cape of Good Hope towards the United States or Europe may find her voyage extended by two to three days due to the bad weather or adverse currents. Once all these distances and times have been assessed you can now total the days at sea and the corresponding fuel and diesel oil consumption where applicable. Now we can allow for any time at a bunker port if required.

Consumption for heating cargo is a consideration. Heating may just involve maintaining the cargo at its loaded temperature or it may involve upgrading the cargo from the loaded to its required discharge temperature. This could involve quite heavy consumption of fuel oil. It is possible that some cleaning will be required between different grades of cargo and this will involve consumption of fuel and possibly diesel.

Next we allow for canal transit time and its consumptions. Remember that the voyage leg distances might have taken account of the distance transited in a Canal, but Worldscale does NOT include this distance only allowing time (24 hours for Panama, 30 hours for Suez). Otherwise extra time should be allowed for, also bunker consumption during transit. In an ideal world all laydays would commence just as soon as a ship was ready to load, however there are frequently occasions when a vessel's ETA pre-dates commencement of the laytime and so we can allow for that in the estimate here, under waiting time.

4.3   PORT TIME

Typically in tankers the laytime is 72 hours plus 6 hours notice of readiness at each port. Therefore port time here could be computed as 3.5 days. However, Worldscale's estimate allows 4 days (plus 12 hours) sometimes you may wish to allow for periods that may be excepted such as inability to move from anchorage to berth due to weather. We can now total the time on the voyage, the fuel and diesel oil consumed.

4.3.1   Cargo Calculations

The calculation of how much cargo can be carried is fundamental. Sometimes the cargo available is less than the capacity of the vessel and such calculations are unnecessary. However, in such a case perhaps the vessel can be supplied with low cost extra bunkers or obviate the necessity of bunkering on route. If the vessel is being paid freight on a lumpsum basis, provided the Charterer has not asked for a guaranteed minimum cargo that can be lifted, this calculation is only of value as a comparison with other business that may involve a full cargo.

If the estimator has to examine various alternatives with the object of maximum cargo lift, thereby increasing the profitability of the venture, he will first have to find out whether any of the ports or berths intended to be used and almost certainly and properly included by name in the charter have a draft restriction. Consideration must then be given to the load line zones for the proposed voyage, which may also affect bunkering plans.

Description of the load line zones has already been given and it is at this point that the estimator has to check to see which, if any, of the load line zones will restrict the draft.

Where a draft restriction will come into effect the summer draft is compared with the available draft and the difference in the centimetres multiplied by the TPC (tonnes per centimetre). TPC x difference in draft, gives a quantity which is deducted from the summer deadweight giving the available deadweight. After making allowance for bunkers, fresh water and constants, the vessel's DWCC is found. For example:

40,000 SDWT	on 11.20 m. Summer Draft	TPC 41 mt
Draft restriction	9.50 m.	
Loss of draft	1.70 m. = 170 cm	
Loss of DWT		= TPC x 170 cm
		= 41 x 170
		= 6,970 mt.
DWT on 9.50 m		= 40,000 – 6,970
		= 33,030 mt.
Less bunkers	1,500 mt	
Less F.W	200 mt	
Less constants	400 mt	
	2,100 mt	
		2,100 mt
DWCC		30,930 mt

In the previous paragraphs we have referred to salt water drafts but there are certain areas of the world where the water is either 'fresh' or 'brackish'.

The density of salt water is 1,025 kilograms per cubic metre and the density of fresh water is 1,000 kilograms per cubic metre. Going back to basic physics we remember that all floating bodies displace their own weight in water, thus to displace her weight in salt water, a vessel will reach a particular draft, but when she transits into fresh water she needs to displace more water or a greater volume and therefore her draft increases. Similarly, if she is loading in fresh water and transits into salt water her draft will decrease. The amount that any ship's draft changes when moving from salt to fresh water and vice versa is known as the fresh water allowance (FWA). On a 60,000 ton tanker the fresh water allowance may be as much as 30 cms.

When a vessel is in a river port close to the sea the water is frequently neither fresh nor salt but in between and this is known as 'brackish water'. The term 'brackish' is, however, imprecise and could, for example, mean any gravity between 1,001 and 1,024, therefore if you are told that a port has a brackish water draft restriction it is essential to find out what the specific gravity of the water actually is. Once you have the specific gravity it is an easy matter to calculate the additional draft to which a vessel can be loaded and is known as the Brackish Water Allowance (BWA).

Assuming:

Density (d) 1,020   FWA 300 mm

BWA mm $= \text{FWA} \dfrac{(1025 - d)}{25}$

Therefore BWA mm $= 300 \text{ mm}. \dfrac{(1025 - 1020)}{25}$

$= 300 \text{ mm}. \dfrac{5}{25}$

$= \dfrac{1500 \text{ mm}}{25}$

$= 60 \text{ mm}$

Therefore the increased draft the ship can load to is 60 mm

4.4   BUNKERS

Tankers usually load in an oil producing and/or refining port, where bunker prices may be low enough to bunker for the round voyage, but if the vessel needs to bunker elsewhere the cost, including deviation and port costs need to be included.

Some smaller and/or older ships may burn diesel oil in the main engine rather than fuel oil when manoeuvring in ports or canals, i.e. to make sure the main engine reacts quickly and allowance should be given also for heating, discharging and any delays.

Beware of published bunker prices they may not include barging costs to vessel as many Owners have discounts from contracted suppliers overall or based on quantities supplied per annum.

4.5   PORT DISBURSEMENTS

Most shipowning companies will have a good idea of the disbursements payable by their vessels loading and discharging at the ports regularly used and will usually have no objection to advising the Broker involved in their negotiations of such costs for estimating purposes. If nothing is entered on those files a check can always be made with BIMCO or INTERTANKO to see what, if any, estimates they can provide which are current. If time permits, however, an Owner will have checked with local agents in the port involved just to make sure he has the most accurate figures available. When enquiring on estimated port disbursements the Agent will normally need to know the vessel's name, flag, deadweight, draft, LOA, GT and NT. The

Agent is then in a position to forward by e-mail or fax an accurate breakdown of port costs. When checking your own files for previous calls it is important not to confuse an Owner's voyage expenses and running costs. Such items as pilotage, towage, line handling, light dues and agency costs are all attributable to the voyage, but also in the disbursement account may be such things as crew expenses, repatriation, air fares, cash to Master, spare parts, repairs and servicing, which are all running costs. When considering canal transit costs there are two elements; the first is the transit tolls and the second is the vessel's disbursements.

4.6   INSURANCE AND CREW EXPENSES

The next item is the insurance and crew expenses involved with a particular voyage. There are three types of extra insurance premium which may be incurred during the voyage.

First, if a vessel is required to break the Institute Warranty Limits (IWL) or International Navigating Conditions as it is now called, possibly to enter the Baltic Sea or St. Lawrence Seaway in the wintertime.

Second, War Risk Additional Premium (WRAP).

The vessel's Hull and Machinery insurance covers war risks for all except certain excluded areas where, if the vessel does enter one must check with the underwriters and establish the levels of Additional Premium (AP) before proceeding. A good example recently was a vessel going to the Gulf war area where additional premiums were paid as the vessel transits certain areas of the Gulf

Third, Over age Premium.

This extra insurance premium concerns ships which are classified as 'over age' by cargo underwriters. Initially this extra insurance premium would fall upon the Charterer as the insurer of the cargo, but in weak markets Charterers will try to impose such a cost onto the Owner arguing that if the Owner does not pay this charge the Charterer might as well fix a more modern vessel. The Owner might therefore agree to this but should try to insert a maximum amount of premium that will be charged and such an amount should be entered in the voyage estimate.

Proof of the additional premium should be provided to Owners, but there have been cases where locally an AP is charged which the insurer re-insures elsewhere without incurring an AP, so it is worth checking insurer's attitudes internationally.

Also included here as a cost should be a crew war bonus which an Owner may have to negotiate with his crew, or the extra expenses incurred with sending a vessel to an icebound area where perhaps the crew needs to be kitted out with cold weather gear. The last line of this section, total daily costs, can be tackled in two ways. Either the estimator can enter the daily running costs of the ship multiplied by the total number of days on the voyage or if the Owner has given you a time charter rate which he wishes to achieve for a particular voyage, say $10,000 a day then you would multiply that figure by the number of days to give you the total 'daily costs' at the required timecharter rate. The sum of all these costs is now added together to give the gross voyage expenses.

Usually running costs (which a Broker may not know) are omitted, but if the resultant income per day does not cover the Owner's costs or expected income they will not take the business, unless for a particular reason, such as positioning, they are prepared to take a loss.

To calculate the earnings we can now go to the Worldscale book to establish the flat rate for the voyage involved and this is entered in the space available. (Remember Worldscale 100 = flat rate). For ease of illustration let us say the flat rate is $10 but the Worldscale rate for the voyage is W85. Therefore alongside the cargo quantity we put Worldscale 85 which equates to $8.50. Multiply 8.50 by the cargo quantity to achieve the gross freight. Deduct commission giving the net freight. For ease of calculation and when making rate adjustments do not put commission under 'voyage expenses'.

To calculate the voyage result the gross voyage expenses are now deducted from the net freight giving us a voyage surplus. The voyage surplus is now divided by the number of days to give the daily surplus. Now the daily surplus is added to the running costs used in the total daily costs to give us a Time Charter Equivalent (TCE). Had we used for instance $10,000 a day as being the Owner's required rate then we would add $10,000 to the daily surplus which would give us the applicable time charter rate for the ship.

We have run this section of the estimate at Worldscale 85 but perhaps the market is rising and we hope to achieve a higher rate. We can now calculate the freight at Worldscale 90 and we can see what a five-point differential will make to the time charter rate. Worldscale 90 equates to $9 x the cargo loaded which gives us a gross freight less commission giving us the net freight. We can then establish the voyage surplus divide it by the number of days giving us a daily surplus, adding that to the running costs used gives us another, higher, time charter rate. Thus we now have a time charter rate for WS 85 and another for WS 90.

We can now compute the difference each 5 Worldscale points make to the time charter return, or you can take the extra freight $0.50 x cargo **less commission** divided by the number of days to get the increased daily income for 5 Worldscale points. (Running and voyage costs are constant.)

Before we look at any examples remember 'despatch money' is not paid in tanker charterparties. A Broker should know or be able to find out quickly the Worldscale "market" rate level for a particular voyage usually based on the last business concluded. It is easy then to calculate percentage variations on possible rate levels and relative income per day, as shown above.

Now we go through an estimate for a voyage on VLCC WALRUS loading at Ras Tanura and discharging at London (see **Appendix 4**). The details of the Charterer, Broker and date are entered together with those of the ship (see **Appendix 3**). On this voyage we assume the vessel will load 260,000 mt. of cargo. The voyage will be via the Cape of Good Hope loaded and return via the Suez Canal in ballast. An allowance of 4.49 days has been made for bad weather – this is a matter of choice, some estimators would allow a percentage of the time on the laden leg. The time at sea is therefore 59 days. One day is allowed for Suez Canal transit southbound and four days for time in port. We are assuming we do not have Load Line Zone or draft restrictions at any point. We now calculate the War Risk Additional Premium (WRAP).

The Insured Value (I.V.) is $60.0 million and the applicable WRAP for Ras Tanura is 0.03%; i.e. $18,000 plus an allowance of $5,000 for crew war bonus.

The bunker price is $620 for 3,722.14 mt.

The port costs are $70,000 at load and $200,000 at discharge.

The Canal transit southbound in ballast is $265,000.

The total daily costs allocated are $10,000 per day, thus Gross Voyage Expenses are $2,128,489.63.

The 'Flat Rate' Ras Tanura to London Cape/Cape is $30.17/mt (see page 58) – do you understand why we are using this rate (C) even though we are returning via Suez?

The rate we are calculating is WS65, that is 65% of 30.17 = $19.6105/mt (use all the decimal places) less commission of 2.5%, the Nett Freight = $4,971,261.75.

The voyage surplus over the 64 days is $1,465,537.40 or a daily surplus of $22,898.18 per day.

Calculating the revenue at WS62.5 shows a daily surplus of $19,910.76 per day. Thus for each 2.5 points the daily surplus alters by $2,987 per day.

Now if you would like to do some examples turn to **Appendix 4**, where you will find the details of three types of tanker the: VLCC, Suezmax and a product tanker.

Here are some examples for you to try (use WS extracts from Chapter Three or **Appendix 6**. Other information is on the datasheet, **Appendix 7**).

Voyages on the *WALRUS*

		Quantity	Rate
i)	Kharg Island/Yokohama	260,000 mt	W 80
ii)	Ras Tanura/Ain Sukhna	260,000 mt	W 75
iii)	Ras Tanura/Loop	260,000 mt	W 60

Voyages on the *DOLPHIN*

i)	Mina al Fahal/Genoa	125,000 mt	W115
ii)	Mina al Fahal/Singapore	125,000 mt	W105
iii)	Bonny Loop	130,000 mt	W110

Voyages on the *OTTER*

i)	Punta Cardon/Philadelphia	30,000 mt	W400
ii)	Punta Cardon/Genoa	30,000 mt	W310
iii)	Augusta/Fawley	30,000 mt	W290

4.7   A LUMPSUM RATE (LS)

Having done a number of estimates using the Worldscale Schedule, we are aware that the big advantage of Worldscale is that if we have agreed a rate to a range of ports, let us say one or two safe ports Japan, or one or two safe ports UK.Cont Bordeaux/Hamburg range we are confident that the return achieved by the Owner on any one of those voyages will be approximately the same as the return calculated for any other of the ports within the range. Sometimes though charterers require a Lumpsum rate for their business. Examples are:

Voyages from Indonesia to Europe or USA

Voyages from Med., UKC, or WAF to Far East.

In fact any aberration in oil prices is liable to create a temporary demand in unusual directions which call for Lumpsum rates. Here the estimator has to adopt a rather more conservative approach to the distances and port costs involved because we are not going to be covered by Worldscale for any anomalies within the port costs and distance ranges.

Let us consider an example of an Indonesia to USAC or USG a cargo of approximately one million barrels. The Indonesian Archipelago is very large, as is the United States Atlantic Coast or United States Gulf. To calculate the Lumpsum rate correctly, you need to take the load and discharge ports which are furthest apart. In addition you must find out from the Charterers whether they intend to load at one or two ports and whether they intend to discharge at one or two ports, so that at the outset you can allow for those costs in your figures; also is any heating of cargo required? These specifications must be clearly stated in your offer So you must look carefully at the voyage route and port disbursements, taking the most pessimistic figures you can now calculate the gross voyage expenses using the time charter return required by the Owner for this particular voyage in your total daily costs.

The net freight = the gross voyage expenses, therefore you have to make allowances for the commission payable, for example if there was 5% commission payable you would divide the gross voyage expenses by 95 and multiply by 100 to give you the gross freight figure to achieve the net freight required.

e.g. Assume gross voyage expenses are $1,550,000 at the Timecharter return required by the Owner, that is the net freight figure which should be received by the Owner. Thus assuming 5% commission:-

$$\frac{\$1,550,000}{95} \times 100 = \$1,631,578$$

As an Owner it is important with Lumpsum freights to make sure that you specify the range of ports covered or nominated and that your rate applies to one load to one discharge (or two loads to one discharge) or a differential is added for each extra port so that there can be no misunderstanding at a later stage. Remember that allowing for a second load or discharge port is not just a matter of adding on the port disbursements, you need to allow for the extra steaming involved with two or more ports. Where multiple ports are required in a Lumpsum rate also specify 'Geographical rotation' to ensure that the vessel does not retrace her steps, adding to the length of the voyage without additional earnings.

In the past a Lumpsum rate has caused confusion amongst Owners and Charterers as to whether it includes any canal tolls involved with the voyage when the lumpsum rate is combined with Worldscale terms and conditions.

It should be made clear by the Broker, but Worldscale states "Fixed and variable rate differentials ………… must be taken into consideration when using Worldscale rates" also "Terms and Conditions are matters which are solely the concern of the contracting parties".

It has been held under English Law that a LS includes the canal tolls thus no FIXED DIFFERENTIALS may be added.

Even if the parties concerned do not do so the good Broker will always make sure that this point is covered which might otherwise lead to a dispute. It is the Brokers job to make sure that no problems arise in interpretation of the contract.

4.7.1 Calculation of Wordscale Break-Even Rate

When an Owner has stipulated a time charter rate that he requires for a particular voyage, we can obviously do the calculation at two Worldscale rates and then just calculate the difference required to show the variation per Worldscale point to give us a rough idea of the break-even rate. However a quicker way of achieving this is once we have established the gross voyage costs on the basis of the Owner's required T/C return we multiply the cargo lifting by the Worldscale Flat Rate (W100), deduct the commission applicable then divide the costs by the earnings. That is to say divide the gross voyage expenses by the net rate at Worldscale 100 and you will see from the example (at the foot of **Appendix 4**) we arrive at the break-even rate just by pressing a few buttons on the calculator.

4.7.2 Thoughts on Voyage Estimating

The estimates we have done thus far have concentrated either on round voyages or trips from the discharge port through the load port to the next discharge port. To face the facts in estimating it is essential to consider the market as it stands at that moment and look for the best income for the ship in her actual position, whilst allowing for any benefit or loss of position after discharge.

For example if the Caribbean market is strong it may pay an Owner to take a poor freight to reach that market.

There is no point in applying the three days the ship waited off Malta to the income arising from a two-day voyage from Libya to Genoa. That voyage has to be considered on its own.

This is logical as on a poor market after extended delay an Owner would never be able to relate income on the next fixture to the cost of waiting – so he would never again fix his ship!

Spot employment is a risk with highs and lows, which are meant to average out as an income, somewhat above that offered by a secure timecharter, but market variations can wildly upset such a theory.

It is fair to say that a lot of tanker estimating done on the round voyage basis is historical from the time when with the limited number of load areas, for instance The Gulf and the Caribbean, ships would have to ballast back to that place for loading the next cargo. These days with other load areas such as the Mediterranean, the North Sea, the Far East, quite often results can be dramatically improved by doing a multi-leg voyage instead of just the round voyage, However, you do not really know whether this is achievable until after the event. Just to illustrate this, try a million barrel voyage from West Africa to the US Gulf and then back from East Coast Mexico to the Mediterranean. It will happen however that the rates for voyages in a direction that is often a ballast voyage will be severely discounted.

The final task for an Owner's voyage estimator is to re-run the figures once the voyage has been completed to see how they compared with those anticipated prior to fixing the voyage. This does two things. It gives you a much better idea of how accurate your port disbursements records are and overall how ships are generally performing vis a vis the figures you use in your voyage estimating.

4.8   SELF-ASSESSMENT AND TEST QUESTIONS

Attempt the following and check your answers from the text.

1. What costs would you include in:

    a) Voyage Costs and,

    b) Running Costs?

2. Why does a vessel's draft reduce when passing from fresh to salt water?

3. What factors determine a vessel's cargo lifting?

4. Itemise the costs to be included in a voyage estimate. Where would you obtain accurate figures for each of the costs?

Having completed Chapter Four attempt the following and submit your answers to your Tutor:

1. What data is needed to prepare a tanker voyage estimate?

2. Using information of your choice demonstrate how you would calculate a Worldscale break even rate for a specific voyage?

Chapter 5

CHARTERING MARKET PRACTICE

5.1   INTRODUCTION

In this Chapter we look at the typical steps and circumstances from an order being quoted up to a fixture. We look at the ways the orders are put into the market, highlight the pitfalls, examine the options and the ways to work the market and the requirements for a successful voyage.

There are many ways that an order may be quoted, negotiated and fixed. The approach adopted is dictated by the Charterer, the type of business and will depend on whether they need to keep the order and fixture private and confidential. If it is a market order perhaps they have to be seen to quote the whole market, to be openly giving all suitable vessels a chance to offer. Alternatively the Charterer has so many cargoes that the Brokers keep them informed of available ships and their rate ideas (just in case he can put the business together on a date and a rate at which it will 'fly'). In certain circumstances the requirements may even be quoted as a tender, perhaps even starting with an advertisement in Lloyd's List and the issue of tender documents which have to be submitted in sealed envelopes by a given date and opened at a set time, although this is rare.

Just a reminder, ethics are important for the smooth operation of the market. Read **Appendix 7** to give you an idea of the 'ground rules'.

We will look first at a normal market quote, typically a Major Oil company for a main trade route. The order will first be quoted to the Oil company's panel Brokers usually by telephone or e-mail – just sufficient information to fill one line of computer screen:

> "VLCC AG/WEST 15/17 OCTOBER ACCT EUROPEAN ENERGY".

The Brokers will then be galvanised into action to quote all the Owners they speak to with a ship in position and later to owners with similar ships out of position to keep them informed of market activity. Depending how far ahead the dates may be there could be a lot of ships that can achieve the laydays. For the next half an hour or so the Owners with ships in position will be inundated with phone calls and any other acceptable means of quoting, giving them these barest details.

The rush to quote the business is a throwback to the days when many Owners worked "first come first served" as a fair basis for deciding with which Broker to work the business. However, Owners for a number of reasons do not always use this system. Luck is of some consequence.

1.   The Owner may have a preferred Broker who keeps him well informed on all market developments.

2.   The Owner may consider the broker quoting to be second rate.

3.   The Owner could have a policy of turns amongst a number of Brokers.

4.   A particular Broker may have an excellent reputation for knowledge of the particular trade.

5.   A Broker may have the reputation for acting in favour of the Charterer.

Some Charterers also give turns in quoting first to a Broker and may even allow them a tew minutes before they quote others. What the Owner's Broker will need to know now is what is the cargo size and description preferred, the load port range and discharge port range required, any restrictions, breakdown of the grades, Charterer's rate ideas, commissions and whether the cargo is firm and ready to work.

The Owner's Broker might ask one, two or more Brokers to give a full run-down of the order as soon as they can get it to see which one can come back quickest with the information required. What the Owner's Broker really needs to be able to do is tell the Principal whether or not the ship is 'definitely' or 'maybe' workable. The dimensions, deadweight, dates or other factors may make another vessel preferable. There is no sense in getting an Owner very interested in the business, if the ship is not going to be suitable.

On the other hand a Charterer will be reticent to publicise too many restrictions or preferences, because that will show the Charterer's hand and limit the number of ships that will offer thereby reducing competition and the chances of keeping the rate down. If European Energy has nine offers they will have more influence on the rate than if only one or two ships have come in firm. What the market may not know is that only one or two of these ships could be actually workable.

When making the decision as to which Broking channel to use some Owners will not use any broker who has put another ship in for the same order. They argue that if they are the only ship in through a particular Broker that Broker will work very hard to get the Charterers to counter for 'his' ship. Other Owners will prefer to offer through a Broker who has more than one ship in because they will have more information from the Charterer due to the number of vessels they have offered.

Sometimes it is obvious to an Owner's Broker which Broker is being given the greatest help by the Charterer in order to fix an order. Maybe, they received the order a little earlier than everybody else, maybe they are being given the back up information much quicker than every other Broker and there may be very valid reasons why a particular Broker has preference for the order. This could be because they have given very good service to a Charterer but not managed to fix a ship with them. It may mean that the Broker concerned will lean towards the Charterer in negotiations and it is up to the owner to weigh the relative pros and cons of the situation.

Some Owners will tell Brokers they are committed to others or it is not their turn, but some also will continue to take information from all Brokers without admitting they are already under offer. Naturally, this can cause irritation when the facts are known and the offended Broker will hardly be supportive of that owner in the future. A clear turn basis is in many ways the most satisfactory method when Brokers are providing equal service as those who do not have the turn are obliged to continue to give information in order to get a subsequent turn.

If a Broker is offering more than one ship he should on no account disclose details of one offer to the others as he is then putting the first Owner at a disadvantage, others could offer even half a point lower on a weak market. They may have trouble taking this attitude, but it should be easily understood that no Owner would like his Broker to disclose an offer made on private terms.

A Broker, however, acting as a Charterer's Agent will deliberately broadcast such information in order to try to get the rate down even if he denies he has done so.

A good Broker should have a strong sense of what is fair in spite of his need to earn commission and particularly first class Principals will avoid a Broker with a bad reputation, so that the Broker will end up only working the most difficult end of the market.

It should be remembered, particularly in competitive Broking, that the failure rate on negotiations is very high due, to the size of the market and the alternatives available. A Charterer may often withdraw an enquiry completely if market conditions prevent a profitable cargo sale. This occurs less with major companies operating in a regular trade to their refineries, but two or three trading companies can all be competing for the same cargo sale causing great difficulty for Owners in judging which Trader to support.

It is advantageous for a Broker to know how a chartering Principal operates when opening negotiations under weak or strong market conditions.

On a weak market a Charterer may wait until he has several offers before countering and may even try to get a Broker to persuade an owner to reduce an offer in order to have a chance of the first counter. On a strong market it can happen that the Charterer receives no offers at all and must exert pressure on the Brokers. All these circumstances are difficult and it is essential for a Broker to listen carefully to his Principals in order to assess their attitude and not dominate the conversation. A moment of silence can sometimes draw a very useful comment!

The next decision for the Owner is at what rate should the offer be made. For a market cargo or well-known trades the Brokers and the Owner will usually know the level of last done as well as the market level, then the decision will be further influenced by the number of ships available and whether their perception of the market is rising, steady or falling.

Taking these factors into account, the actual offering rate has to be decided. It is dangerous to think that when two parties negotiate, they anticipate reaching an agreement at a mid point. For example if an Owner offers at W150 (say last done was W140) on a firm market a counter from charterers at W130 might lead the unwary to believe the fixing level will he "same as last time" (W140) albeit after a suitable period of negotiations.

The Chartering Market is not a bazaar. One party may in fact refuse to budge from the rate in the first offer, having opened negotiations at the 'fixing rate' perhaps with a view to finishing negotiations quickly. The Broker must, of course, be able to understand his own Principal's way of working and must also develop the skill to know whether or not the other side is bluffing.

It is important to remember that rate level is only ONE element of the negotiations. We have to consider what is included in the Charterer's terms. For example, suppose Owners wish to fix their AFRAMAX from the Mediterranean to the US Gulf. To fix with the US Gulf discharge range only he may be prepared to do 70,000 tonnes at W100. But, if the Charterer wants other discharge options, say European Med/ UK Cont and USAC the business as a whole is less attractive to the Owners and if they are prepared to grant the options the USG rate may well be W110 as part of the overall package, or a different rate will be given to each range. This will often enable the Owner to judge, which is the intended range, as the Charterer will try to keep that rate low. Cargoes that are unsold will frequently be worked with as many options as possible giving the Trader increased flexibility as circumstances change. It is not unusual for the larger trading organisations to be unsure where their cargo will be loaded and there are times when the load range (it is usually singular) is very wide and spread out geographically so that the Owner must be careful that he can make the cancelling date at all possible load ports! Remember in the AG it takes about two days steaming to reach the northern most ports from Quoin Island.

There are some occasions when a very brief offer will be sufficient but normally a full offer is best and it can be given for a short duration, say ten minutes. For those of you familiar with the Dry Cargo market an offer for this short period will seem strange – however it is perhaps best thought of as the tanker equivalent of a "firm indication", that is to say, it registers definite interest and puts the ship in front of Charterers.

Typically, the first firm offer will be sent by e-mail or fax and perhaps then negotiations continued by telephone. The Owner's Broker will have a firm offer prepared on the computer which can be sent by the Owner to the Brokers very quickly by e-mail or fax. The Owner makes the first offer in 999 cases out of a thousand and, when the Charterer gives the first counter it will invariably be on Charterer's standard terms. That is to say, the format of the first offer (from the Owner) and the first counter (from the Charterer) will be substantially different.

The Owner's first offer may just as well be in the form that suits him best and an example is given in **Appendix 8** So let us see how this might be prepared for our VLCC ready to load in The Gulf.

Referring to the form, it can be considered in three parts:

1.   Information on the Charterer's/Broker's/ship's details.

2.   The cargo and voyage, load, discharge, laydays.

3.   The terms.

We will look at these in some detail. Think of this form as part of a record of events that will lead to a fixture, possibly negotiations will take some time and maybe, at a later date you will be asked for times and details which you will not be able to recall without a written record to refer to. (Also if you are out of the office when a counter is received, one of your colleagues can take up the file).

Therefore, enter the Charterer's and Broker's names and time/date of the offer.

Full description of ship:

The amount of information actually required will vary with the particular order or possibly charterer's intended ports but in the majority of cases the following information is what would be required'

Name: (Ensure correct spelling, there could be two vessels with similar names). There is the famous story of the owners offering the 'MYRTEA' but the Charterers wrote down 'MERTIA'. It was not until the recap was sent – incidentally after the subjects were lifted – that the mistake was spotted, and unfortunately the 'MYRTEA was not acceptable. This is how lawyers become rich.

Year of Build	Flag	Class

SDWT on Summer Draft.

	LOA	BM

IGS/COW/SBT/COILED/COATED (delete if not applicable)
Cargo Capacity at 98% (including slops?)

BCM	Derricks/cranes	TPC	SCNRT

Last Three Cargoes/Charterers

Oil company acceptability.

Using the 'WALRUS' (Chapter Four) enter as many details as possible in the above format.

5.2   CARGO DESCRIPTION

The cargo is described in terms of quantity and type, for instance in this example:

250,000 5% MOLOO 1 grade Crude Oil No Heat

or if two grades are intended-

250,000 5% MOLOO 1-2 grades WVNS Crude Oil No Heat

The term WVNS (Within Vessel's Natural Segregation) allows for the situation where the exact split of grades cannot necessarily be loaded due to tank configuration and seaworthy trim requirements when steaming between combination load or discharge ports with a part cargo. Perhaps a certain proportion of the cargo might have to be handled through common pipelines and pumps so there will be some "line and pump contamination". The Charterer should be made aware of this, preferably at an early stage.

In the event that the cargo needs heating, say a fuel oil or a heated crude, the description could read:

"1–2 grades WVNS Crude Oil vessel to maintain loaded temperature but maximum 100°F" (the actual temperature will depend on the grade of cargo but most shipowners will want to limit temperature to maximum 135°F, perhaps in certain cases 145°F).

5.2.1 Load Range

The description of the load range will depend upon the Charterer's intended load port, if known, together with any political restrictions imposed. In the autumn of 1990, after Iraq had invaded Kuwait, the determination of the AG loading range was quite an interesting exercise. No cargoes could be loaded or discharged in Iraq or Kuwait and there are various War Risk Additional Premiums (WRAP) applicable to different load areas, so the load port has to be tied as closely as possible whilst still leaving the Charterer maximum flexibility if such is required, e.g. suppose Kharg Island is the intended load port, the description could be as follows:

"One Safe Port AG not North of but including Kharg Island excluding Iraq and Kuwait."

Suppose the intended load ports are Ras Tanura and Mina Al Fahal the following description should suffice:

"1–2 SP AG not North of but including Ras Tanura excluding Iran but including Mina Al Fahal" (which is in Oman but outside the AG).

5.2.2 Discharge Ports

There are ports and ranges which some owners do not like to give. In the USA many owners want to exclude Florida due to onerous state legislation; if New York, not North of George Washington Bridge due to dimensions. In the Mediterranean Owners like to exclude Albania, Israel and perhaps some of the exposed weather ports, for example Falconara, Fuimicimo and Ravenna. The Owner can include all exclusions in his first offer – there is usually a cost implication involved. In the Charterer's counter there may be a demand for fewer exclusions. The Owner will build this requirement into his rate terms. In the example the discharge ranges could read:-

"1–2 SP Egyptian Red Sea or CHOPT."

"1–2 SP European Med excluding Albania, Falconara, Fuimicimo and Ravenna or CHOPT."

"1–2 SP UK Cont Gibraltar/Hamburg range or CHOPT".

"1–2 SP Caribbean Sea excluding Cuba Haiti and Orinoco."

5.2.3 Laydays

If the ship is going to be ready earlier than the first day of the laydays quoted, the Owner would try one or two days earlier in the first offer, and sometimes Charterers can accommodate the earlier commencement. Of course, in a very strong market the Charterer may have no choice but to accept the earlier commencement and then have the vessel's laytime commence 24 or 48 hours earlier than loading.

5.2.4 The Terms

We will be looking at the clauses in more detail in the next Chapter, but for clarity some explanation is given here as necessary.

With an unknown Charterer as a first choice the ASBATANKVOY Charter party is preferred by many Owners, not that it covers everything, however it is not very strongly in Charterers' favour either.

5.2.5 Freight

Payment details should be spelt out in order to reduce the risk of fraud. By specifying an account in New York or London emphasises that in order to be considered 'paid' on the due date the money must be received at that place – not just transmitted from somewhere else. Even first class banks have been known to deny that they have received money, when it is subsequently proved that they have done so.

Place of General Average and Arbitration should be stated and which law to apply thereby avoiding misunderstanding.

York – Antwerp 94 (YA 94) incorporates the latest York- Antwerp Rules.

Conoco Weather Clause covers the problem of delays at load or discharge ports caused by bad weather. Any time thereby lost counts as 50% laytime.

Federal Maritime Commission – US Coast Guard (FMC – USCG). These clauses are required for vessels calling at US ports and would not be required for discharging elsewhere.

ITOPF. This confirms that the vessel is entered in the ITOPF scheme.

5.3 WORLDSCALE HOURS TERMS AND CONDITIONS (WSHTC) AND SPECIAL RATES TO APPLY

This ensures that all Worldscale Schedule including the preamble is incorporated in the contract. With regard to special rates we need to look at TRANS – SHIPMENT AREAS **Appendix 1** of the Worldscale Appendix in Chapter Three. The final paragraph refers to any transhipment areas, which are not designated. Worldscale will provide rates for discharges, which include these areas but, in summary, it says "such rates must be agreed by the two parties if they are to apply"; hence mention must be made at this point in the offer.

5.3.1 Rate and Extras According to Worldscale "X" (REWS "X")

This is the rate you will be offering and you must specify if applicable on which route you are basing your offer, for example Cape/Cape or Suez/Suez. (Remember that without agreement to the contrary the rate applicable is that for the route which gives the lowest flat rate – usually the shortest.)

5.3.2 Demurrage Rate

Although there is a table of demurrage rates which can be found in Worldscale (Preamble 15) this is usually negotiated on a lumpsum per day or pro rata basis. Here you must remember that if the Conoco weather clause is agreed and delays occur due to weather the agreed rate will be reduced by half for the period of bad weather.

Chevron War Risk Clause. In the voyage estimate for the trip you will have received a quote for WRAP covering the intended load ports. Typically, quotes will be valid for calls within 48 hours. That is to say, the vessel will have to enter the war zone en route to load within 48 hours. However, possibly the laydays are a week or more away and if the WRAP is increased in the interim then the Owners will have extra unbudgeted expenses. The quote given will usually stipulate maximum time that the vessel can be in the War Risk Area (say seven or fourteen days) before incurring costs. The Chevron War Risk Clause covers these eventualities by stating further that additional time and any increases will be for Charterer's account.

5.3.3 Commission

This is the amount the Owner is agreeing to pay either from the freight or the total of all monies earned, a matter to be agreed at the outset. Some Owners decline to pay commission on demurrage but this can depend upon the effort put in by the Broker to settle the claim.

5.3.4 Reply Time

Perhaps for special reasons the Charterer needs an offer for a given period longer than, say 10 minutes and this could possibly be agreed. Remember that a ship cannot be offered elsewhere (except perhaps "sub open") whilst already firm to one Charterer. The same applies to counter offers to Owners, but some Charterers have been known to make more than one "subject" counter at the same time. There is a possibility that the Owners offer could be accepted in full and within time. Such instances are rare today but talked about with nostalgia by Brokers involved in the heady market of 1973 and before.

If the above offer were to be accepted the Owner would be fully covered by the terms of the ASBATANKVOY and those spelt out – therefore it is not necessary to say, for example "subject details". However, some Owners favour offering with a subject just in case there is a mistake in the terms or even in the rate!

A rapid reaction from a Charterer may result from the fact that there is more than one similar cargo, that it is expected others will enter the market or that the feeling is that the market is likely to rise.

With a "sub details" offer, for a short reply an Owner would be in a position to drop negotiations and offer elsewhere if the subjects were not cleared, but a Charterer could still confirm in expectation that the "details" were not too onerous. The Owner would be obliged to state the details – which the Charterer's intended to accept – but the Owner would not normally, at that stage, introduce a new major factor or amend the rate having only referred to "sub details".

There are a number of legitimate reasons why a ship offers at low levels:

1. The Owner may have more than one ship on a similar position.

2. Perhaps the Owner thinks the market will decline and wants to be fixed before a general decline is apparent.

3. The vessel may have a dry-docking stemmed near the destination of the cargo and fixing the particular voyage will reduce to eliminate ballast cost.

The offer, as discussed would cover the case where an Owner either has not fixed with a Charterer before or not for a long time and perhaps Charterer's terms have changed. The offer could be much simpler if the Owner/Charterer has a recent fixture on this or another vessel in the Owner's fleet. In that case all that would need to be specified is the ship, cargo type and quantity, load/discharge ranges, lay days, rate, demurrage, reply time and then "otherwise as per terms of ship's name/Charterer's name/CP dated ....with logical alterations".

The term logical alterations may sound quite straightforward but it is worth thinking about what it means and can be dangerous in interpretation. For instance, suppose the previous fixture was for a Fuel Oil cargo that requires heating and this cargo is a crude oil which is fixed basis no heat. If there had been a heating clause in the first charter party it should be deleted in the second and of course vice versa. Otherwise logical amendments would include the ship, her description, dates and rates.

All Ship Brokers should have on file the current standard terms of those Charterers with whom they are active and should easily be able to send those terms to an Owner immediately after quoting an enquiry, if needed, and before the Owner has offered. If time permits, this puts the Owner in a stronger position with his initial offer accepting or making minor alterations to known terms, so the Charterer is confident when making a counter offer that no misunderstandings will occur. On many occasions the Owner knows the terms, but it is always wise to identify the date in case terms have changed, e.g. as per terms C/P dated.

The counters given during a negotiation will usually take one of three forms:

"Decline and offer"

"Accept/Except" or

"Repeat Last/Except"

It is important that the Broker is in no doubt as to which way the Principal is countering, and before passing the counter should ensure the person giving the counter agrees with the Broker's understanding.

Remember *it is not what you said, or what you thought you said but what they understood from what you said.*

Typically Charterer's first counter will not be received within the time limit and the situation in the market may have changed.

When given, the counter will often be a "decline and offer" with Charterer's full terms spelt out. The one agreement at this stage should be the ship's description, except that further questions may be asked such as an estimated lifting on a given draft, air draft or distance from waterline to centre of manifolds or distance from Bow to Centre Manifold (BCM).

Obviously, the elements of the offer need to be examined, but in addition the Owner's Broker needs to see if any points from the first offer are agreed or not mentioned (i.e. not agreed) so that they can be included in the next counter offer if necessary. Particular attention must be paid to which subjects are involved and when are they to be declared. In the majority of cases it is necessary to work – and I am not suggesting agree in full – on the basis of Charterer's terms. This is not necessarily a concession on the part of Owners, but rather to make it easier for the Charterer to cover "in house" information. For example, a fixture concluded in London may involve discharge in Singapore and if the Charterer's office in Singapore knows it is on standard terms with a few alterations, the exchange of information and operation of the voyage will be more efficient.

Some Charterers have many additional clauses and in the speed required to negotiate main terms regarding cargo size, description, laydays, rate and demurrage it may not be possible (time is too short) or necessary (you are too far apart on money) to go through the clauses, thus Owner's counter could be made "subject terms".

The pressure arising from Oil Traders trying to buy and sell before their competitors has created the impression that speed is efficient, but it is not always the case.

If the market goes through a phase when Shipowners have a degree of control, they will properly feel that a ten minute offer cannot be serious; as they have no time to make sure that all aspects of the venture have been checked. In many respects Worldscale is accepted as blanket coverage leaving only the rate and the Charter form to be agreed. What would happen, however, if due to speed of negotiation the Owner had no time to check on bunker availability and for some unexpected reason no bunkers were available on the intended voyage?

Through the whole of the negotiating stage, very careful record keeping by Owners/Charterers is important, but it is vital that the Broker makes a very careful note as and when points are agreed and keeps the outstanding points to the forefront.

On a practical note it is very useful to start drawing up a 'recap message' as soon as negotiations start, and no later than when you realise that the two parties are likely to come to an agreement. You start by entering the ship's details, cargo size, etc. other points as and when they are agreed. Depending upon the technology available in your office you should either have a draft e-mail or Fax ready which you have prepared during negotiations, to be despatched just as soon as the very last point is agreed, whether that is the rate or a particular sticky term that has caused problems. The majority of negotiations will come down to one or possibly two points. The Broker who says, albeit late in the evening, "I will send you a recap tomorrow morning", is to be charitable, way behind the times and is certainly not giving a good service to the Principals upon whom he depends for his livelihood. The recap may be the first written record exchanged between the parties and should be checked very carefully.

Anyone who deals regularly in dry cargo chartering will be familiar with the practice of fixing "subject details". This frequently means that the main terms are agreed: ship, cargo, ports, dates, rate, demurrage, etc. The Charterer then clears the subject stem and perhaps shipper's/receiver's approval before working the charter party details. The length of dry cargo charter parties may well give a clue to the reason for this practice. A large printed form followed by 72 additional clauses is not something to be tackled lightly so why waste time if the Charterers cannot confirm the stem?

Many oil companies created their own form of charter party (Asbatankvoy was based on an Exxon charter that was in turn based on Warshipoilvoy – a voyage charter used during the second World War) and after circulating those forms they were able to charter ships without having to include additional side clauses that might cause fixtures to be concluded "subject details".

Unfortunately many companies, particularly traders, have introduced many side clauses, some of which may even be superfluous. As a result, and also due to the speed at which negotiations are carried out, it is common for initial basic negotiations to be carried out "subject details".

This can and if possible should be avoided if the Owners know the terms or if they have had a previous fixture with the same Charterer on which terms can be based. Otherwise, during negotiations the Broker should try to get terms approved by the parties or at least get as far as possible towards approval.

For example a Trader may say to the Broker "otherwise same terms as our last fixture". If the Broker can then e-mail or fax a copy of those terms to the Owner, there is a chance they can be agreed "with logical amendments", e.g. descriptions, rates and dates.

In general terms of negotiating, it is important to bear in mind one vital point. What we refer to as a "counter-offer" is in fact saying "I decline your offer and now offer you firm....". Unless, therefore a clean acceptance is received within the time limit, the other side is free. He may change terms previously agreed, even drop negotiations entirely and pursue other business. This possibility exists right up until the final point is agreed. Having said that, no Owner or Charterer worth the name would like to have a reputation for pulling out of negotiations capriciously but, let us face it, there could be genuine changes of circumstances that may cause either party to call a halt. On a strong market an Owner may even hope for a counter offer making him free to offer elsewhere.

Once the vessel is on "subjects" be they Charterer's management approval, Shipper's, Receiver's approval or stem, the vessel cannot be worked elsewhere. If subjects cannot be lifted timely the Charterers may ask for an extension of the time limit. The Broker should try to find out as much information as possible as to why the extension is required – as much as anything to see if the request for the extra time will be long enough – perhaps a European Charterer is trying to contact an American Receiver. The Owner will make his decision on whether to grant the extension partly on the time required and partly on the likelihood of subjects finally being lifted. It sometimes happens that Charterers do not know whether they will eventually lift subjects and they may say they will revert if they can make contact with the right people but are not asking to hold the vessel firm for an extended period.

Remember that no contract exists until all "subjects" have been lifted. That is to say the business is not "fixed" until ALL subjects are lifted. It is of great value to all parties, including the Broker to keep "subjects" to the minimum and make sure each "subject" is clear and understood.

The expression "subject stem" has at times been used loosely when really they mean "subject to us being able to buy and sell this cargo". It has happened, when it is definitely "subject stem" and, say, a reply is awaited from a Middle East supplier, that the Charterer will agree that the Owner's local agent may try to contact the supplier for information. Such permission tends to prove that the stem situation is genuine and Owners can be lenient in offering extension of time.

5.4   PRODUCTION OF CHARTER PARTY

Many major Charterers no longer require a completed signed charter party following the fixture but either party has the right to call for full documentation if needed, e.g. in the event of a dispute. An "Administration Clause" will be included in Charterer's terms and states that the full terms and conditions are evidenced in a 'fixing confirmation' or 'Recap' message.

If required, the charter party will be drawn up (drafted) by the Broker and if more than one Broker is involved then by the one who works the Charterer direct. This is because he is the one most likely to have drawn up many charter parties for the Principal and the experience factor reduces the chances of errors, typographical or otherwise.

The charter party will usually be drawn up in duplicate, the two originals being sent to the Owner first for checking and signature before being forwarded to Charterers for their signature. Charterer and Owner usually keep one original for their records and the Broker will supply each Principal with the number of photocopies required for their files. Sometimes the Broker will retain the signed original(s) and the Principals accept copies.

Once the subjects have been lifted the whole file will usually be passed from the Chartering Department on to the personnel responsible for the administration of the charter party performance, usually known as the operations department in tanker brokers offices. To give you an idea of the information that is needed for the efficient running of a voyage, two check lists used in the gas trades are included in **Appendices 9** and **10.** The Operations Department of the Owner will be responsible for ensuring that the Master and agents are advised of the relevant information regarding the terms of the charter party and this process is started with the voyage orders sent by Charterers.

The voyage orders are generally very detailed instructions covering such items as where the vessel will load, how much cargo and which grades to load, what notices/ETAs are to be given, what the Master should do with regard to cargo quantities, Bills of Lading, terminal orders, what protests should be noted, etc. As you will appreciate, the voyage orders and their implementation are vitally important to a successful voyage and some charterers find it necessary to include a clause in the charter party stating that the strict compliance of the voyage orders form an integral part of the contract.

An increasing number of vessels are fitted with satellite communication systems e-mail or telex machines allowing swift accurate receipt of all messages, but the voluminous voyage orders transmitted direct to the ship, instead of via a radio station using radio telegraphy, has avoided many problems and misunderstandings. If you become involved in tanker chartering it is likely that during your career you will spend many hours in the office during the evenings waiting for the elusive "Voyage Orders".

The information that passes between Owners and Charterers will go through the broking channels – possibly duplicating information passing from the ship to Charterer and vice versa. The job of the broking company now becomes very much a service to his Principals ensuring that, when required, questions are answered promptly. A note here, if a question is posed by a Charterer or Owner, it is tempting for the Operations Department to telephone the query without written confirmation – DO BOTH – Telephone and follow up in writing to ensure it is not forgotten. It is very useful that messages in and out are timed automatically, if a Broker could be shown to be dilatory in passing instructions he could be liable for costs arising from the inefficiency. Once the vessel has completed loading, unless already stated in the voyage orders, she will probably be sent, for example, to "Land's End" or possibly to a port for orders. Remember the cargo may be sold more than once en route, nevertheless the Charterer remains responsible for the liabilities and duties under the charter party even if he has sub-chartered, but at this stage the more discharge port options that an Owner has given, the more flexibility the seller has of canvassing the market for a good deal. Very often the Charterer has an option to discharge at a port or ports within a range, and once that option has been declared the charter party is operative in effect to named ports.

However, it is also likely that the terms allow the Charterer to change the orders provided he pays for any deviation and other costs arising to the Owner. For example the Owner may have organised repairs or a crew change at the nominated port and incurs expense when the port is changed.

Providing there are no emergencies encountered during the voyage, once the discharge port(s) has been nominated the freight invoice can be prepared. This may be done by the Broker or by the Owner and will usually be submitted by e-mail, fax or telex followed by a printed copy. Late payment of freight is one of the ways that a Charterer will soon get a bad name in the market, so it is usual that all efforts are made to ensure prompt accurate payment.

One of the important pieces of information required by Owners is whether there will be an original Bill of Lading at the discharge port to be presented to the Master for the release of the cargo. If not, then the Charterer will issue a Letter of Indemnity (LOI) holding the Master/ Owners harmless against all consequences of discharging the cargo without presentation of an original Bill of Lading. In addition, if required, a Letter of Indemnity for change of destination will be issued. This would be required for instance if the Bill of Lading stated Rotterdam and the vessel was ordered to discharge at Le Havre.

5.5   DEMURRAGE

Once the discharge has been completed the Owners would need the statement facts from each port to enable the laytime statement to be prepared and demurrage, if any, calculated. The majority of charter parties have some form of time limit agreed for the submission of demurrage claims. This is because the Charterer usually has a time limit within which he can submit such claims to his Shippers or Receivers. At times Charterers require their own Agents to be used (possibly due to difficult conditions on the oil sale) and if this is the case Owners should include a provision that the laytime statement must be received by them in good time to prepare a demurrage claim. Sometimes Owners appoint their own Sub Agents to be sure of the service obtained.

5.6   CONTRACT OF AFFREIGHTMENT (COA)

Strictly speaking all charter parties are Contracts of Affreightment but in broking parlance the term usually refers to the contract covering a quantity of cargo carried over a given period of time in several vessels. The essential details of an offer for a COA are similar to a voyage except the names of the vessels to be used may not be known. Perhaps, "Named Ship or similar substitute" otherwise "Shipowners named tonnage to be nominated" would be sufficient.

The total quantity to be lifted over what period, the size, margin and regularity of each shipment, notices required to be given by Charterers and Owners would also need to be spelt out.

If the contract is to cover more than one load and/or discharge ports the calculation of freight rates is likely to be very complex and the computer really comes into its own.

It is worth remembering that a small error in costs in a single voyage charter party may be overcome on the next fixture, whereas in a COA one small error multiplies with the number of voyages. It is essential for the Charterer to ensure that an Owner fixing the COA has the skill, experience and standing to perform well. The Owner would try to build some protection for bunker price rises and depending on the intended voyage, perhaps cover for any increases in war risk premiums.

As far as a "similar substitute" is concerned in contract litigation could easily occur if an attempt was made to substitute a ship that was clearly of poorer quality, whereas the contract will certainly impose a 5 or 10% variation in the size of ship.

Here is an example of a Bunker Adjustment Clause:

Freight rates in this contract are based on an average of the bunker prices at Hong Kong, New York and Rotterdam for MFO grade bunkers in US dollars.

Should the average price of the PLAITS Oilgramme Bunkerwire for the above ports at the commencement of laydays vary more than US $10 per metric ton from the base price, Charterer will benefit or contribute from the cost variant as per the following formula:

For every 7% increase in bunker price the freight to be increased or decreased respectively by 1%.

5.7   TENDERS

Some Charterers, usually government agencies, find it necessary to put their chartering requirements out to tender. This may involve an advertisement in the shipping and local press inviting applications for pre- qualification, to establish the good standing of the organisations that wish to participate in the tender. It is likely that those who offer will need to put up a bank guarantee, which will be valid for the period of the offer.

The tender will be based on a standard document the terms of which are not negotiable. The calculations that the Owner carries out and subsequent offer have to take all the terms and their cost implications into account so that all offers can be judged on the same basis.

It can be a time consuming process to study the terms and ensure the offer is prepared exactly as required. Once the full firm offer is drawn up on the necessary tender documents they will be submitted in sealed envelopes to be opened at the stated time.

The idea would be to check all offers are submitted correctly and then take the lowest rate of the valid offers. Frequently, the Owner with the lowest offer finds that he is in the difficult position of discovering that the Charterers intend to negotiate his rate even lower still. Perhaps all his 'lowest rate' has achieved is to give him 'first refusal' possibly leading to a further round of negotiations.

Not all Shipowning organisations are prepared to become involved in such methods of chartering. The business is often left to companies who understand the local market and are able to avoid many of the pitfalls and traps that are in the terms of difficult tenders.

5.8   SELF-ASSESSMENT AND TEST QUESTIONS

Attempt the following and check your answers from the text:

1. What information does a Broker need from the Charterer regarding a newly quoted order?

2. What factors could influence an Owner's choice of Broker when offering for a market cargo?

3.   Write down the headings for a voyage firm offer.

4.   When is a charter party fixed?

5.   What would you check for in the recap?

Having completed Chapter Five, attempt the following and submit your essay to your Tutor:

A major Charterer has just quoted to your broking office an order for a single voyage requirement. Explain how this would be handled and what factors would be likely to determine an Owner's choice of broking channel when offering for the cargo.

Chapter 6

TANKER VOYAGE CHARTER PARTIES

6.1 INTRODUCTION

What you should learn from this Chapter are the points which can cost money to an Owner or a Charterer, so that during negotiations you will have an understanding, as to why one or other party is sticking to a point.

This Chapter is devoted to voyage charters and in the tanker industry, we see that the Oil Majors have their own standard forms.

6.2 ASBATANKVOY

A voyage form well known and often used which may have a great number of additional, or rider side clauses, which were added by Charterers as their trade developed. In practice, you will see that quite often a rider clause re-states what is in the main body of the charter party and is therefore an unnecessary addition.

All charter party forms have their pros and cons but, while most are reasonably well balanced, a few appear heavily weighted in favour of one party or the other. Oil company Charters tend to be well written and kept up to date so that even trading companies may use a major oil company form, but still with additional side clauses. Unless such additional clauses are carefully drafted and related to each other and to the clauses in the printed form there is inevitably scope for error, duplication, inconsistency and subsequent litigation.

The earliest tanker voyage charter parties were developments of the existing dry cargo forms and the differences between the forms were then comparatively modest.

In essence, these were:

i)   The cargo to be pumped into the tanker by the Charterer and pumped out of the tanker by the tanker – the vessel supplying the pumps and steam wherever the discharge port regulations permitted fires on board.

ii)   The Owner's responsibilities, or lack of them, if more than one grade of oil was loaded or if there was any leakage.

iii) A declaration regarding the type and nature of the previous cargo.

The fundamentals of both form of charter party are still the same but much of the modern bulk liquid charter is tailored for its specialised purpose. After the 1939/45 War, some of the major US oil companies developed their own house charter parties from Government's Warshipoilvoy form and in Europe the London form was the basis for the European Oil Companies' forms. The charter party forms of the major oil companies such as ExxonMobil, Shell and BP **Appendices 14, 15** and **16** have been thoroughly revised a number of times in order to incorporate terms and provisions addressing their changing needs and trading conditions and taking account of new statutes and regulations.

Let us consider where the charter party fits in to the needs of the commercial tanker industry.

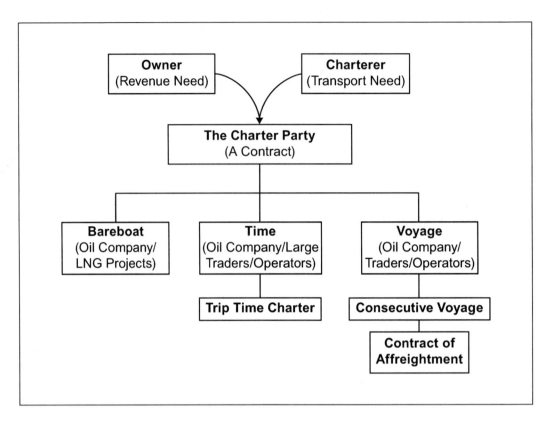

Firstly, note under English law it has been held that the parties entering a shipping contract both intend to make every reasonable endeavour to make it succeed. Fundamentally, they are both on the same side aiming to move valuable cargo across a dangerous sea successfully.

From the diagram you will see that we are looking at the Owner's requirement which is revenue need versus the Charterer's requirement which is a transport need and they are brought together by the charter party. The forms of charter party used are bareboat, time and voyage charters.

Bareboat charters basically lease the hull and machinery of the ship for usually a long period of time (like the lease of a building) and the Charterer then acts as if he was the Owner of the ship. Some evidence must be provided that he is covering the insured value and conditions on redelivery must be stipulated, e.g. fully classed.

Time charters enable the oil company or operator to know that they have covered their shipping requirements at a stable price other than bunker costs. Owners who need a secure income over a period often to cover loan liabilities have also sought to time charter out their shipping fleet.

Voyage charters are used for spot requirements and leave the ship management totally in the hands of the Owners, whereas under a time charter, the Charterers programme and issue instructions to the ship within the confines of the time charter terms.

Consecutive voyages (CONSECS) and Contracts of Affreightment (COAs) offer both parties cover over a period of time but leave the ship operation to the Owners, as under a single voyage charter.

The implications of costs and responsibilities between the Owner and the Charterers are summarised in the following diagram:

TANKER CHARTER PARTY RESPONSIBILITIES

Cost element	Bareboat	Time charter	Voyage charter
Pumping			
Load port			
Discharge port			
Voyage Expenses			
Fuel			
Port disbursement			
Canal tolls			
Cleaning			
Heating			
Insurance AP			
Operating Expenses			
Crewing			
Stores			
Spares			
Lube oil			
Repairs			
Surveys			
Insurance/P&I			
Management			
Capital cost			
Interest			
Capital repayment			
Insurance			

Charterer	
Owner	

The elements common to all oil charter parties are summarised below, and for illustration we use the ASBATANKVOY charter party form.

Refer to the ASBATANKVOY charter party in the **Appendix 11**

1. **Place Where Contract Made:**

This is important as, in the absence of a clause to the contrary, it will govern the law to be applied to the charter party in the event of a dispute. The "Place" can be defined as "where the contract is made", the domicile of the Charterer's Broker not necessarily the place of business of one or other of the Principals involved.

To ensure certainty that any dispute be heard under a given jurisdiction, it is advised that a contract includes an "exclusive jurisdiction clause".

2. **Date of Charter Party:**

The date entered here is that date on which the negotiations are concluded with all subjects lifted.

PREAMBLE

3. Names and Domiciles of Contracting Parties:

The names of the contracting parties (i.e. their full styles and domicile) and the name of the vessel.

PART I

4. Description and Position of Vessel:

Typically the description will include the deadweight of the vessel. Classification. Summer loaded draft in salt water. Cargo capacity on her summer draft, taking into account deductions for such things as bunkers, stores and water. Is the vessel coated/coiled? Last three cargoes. What oil company acceptabilities does the tanker have? Vessel's present position and expected readiness to load.

5. Laydays/Cancelling:

The spread of dates during which the vessel is to present herself at the first (or sole) load port. (NB. See clause 5 for the applicable times and rights of cancellation).

6. Voyage:

Names of loading and discharging ranges or places (NB. See also clause 1, clause 4 and clause 9).

7. Cargo:

Quantity may be stipulated as minimum, or with a margin, say 5% or 10% in either Owner's or Charterer's option or as a minimum or maximum. For example min 80,000 metric tons or 80,000 metric tons 5% MOLOO or 80/85,000 metric tons min/max at Charterers's option. (CHOPT)

8. Description of Cargo:

This will include number of grades and heating requirements if any, plus "No Heat Crude Oil" or "Fuel Oil vessel to maintain loaded temperature but maximum 135°F". The number of grades may read simply:

"Maximum 3 grades, within vessel's natural segregation" or possibly,

"1/3 grades in Charterer's option WVNS".

9. Rate/Billing:

Enter here the Worldscale rates as agreed for the various discharge ranges to be included is the full freight payment details specifying the bank where freight is to be received, full name and account number. This reduces the risk of fraud and remember that freight is not deemed paid until it is in the Owner's bank account ready for use. Clause 2 specifies how the cargo quantity, used to compute the freight, will be arrived at. Clause 3 covers deadfreight.

10. Laytime:

Here is entered the laytime allowed, and, under the Worldscale hours terms and conditions, 72 hours would be the laytime allowance. (This may be varied during negotiations). Laytime is the time allowed to the Charterer to carry out various operations required to load and discharge the cargoes without incurring extra costs.

Laytime is referred to again later in the charter party under clause 6 which allows the Charterer to have six hours Notice Of Readiness (NOR) at each port of loading and discharge. Clause 7 specifies the excepted periods and clauses 9, 10 and 11 all include stipulations regarding laytime.

11. Demurrage:

Daily amount of liquidated damages (demurrage) payable by the Charterer in the event that the vessel is delayed in port beyond the permitted laytime.

12. Commission:

Some Charterers require this to be deleted as being an agreement between the Owner and the Broker. Under English Law, the Rights of Third Parties Act gives any third party who anticipated to benefit from the contract the right to claim for the payment of that benefit. In this case a broker or brokers expects to earn a commission upon payment of freight therefore they have a right to claim for the commission if it is not paid by the Owner.

13. General Average/Arbitration:

Place of proceedings.

14. TOVALOP

No longer applicable and replaced by ITOPF clause. (See **Appendix 12)** for an example

15. Special Provisions:

Space is provided here to enter the special provisions but from a quick glance you will see that not much space is available so it is usual practice to enter a phrase along the lines of "additional clauses numbers............as attached are deemed incorporated in this charter party".

16. Signatures:

Space is provided for the Owner's and Charterer's signature as well as a witness for each. You will notice that it states that the charter party is to be executed in duplicate.

Where contracts are agreed between Principals who are geographically wide apart, for example Tokyo and New York, it is not unusual for one of the Brokers to be given authority to sign the charter party on one or other of the Principal's behalf. In order to do this the Broker must have a written authority either by letter telex or e-mail, enabling him to sign on behalf of that Principal. Such authority ought to be clearly stipulated on the charter party and will normally be shown as "by written authority of Charterer (or Owners)" and at the end of the signature, the words "as agents only".

PART II

17. Warranty:

The Shipowner (or Disponent Owner) confirms that the vessel is in a suitable condition to safely and properly perform the contracted voyage.

18. Freight and Deadfreight:

Clauses 2 and 3 cover the quantity and measurement of cargo on which freight is paid and the right of Charterers to deduct advances (made to the Master or Agents) from the freight.

19. Berthing, Pumping and Mooring:

Clauses 9, 10 and 11 cover the conditions applicable to the loading and discharging place and the responsibilities for pumping cargo and mooring at sea terminals. These clauses can affect the time used as laytime.

20. Dues and Other Charges:

Clause 12. This states that dues and other charges on the vessel including those assessed on the quantity of cargo loaded or discharged shall be paid by the Owners. Other dues and charges on the cargo being paid by Charterer. Reference should also be made to Worldscale terms (Rate Differentials) when making the voyage estimate.

21. **Ice:**

Clause 14. In many trades it is not necessary for the ice clause to be included in the charter party. However, it is unlikely that it will be deleted. The object of the ice clause is to prevent an Owner and his Master being left with no alternative but to attempt to proceed to a contractual destination irrespective of ice conditions and to avoid damage that may be caused to ship and cargo as a result.

22. **Cleaning/Grades:**

Clause 18. This states that the Owner shall clean the tanks, pipes and pumps of the vessel to the satisfaction of the Charterer's inspector. This implies that the Charterer's inspector will ensure that the vessel is ready for the cargo which they intend to load. The cleanliness required will vary whether the intended cargo is crude oil or a clean petroleum product. Although the Owner remains responsible for the vessel's fitness to carry the specified cargo, the Charterer and sometimes the supplier may not be prepared to commence loading once the vessel has been inspected. A good cleaning clause will include the allocation of responsibility for the time taken de-inerting, inspecting and re-inerting. It is a clause the use of which, Owners suspect, is abused from time to time by a requirement for further cleaning being made only to disguise the fact that the cargo may not be ready for loading. In doubtful cases an Owner may even send his own inspector to verify the facts.

23. **Advances:**

Clause 2. The freight payment clause allows the Charterer to deduct from freight money advanced for ordinary disbursements at the ports of loading and discharge.

24. **Bills of Lading:**

Clause 20 specifies the manner in which the Bills of Lading shall be drawn up and signed. Also states that Bills of Lading shall be without prejudice to this charter.

6.3   PROTECTIVE CLAUSES

Clauses commonly included in the printed form of a charter party.

25. **Clause Paramount:**

Clause 20 (b)(i) has been amended to include the Hague or Hague/Visby Rules into the contract and into the bills of lading issued thereunder. These govern the rights and responsibility of the carrier. This charter party only contains the USA clause paramount which covers voyages involving the USA. (See **Appendix 13**)

26. **Jason Clause and General Average Clause:**

Clause 20 (b)(ii) and (iii) covers general average law and practice for adjustments made in the United States. You will note that the printed form refers to the York/Antwerp Rules 1950. This date should be amended to "1994".

27. **Both to Blame:**

Clause 20 (b)(iv) covers the Owners rights in respect of vessels colliding within American waters.

28. **War Clauses:**

Clause 20 (vi) cover the rights to deviate in the event of war risk.

(Do not confuse with the Chevron War Risk Clause)

29. **Lien:**

Clause 21 This gives the Owner the right to put a lien on cargoes for all amounts due under the charter.

30. **Agents:**

Clause 22. This gives the Owner the right to appoint vessel's Agents at all ports. (Frequently amended in the rider clauses).

31. **Assignment / Sub-let:**

Clause 25. This clause gives the Charterer the right to sublet the vessel, but stipulates that the Charterer shall remain responsible for the fulfilment of the charter.

32. **Clean Seas:**

Clause 26. This covers the anti-pollution measures required and forms an important part of any modern tanker charter party. (See **Appendix 12** and Chapter 7)

33. **Arbitration:**

Clause 24. This stipulates that the interpretation of the charter, the rights and obligations of the parties shall be governed by the laws applicable to charter parties made in New York or London and that arbitration shall take place in either city as nominated in Part I of the charter.

These are the elements of Tanker voyage charter parties and it is fair to say that most people do not make much effort to study the clauses apart from those elements which we might call the main terms.

6.4   DRAFTING ADDITIONAL CLAUSES

Clauses which are most frequently subject to negotiation are the rider clauses or additional clauses which are added to the printed form. It is now worthwhile spending some time to look at the rider clauses which are commonly used today.

There should be no particular problem in drafting additional clauses provided the language is clear and certain basic points are borne in mind. In general, where there is inconsistency between the various terms of the charter party, the written or typed clause will prevail over the printed clause, but inconsistency or uncertainty are precisely what one should seek to avoid.

It is important to be aware of the other relevant provisions of a charter party and to make clear which clause prevails. It may be necessary to start an additional clause with the words "notwithstanding the provisions of Clause x" or possibly "notwithstanding the provisions of any other clause of this charter party" in order to reduce the possibility of uncertainty or conflict.

If a general statement is sufficient, it is better not to detail items or examples for fear that something else not specifically mentioned shall be deemed excluded. If there is good reason for detailing specific items it should be made clear that these words do not limit the width of the preceeding words.

Those of us involved in day to day chartering are led to wonder sometimes whether the person drafting certain clauses really did intend to build in a conflict or an uncertainty! In good clause drafting the aim should be to be clear rather than clever.

It is worth noting the following observation of Lord Reid:

> "As a general principle, when considering a contract, weight should be given to the unreasonableness of the result of a particular situation The more unreasonable the result the more unlikely it is that the parties can have intended it and if they do intend it, the more necessary it is that they shall make that intention abundantly clear."

Having looked at the clauses that are included in the printed forms of tanker charter parties, we will now look at the additional clauses which are new and others which are longer established.

All are included to cover one of the changing aspects of the trade. Some of the clauses have evolved because of practical, operational problems while others because of decisions taken in a court of law over the interpretation of a phrase. Some of the clauses we will examine cause little argument; others can cost money. As far as negotiating terms is concerned, in a rising market Owners influence terms, and in a falling market Charterers influence terms.

6.4.1 Conoco Weather Clause:

"Delays in berthing for loading or discharging and any delays after berthing which are due to weather conditions shall count as half laytime or, if on demurrage, half demurrage."

This clause is included in charter parties because there have been a number of decisions in courts whereby delays caused by weather are held to be delays beyond the control of Charterers. At first glance this seems quite a reasonable approach but it does not take into account the fact that Charterers could send the cargo to any one out of a range of ports. There are a number of ports which are notorious for delays caused by bad weather. Quite often it is not just the wind, no matter how strong that may be, but the swell or the height of the waves entering a port which means that the vessel cannot be held safely alongside the berth. Either the vessel has to stop pumping or leave the berth altogether. Such ports, for instance, Falconara, Fiumicino and Ravenna could possibly be excluded during negotiations. However, should a Charterer wish to have to option to send ships there, the Conoco Weather Clause will go some way toward fairly attributing costs of delays. The Conoco Weather Clause does not, however, cover the cost of shifting a ship should she have to come off the berth due to heavy swell and without a provision to the contrary the Owner may well find that such costs are for their account. At these ports then the Owner would try to negotiate that all costs of shifting would be for Charterer's account and, if possible, settled directly by Charterer. Because such a port has been regularly used it is difficult or even impossible to show that the port is not a "safe port".

6.4.2 Amoco Cargo Retention Clause

"In the event that any cargo remains on board upon completion of discharge, Charterer shall have the right to deduct from freight an amount equal to FOB port of loading value of such cargo plus freight due with respect thereto provided that the volume of cargo remaining on board is pumpable as determined by an independent surveyor. Any action or lack of action in accordance with this provision shall be without prejudice to any rights or obligations of the parties."

When considering this clause perhaps we should remind ourselves that there are two basic trades within tanker chartering, that is dirty and clean. In the clean trades we can readily understand that the residues of cargoes are liquid. Crude oil, however, has a lot of sediment and foreign matter which is not liquid, suspended in the cargo whilst it is loaded. During the voyage this sediment and even water settles to the bottom of the tank and during discharge a certain amount will cling to the sides of the tank so that upon completion of discharge there will be residues within the cargo space. This does not cause a problem if the next cargo to be loaded is also crude oil. Therefore vessels which are in the crude oil trades regularly will have a certain amount of residues within the tank at all times which it is impracable to remove. By looking at the internal structure of a crude oil tanker you will realise that there are a large number of areas within the tank and that at certain lists or trims cargo will not run towards the suction. In theory, it would be possible, given time, to ensure that these residues ran to the strum and were discharged. However in practice, the terminal wants the vessel to be off the berth quickly once the majority of the cargo has been discharged so that they can bring the next vessel on, meaning that there are times when there is liquid on board a ship which is not pumpable because it cannot be reached. To cover such an event the words "and reachable by vessel's fixed pumps" should be inserted between "pumpable" and "as determined" so that particular phrase reads "pumpable and reachable as determined by an independent surveyor".

6.4.3 Chevron War Risk Clause

"War risk insurance for the first fourteen (14) days to be for Owner's account. Thereafter for Charterer's account. Any increase of hull and machinery war risk premiums over and above those in effect on the date of the charter party, will be for Charterers's account.

Any premiums or increases thereto attributable to closure (i.e. blocking and trapping) insurance shall be for Owner's account."

The Owner's normal hull and machinery policy will cover the event of damage or loss caused by a warlike act providing the vessel is not in an area actually designated as a war risk area. If a vessel is to proceed into such an area the war risk underwriter will need an additional premium to cover the vessel during her temporary stay; the underwriter will estimate how long it will take for a ship to enter, load or discharge and return to a place of safety to calculate the premium required on such a duration. Quite often this will be ten or fourteen days, and if the situation does not worsen extra days can be covered at a pro rata daily rate. Other ports which are close to the safe area may only be given seven days cover for the basic rate. In areas where the risk of warlike activity is heightening underwriters will usually only give a quote valid for forty-eight hours. That is to say, the vessel must enter the war risk area within the next forty-eight hours.

When negotiating charters it is quite usual that the vessel will not be arriving in the war risk area within that 48 hours period. Thus from the time of receiving the original quote the rate may be increased due to an increased risk of hostilities. The Owner is therefore at risk on two counts. Firstly the vessel may stay in the war risk area for longer than the period at first contemplated and secondly that the war risk rate may increase between the quote included in the first voyage estimate and the time that the vessel actually arrives at the war risk area. To cover such eventualities the Chevron War Risk Clause stipulates that any increase of hull and machinery war risk premiums over and above those in effect on the date of the charter party will be for Charterers's account. It would be as well to also include a phrase here to say that any time in excess of the fourteen (or seven) days will be for Charterer's account to avoid any misunderstanding.

It is sometimes possible that Charterers will agree that a rate applicable sometime prior to the charter party date, say for instance when the first voyage estimate was run, should be for Owner's account and any increases for Charterer's account. Under many circumstances it is necessary to tell the Charterers what war risk premium is applicable at the time of fixing so that they can check how much it has increased by the time the ship arrives in the war risk area. Also, the meaning of "first fourteen" can lead to misunderstanding, so that it should be made clear that it applies from the time that the vessel enters the area and not from some earlier date.

6.4.4   Cleaning

A typical cleaning clause is given here.

> *"Without prejudice and in addition to Owner's obligations elsewhere in this charter to present vessel with clean cargo tanks, pumps and pipes, vessel shall arrive at load port with all cargo tanks, pumps and pipes cleaned to Charterer's Inspector's satisfaction. Further, Owners shall ensure that all traces of sediment, tank washings or chemicals, if used, are removed from tanks, pumps and pipes intended for the carriage of designated cargo. If the vessel is unclean at cancelling deadline, Charterers will retain its cancellation option until twenty-four hours after the cancelling deadline or until twenty-four hours after the Inspector first rejects the vessel, whichever is later."*

Again, we need to remember that there are two practices; one for dirty trades and one for clean trades. In the clean trades we can easily understand that all sediments from tanks, pumps and lines must be removed to avoid the risk of contamination. However, in the dirty trades and particularly in the large crude oil carriers, it is in practice impossible to remove all sediment from previous cargoes. Thus, the Owner of a crude oil carrier would not be wise to agree to remove all traces of sediment from tanks, and perhaps in 999 cases out of 1,000 no inspector or surveyor would ever question the fact that there were sediments at the bottom of a tank. However, suppose for some reason the ship's cargo is not ready or there are problems at a terminal it would be possible for a Charterer to invoke this clause by saying "there are sediments in the tank and therefore the vessel is rejected until you have cleaned again and removed all sediment." In theory this could be done but then it is down to the Owners to pay all the costs of cleaning and delays which would make the whole exercise uneconomic. You will appreciate that prior to cleaning, a tank will need to be de-inerted and ventilated. This takes a great deal of time, perhaps twenty-four hours and once the cleaning operation is completed the tank has to be re-inerted, taking perhaps again another twenty-four hours. Typically, cleaning clauses are silent as to who will pay for such delays, meaning that the Owner will be the one to cover the cost. Thus in practice for crude cargoes, it would be better to delete the words *"that all traces of sediment"*, or delete the phrase *"that all traces of sediment tank washings or chemicals, if used, are removed from tanks, pumps and pipes intended for the carriage of designated cargo"* and insert *"that all tanks, pumps and pipes will be suitable for the carriage of the designated cargo.* "Thus, in practical terms the vessel will present with the tanks fit for the cargo to be loaded.

For dirty product it would probably be acceptable to describe the ship as *"clean for fuel oil"*, which would mean that the tanks were "dirty", but without low flash crude oil residues in the tank bottoms.

For clean cargo any risk of alteration of flash point is a serious matter (imagine diesel polluted with gasoline). Other problems that can arise are from leaded gasoline, which has a dangerous effect on jet fuel and of course edible oils. It is also not appreciated that discolouration of clean gas oil means down grading, as the colour cannot be removed without re-refining.

Some oil companies have taken the attitude that in fixing a ship for clean cargo a cleaning clause is to be avoided, so that the responsibility for presenting the ship fit for loading the cargo remains with the Owner without any reservations.

Cleaning of tanks by washing will cause the vessel to retain the washings on board in a slop tank. Once the tank has settled free water can be pumped overboard, but areas in which such an operations is not allowed are numerous covering enclosed waters and seas such as the Mediterranean. This can present problems in short sea trades.

6.4.5 Over Age Insurance (Cargo Insurance)

> *"Any additional premium which might be placed on the cargo insurance by reason of the vessel's age and/or condition shall be for Owner's account, and Charterers shall be entitled to deduct the cost of any such additional premium from the freight."*

With the increasing age profile of the tanker fleet this clause is becoming more important to Charterers and Owners alike. We must remember that it is the cargo Owner who will be placing the cargo insurance with their own underwriters. Owners are not able to take part in any of the negotiations leading to the placing of such insurance. Thus, as written, the clause is open ended. The Shipowner does not know the value of the cargo nor does he know what premium is applicable or, for that matter, whether it is even paid. In addition, Charterers are entitled to deduct the cost from the freight. What deduction can the Shipowner expect? $1,000, $5,000, $50,000? Thus to avoid these unknowns if it is necessary to agree anything on this clause it would be prudent to agree a maximum premium say, $5,000 and specify that it should be paid against proper documentation, that is to say, an invoice or receipt from the underwriter for the insurance of the cargo on the voyage in question. Thus, such monies cannot be arbitrarily deducted from the freight. Comment on this was made in an earlier Chapter.

6.4.6 Clean Ballast

You will appreciate that his is not a problem for vessels fitted with SBT (Segregated Ballast Tanks)

> *"Vessel shall arrive at load port with clean Ballast."*

In this clause clean ballast means ballast which is not contaminated with oily residues and has been included in charter parties because many ports do not have dirty ballast reception facilities. This is one of those cases where Owners have had to adapt to marine pollution regulations but some terminals and ports have done very little to assist the process of cleaner seas. An Owner's broker therefore has to check that the vessel does indeed have, or will have, clean ballast on board the ship prior to agreeing this clause. There is a new development, however, which goes beyond just having clean ballast on board the vessel, because there are an increasing number of ports which will not allow even clean ballast to be discharged into their waters and for good reason. Take the example of a vessel which is fitted with SBT tanks and whilst discharging she loads ballast which of course is the sea water or river water in which she is lying. Such water, although it will be free of oily residues, may well have other pollutants or chemicals in it, or if it is lucky enough not to be polluted by industrial waste, may contain bugs or micro-organisms which will continue to live and breed within the segregated ballast tank. If such is discharged into an area that has a sensitive marine environment either the chemical pollutant or the micro-organisms may cause irreparable damage to the marine environment at the subsequent load port. These sensitive ports will frequently have clean ballast reception facilities but will make a charge for their use but it is a development, which we must watch closely.

6.4.7 Inert Gas

"Owner warrants that the vessel has operable Is an inert gas system aboard the vessel and said system shall be operational during duration of this charter party. Master may be required by terminal personnel, Charterer or Independent Inspectors to breach the gas system for the purpose of gauging, sampling, temperature determination or determining the quantity of cargo remaining on board after discharge. Master shall comply, consistent with the safe operation of the vessel and regulations of the port."

This clause does not specify whether laytime will count during such operation and suitable wording should be added.

6.4.8 Crude Oil Washing

"Charterer shall have the right to require the vessel, if it is so equipped, to crude oil wash the cargo tanks and, in such case, the allowed pumping hours shall be increased by... hours. If less than all of the tanks are washed, such extra hours shall be pro-rated on the basis of the number of tanks washed to the total number of cargo tanks and the hours resulting from such pro-ration shall be added to the allowed pumping hours. If crude oil wash is not conducted, Charterer shall have the right to require the vessel to remain at berth for clingage rundown or other cargo recovery technique. The time for such clingage rundown or other cargo recovery technique shall not exceed ten hours and the time so used shall count as laytime or, if the vessel is on demurrage, as time on demurrage."

To understand this clause we have to remember that crude oil washing is conducted by re-circulating approximately 10% of the cargo from the tank through the crude oil washing gun to wash down the sides of the tank. It is easily appreciated that this slows the net discharge rate by a certain extent. The next point to remember is that the Owner has undertaken to discharge the entire cargo within twenty-four hours and any pumping time in excess of that will not count as laytime. The operation of this clause is to increase the allowed pumping time in which laytime will count. The number of hours inserted really is dependent upon the size of vessel and should not be less than six hours for a vessel of 80,000 tons and should be twelve hours for a VLCC. Oil companies frequently allow a fixed time per tank to be crude oil washed thus Shell has allowed 0.75 hours per tank which is crude oil washed. You will appreciate that the extra pumping time will cause the terminal to achieve a slower discharge rate overall and may not encourage vessels and receivers to carry out the crude oil washing procedure.

6.4.9 Worldscale Clause

"Worldscale hours, terms and conditions as per date of loading to apply to this charter party"

Worldscale terms and conditions are periodically amended. Therefore, it is important to establish which will apply. Certain variations of this clause do not have the required precision. Worldscale lays down the rate applicable as at date of loading; some Charterers specify the bill of lading date, whilst others the date of the charter party. If a vessel is likely to load around the end of December or beginning of January it would be advisable to specify which Worldscale rate will apply, the year ending or the year beginning. Remember that the Flat Rate is calculated using bunker prices that can go down as well as up, so next year's rates on some voyages could be lower than the previous year.

The words *"and special rates"* should be added after "conditions" to cover the event of a vessel loading or discharging a transhipment area not included in the WS terms.

6.4.10 Pumping Clause

"Owner warrants that the vessel will discharge her entire cargo within twenty-four (24) hours or will maintain 100 PSI at the ship's rail."

Delays in pumping the cargo during discharge (except when due to the crude oil washing operations) are mainly caused by:

(a) Vessel's boilers or pumps operational condition fails to provide the rate or maintain the pressure as required in charter party.

(b) Residues on tank's bottom may extend stripping time especially if cargo has high viscosity.

(c) High back pressure due to distance from the vessel to the shore tanks, or perhaps the elevation of the shore tanks with respect to the tanker, or reduced number and size of hoses provided by the terminal or deliberate closing of shore valves.

(d) Tanker has to reduce the pumping pressure due to shore instructions (calling for a protest from the master).

It is therefore necessary to add at the end of the paragraph the words "providing shore facilities permit."

In practice, it seems that it is difficult to persuade Arbitrators that a pumping performance of a tanker was sub-standard against the Owner's declaration that the vessel has maintained a pressure of 100 PSI, when documentary proof of this is not produced. To get a full picture of the circumstances further information is required, such as:

(a) Pumping logs from the vessel showing hour by hour the back pressure at the manifolds and the pressure at the cargo pumps. If this can be countersigned by a shore representative, it is excellent evidence.

(b) The viscosity of the liquid being pumped has a greater effect on pumping rate than a specific gravity.

(c) Besides the diameter of the pipelines their length under the sea, overland or buried and whether they are insulated or not, could be established.

(d) The ambient temperature should be recorded throughout the pumping operation.

(e) The temperature of the product as it leaves the ship and on arrival at the storage tank could be recorded, if such inspection is allowed.

(f) The height of the storage tank above sea level and the height of any product in the tank as the cargo enters the tank.

Finally, the Receivers should be prepared to show that every valve on the lines through which the cargo passes from the ship to the storage area has remained open throughout the whole operation. It has happened that shore deliberately slowed discharge in order to load barges from their installation. The above factors which influence the speed of discharge can all be covered **so long as the vessel has maintained the agreed pressure at the manifold.** It is important to remember that the viscosity and the time taken to strip the tank also have an effect on the period of discharge, both are interrelated. The higher the viscosity the more laborious and difficult the stripping process is. It is worth noting that it is unlikely a vessel can maintain the required back pressure during the stripping process. (NB. Stripping pumps are smaller pumps collecting the small amounts of cargo at the bottom of the tank).

6.4.11 Speed

Usually an agreed economic speed or range of speed is included in the charter and the ship is expected to perform at that speed "weather and safe navigation permitting".

6.4.12 Speedup Clause

"Unless otherwise directed by the Charterer, the vessel shall proceed from loading port to discharge port at an average speed of............(12 knots) ("slow speed")."

Charterers shall have the right at any time during the loaded voyage to order the vessel to increase speed to "full speed" of up to ... (15 knots) weather and safe navigation permitting, or to any interim speed between slow and full speeds. The charterer may also order the vessel at any time to arrive at the discharge port on a certain date, in which case the vessel shall make whatever adjustments to speed may be necessary in order to arrive at the specified date, as long as speed necessary to do so is between the above-mentioned "slow" and "full" speeds.

The applicable freight rate set forth in clause . . . shall be applicable during all periods when the vessel is proceeding at slow speed. This freight rate shall be increased ... (1.5) WS points for each knot of increased speed above slow speed on a pro rate basis for fractions of a knot, up to the applicable full speed rate of Worldscale.

When any alterations in speed have been ordered during the loaded voyage the freight rate for the voyage shall be calculated in accordance with the following example:

Example

The vessel proceeds at slow speed of 10 knots, the rate for which is Worldscale 40. After ten days vessel is ordered to complete voyage at interim speed of 12 knots. Remainder of voyage taking 20 days. Increased speed option provides for a premium of 1.5 WS points per knot of increased speed over slow speed.

Freight rate for above voyage:

Voyage freight rate =

$$\frac{(WS40 \times 10 \text{ days}) + (WS43^* \times 20 \text{ days})}{30 \text{ (total voyage days)}} = WS\ 42$$

(*3 points premium for 2 knots)

Should the vessel not maintain speed ordered, due to weather or breakdown of the vessel or any other reason beyond the Charterer's control, the freight rate shall be calculated based on the speed actually performed by the vessel using BP distance tables and the voyage time between pilot stations at the load and discharge port, but such freight rate shall not be less than the slow speed rate.

The above means that although the Owner will have used more fuel to increase speed, unless such speed is actually achieved he will not be recompensed.

There are a number of reasons why, even by increasing revs the vessel will not increase her speed over the ground. Adverse currents or bad weather are examples. Ships cannot be considered as vehicles which can increase or decrease speed as required so a more realistic speed-up clause would allow for increased bunker consumption to be paid for by Charterers, even though the vessel may not have been able to achieve the whole increased speed as required. A motor ship will also have "critical" speeds at which vibration occurs at certain revolutions of the main engine.

6.4.13 Exxon – A Mobil Drug and Alcohol Policy Clause

"Owner warrants that it has a policy on drug and alcohol abuse ("policy") applicable to the vessel which meets or exceeds the standards in the Oil Companies International Marine Forum Guidelines for the control of drugs and alcohol on board ship ("OCIMF Guidelines"). Owner further warrants that this policy will remain in effect during the term of this charter and that Owner shall exercise due diligence to ensure that the policy is complied with.

For the purposes of this clause and the OCIMF Guidelines, alcohol impairment shall be defined as a blood alcohol content of 40 mg/100 ml or greater; the appropriate seafarers to be tested shall be all vessel officers and the drug/alcohol testing and screening shall include random testing of the officers with a frequency to ensure that each officer is tested at least once a year."

This clause met with almost universal condemnation within the industry, not because anybody disagrees with the aims of the clause but it brings into focus problems of civil liberties. At the time BIMCO issued the following warning to its members:

"Owners should be aware that under most legal systems no crew member is obliged to submit himself to random testing of alcohol content in the system. This is supposed to interfere too much with personal integrity and can consequently be refused by the crew members. In order to be allowed to insist on random testing, this must expressly be permitted by law (presumably by the law of the flag of the ship), where it must be agreed beforehand with the crew members or alternatively be agreed in the collective agreements to which the crew members are bound. For the time being it is therefore our recommendation that Owners should refuse to include Exxon's Drug and Alcohol Clause in their charter parties because Owners cannot guarantee that they can comply with the clause."

The key to this issue obviously lies in the wording of the contracts which the crew members sign either with the Owner or the crewing agency. By agreement a policy can operate where all active personnel are automatically tested whenever any form of incident occurs in order not only to protect the company concerned but also the individual.

6.4.14 In Transit Loss Clause

"In addition to any other rights which Charterer may have, Owner will be responsible for the full amount of any in transit loss if in transit loss exceeds 0.3% and Charterer shall have the right to deduct from freight an amount equal to the FOB port of loading cost of such missing cargo plus its pro rata cost of freight and insurance. In transit loss is defined as the difference between gross standard vessel volumes after loading at the loading port and before unloading at the discharge port."

This clause is often included as a part of the cargo retention clause. However, with the increasing cost of crude oil and products these days this clause is becoming more important and features in more and more rider clauses. The important aspect to watch here is how the in transit loss shall be calculated. The clause here specifies gross standard vessel volumes at the load port and discharging port. Some Charterers will want to use shore meters or tank measurements from ashore, perhaps even trying to measure net volumes. In practice providing a ship has accurate calibration tables, it is better to use vessel's volumes at each end because then you are comparing like with like. There is some discussion these days as to whether the amount 0.3%, is in fact acceptable for all liquid cargoes. For instance crude oil cargoes can perhaps stand such a tolerance whereas chemicals maybe require a smaller tolerance.

Water content can cause problems as it tends to settle out during the voyage and the Receiver may maintain that valuable cargo has been replaced with sea water or leaking heating coils have increased water content. Gross measurement of on board quantities is essential and care should be taken that the Inspector is clearly independent. Water content of crude or fuel is often inaccurate due to suspension, but one sure way of checking is to take samples of any settled water whereby its chemical solvents (salts, sulphates etc) may demonstrate its origin as compared with sea water.

6.4.15 Privacy

"All negotiations and details of this fixture shall be kept strictly private and confidential."

This clause ought to be observed strictly by all parties involved in a fixture. Oil trading organisations, whether independent or oil company owned, frequently need this clause to reduce the chances of their competitors knowing what they are doing. Sometimes a fixture has been concluded at a very low level and an Owner would want the fixture to be private, but for whatever reason, parties should honour this simple clause. If the details of a fixture do leak to the market, a broking company may need to try to prove that the information did not come from them. Sometimes the details are on the market so quickly and accurately that you would think someone has taken *"P + C" to* mean *"Publish and Circulate"!*

Turning to **Appendix 18,** you can see a recent recap detailing the charter party agreement listing the agreed amendments and additional clauses. All commercial information has been removed to protect the parties involved.

6.4.16   Questionnaires

Questionnaires were initially introduced where vessels would have to call at berths with special requirements. The scope of the questions became wider and wider and today under the BEEPEEVOY 4 **(Appendix 17)** you will see that the questionnaire known as Appendix 1 to the charter party forms a part of the charter party itself and covers everything from the vessel's name and previous names, vessel's details, details of the Ownership, confirmation on the validity of the trading certificates, history of accidents and pollution incidents, information about Master, Officers and Crew, through to the last time that the vessel was fixed to a BP company, etc.

As oil companies become more aware of their exposure to the media and oil pollution liability the feeling is the questionnaire will form a greater part of the choice of vessel fixed as time goes on.

6.4.17   Letters of Indemnity

The nature of the tanker market is such that a cargo will be sold a number of times prior to delivery. To enable the sellers to trade the cargo they need a complete set of Original Bills of Lading, forming part of the documentation required by a bank under the terms of their letter of credit. In practice this means that the vessel will have to discharge before the original bills of lading arrive at the discharge port. There is no need to remind you of the trouble in which an Owner can find himself if he delivers the cargo to the wrong party.

The problem is overcome by Charterers issuing a Letter of Indemnity (LOI) which although not recommended by P&I Clubs is recognised as a necessity for commercial expediency.

Thus, in the charter party there will normally be a clause allowing for the cargo to be discharged without production of an original Bill of Lading against a Charterer issuing an LOI as per the Owner's P&I Club wording and, if the Charterers are unknown or little known, such indemnity to be countersigned by a first class bank.

The Clubs insist on a bank guarantee for lesser-known Charterers because the amount of money that could arise from a claim may be extremely large. For instance, the claim could involve CIF value of cargo plus consequential damages, e.g. because a refinery is closed due to lack of product. This also underlines the point that no maximum monetary limit should be inserted in the LOI

There are two instances when an LOI will be required.

i)   Non production of Bills of Lading,

ii)   Actual discharge port different from that shown on Bill of Lading.

A typical LOI is in **Appendix 18 and 19** and you should note that there is no time limit stated. That is to say the Letter of Indemnity does not become null and void after a period of, say, 13 months which is frequently requested by Charterers. The reason for this of course is that claims can be made until six or seven years after discharge and an Owner would be leaving himself open to a large claim sometime after the Letter of Indemnity expired.

6.5 THE CONTRACT OF AFFREIGHTMENT

You can readily understand that the traditional voyage charter covers one agreement – one voyage. There are often occasions, however, when there is a need for a contract that covers several shipments. Possibly these could be arranged by time chartering or by voyage chartering for consecutive voyages, and in both cases such would normally be performed by one vessel in direct continuation. Such agreements do not give the Owner any flexibility to bring in alternative or substitute vessels. Another solution, which is popular with large Owners or operators, is to enter into a so-called Contract of Affreightment (COA).

Agreements, which intend to cover more than one shipment or voyage give rise to several questions over and above those already covered for the single voyage.

Strictly speaking, all charter parties are forms of a Contract of Affreightment but in commercial shipping the term COA refers to a contract which is.

1.   That the carriage is of a specified type and quantity of cargo

2.   Covering two or more shipments

3.   Running over a protracted period.

Some examples may help to illustrate. An Owner undertakes to carry between X and Y metric tons of crude oil from B to C during a twelve month period. The Owner agrees to carry all cargo shipped by the Charterer from a load port to the given discharge port during a given period.

In the COA it is the cargo, which determines the nature of the contract and as such it is built up without a specified ship. Thus, under a traditional charter party, if a vessel is lost the contract is usually abandoned whereas a COA would still be in force. The descriptions of the suitable vessels for the contract are of course important, so should his ship be lost, the Owner must find a suitable substitute because he has not been relieved of his obligation to carry the cargo.

The number of voyages is an important factor of a COA. The total quantity and the size of ship used will be an important determining element when it comes to deciding the number of voyages which are to be involved in the COA. Quite often this will be determined by the storage facilities either at the Shipper's or Receiver's end. Whereas, as we have already seen, there are a number of standard forms of voyage chartering, this is not the case for contracts of affreightment, probably because in most cases the contract needs to be designed for the specific circumstances of the Charterer.

As may be expected the COA will include a number of clauses dealing with questions, which are specific for a specialised contract. Typically, the parties will use a standard form of voyage charter to form a basis for the COA. Thus, once there is an overruling COA dealing with cargo quantities, period, Owner's remuneration, type of vessel, etc. the standard form of charterparty can be used for a specific voyage and for the administration of the charter party for each ship as nominated under the contract for specified dates.

An alternative solution could be to have a standard charter party with additional clauses specifically dealing with the COA terms.

In short, Contracts of Affreightment can be flexible, but are less widely used in the crude trades than they are in the product and chemical trades. One major advantage for the Charterer is that unless the contract is for one named vessel the loss of a ship or even delay to a ship does not end the contract or remove the liability to perform as scheduled.

If a Charterer, seeking flexibility, negotiates tolerances in quantities, loading dates and voyages, under a COA he can ship the required quantities at a stable freight rate and avoid the problem of trying to find countinuous employment for vessels owned or time chartered by him.

The tolerances permitted in quantities, loading dates and voyages, which are so useful to the Charterer, are also a potential source of disputes. It is very important to both parties to ensure that the contract details clearly and precisely the number and timing of notices regarding cargo size, type and readiness and/or vessel size, readiness and quality.

Such notices are essential to facilitate matching vessels and cargoes. The very flexibility of contracts of affreightment can otherwise lead to acrimony because of one party or the other taking full advantage of the letter rather than the spirit of the agreement, in respect of the tolerances available.

It is common practice to have minimum and maximum quantities to be shipped, say in each quarter, and a minimum and maximum quantity which must be shipped in a year and provision for over-lifts and under-lifts, perhaps with some tolerance for carrying forward to the next contract year.

The contract may be structured in one part containing all the clauses governing the overall agreement as well as the individual voyages, or in two parts. The first part contains the main terms such as cargoes, voyages, vessel size and type, notice and nomination requirements, freight rates and governing law and the second part a voyage charter, the terms of which come into force for each individual voyage as it arises.

As with any form of period charter, careful consideration must be given to war risks, failure to pay freight on time, cancellation rights and exceptions clauses.

6.6 CONSECUTIVE VOYAGE CHARTERS

Charterers seeking protection against the fluctuations in single voyage market may turn to consecutive voyage chartering to obtain a commitment of tonnage on agreed terms over a period of time.

A consecutive voyage contract may take the form of a single voyage charter with a clause added to provide for one or more further voyages in direct continuation, or a charter form designed specifically for consecutive voyages. The popular fashion in this respect has tended to vary over the years and at the moment the full consecutive voyage charters such as the Shellconsec and Caltexconsec seem to be less widely used and the adapted voyage charter is in favour

There is no overriding reason for using one approach as opposed to the other, provided all the necessary terms are included. At the end of the day there is very little difference between a single voyage form with a number of additional clauses designed to cover the parties' needs in respect of a series of voyages and a standard consecutive form. However, because the standard form should already contain all the appropriate provisions there is, with that, less chance of the parties failing to remember to cover some contingency that subsequently proves relevant.

The basic consideration for the parties is how to approach the question of duration of the charter. The charter may for example, be for a stated number of voyages or for as many voyages as the vessel can perform in a stated period of time.

With an agreement for say six voyages and wide discharge options, then if the Charterers opts for six short voyages the duration of the charter and the Owner's income will be much less than if the Charterer had elected to have the vessel perform the longest permissible voyages. If the Charterer has complete flexibility in this respect, the market level will no doubt influence his decision on the length of the voyage. Apart from the effect of the length of voyage on the Owner's income, the Owner wishes to have some reasonable idea of when his vessel will again be free for charter.

If the charter is for as many voyages as the vessel can perform within a set period, then the overall time factor is more definite, but it is essential to clearly spell out the cut-off point. It is usual to use some form of wording referring to the number of times the vessel can present for loading within the agreed period. It is important to be quite specific in this respect and refer "to arrival at or off the port", "presentation of notice of readiness" or, "commencement of loading".

With a single voyage charter the agreement of a cancelling date is straightforward, as indeed it is for a first loading under a consecutive voyage charter. However, under a consecutive voyage arrangement it is prudent to have some suitable formula for agreeing a cancelling date for each succeeding voyage which arises. If not, the arrangement will be loose and too much latitude invariably leads to problems.

The application of any cancelling option must also be considered. In a consecutive voyage charter the terms have to make it clear whether late arrival on any voyage will lead to cancellation of the remainder of the charter or only to cancellation of that particular voyage. It has happened with a major oil company that a ship took so long to perform three voyages, that when she presented for the third they had forgotten they had her on charter!

For similar reasons, the possibility of late payment of freight (and demurrage) needs special attention. The terms of the charter should be such that the Owner will not find himself obliged to load a further cargo if the Charterer has failed to pay the freight due on the previous cargo. At the same time, it would hardly be reasonable for an accidental late payment to provide opportunity for an Owner to cancel the remainder of the contract. One equitable basis is for the Owner to have to give notice if payment is overdue and then some days of grace be allowed, in which the position may be remedied. The Owner should not be obliged to load a further cargo in the meantime and he should be entitled to interest to compensate for any such delay.

Two other significant matters are ballast voyage length and war risks. It would be a poor charter for the Owner if Charterers could get away with performing short laden voyages and long ballast legs. The other side of the coin is the possibility of the Charterer obtaining back-haul cargo from at, or near, the discharge port. If the Owner is paid a round voyage freight in both directions, it is a bad deal for the Charterer. A provision for war risk insurance and war bonuses or a right to cancel should be considered having regard to the duration of the charter.

6.7 SELF-ASSESSMENT AND TEST QUESTIONS

Attempt the following and check your answer from the text.

1. What costs are for Owner's account under a voyage charter?

2. What sre the main terms of a voyage charter party?

3. Which of the Rider Clauses have an effect on the laytime calculation?

4. What are the advantages of a COA for a Charterer and an Owner?

5. What are the problems that may be encountered in consecutive voyage charters?

Having completed Chapter Six attempt the following and submit your essay to your Tutor:

If you were a newly established Charterer and not well known in the market, what charter party form and additional clauses (if any) would you prefer to use as your pro-forma?

Chapter 7

TANKER TIME CHARTERS

7.1 INTRODUCTION

From the charter party family tree in Chapter Six you will see that two types of time charter are shown, time and trip time charter. At the present time it must be said that 'trip' time charters are rare in the tanker industry but perhaps the situation will change, so a short explanation is given here to fill in the background.

A trip time charter is for a voyage (or if you like, a very short period, maybe only a few days, up to 4/5 months). Typically, good examples would be found in the dry cargo trades, the first a fully fitted containership being taken from a port on the continent to a port on the US Atlantic coast, the Charterer being a liner company, wanting to supplement the tonnage on its service and have the flexibility of ordering a vessel to any port in any order within the load and discharge ranges at a speed to suit their own schedule and delivery dates.

A second example would be a government organisation chartering a panamax vessel to carry bulk grain from one or more ports in the United States Gulf to discharge one or more ports anywhere between the Black and Baltic Seas. The time charter element gives the Charterer the flexibility required for his transport and delivery needs.

In the tanker industry, it used to be necessary on a voyage charter to agree a wide range of options including one to three discharge ports within a given range at stated rates per ton which might have been better covered by a trip time charter. Oil company promotion of Worldscale, giving a theoretical income per day on a certain size and performance of ship on a round voyage, tried to equate any voyage income per ton of cargo loaded with a daily income. In effect the use of Worldscale made a trip time charter unnecessary. However no Owner likes to enter a trade with a tanker (that normally has a fast turn round) where charter conditions involve a very large demurrage claim that will be disputed, settled many months or even years after the voyage and may end in arbitration. So entry into a complicated voyage commitment may be better converted into a trip time charter, although on a weak market that may not be possible, as the Charterer is only interested in a definite cost per ton delivered.

Four trades in which it can occur are vegetable oil, chemicals, areas where an Owner may have bunkering problems (bunkers on time charter being for Charterers account) and local area employment within a Charterers programme, where delay and last minute alteration is probable.

In vegoil the ship may be delivered, say, Far East for a voyage to Europe, but the Charterers need to be able to off load, reload and delay the ship during the voyage if necessary in order to pick up a parcel of vegoil.

Much the same situation applies with chemicals in the parcel trades with a ship chartered in for a voyage in a particular direction, but with the probability of discharging and reloading parcels en route. This type of trade makes individual tank segregation almost essential.

For occasional voyages to Chile with about 130,000 tons of crude oil from West Africa, Charterers have used a trip time charter due to the risk of high bunker prices and supply insecurity on a voyage round Cape Horn, but redelivery may be agreed, say, off Montevideo, so it is not a round voyage time charter.

In local area employment, say, involving bunker supplies in The Gulf, the intention to load at a port and to proceed south to one or more ports or places may be disrupted, making a type of trip time charter easier to operate than if performed on a voyage basis which would be liable to create considerable demurrage claims.

We are now going to concentrate on period time charters which are usually entered into by oil companies, larger traders or operators. That is to say, very large organisations with good financial resources acceptable to the Owners taking the commitment.

The time charter is an agreement to hire a particular vessel or vessels for a certain period during which time the Time Charterer is responsible for the commercial operation of the vessel. The Charterer arranges for payment of bunkers, port and canal dues, fixing the cargo and arranges for the requisite voyage orders to be given to the vessel. Except to the extent of any rights to stop or reduce the hire, the Charterer takes the risks on any time lost in port or at sea. Thus the profitability or otherwise of the charter will depend not only on the market rates and the ready availability of cargo, but also on weather conditions and the Charterer's ability to maximise the employment of a vessel by good programming.

You will appreciate that the very important aspect of a vessel's worth can only be determined from the description of the vessel. You should consider anything from physical dimensions of beam and draft through to cargo capacity, types of cargo she can carry and the cost of running the vessel, i.e. speed and consumption, including GT and NT which are important for the port costs. Commercially, two sister ships under different Ownerships may be worth a different rate of hire. If Owner "A" is prepared to agree a very wide trading area, is generally co-operative and agrees to carry many different cargoes, his ship could be worth more than the vessel of Owner "B" who gives only a limited trading area and less cargo types and is awkward. Thus to evaluate accurately reported fixtures or any business which is proposed, the fullest possible details of the ship and/or the trade should be ascertained.

Let us now look at the main clauses of the time charter, using the relevant parts of the Shelltime4 as an example and adopting a similar approach to that employed in the previous Chapter on Voyage Charter Clauses. (See **Appendix 20**)

Place where contract made.	see
Date of charter party.	voyage
Name and domicile of contracting parties (1.1-5)	charter
Description and Condition of Vessel (Clause 1 1.6-24)	clauses

The amount of information required in the description depends upon the complexity of the intended trade and in addition to the requirements laid out in this clause you will note mention is also made of Form B which is a comprehensive list of particulars of the tanker and such description forms part of the charter party. You will of course say that a time charter description should include a speed and consumption and in fact this is covered later in this particular charter party under Clause 24 which we will come to later. Some charters call for the plans of a vessel to be submitted to Charterers. It will be important to Charterers to know which oil companies the vessel is acceptable to and that the vessel will remain acceptable throughout the period of the charter.

7.2   SHIPBOARD PERSONNEL AND DUTIES (Clause 2 l.25-43)

The Charterer is not only hiring the ship he is hiring the crew. As such it probably makes good sense to spell out in the charter party what the Charterers expect the crew to be able to achieve and what they want them to do to perform all the voyages with the utmost despatch. Without such a clause the Charterer has little power to deal with an inefficient crew.

7.2.1   Duty to Maintain (Clause 3 l.44-64)

This clause requires the Owner to take steps to exercise due diligence to maintain and restore the vessel to its required condition stated in the Form B. Should the Owners fail to maintain the vessel the Charterers have the right after a 30 day period of notice to put the vessel off hire. Here is the sting in the tail: once the vessel is off hire under this clause, Charterers have the option to terminate the charter.

However Owners "must have failed to demonstrate to Charterer's reasonable satisfaction the exercise of due diligence", so that given the impossibility of making an unexpected minor repair where the ship is lying and Owners planning such a repair as soon as possible, Owners have exercised due diligence.

7.2.2   Limits of Trading Period (Clause 4 l.65-84)

The traditional way to describe the period is to fix a certain number of months or years, for instance twelve months or two years, etc. Since it is difficult to determine beforehand exactly when the ship can be redelivered (i.e. at the completion of discharge) it is usual to have a certain flexibility built in by adding a phrase such as "fifteen days more or less in Charterer's option", possibly even adding the word "about". When establishing the meaning of "about" several factors will be taken into account, in particular the length of the initial period.

Sometimes the Charterers have the option to prolong the charter period, such an option will be for the benefit solely of the Charterer. Should the market rate go down during the period, the Charterers will probably not exercise their option and the Owners will have to find new employment for the vessel at the lower market rate.

The Charterers may choose another ship, or maybe the same ship, at a lower level than in the original charter. Should the market rate go up during the charter period, the Charterers are most likely to exercise their option and thereby keep the vessel at a rate lower than that existing in the market place. Especially when there is a big difference between market and charter party rates, disputes can easily arise concerning the length of the period.

7.2.3   Final Voyage (Clause 19 l.185-197)

Sometimes a vessel is redelivered before and other times after the agreed delivery date or period. In the first case it is an underlap situation and in the latter an overlap.

Owners cannot refuse to take the ship should Charterers redeliver prior to the agreed date even though this is a breach of contract on the Charterer's side. The Owners have an obligation to minimise their loss by seeking alternative employment for the vessel but should they fail, or if they get a lower revenue compared with the existing charter, they are entitled to compensation from the original Charterers and have a case for damages against them.

When Charterers are planning the last voyage for the vessel they need to take into consideration where and when she has to be redelivered under the agreement in the charter. It is often difficult to plan or estimate exactly when the vessel can be redelivered particularly in a long period time charter, and so this problem is covered in the Clause 19. Some charter parties are silent on the point, Other charters say that the vessel should receive the market rate for any period in excess of the charter period. Whereas this is an attempt to be fair, it can be a tricky problem to decide what the market rate is and in this clause the vessel receives the charter rate.

Note that the Charterers have the continued use of the vessel (only) if she is ballasting to redelivery port or is on a laden voyage, which could incur a subsequent ballast to a redelivery port. This could give rise to argument as the ship on the last voyage could be sent to a distant port to load just before the redelivery date, so she then does a long laden voyage possibly followed by a ballast, thereby considerably extending the charter. This question should be borne in mind when agreeing a margin on the period in Clause 4.

Charterers are not entitled to extend the base period because of off-hire incidents that may have occurred during the charter unless it is expressly agreed. If such a clause is inserted it would be advisable to have an agreed time at which the Charterers must notify the Owners whether or not they intend to exercise their option to extend the period.

Should you ever become involved in trip time charters for a specific voyage it is usual to insert an approximate duration e.g. 30-50 days, and this will often be qualified by adding the words "without guarantee".

It is usual to state in line 67 what will be the intended cargo or cargoes and how many grades. (See also Clause 28 1.387-390).

7.2.4   Trading Limits (Clause 4 I.65-84)

Without amendment Charterers may use the vessel in any part of the world "Within Institute Warranty Limits" (WIWL). However, it is usually necessary to limit the trading of a tanker in particular. You will recall that, under the current political situation tankers that have traded to Israel will not be accepted in such places as The Gulf. For these reasons it would be necessary to exclude Israel from the Trading Limits. In addition there could be other places where a vessel would not want to trade, such as Cuba, currently a vessel which has traded to Cuba will not be able to call at USA ports for 180 days hence unworkable by American Charterers; Scandinavia, Australia, New Zealand if her crew is not employed on an ITF agreement (See Chapter Ten). Such trading exclusions are included at this point. The final part of the clause states where the vessel shall be delivered to the Charterers and redelivered to the Owners.

7.2.5   Laydays/Cancelling (Clause 5 I.85-86)

You will notice that unlike voyage charters no mention is made of the need to tender notice of readiness prior to time counting, or for any time on the cancelling date that the vessel has to present.

It is customary for a vessel to be inspected prior to delivery to the Charterer to ensure that she complies with what is agreed in the charter and what the Charterer had expected of the vessel. Some charter parties allow the Owner time to rectify any faults, whilst others give the Charterer the right to cancel the charter party without any claim against them.

7.2.6   Owners to Provide (Clause 6 I.87-96)

This clause specifies that Owners are to provide and pay for all provisions, wages, etc. so long as these costs relate to the Master, officers and crew. It also goes on to specify such things as the insurance of the vessel, stores, water, drydocking.

7.2.7   Charterers to Provide (Clause 7 I.97-103)

This clause spells out in full what the Charterers shall provide and pay for. Note also that the clause states that whilst the vessel is off-hire specified items will be for Owner's account. In short this means that the Charterers will provide all those items "whilst on hire", a phrase that the dry cargo Brokers are very familiar with.

7.2.8   Rate of Hire and Payment of Hire (Clauses 8 & 9 I.104-128)

Hire can be described as a financial payment to the Owners for leasing the manned and equipped vessel to the Charterers. Essentially, hire shall be paid from the moment the ship is delivered to the Charterers until she has been redelivered to the Owners on termination of the charter period. The Charterer pays hire in advance and can only recover hire in respect of idle time if he can show that time was lost for one of the causes specified in an off-hire clause (see Clause 9 lines 110/115).

Most off-hire clauses have a threshold and only if the time lost by the vessel exceeds such a threshold of say six hours, may the vessel be put off-hire. When the time lost exceeds the threshold, the vessel is off-hire from the commencement of the delay. So, with a six-hour franchise, if the vessel breaks down for seven hours, the off-hire is seven hours, but if the breakdown lasts only five hours, no off-hire arises.

However if the vessel stops at sea a deduction of hire could occur through the performance Clause 24. The general principle is that any expenses that are stated to be for Charterer's account remain for Charterers's account, even when the vessel is off-hire, unless the charter provides otherwise. Hence under the Shelltime charter party it is provided that Punkers consumed during off-hire etc. shall be for Owner's account.

You will note that the payment of hire must be made in immediately available funds, meaning that the money must be in the Owner's account free for his use (otherwise it is not deemed paid). To this end it is necessary to give the details of the Owner's bank account to which the funds must be remitted, thereby allowing enough time for Charterers to arrange such payment and minimising the chance of fraud. By specifying in the charter party where hire or even freight payments are to be made, means that the Charterer cannot change payment instructions without prior notice and an addendum to the charter party being agreed. By the same token it is necessary to agree in which currency hire payments will be made. The Owner does not want to receive funds in a foreign currency and then find that he has to have them exchanged for the currency he requires, thereby experiencing delay and extra costs. The Shelltime charter party calls for hire to be paid per calendar month in advance. Some Charterers try to reduce the period paid in advance to fifteen days or possibly less. Hire should be paid in full unless it is agreed that certain deductions can be made and such event is covered in lines 110-117.

Should the Charterers be in default by paying either too late or too little, the Owners would be entitled under English law, and in accordance with the majority of time charter party forms, to cancel the charter agreement. The Charterer's obligation then is to pay the hire money into the account named by the Owner by midnight on the due date. If the due date falls on a weekend or any other holiday, which is not a banking day, hire must be paid on the preceeding banking day. Thus if hire falls due on a Saturday or a Sunday it would have to be paid no later than the preceeding Friday.

As hire is paid in advance any recoveries that may become due can only be made by deduction from a subsequent month's hire payment. Even when it is known that the vessel will be off-hire at the due date for payment, hire must be paid in full. It is not permitted to withhold the anticipated off-hire. However, a reasonable assessment of hire due on the final voyage, less disbursements, is allowed under Clause 19.

All tanker charters contain a withdrawal clause. This is an important protection for the Owner, enabling him to regain control of his ship if the hire money is not paid on time. This right of withdrawal can present a tempting opportunity to an Owner, with a vessel on at a low rate, in order to take advantage of a higher market if for any reason the hire money is overdue by even a short space of time. Unless expressly agreed otherwise, the Owner does not need to notify the Charterer that a payment is due or overdue. However, he must give notice of withdrawal within a reasonable time. What is a reasonable time is not easily defined because it will vary depending on circumstances. An Owner can by his conduct lose his right to withdraw a vessel. For example, regular acceptance of late payment over a period could amount to a waiver or, if the Owner accepts the late payment, as if it had been tendered on time.

It is usual these days for tanker time charter parties to deal with late payment by including a requirement that the Owner must notify the Charterer if hire money is overdue and the Charterer then has a period of grace in which to remedy the situation before the Owner is entitled to withdraw his ship. The wording of the reference to late payment is important. If the charter relates to the right of withdrawal of the vessel to "in default of payment" this right is lost once the hire has been received. If the charter relates to the right of withdrawal to default of "regular and punctual payment of hire" a Charterer who fails to make a payment on time cannot avoid the consequences of this failure by making late tender of the payment.

A late payment does not have to be deliberate and may occur because of a variety of reasons from an oversight in the Charterer's office to a banking error, and in the Shelltime charter party Charterers have seven days to make good the payment after receiving notice from the Owners that payment is late (Clause 9(a)).

7.2.9 Instructions and Logs (Clause 12 I.136-141)

A small but important clause for Charterers because it enables them to monitor how the vessel is performing with respect to speed and consumption.

Some charters call for the Charterer's own log books to be completed by the vessel and for same to be returned to Charterer's office at regular intervals. This is an important element in the commercial running of the vessel.

7.2.10 Direction and Conduct of Vessel's Personnel (Clauses 13-14 I.142-159)

Under a time charter the Master is in a difficult position. He has to follow the instructions of both the Owner and the Time Charterer. Therefore he represents two parties and has to look after the interests of them both, although in fairness it is true to say these interests frequently coincide.

Although, the Master will receive his sailing instructions from the Time Charterer and he should comply with such instructions, there are occasions when he may not necessarily follow such orders. The Master is primarily responsible for the safety of the crew and in addition he will have responsibilities with regard to the cargo Owners and other third parties.

If, according to the Master's opinion and experience, such orders or instructions jeopardise the crew, ship, cargo or other persons, he has an obligation not to obey such orders. In such a situation the Master would contact not only the Charterers but also the Owners and try to deal with the situation without causing any additional costs for any of the parties involved.

In the event, that the Master does not receive clear or acceptable orders from the time Charterers or the cargo Owners, he should follow those received from his Owners providing the same are in the above-mentioned parameters. Many time charter party forms have a clause covering the situation where Charterers are not satisfied with the Master, officers or crew. In some charter parties the clause is as severe as obliging the Owner to make any changes in the appointments which Charterers deem necessary and this applies in Clause 14.

7.2.11 Bunkers (Clause 15 I.160-167)

This clause states that the Charterers shall accept and pay for the bunkers as on board at the time of delivery and likewise Owners shall accept and pay for bunkers as on board at time of redelivery at the current market prices at the relevant ports. At first sight this may appear reasonable but it may cause difficulties.

Perhaps the ship is delivering at a port where bunkers come by road tanker at a high price or even where no bunkers are available and without sufficient bunkers on board to reach a main bunkering port. Lines 163/164 cover this point to some extent.

If the vessel was in effect stranded without bunkers, it is most unlikely that Charterers would accept delivery. It is therefore important to spell out the estimated quantities of bunkers on delivery and redelivery thereby highlighting any potential problems before they arise.

The agreed prices for bunkers will usually not cause a problem on long period charters. However, for shorter periods the negotiation regarding bunker prices may well be influenced by the volatility of the bunker market. Due regard should be paid to the ongoing bunker prices at areas of delivery or redelivery.

It is important to bear in mind that the supply of bunkers is the Charterer's responsibility. The quality is very much a concern of the Owners. The quality of bunkers is a factor affecting the wear of the engines on a motor ship, maintenance costs and the vessel's performance.

More often than not, the Charterer only states the maximum viscosity limit for the bunkers to be supplied, but in so far as the grade of bunkers is included in Clause 29 and the Form B attached to the charter and which forms part of the charter, the Charterer would be exposed to risk if a lower quality was supplied.

7.2.12 Supernumeraries (Clause 17 l.180-182)

This gives the right to put representatives on board the vessel who will be accommodated in the available accommodation and provided with necessary victuals and requisites at a given rate in dollars per day.

7.2.13 Sub-Letting (Clause 18 l.183-184)

Although the original Charterers remain responsible, they can at times tend to hide behind the sub-charterers and it is up to the Broker to make sure that the head Charterer is well informed of any liabilities that may arise from malperformance or differences in terms (although wisely a sub-charter is back to back).

7.2.14 Loss of Vessel (Clause 20 l.198-204)

This clause spells out what will happen should a vessel become a total loss or a constructive total loss and further states that should any hire have been paid in advance same should be returned to Charterer.

7.2.15 Off-Hire (Clause 21 l.205-256)

This is a comprehensive clause in the Shelltime form specifying that where there is a loss of time, the Charterers will have the right to put the vessel off-hire from the commencement of such loss of time until she is again ready and in an efficient state to resume her service.

In fact this clause should operate in a very fair way and allowance is given by Charterers for benefit of position while off hire and any time involved under this clause is to be excluded from any calculations made under Clause 24 (Performance). Off hire counts as part of the charter period.

7.2.16 Periodical Drydocking (Clause 22 l.257-291)

Such a clause is usually deleted in a time charter for a short period. However, if the duration of the charter is going to be two years or more, there will definitely be a need for careful consideration of this clause. Owners may need to specify that the vessel has to be in a certain area for a dry-docking, particularly if it is a newbuilding and will have to present herself for a guarantee drydock.

Note that the docking port must have slop facilities, but as Charterers are not obliged to present the ship fit for hot work in the tanks, some co-operation on the last cargo carried can be invaluable. Owners may be advised to have their own independent inspector available to differentiate between gas free for painting and "entry to cargo tanks" (1.276).

As Charterers allow the time taken from last discharge port to next loading port when a vessel is deviating to a "special port" for dry-docking, it is valuable for a Broker to try to obtain a forward programme from Charterers before the vessel is committed for docking. For example from UK/Cont Lisbon would be no problem if next loading West Africa and Malta if ballasting through Suez.

7.2.17 Performance Clause (Clause 24 l.302-352)

Obviously, it is to the Charterer's benefit to maximise the employment of the vessel. The Charterer wants the most efficient service he can obtain. The sea performance will be warranted by the Owner in terms of speed and bunker consumption and most tanker charters now have detailed and very tight performance clauses, although in some charters the performance will be qualified by an "about".

Some charters provide for hire to be adjusted only for performance shortfall, but this charter gives Owners the benefit of any lower bunker consumption at the assigned speed. Therefore the Charterer will have the right to reduce the hire rate or deduct from hire the amount of any performance penalties or pay any savings made to Owners.

To recap, for a moment, remember that when contemplating a time charter, the Charterer will wish to calculate the vessel's freighting performance, in Worldscale points for a standard voyage. In his calculation he will use the speed and consumption as declared by the Owner, to establish the steaming time and total bunker consumption of the vessel for the voyage selected. He needs to cost the time at the daily hire rate. The total cost of the time at sea, in port and the cost of bunkers and port charges for the voyage, divided by the amount of cargo that the vessel could carry on that voyage will equate to the cost per ton of cargo. This figure, divided by the Worldscale flat rate for the voyage, gives the Worldscale percentage level when multiplied by 100 (Worldscale flat = W100) for the time charter rate applied.

By this means the Charterer can compare the freighting cost to him of the vessels offered and choose the cheapest suitable vessel. However, if in service, the vessel does not achieve the declared performance, the Charterer may find that he does not have the cheapest vessel, so he needs some means of indemnity. Thus, modern tanker charters contain detailed and stringent performance clauses, so that if the vessel does not give the warranted performance, the Charterer has some redress. These performance clauses may include pumping rates and other aspects of port performance, but their most significant feature is speed and bunker consumption.

7.2.18 Salvage (Clause 25 l.353-359)

This clause covers the apportionment of expenses and rewards in cases of salvage that as is normal practice, will be shared.

7.2.19 Lien (Clause 26 l.360-362)

This specifies each party's rights of lien.

7.2.20 Exceptions (Clause 27 l.363-386)

This clause is relatively standard, but a provision is made that although breakdown etc is an excepted risk it does not alter the provisions of the off hire Clause 21.

7.2.21 Injurious Cargoes (Clause 28 l.387-390)

Although many oil cargoes could in conjunction with air create explosive gases they are not in themselves explosive although the loading of butanised crude was criticised by Owners under this clause (crude oil with butane gas injected into it).

7.2.22 Laying-up (Clause 31 l.400-404)

During a long period time charter it is possible that the market will be such that the Charterers will contemplate laying a vessel up. This clause allows for the Charterers and Owners to consult and the vessel to be laid up at a place nominated by Charterers and the hire provided for under the charter to be adjusted to reflect any net increases in expenditure reasonably incurred or any savings which can reasonably be made by Owners. Naturally maintenance of the vessel in lay up will be cheaper at a port convenient to Owners and where mooring costs are low.

Many Owners dislike a ship being out of operation as it requires management reorganisation and a working ship always seems to be a little better than a similar ship out of lay up Disputes can occur on the savings and altered cash flow can be a problem.

7.2.23 Requisition (Clause 32 l.405–408)

This clause covers the event of the vessel being requisitioned by any government during the period of the charter party.

Protective Clauses

Clause 36 Both to Blame Collision Clause

Clause 37 New Jason Clause

Clause 38 Clause Paramount

7.2.25 TOVALOP (Clause 39 I.494-527) (and ITOPF)

Tanker Owners belong to ITOPF (International Tanker Owners' Pollution Federation Ltd.) and this clause is replaced with the ITOPF clause (see **Appendix 12**), which states that the Owners warrant the vessel is entered with ITOPF and is also entered with a named P&I Club and will remain so during the currency of the charter party.

The cost of cleaning up and the fine following a pollution incident can be considerable and many governments have introduced legislation based on 'the polluter pays' which do not allow the Owner to limit his liability tand also introduce the concept of penal damages or fines at immense financial levels.

The USA enactment Oil Pollution Act of 1990 (OPA 90) is the leading example of such legislation, which not only deals with liability but also establishes specific operational response plans and nominated persons to be responsible for the response. However, this book cannot deal in depth with the very large subject of Marine Pollution and the International Marpol Conventions. Having said that, contracts therefore specify the rights and responsibilities of the parties as well as perhaps listing the certificates required to be onboard the time chartered ship.

P&I Clubs provide the insurance cover for entered vessels against spillages and fines and clean up expenses. Certain countries insist that Owners of all vessels calling at their ports (including dry cargo because they carry significant quantities of bunkers) provide evidence of financial responsibility for pollution liability in the event of an oil spillage – evidence usually being in the form of a certificate of financial responsibility. Potentially, amounts demanded as security can be very large and entail tying up large sums of capital against relatively small risks of pollution.

The result is that P&I Clubs do not encourage countries to insist on their own, individual demands for security, instead providing Owners with just two certificates of insurance for pollution liability; one required internationally under the 1969 Civil Liability Convention (designed for tankers); the other (for all vessels) in conformity with the requirements of the United States Oil Pollution Act of 1990 (OPA90).

Further P&I Club help with certification to comply with any requirements of individual governments or countries for evidence of financial responsibility for pollution liability is not tendered.

7.2.25 Law and Litigation (Clause 41 I.547-573)

This clause states that the charter shall be construed in accordance with the laws of England. Any disputes shall be decided by the English courts but parties have the right to refer the dispute to arbitration by a single arbitrator in London.

7.3 THE LAW AND DISPUTES

According to London arbitrators the major areas of dispute under a charter party are the following:

> *"Withdrawal, set-off, performance claims, off-hire incidents, liens for subfreights, safe port warranties and condition of vessel on delivery and redelivery".*

We will look at these in a little detail to see where the problems arise.

7.3.1 Withdrawal

There are three reasons for premature determination of a charter party

1. Frustration
2. Result of repudiatory breach. These are both essentially legal problems.
3. Exercising a right given under the charter party.

Charterers have the right to cancel if the vessel does not arrive at the delivery point by the cancelling time and date. Charterer may be entitled to cancel if the vessel does not present in the condition required by the charter party, for example "in every way fitted for the cargo service".

The Owner's right to withdraw, however, continues throughout the charter party and centres around non payment of hire, late payment of hire or part payment of hire.

To recap what we have already covered, hire is payable in advance. The timing of the first payment may be difficult if the Charterer does not know exactly when the vessel will deliver and what the bunker quantities will be on delivery. For subsequent regular payments the Charterer has to work back from the time when the hire must actually be in the Owner's bank ready for his use. Allowance must be made for banking transfers and holiday delays. Acceptance of one or more late payments may not be construed as the Owner waiving the right to withdraw.

As an Owner, the following rules should be followed:

I.   Decide quickly whether or not to exercise the right to withdraw.
II. Instruct the bank to refuse the payment.
III. Inform Charterers immediately of your decision.
IV. Inform the Master.
V.   If payment is consistently late give notice that in future, payments must be made on time.

Charterer has one rule, particularly in a rising market: pay hire before the due date.

7.3.2 Set-off

In this instance Charterer feels he has a legitimate claim on the Owner and prior to paying the next period of hire deducts an amount which he feels covers the value of his claim, thereby setting off against his next payment. Without specific agreement to the contrary (which may be covered under a performance clause for example), such an act is not allowed under normal terms of chartering practice governed by English law. Such an action can cause the Owner and his bankers a great deal of frustration and annoyance.

Where such an action is taken when one vessel is involved the situation may be easily resolved by the judicious interjection of the Brokers. However, situations have arisen where there have been a number of vessels on charter with various claims outstanding on all ships. The Charterer arbitrarily deducted the total value of the claims from one of the vessel's hire payments meaning that virtually nothing was transferred to the Owner's account. It is fair to say that such an action will probably only take place when there is bad feeling between the Owners and the Charterers.

7.3.3 Speed and Consumption

The stringency of the wording of speed and consumption warranties differs between the various clauses in the principal charter forms and so does the actual method of calculation. Broadly speaking, the more modern the charter form the stricter performance warranty. The most comprehensive method of calculation is to compare the total mileage steamed and the total bunkers consumed at sea during the period in question, with the time the vessel would have taken and the bunkers the vessel would have consumed over the same distance at the charterparty speed and consumption.

Any excess time taken and any extra bunkers consumed are then respectively valued at the time charter rate and at the average price paid for bunkers during the performance period. The total cost of the time lost and the bunker excess is the amount of performance shortfall that the Charterer wishes to recover.

The Charterer may make his recovery by deduction from hire, but some charters also provide for a reduction in the hire rate to correspond to the under-performance.

The clauses vary and in particular some provide for a bonus payment to the Owner if the performance is better than warranted. A vessel may not achieve a better or worse performance in both speed and consumption. It may, for example, gain in speed but over consume, or be down in speed and make a bunker saving. In clauses that provide for a penalty only and do not pay a bonus for better performance, some look at speed and consumption together, and allow a gain to be offset against a loss. Others look at the two separately and no credit is given for that aspect of the performance, which turns out to be better than warranted.

A lot of clauses introduce a margin of tolerance by qualifying the declared performance e.g. "about 15 knots". The tolerance allowed by "about" depends upon the circumstances but is taken quite often to mean 5% more or less. When the performance is assessed the affect of this is that the vessel is not below the warranted performance unless her speed falls below 95% nor above if it does not exceed 105% of the warranted performance. The other usual interpretation of the word "about" is that it allows the speed to reduce by 0.5 of a knot without any penalty being attached.

In declaring a vessel's performance it would be necessary to take into account the deterioration that occurs between dry-dockings. Unfortunately for the Owner, factors outside his control can affect performance. In general it is said that currents can be ignored on the basis that they balance out but the following items should be noted as factors that will reduce speed:

Idle Time, particularly in tropical waters, increases the risk and rate of fouling of the vessel's underwater parts.

Adverse weather, such as is often experienced in winter conditions in the North Atlantic, will reduce the speed and may necessitate a reduction of revolutions for safety reasons,

Fog or any other reason for poor visibility, particularly in busy shipping lanes,

Canal passages, coastal or river steaming, or where ice may be encountered.

Very short voyages, in which gaining full speed at the beginning and reducing speed at the end, becomes relatively more significant and,

The poor quality of bunkers supplied.

Some of these factors may be excluded from performance calculations, e.g. "weather and safe navigation permitting" (see below).

Some charters make allowance for a number of the factors mentioned above. Others take the view that the Owner must take the average conditions into account when declaring the performance of the vessel and they make no concessions for any factors adversely affecting such performance.

In period charters performance is most often calculated on an annual basis. Over shorter periods the chance of all good or all bad weather is perhaps greater and in these circumstances it is often agreed that the vessel's performance will only be warranted up to and including a certain wind speed e.g. Beaufort force 5. Voyage distances and times are usually measured from 'full away' on the engines to first reduction of speed or, less accurately, from dropping the pilot on sailing, to arriving at the pilot station at the next port.

7.3.4 Off-hire

Remembering that the rule is Charterers' pay hire in advance from the time the vessel is delivered until redelivery, the financial risk for delay to the vessel due to bad weather, strikes, etc. during the charter, normally rests with the Charterers.

There are certain conditions, agreed in the charter, and usually attributable to the crew or breakdown of the vessel, when the Charterers may be entitled to suspend the hire.

Charterers are entitled to off-hire only if the ship is delayed for reasons which are in accordance with an off-hire clause or Common law. Some people would compare off-hire with liquidated damages, meaning that it is damages agreed prior to the event. The compensation to Charterers is based on the charter hire and Charterers do not have to prove the quantum of their loss. It may be that the off-hire event leads to the Charterer being entitled to make a deduction from hire even if the Owner has not been negligent or caused any breach of the contract.

The charter may therefore specify what events constitute an off-hire period but if not in general terms to establish whether a vessel has been off-hire the following points should be answered:

- Has the delay been caused by an event listed in the off-hire clause?

- Is there any franchise period, e.g. is the Owner allowed six hours off-hire prior to off-hire time commencing?

- The loss of time? How much time has actually been lost by the Charterer is the next question to be answered.

If a vessel is at sea and breaks down for six, ten or twelve hours, the off-hire time with reference to the franchise will soon establish the time that the Charterer has lost.

However, should a vessel have to divert either to a port of refuge, to put ashore an injured seaman or for any other purpose over which the Charterer has no desire or control, then the time off-hire is more complicated to establish. Reference must then be made to the time that the vessel deviated from the course which she was sailing, the time spent in port either undergoing repairs or for whatever reason, and the time to get the vessel back to a position equivalent to her original one.

Perhaps the easiest way to think of this position as being an equivalent distance to the next port of call as the deviation point and one may approximately be comparing the length of the hypotenuse of a triangle (the direct distance) with the length of the other two sides (the deviation distance).

Time lost in port may be quite straightforward, for instance if the vessel's pumps break down for a given period, then the time so lost is easily determined. However, suppose a ballast pump breaks down five hours prior to the expected completion of loading, three hours later loading has to be stopped because of a draft restriction and it is another six hours before the ballast pump is repaired and loading is completed. However, the vessel is then held alongside due to non-availability of tugs or pilots, which are working with another vessel. This chain of events is a lawyer's dream when it comes to determining the time off-hire.

The loss of money? Once a loss of time has been determined the same can be converted into money by simple multiplication of the rate of hire. However, if we consider again the vessel with ballast pump problems, we may find that the Charterer had to pay the tugs to stand by, possibly bringing the ship into overtime rates for tugs, boatmen and line men and we can soon see that the money involved is not necessarily just a pro rata of the daily hire. Normally any expense incurred by the vessel whilst off-hire is for account of the Owners, so in the above case perhaps Owners would be called on for the stand by charges until hire resumes.

The deduction of off-hire? The question now is can the Charterer deduct the off-hire time from his next hire payment? In simple terms he cannot do so without prior agreement. This means that there is probably an agreement in the charter party which gives him the right to "reasonably" deduct these off-hire periods. If not then he must go to the Owner with his claims and seek his agreement before making any deductions for the next hire payment.

7.4   LIENS FOR SUB FREIGHT

If the Owner does not receive his freight or his hire, he may still have some remedy if he has a lien on the cargo, freight or sub freights. The Ship Owner, as carrier, has a Common law right of lien on the cargo but the terms of his contract may be inconsistent with the exercise of this right. There is also the practical problem in the oil tanker trade that it may be impossible at some places to find a suitable cargo reception facility that is not controlled by the cargo interests. It is more important to remember that the right of a lien is lost if freight pre-paid Bills of Lading are issued, which could be inconsistent with the fact that charter terms are incorporated in the bill of lading covering freight payment on delivery.

In fact this is a very practical problem. If Charterers indemnify the master against the consequences of signing bills of lading as presented by them (as is normal in a time charter but may require a side clause in a voyage charter) the Master and Owners are covered.

A Charterer may well have sold the cargo C.I.F., so the Receiver insists that the Bills of Lading are marked freight prepaid. The Charterer however is reluctant to prepay freight due to risk of shortages, delays etc that may affect delivery. The letters of credit, irrevocable, set up with a bank by the receiver will require proof of delivery – a discharged Bill of Lading and probably cargo inspectors' certificates. This means that the Owner must trust the Charterer in performance because the courts at the discharge port/country will accept the pre-paid bills as evidence of payment and refuse a lien. With freight payment before breaking bulk there is no problem, but on a weak market such a term would be difficult to obtain and if obtained may suggest that the Charterer has difficulty finding ships.

At times a Charterer may ask a ship to stand-off a port outside national waters, probably because cargo payment delay or unsatisfactory documentation has occurred making him fearful of the local effect of a prepaid bill.

Most charters purport to give the Owner the right of lien on the cargo, freight and subfreights and this right may be incorporated into the Bill of Lading by a suitable clause in the bill. The possibility of exercising the lien, however, will largely depend on when the freight is due. If the freight is due after delivery of the cargo there cannot be a genuine lien. If it is due after completion of discharge, then an effective lien can be exercised, but only if it is possible to discharge into storage not controlled by the Charterer or cargo Owner. If freight is due concurrently with discharge or delivery, it may be possible to stop discharging and require part payment and this can be a useful compromise. The Broker may even offer to handle the freight in such circumstances, so the Owner knows it is paid, but any major fault in discharge has a chance of fair redress.

The factor affecting the right of the carrier to exercise a lien on sub freights is that, in England, Wales and certain Commonwealth countries, such a lien has to be registered within twenty-one days of creation or it will be void against a liquidator or creditor. This is because the lien may be regarded as a floating charge against the assets of the head Charterer if he has his place of business in or registered in, one of these countries. Registration of every lien, other than that in respect of period charters, is scarcely a practical proposition.

7.5 SELF-ASSESSMENT AND TEST QUESTIONS

1. What factors of a ship's description influence the cost of the vessel to a time Charterer?

2. To fix a vessel for 2 years how would you describe the period to reduce the chance of misunderstandings?

3. As an Owner, what trading limits would you like to impose when fixing your vessel for a 2-year period?

4. What steps would an Owner be able to take if hire payments are received consistently late?

5. A tanker is on a 12-month period time charter trading between ports in the Red Sea with about 2 weeks at anchor each month. Which of the above mentioned factors may influence speed?

Having completed Chapter Seven attempt the following and submit your essay to your Tutor: Whilst a vessel is on time charter, what are the points most likely to cause problems and why?

Chapter 8

TANKER LAYTIME

8.1   INTRODUCTION

Laytime affects earnings on all voyage charter parties and has been a central thread running through nearly all Chapters in this publication. In Chapter Three we looked at Worldscale which has set the industry standard of 72 hours laytime. In Chapter Four we carried out voyage estimates allowing time in port as an integral part of the voyage duration and costs. In Chapter Five, whilst examining chartering market practice, we looked at a firm offer where laytime was covered under the heading WSHTC. In Chapter Six, by investigating each charter party you may have begun to notice that there are clauses covering commencement of laytime, periods when laytime does not count, incidents that lead to laytime being stopped and the time that laytime terminates.

In this Chapter we now bring these elements into focus and, without providing all the answers, we look at the pitfalls and problems.

In simple terms, laytime can be considered as the port time available under a voyage charter for the Charterer to carry out the cargo and associated operations (e.g. waiting, loading and discharging). If laytime is exceeded the Charterer pays liquidated damages "demurrage". In tanker chartering if the full laytime is not utilised the Owner does not pay despatch, which is one of the major differences between dry cargo and tanker laytime. You can understand by its very nature that laytime only applies to voyage charters and not to time charters or bareboat charters.

The interpretation of laytime causes many disputes. There are four stages to any laytime calculation

i)   Commencement of laytime
ii)   Interruptions to laytime
iii) Duration of available laytime
iv)   Calculation of demurrage

To calculate laytime one has to look for the clauses which cover the above subjects and it is the interpretation of the relevant clauses with regard to exactly what time is available for loading or discharging, when laytime commences or is interrupted or ceases. Ideally the charter party clauses should be clear and concise. Unfortunately this is not always the case and the laytime calculator perceives his job as interpreting the clauses to the maximum benefit of his employers.

Statement of Facts

In addition to the charter party clauses concerned with laytime, the Statement of Facts form (see **Appendix 21**) will be required which is prepared and issued by the ship's Agent upon completion of the vessel's call at his port. The Statement of Facts will include information important to the calculation of laytime including dates and times of tendering notice of readiness, commencement and completion of cargo operations, details of pumping times and delays, together with reasons for such delay. All parties concerned with the port operations should sign this form including the representative of the Charterer and/or Receiver. Since this is the 'Statement of Facts' there is normally no objection from anyone to signing this document. Usually the problems arise in the interpretation of the facts which are presented. Should there be a case where one party feels unable to agree with anything in the Statement of Facts it is best for him to sign "under protest" and draw attention to the objection, providing a reason for such disagreement. Some ports may only provide a "port log" which will list events in chronological order, and the experienced laytime practitioner will be able to interpret this form easily. In all cases it is essential that the local Agent appointed will produce a proper statement of facts and if there is any doubt an Owner may be advised to appoint a protecting agent and also to make sure that every incident is noted in the ship's logs.

Cargo surveyors usually issue their own report, but this is usually retained by Charterers, although in the event of difficulty there should be no reason for non-disclosure as if a dispute goes too far such reports would have to be provided as evidence in court.

Laytime Statement

Using the charter party clauses and Statement of Facts a Laytime Statement can now be prepared which will show how much laytime has been used. (See **Appendix 22** for an example of a Time Sheet) In practice, the Owner will receive all the documentation including letters of protest and prepare his demurrage claim which he will present to the Charterers for their consideration. You will recall that in many charter parties such claims must be submitted by the Owner within 90 days of the completion of discharge of the voyage.

The reason for this is quite simply that the Charterer may find himself in the middle between Shipowner, Shipper and Receiver.

The Charterer may have three different sets of laytime to consider:

1. With the Shipowner,

2. The time agreed with the Shipper and,

3. Time agreed with the Receiver.

The exact relationship with each depends to some extent on whether the cargo is sold CIF or FOB. Under these contracts there will inevitably be a time in which the Charterer can seek recompense for excess port time and yet he is relying on an Owner to collate the facts and present them as a claim.

8.2   COMMENCEMENT OF LAYTIME

In general, laytime commences when a vessel is an "arrived ship". Simply put it could be considered the time that the vessel arrives at the agreed place. Therefore, the more detailed the description of that place the more careful the Owner must be to reach that place.

"The vessel shall proceed to Ras Tanura" is less onerous than "The vessel shall proceed to No.2 berth Ras Tanura".

The former is known as a "port charter", the latter a "berth charter". If the vessel berths on arrival without delay there can be no disagreement as to when the vessel is ready and the "clock starts" but if there is a delay the situation is less clear. The English courts hold that the vessel must be within the commercial area of the port and perhaps this can be slightly amended to mean the "normal waiting area for a port". The importance, of course, being as to who will pay for the time waiting for a berth or the commencement of the cargo operation. However, another complication arises should a vessel arrive prior to the agreed laydays. The purchase of an oil cargo typically requires a ship to be at the load port within perhaps only a three day spread say, 14/16 (i.e. 14/15/16).

Let us suppose the Laydays Cancelling – frequently referred to as LAYCAN for short – are 14/16 September and the vessel arrives at the load port on the 12th, the Master may tender his notice on arrival. Without a clause to the contrary the laytime would then commence at midnight on the 13th (that is to say, 13th, 2400 hours or 14th, 0000 hours). However, the Charterer will usually want the benefit of six hours "notice time" e.g. to allow the terminal time to get ready for the ship. Thus in ASBA II clause 5 states "laytime shall not commence before 0600 hours local time on the commencing date............unless with Charterer's sanction".

The last phrase gives us a clue to another possible problem in oil trading. Consider the case of the vessel tendering her notice on the 12th, perhaps the terminal will call the vessel in to load immediately, but, particularly if the sale contract is FOB the load date may be important in determining price and if the ship loads early this could well upset the economics of the deal for the Charterer. Not only may there be disagreements about whether or not laytime counts there is likely to be a claim against the Owners if there has been any monetary loss.

There are occasions when a vessel arrives within the laydays and the Charterer does not want to proceed to the berth. Under these circumstances, time would count but the Master will probably be under a lot of pressure from the terminal to berth immediately. The golden rule is for the Master to keep the Charterer fully advised of developments at the load and discharge ports.

If a vessel misses her cancelling i.e. under BP VOY 4 ... has not given Notice of Readiness to load by 1600 hours local time.

Thus if the Charterer does not cancel the charter party no new time limit is set and this cannot be considered satisfactory in the majority of cases. BEEPEEVOY and SHELLVOY consider this eventuality in slightly different ways. When it becomes clear that the vessel cannot arrive before cancelling date, the Owners may, as soon as they are able to state with reasonable certainty a new date when the vessel will be ready, give notice to Charterers declaring the new readiness date and asking Charterers to elect whether or not to terminate the charter. BEEPEEVOY 4 gives 96 hours, Sundays and holidays excepted. The option to cancel is maintained if no notification is given.

Without specific clauses the vessel would have to present at the load port no matter how late she is before the Charterer would have to declare whether or not the ship would be maintained on the charter party. However if, say, some accident or bad weather had occurred delaying the ship, i.e. not due to gross misrepresentation by Owners, and Charterers knew very well that the cargo would not be loaded due to the delay, they may lay themselves open to a claim for non mitigation of losses if they deliberately failed to advise the Owners. The notification of delay should avoid this problem.

You will have seen from the foregoing that the tendering of Notice of Readiness (NOR) is an important element in the prosecution of the voyage. Thus the question arises, when can the NOR be tendered? ASBA II Clause 6 states "upon arrival at customary anchorages at each port of loading and discharge.by letter, wireless or telephone that the vessel is ready to load or discharge cargo, berth or no berth and laytime shall commence...6 hours after receipt of such Notice..." Note that under English law if there is not a clause to the contrary the vessel would only be required to tender NOR at the first load port and not at the second or subsequent load ports or at a discharge port. Note also that this clause states "after receipt of such notice". This may cause problems if the notice is transmitted by radio through a distant shore station then passed on by telex to the shipper, receiver or agent as applicable. The master is careful to log the presentation of NOR.

SHELLVOY 5 combines tendering NOR with the vessel being "securely moored at specified loading or discharging berth". It does not preclude laytime from running at "the area where she (the vessel) was ordered to wait or, in the absence of any specific order, in a usual waiting area" provided "the specified berth is accessible".

BP VOY 4 (clause 6) states that the NOR is not effective unless certain conditions are met:

1.   ... she is securely moored and her gangway is in place.

2.   ... not berthing on arrival ... she has completed anchoring at the customary anchor.

3.   free pratique has been granted.

Many disputes originated from different interpretations of accessibility of berth. SHELLVOY 5 leaves no doubts by enumerating such conditions: bad weather, tide, ice, awaiting daylight, pilot or tugs or port traffic control requirements (except those resulting from the unavailability of the berth or the cargo). When a vessel does not proceed to the berth immediately it is almost inevitable that there will be a dispute about the arrival time and when the NOR was accepted.

According to a leading London maritime arbitrator "there is no subject which has been more messed around over the years, than the arrived ship approach, which is basically quite a simple point: so long as a ship gets as near to her destination as she reasonably can and is prevented from going any further for some reason of the Charterer's, then the test is very easy, and that is the test brought in now by way of special added clauses. Problems now are not so much regarding the arrived ship but whether the vessel can get into the berth when she gets off the port because of bad weather or congestion." In addition, the interpretation of the general expression "where delay is caused...for any reason over which the Charterer has no control" gives rise to long disputes as is illustrated by the case of the "LAURA PRIMA" case. The "LAURA PRIMA" arrived at her Libyan load port on 27th November 1978 but could not proceed to the berth since they were all occupied. She berthed on 6th December and therefore suffered nine days delay. It was found as a fact that the Charterers were not responsible for congestion at the load berth, nor was it in any way within their control. The fact, therefore, gave rise to the simple issue; under the ASBATANKVOY is clause 6 or clause 9 to prevail?

> **Clause 6. Notice of Readiness.** Upon arrival at customary anchorage at each port of loading or discharge, the Master or his agent shall give the Charterer or his agent notice by letter, telegraph, wireless or telephone that the vessel is ready to load or discharge cargo, berth or not berth and laytime, as hereinafter provided, shall commence upon the expiration of 6 hours after receipt of such notice or upon the vessel's arrival in berth (i.e. finished mooring when at a sea loading or discharging terminal and all fast when loading or discharging alongside a wharf), whichever occurs first. However, where delay is caused to vessel getting into berth after giving Notice of Readiness for any reason over which Charterer has no control, such delay shall not count as used laytime.

> **Clause 9 Safe Berthing – Shifting.** The vessel shall load or discharge at any safe place or wharf, or alongside vessels or lighters reachable on her arrival which shall be designated and procured by the Charterer, provided the vessel can proceed thereto, lie at, and depart therefrom always safely afloat, any lighterage being at the expense, risk and peril of the Charterer. The Charterer shall have the right of shifting the vessel at ports of loading and/or discharge from one safe berth to another on payment of all towage and pilotage shifting to next berth, charges for running lines at arrival at and leaving that berth, additional agency charges and expense, customs overtime and fees and any other extra port charges for port expenses incurred by reason of using more than one berth. Time consumed on account of shifting shall count as used laytime except as otherwise provided in clause 15. (Clause 15 deals with "two or more ports counting as one").

This was a question upon which there was already a conflict of opinion amongst London arbitrators – the umpire decided that the Charterers had protection under clause 6.

The case went to appeal before Mr Justice Mocatta and the decision was reversed. The Judge held that the last sentence of clause 6 only applied and prevented laytime from running if the Charterers pursuant to clause 9 had complied with their separate obligation of designating a berth reachable on arrival. The Charterers would be protected from liability only if there were then some intervening event, the effect of which was although the berth was reachable when it had been nominated, it ceased to be reachable thereafter.

The Charterers appealed and the Court of Appeal held that clause 6 was a general exception in favour of Charterers which applied to any delay provided it was beyond Charterer's control and the Judge's decision was reversed.

The House of Lords reinstated the Judge's decision where Lord Roskill resolved the problem by deciding that the word 'berth' in the penultimate line of clause 6 meant a berth which has already been designated and procured by the Charterers in accordance with their obligations under clause 9. Thus the last sentence of clause 6 had to be read as though it said "where delay is caused to vessel getting into the berth designated and procured in accordance with clause 9 after giving Notice of Readiness for any reason over which Charterers have no control, such delay shall not count as used laytime".

8.2.1 Interruptions to Laytime

Without agreement to the contrary, once laytime has started it should continue uninterrupted until completion of cargo operations or, until it has expired. The tanker industry almost universally adopts 72 hours, Sundays and Holidays Included, (SHINC), as the laytime allowance.

Some traders have 96 hours in their terms. The reason stated for this is that so many demurrage claims were for periods between 72 and 96 hours that it was more realistic to use the longer time and the Owner would include it in his voyage estimate thereby avoiding protracted negotiations and paperwork at a later stage, thus making allowance for the NOR time (typically 6 hours at each port).

The calculation of allowed time in the tanker trades is straightforward. The same cannot be said of the excepted periods although in truth it is much easier than in the dry trades.

Using the ASBATANKVOY charter party as the proforma we will identify the occurrences in which time so lost will not count as laytime.

(a) Delay in getting to berth after giving NOR for any reason whatsoever over which Charterer has no control.

(b) Delays resulting from conditions at the ordered ports, places not caused by Charterer's fault *or* neglect or which could be avoided by the exercise of reasonable care on the part of the Master.

(c) Inward passage (i.e. from anchorage to berth).

(d) Handling ballast.

(e) Breakdown, inefficiency or other causes attributable to the vessel or Owners.

(f) Inability to maintain the temperature required.

(g) Delays as result of labour dispute or strikes involving Master, officers or crew of the vessel, tugs or pilot.

(h) Owners or port authorities prohibiting loading or discharging.

(i) Due to quarantine unless quarantine was in force when such place was nominated by Charterers.

To remind you, the above refers to the ASBATANKVOY charter party. Now try doing the same for the other charter parties. In addition to the laytime demurrage clause 14, 21 other clauses contain reference to the laytime/demurrage calculation.

The study you have done should enable you to categorise the instances in which the Charterer is not liable for time or demurrage. These are:

i) Specific release clauses in charter parties.

ii) Delays attributable to the fault of the Shipowner or those for whom he is responsible,

iii) Force Majeure resulting in sudden or unforeseen interruption or prevention of loading or discharging not the fault of the Charterer.

A special mention here with reference to strikes. Those of you used to dry cargo charter parties will be familiar with the fact that strikes have a clause all to themselves in the majority of dry cargo proformas. Not so in tanker charter parties. Perhaps because historically very little time has been lost through strikes in the oil terminals, which if not privately owned by the major oil companies are usually operated by them under a contract with the terminal

Owner. The words "...strike, labour dispute...." are typically included in a general clause stating that any delays arising from various causes will count as half laytime or half the demurrage rate. Should a vessel be affected by such a stoppage it is first necessary to confirm that it is caused by a strike. The accepted definition is "a general concerted refusal by workmen to work in consequence of an alleged grievance". It is understood that this is extended to include stoppages in support of some other body of workers who have an alleged grievance. The lawyers then like to take issue with the words "...within reasonable control....". Suppose workmen are on strike for more pay or for safer working conditions, the question arises, is the employer (whether Charterer or Owner) being reasonable in not agreeing the demands?

Noting the words "lock out" are included in some charter parties. This is an instance where the labour wishes to come to work but the employer either refuses to allow the men to enter the premises or to do their work. The final problem that occurs in this category is when labour is "working to rule". Perhaps accepted working practice is 24 hours where possibly 8 hours are counted as overtime. Thus, if workers decide to ban overtime or perhaps working hours are restricted due to some other rule, how much of the lost time will count as laytime?

8.2.2   Duration of Available Laytime

In tanker chartering this is determined by Worldscale to be 72 hours, subject to whatever qualifications, if any, that are stated in the charter party.

8.2.3   Calculation of Laytime Used/Demurrage

This calculation is relatively easy by comparison with dry cargo computations. I have heard "professional demurrage" personnel say they take the arrival and departure times of a tanker at each port, deduct the notice periods and if the total time is over 72 hours (96 hours in some cases) find reasons to deduct time and hopefully bring it below 72 hours.

In truth the starting point is the Statement of Facts which is used to prepare the laytime statement. By reference to the relevant charterparty, deductions are made (e.g. time shifting from anchorage to berth). At the discharge port you will recall that the Owner undertakes to discharge the cargo in "24 hours or maintain 100 pounds per square inch provided shore facilities permit". Thus, if pumping takes more than 24 hours it is up to the Owner to show that the vessel maintained a minimum 100 pounds per square inch (100 PSI) at all times during discharge. This is not taken to mean the average over the period viz 150 PSI for 18 hours and 50 PSI for 6 hours could not be taken as in excess of 100 PSI for the 24 hours. The 6 hours at 50 PSI would not count as laytime unless the vessel could show that the receiver or terminal requested a slower discharge rate. In simple terms the effect that the pumping warranty has on laytime is that any time in excess of 24 hours of a discharge, or any time when pressure at manifolds is below 100 PSI will be deducted from the laytime. If the vessel is pumping at 100 PSI and takes 48 hours all that time would count, but once the pressure is below 100 PSI the 24-hour time limit would tend to be in effect although pumping for 36 hours at 100 PSI followed by a lower pressure would no doubt call for the 36 hours to count. A ship often protests at the size of the cargo hoses used for discharge, but this is of no consequence under a 100 PSI clause even though discharge may be slow. When a vessel is discharging crude oil and is employing COW this pumping warranty is usually extended. Perhaps, as in SHELLVOY 5, by 45 minutes per tank which is crude oil washed, or just a fixed time of 6/8 or 12 hours depending upon size of ship.

When does laytime stop? Typically when the hoses are disconnected "or until ballasting begins at the discharge port(s), whichever occurs first". This phrase harks back to the days when vessels could only ballast when cargo was completed or that cargo operations were interrupted by the ballasting. Modern vessels fitted with SBT facilities can ballast concurrently with cargo operations and no time is lost. Thus this phrase can be deleted with no loss to the Charterer.

MT WAYFARER

From the following information and the attached extract from the relevant charter party, prepare a laytime statement and calculate any demurrage due. Check your workings with Appendix 23.

MT Wayfarer 89,000 mt.

Laycan 23/25 April

Demurrage rate $12,000 per day pro rata.

Saturday 23 April	0300	Arrive Bonny Pilots, NOR tendered, waiting Berth
Sunday 24 April	1500	Anchor away, proceed to Berth
	1830	All Fast
	1900	Tanks inspected, commenced Deballasting
	1930	Hoses connected, loading commenced
	2130	Deballasting completed
Monday 25 April	2330	Completed Loading
Tuesday 26 April	0030	Hoses disconnected
	0100	Documents on board, vessel sails from Berth
	0230	Pilot away

* * *

Wednesday 11 May	1415	Arrive Fiumicino Anchorage, NOR tendered, waiting berth
Thursday 12 May	0600	Strong winds, heavy swell, Port closed
Friday 13 May	1200	Weather improved, Port opens
Saturday 14 May	0815	Anchor away, proceed to berth
	0945	All Fast
	1015	Ullages taken, Hoses connected
	1030	Commence discharge – 1 hose shore instructions
	1800	Discharge commenced, 3 hoses
Sunday 15 May	0100	Pump failure, discharge stopped
	0500	Pumps repaired, discharge continued
	0600	Ballasting commenced
	1000	Discharge Completed
	1045	Hoses disconnected
	1130	Vessel sails from berth
	1225	Pilot away

Total Laytime in Running Hours = 72

Commencement or Cancellation

Laytime shall not commence before 0600 hours local time on the date specified in Part 1 (B) unless with Charterer's sanction. If the Vessel has not given notice of readiness to load by 1600 hours local time on the Cancelling date specified in Part 1 (B), Charterer shall have the option of cancelling this charter party within 24 hours. Cancellation or failure to cancel shall be without prejudice to any claims for damages Charterer may have for late tender of the Vessel's services.

Notice of Readiness

Upon arrival at customary anchorage at each port of loading or discharge the Master shall give the Charterer notice by letter, telegraph, wireless or telephone that the Vessel is ready to load or discharge cargo, berth or no berth, and laytime or, if the Vessel is on demurrage, time on demurrage shall commence upon the expiration of six (6) hours after receipt of such notice, or upon the Vessel's arrival in berth (i.e. finished mooring when at a sea loading or discharging terminal and all fast when loading or discharging alongside a wharf or when barge lighter or lightering vessel is alongside when lightering), whichever first occurs. However, where delay is caused to Vessel getting into berth after giving notice of readiness for any reason whatsoever over which Charterer has no control, such delay shall not count as laytime or as time on demurrage.

Laytime

(a) The laytime specified in Part 1(H) shall be allowed free of expense to Charterer for the purpose of loading and discharging cargo. Any delay due to the Vessel's condition or breakdown or inability of the Vessel to load or discharge cargo or due to any other reason assignable to the Vessel or her Master, officers or crew shall not count as laytime or as time on demurrage. Charterer shall have the right of loading and discharging during the night provided that, if regulations of the Owner or port authorities prohibit loading or discharging of the cargo at night, time lost will not count as laytime or as time on demurrage. If the Charterer, Shipper or consignee prohibits loading or discharging at night, time thereby lost will count as laytime or, if the vessel is on demurrage, as time on demurrage.

(b) For the purpose of freight payment the places grouped in port and terminal combinations in Worldscale current at the date of commencement of loading are to be considered as berths within a single port. Time consumed shifting between berths within such a "single port" or any other port shall count as laytime or, if the Vessel is on demurrage, time on demurrage.

(c) Time consumed by the Vessel in moving from loading or discharging port anchorage even if lightering has taken place at the anchorage, to the Vessel's loading or discharging berth, or in discharging ballast water, will not count as laytime or time on demurrage.

(d) If lightering takes place on the high seas or at a place other than the discharge port(s) steaming time and lightering time not compensated for in Part 1 (F) shall count as laytime or if the vessel is on demurrage, time on demurrage.

Demurrage

Charterer shall pay demurrage per running hour and *pro rata* for a part thereof at the rate specified in Part 1 (1) for all time that laytime therein specified is exceeded by the time taken to load and discharge cargo and the time which, under the provisions of this Charter, counts as laytime or time on demurrage. If, however, demurrage shall be incurred at ports of loading and/or discharge for delays by reason of fire, explosion, storm or by a strike, lockout, stoppage or restraint of labour or by breakdown of machinery or equipment in or about the plant of the Charterer, Supplier, Shipper or Consignee of the cargo, such demurrage shall be calculated at one-half the rate specified in Part 1(1). Laytime shall not run or, if the vessel is on demurrage shall not accrue, for any delay caused by strike, lockout, stoppage or restraint of labour of Master, officers and crew of the Vessel or tugboat or pilots or any other cause of whatsoever nature or kind over which the Charterer has no control.

8.3 TEST QUESTION

Having completed Chapter Eight attempt the following and submit the answer to your Tutor

Using the following information to calculate the laytime used and demurrage earned, if any. (Show all your calculations):

MT SUCCESS – Statement of Facts

Load Port

Arrived anchorage	26 October 0600
NOR tendered	0600
Proceeded to berth	27 October 0800
All fast alongside	1130
Hoses connected	1300
Commenced deballasting	1300
Completed deballasting	1630
Commenced loading	1700
Loading completed	29 October 0100
Hoses off	0200
Unberthed	0630
Pilot away	0930

Discharge Port

Arrived anchorage	8 November 1600
NOR tendered	1600
Proceeded to berth	10 November 0500
All fast # 1 berth	10 November 0800
Hoses connected	0830
Commenced discharge	0900
Discharge stopped	2100
Hoses off unberthed	2230
All Fast # 2 berth	11 November 0615
Hoses connected	0700
Discharge resumed	0715
Ballasting commenced	12 November 0830
Discharge completed	1430
Hoses off	1500
Left berth	1630
Pilot away	1900

Extracts from Voyage Charter Party of M

LAYCAN

26/28 October

LAYTIME

72 Running hours

DEMURRAGE

US $17,500 per day pro rata

COMMENCEMENT OR CANCELLATION

5. Laytime shall not commence before 0600 hours local time on the date specified in Part 1 (B) unless with Charterer's sanction. If the Vessel has not given notice of readiness to load by 1600 hours local time on the Cancelling date specified in Part 1 (B), Charterer shall have the option of cancelling this Charter Party within 24 hours. Cancellation or failure to cancel shall be without prejudice to any claims for damages Charterer may have for late tender of the Vessel's services.

NOTICE OF READINESS

6.   Upon arrival at customary anchorages at each port of loading or discharge, the Master shall give the Charterer notice by letter, telegraph, wireless or telephone that the Vessel is ready to load or discharge cargo, berth or no berth, and laytime or, if the Vessel is on demurrage, time on demurrage shall commence upon the expiration of six (6) hours after receipt of such notice, or upon the Vessel's arrival in berth (i.e. finished mooring when at sea loading or discharging alongside a wharf or when barge lighter or lightering vessel is alongside when lightering), whichever first occurs. However, where delay is caused to Vessel getting into berth after giving notice of readiness for any reason whatsoever over which Charterer has no control, such delay shall not count as laytime or as time on demmurage.

LAYTIME

7.   (a)   The laytime specified in Part 1(H) shall be allowed free of expense to Charterer for the purpose of loading and discharging cargo. Any delay due to the Vessel's condition or breakdown or inability of the Vessel to load or discharge cargo or due to any other reason assignable to the Vessel or her Master, Officers or crew shall not count as laytime or as time on demurrage. Charterer shall have the right of loading and discharging during the night providing that, if regulations of the Owner or port authorities prohibit loading or discharging of the cargo at night time thereby lost will not count as laytime or as time on demurrage. If the Charterer, shipper or consignee prohibits loading or discharging at night, time thereby lost will count as laytime or, if the vessel is on demurrage, as time on demurrage.

(b)   For the purpose of freight payment the places grouped in port and terminal combinations in Worldscale current at the date of commencement of loading are to be considered as berths within a single port. Time consumed shifting between berths within such a "single port" or any other port shall count as laytime or, if the Vessel is on demurrage, time on demurrage.

(c)   Time consumed by the Vessel in moving from loading or discharging port anchorage even if lightering has taken place at the anchorage, to the Vessel's loading or discharging berth, or in discharging ballast water, will not count as laytime or time on demurrage.

(d)   If lightering takes place on the high seas or at a place other than the discharge port(s) steaming time and lightering time not compensated for in Part 1(F) shall count as laytime or if the vessel is on demurrage, time on demurrage.

DEMURRAGE

8.   Charterer shall pay demurrage per running hour and pro rata for a part thereof at the rate specified in Part 1(1) for all time that laytime therein specified is exceeded by the time taken to load and discharge cargo and the time which, under the provisions of this Charter, counts as laytime or time on demurrage. If, however, demurrage shall be incurred at ports of loading and/or discharge for delays by reason of fire, explosion, storm or by a strike, lockout, stoppage or restraint of labour or by breakdown of machinery or equipment in or about the plant of the Charterer, supplier, shipper or consignee of the cargo, such demurrage shall be calculated at one-half the rate specified in Part 1(1). Laytime shall not run or, if the vessel is on demurrage shall not accrue, for any delay caused by strike, lockout, stoppage or restraint of labour of Master, officers and crew of the Vessel or tugboat or pilots or any other cause of whatsoever nature or kind over which the Charterer has no control.

HOSES/SEA TERMINALS

Hoses for loading and discharging shall be furnished by the Charterer and shall be connected and disconnected by the Charterer, or by the Owner at the Charterer's option. Laytime or, if the Vessel is on demurrage, time on demurrage shall continue until the hoses have been disconnected, or until ballasting begins at the discharge port(s), whichever occurs first. When Vessel loads or discharges at a sea terminal, the Vessel shall be properly equipped at Owner's expense for loading or discharging at such place, including suitable ground tackle, mooring lines and equipment for handling submarine hoses.

Chapter 9

FINANCIAL ELEMENTS OF TANKER CHARTER PARTIES

9.1 FREIGHT

Any vessel's earning potential is ultimately determined by its deadweight cargo carrying capacity (dwcc) which is in turn governed by the ability to load fully to its marks, (loadline see **Appendix 25**)

However with regard to the payment of freight there are three main questions which arise:

i)   On what quantity is freight payable?

ii)   When is freight to be paid?

iii) Can a claim that a Charterer may have against Owners be deducted from the freight before payment?

For the purposes of the following discussion we will refer to the Asbatankvoy charter party form.

9.1.1 On What Quantity is Freight Payable?

In practice the first two lines of clause 2 mean that freight is payable on the quantity shown in the Bill of Lading.

"Freight shall be at the rate stipulated in Part I and shall be computed on intake quantity (except dead freight as per clause 3) as shown on the inspector's certificate of inspection."

Sometimes for crude oil, two sets of figures appear – the gross quantity which is the quantity actually loaded and nett, which is the gross figure less the quantity of water and sediment in the crude oil as determined in the laboratory. You will appreciate that many load ports will not have such facilities available. The nett quantity is used by the supplier for invoicing his customer and the gross quantity for the payment of freight because it is the total weight of cargo carried which is of prime importance to the Owner.

"No deduction from freight shall be made for water and/or sediment contained in the cargo."

Independent inspection companies are available for measuring the quantities of cargo loaded but they are not always employed and then the supplier's figures are used.

"The services of the Petroleum Inspector shall be arranged and paid for by the Charterer who shall furnish the Owner with a copy of the Inspector's Certificate."

It is clear that if no inspector is to be used the beginning of the clause needs to be modified as follows:

"Freight shall be payable at the rate stipulated in Part I hereof and shall be computed on the intake quantity except in the case of deadfreight it shall be determined according to clause 3 hereof as shown on the Bill of Lading..."

Irrespective of the quantity received (assuming that more than a token quantity is discharged), freight is due on the quantity loaded and not the quantity actually discharged.

If part of the cargo loaded is lost (a risk insured by the cargo Owner), the Shipowner is only entitled to freight pro rata on the quantity delivered, unless the contract is for a lump sum freight. ASBATANKVOY provides for payment of freight on delivery of cargo, but SHELLVOY 6 is more specific by referring to "receipt by Charterers of notice of completion of final discharge". This leaves the door open for argument if the ship has a considerable ROB quantity in so far as discharge is not final. A lump sum freight is payable in full if any portion of the cargo is delivered but not if no cargo at all is delivered. Only if the vessel is unable to load the agreed cargo quantity may a lump sum freight be paid pro rata.

Unfortunately it can happen that the cargo inspector at loading port is somewhat casual in his assessment of cargo quantities and for example a Charterer regularly shipping clean product on the same route found that the out-turn quantity always showed an unusually high handling loss, causing cargo insurance claims. When they introduced their own independent inspector they found measurement had been inaccurate and thereafter the losses ceased saving considerable expense and trouble to all concerned.

Many Charterers include an in transit loss clause, whereby freight deduction can be made if such a loss exceeds an agreed percentage (say 0.03/0.05%) based on the nett vessel's volume on board after loading and before discharge. This exposes the Owner to the risk that water and or sediment in the cargo held in suspension settles out during the voyage and adversely alters the nett quantity. With crude oil a supplier will often state an arbitrary figure for water content so that strangely enough every cargo loaded from that terminal has the same water and/or sediment content. Careful sampling of cargo is very important in such cases and in the event of dispute such samples should only be tested by first class independent chemists.

The in transit loss clause was created to avoid the risk of cargo being stolen for bunkering purposes and replaced by sea water. Such action can be exposed by a chemist due to the different salinity and chemical content of water originating from an oil field or even different seas and coastal waters.

This principle is underlined in a court case, "The Metula" 1978. Charterers loaded 190,415 l.t. of crude oil at Ras Tanura for discharge in Chile. The vessel grounded in the Straits of Magellan and only 138,195.3 l.t. were finally delivered after a transhipment. Charterers paid freight on this quantity plus 5% but Owners claimed freight was payable on the intake quantity and this claim was confirmed in the commercial court and then in the Court of Appeal which held that:-

(a) The freight was computed on the intake quantity so that it should be ascertained at that moment, although payable later when the vessel arrived at destination and that there was no provision whatsoever for subsequent adjustment of calculations being made at the port of destination:

(b) Although it was not a lump sum freight it was akin to such a freight as it was to be computed on the intake quantity and was to be paid on that quantity even though there was a shortage.

9.1.2   When is Freight Payable?

The ASBATANKVOY charter party is very clear on this point:

"Upon completion of discharge at destination."

In this case if the vessel is lost no freight is due. What then, does "payment" mean? This has been examined by the courts in the case of "punctual payment" in connection with time charter parties where the court has arrived at a stop watch controlled definition which many commercial men find unrealistic. In 1981 the House of Lords decided that although Owners had the use of hire as soon as it was credited to their account it was not the equivalent of a cash payment because it could not be used to earn interest by the immediate transfer to a deposit account, because the "value date" applied by the bank was two days after the account was credited with the payment. Presumably it was not drawn to the attention of their Lordships that even if the payment had been made in cash the value date would not have been the day of payment but the next banking day, the continental banking practice being that the value date of any amount credited to an account is that of the next banking day and on the debit the last banking day before the account is debited. A cheque is not credited to an account until it is cleared, which may take several days. There have also been cases where a bank denied receiving funds and were forced to admit subsequently that they had in fact been received.

This question does not appear to have been examined in a voyage charter party scenario. Whilst time is of the essence in the case of "punctual payment" of hire for a time charter, it is probably not so the case of a voyage charter unless the charter party states so expressly. This does not mean that payment may not be made unduly late and it is accepted that it would be reasonable for the Charterer to instruct his bank on the day following the completion of discharge to remit the freight by telegraphic transfer and this requirement can be included in the charter.

There are other clauses referring to when freight is due, the two main ones being:

1. On delivery (which means physical delivery into Receiver's shore tanks)

2. Upon receipt by the Charterers of the notice of completion of discharge.

If the Owner does not receive his freight or his hire he may still have some remedy if he has a lien on the cargo, freight or sub-freights.

In the context of the above it seems difficult, if not impossible, to exercise a lien on cargo. Freight is paid after the cargo has been released and there is no way to get possession of it again. The Shipowner, as carrier, has a common law right or lien on the cargo but the terms of his contract may be inconsistent with the exercise of this right. There is also the practical problem in the oil tanker trade that it may be impossible at some places to find suitable cargo reception facilities that are not controlled by the cargo interests. The right of lien is lost if freight pre-paid bills of lading are issued.

Most charters purport to give the Owner the right of lien on the cargo, freight and sub-freights and this right may be incorporated into the Bill of Lading by a suitable clause. The possibility of exercising the lien, however, will largely depend on when the freight is due. If freight is due after "delivery" of the cargo, there cannot be a genuine lien. If it is due after completion of "discharge", then an effective lien can be exercised but only if it is possible to discharge into storage not controlled by the Charterer. If freight is due concurrently with discharge or delivery, it may be possible to stop discharging and require payment.

A factor affecting the right of a carrier to exercise his lien on sub-freights is that, in England, Wales and certain Commonwealth countries, such a lien has to be registered within 21 days of creation or it will be void against a liquidator or creditor. This is because the lien may be regarded as a floating charge against the assets of the head Charterer if he has his place of business in, or registered in, one of these countries. Registration of every lien, other than in respect of period charters, is scarcely a practical proposition.

Inconsistency in this matter was clearly shown in the "Fort Kipp" case.

The vessel was chartered on the standard BEEPEEVOY 2 form and on May 13 1983 arrived at New York having on board about 29,000 tons of petroleum from Constanza. After discharging about 26,500 tons the Owners exercised a lien over the cargo remaining on board the vessel in respect of unpaid freight. Six days later the remaining cargo was discharged into a barge. The lien over that part of the cargo, though discharged, was exercised for a number of days until the freight was paid. The contradictory clauses relevant to this dispute were clauses 7 and 22. Clause 7 stated that "Freight shall be payable immediately after completion of discharge..." Clause 22 provided that "Owner shall have a lien upon the cargo for all freight, deadfreight, demurrage and cost of recovery thereof."

The court found, inter alia, that in case of conflict between clauses 7 and 22 the clear language of clause 7 must prevail. The court held that the Owners were not entitled to exercise a lien for freight on part of the cargo remaining onboard. As regards the question of whether the Owners were entitled to assert a lien over that part of the cargo discharged into barge, the court said that a lien was properly asserted .... cargo was still under their (owners) control.

Clearly it is impracticable to complete discharge into a barge and hold that cargo until the freight is paid. It is perhaps considered a precedent but by no means a satisfactory method for regular use.

Dry cargoes are often discharged into warehouses where for a certain period they may be under the vessel's Agent or port custom office control. Nevertheless most dry cargo charter parties frequently have the following scheme for freight payment:

> "90% to be paid upon vessel sailing from the load port, the balance being paid upon discharging."

With fewer and better known Charterers such as major oil companies in the tanker trades such a scheme has never worked. Tanker Owners are expected to give credit to the Charterers, the longer the voyage, the longer and bigger the credit. In some measure it is probably also a reflection of the weak market caused by the surplus of tanker tonnage.

In some countries where exchange control formalities have to be followed, remitting freight will require a certain time, but there is no reason for Charterers to wait until the last minute before approaching any exchange control.

In some countries the exchange control authorities insist that the Owners remit, before the vessel's arrival, sufficient funds to cover the estimated expenses of the ship's Agents. To avoid the practice of partial payment being made outside the country concerned, the authorities will insist on receiving a copy of the estimated account for the ship's call to ensure it is a proper estimate of expenses and a certificate from the bank that the appropriate foreign exchange has been remitted and received. Once all is in order the Charterer will be allowed to remit the full amount of the freight. If no remittance is made or an insufficient amount only is remitted then the authorities will hold back a percentage of the freight as guarantee. The amount held back can either be used for paying the ship's account or the balance of it when the remaining amount of freight can be remitted or the Owners can remit the necessary balance to enable release of the full freight.

It cannot be emphasised too strongly that if payment of freight is delayed or is only paid in part because of such a situation the Charterer is by no means excused unless he has made an appropriate reservation in the charter party.

The words "without discount" are presumably present in order to avoid doubt as in some trades such discounts were recognised. For example there was a custom at one time in Liverpool that three months interest was deducted from freight payable on such shipments as cotton shipped from New Orleans.

The words "...less any disbursements or advances made to the Master or Owner's Agents at ports of loading and/or discharge and cost of insurance thereon..." have been referred to as relics of the past. These days it is expected that such advances will be made by the Ship's Agent who has usually received the necessary funds in advance direct from the Owners. In many countries for Charterers to make such advances would be against exchange control regulations, in which case the clause should be deleted. Having said that, there are Owners who today will ask for the Charterers to advance port disbursements at load and discharge ports making the necessary deductions from the freight payment when eventually effected. The reason why an Owner may make such a request could possibly be found in the loan agreement attached to the vessel. Perhaps there is an agreement that all freight should be paid direct to the lending bank, thereby giving the bank some control over the account and monitoring the earnings of the vessel. As funds arrive in the account perhaps the bank has the ability to apply them for other means beyond payments to port Agents and bunker suppliers. Thus the Owner may feel that if he can get the Charterer to pay for port disbursements and bunkers and deduct the cost of same prior to payment of freight the bank will receive only a small amount of money and the Owner will have very limited exposure.

There are also cases where local agents, particularly Charterers Agents, are notoriously slow in returning any balances to Owners, so it is safer for Charterers (who may be local) to disburse such funds and deduct from freight.

9.1.3 Deductions from Freight

Other than the right, when applicable, to pay only pro rata freight, the Charterer does not have any right to make stoppages from freight for amounts he believes may be due to him. This rule against counter claims is clear, no unliguidated (not adjudicated or quantified) claims may be offset against the freight due, unless there is an express contractual right in the charter Unfortunately for Owners, nowadays there very often is such a right. For many years the only commonly found express provision for deduction was in respect of cash advanced to the Master. This provision is still included in many charters but with modern means of arranging funds can seldom be difficult for the Owner to arrange to transfer money to the Agent or Master.

Other significant deductions for which provision may be found are:-

Additional insurance on the cargo due to vessel's age, flag or class (the cargo interests may incur additional insurance costs because of one of these factors).

Bunkers supplied by the Charterer or an associated company (oil company Charterers who doubt the credit worthiness of a bunker customer may solve their problems this way).

The value of any measurable cargo remaining on board on the vessel on completion of discharge and/or an in transit loss clause. (See **Appendix 24**)

The last of the foregoing items is the most controversial. The increased value of oil has made out-turn shortages of considerable importance and it is now widespread practice for Charterers to insist on the inclusion of an ROB (Remaining On Board) clause. This is referred to at the point of loading as On Board Quantities (OBQs). (See note on **Appendix 24**).

These clauses are controversial because many of them do not give Owners satisfactory assurance that any deduction will only be in respect of pumpable cargo, that this will be accurately measured and that there will not be a further claim by the Bill of Lading holder.

The reason why deductions from freight are not permitted without a clause to the contrary would seem to come from the fact that the amount due for freight is an amount which is easily determined whereas a deduction in support of a claim is not easily ascertained and may or may not be legally due. If the Owners do not accept the claim then there is a dispute which must be settled by proceedings in arbitration or in a court of law in accordance with the charter party terms. To allow otherwise would be to permit the Charterer to judge on his own case.

In the majority of cases Charterers cannot refer the question of payment of freight to arbitration before making such payment. If the Charterer refuses to pay freight or makes an unauthorised deduction in payment Owners can apply for summary judgement. Unless on the hearing of the application either the court dismisses the action or the defendant satisfies the court in respect to the claim that there is an issue which ought to be tried, the court may give such judgement for the plaintiff.

Most voyage charter parties will have the Hague Rules incorporated into them and an often repeated mistake on the part of Charterers in the case of an apparent cargo shortage is to deduct the value of the alleged short delivery from the payment of freight. The wise Owner, in such circumstances, waits for just over a year from the date of delivery of the cargo, i.e. until the prescription period under the Hague Rules has expired, and then applies for summary judgement. When the Charterer seeks leave to defend he finds he has no defence, as any claim he has is time barred.

Two cases on this subject are "The Breed" (1973) and "The Aires" (1976). In the latter case the whole aspect was thoroughly reviewed by the Court of Appeal and House of Lords. The latter held:

(a) The Charterers had contracted on the basis and against the background that the established rule was against deduction;

(b) The rule against deduction had to be applied to the charter party and the Charterer's claim for short delivery could not be relied upon by way of defence;

(c) For an equitable set-off to exist there had to be some equity some ground for equitable intervention other than the mere existence of a cross-claim;

(d) Any equity was really against the Charterers and they had freely made a bargain incorporating the Hague Rules.

Lord Salmon added that the Rule had now stood for so long that it could not be challenged in the English court and it would have to be altered by statute were it to be considered no longer desirable.

9.1.4 Deadfreight

All the major tanker charters make provision for the payment of deadfreight if the agreed quantity of cargo is not supplied. There are variations in the wording of the clauses in all these charters but the results are much the same, i.e. if a full cargo is not supplied, the Charterer shall still pay freight in full. Whether or not the exceptions clause will act to excuse the Charterer, when one of those exceptions, e.g. Act of God, prevents the full cargo being supplied, depends of course upon the wording of the charter.

As the basis of a deadfreight claim is the Charterer's failure to supply the required quantity it is obviously important to be able to establish this as a fact. If not it may be alleged that loading was stopped by the ship or alternatively that the Charterer could have arranged more cargo if notified at the time.

When a number of different grades are to be shipped, tank sizes and segregation requirements increase the possibility of deadfreight arising. It is common practice in the parcel trade for there to be some tolerance in Owner's option, in the parcel sizes. With a tolerance of, say, 5% or in Owner's option the measure of deadfreight, if any, will be based on the maximum parcel size, i.e. 105%.

To establish the exact deadfreight liability the Charterer will want details of the vessel's deadweight, draft and cubic capacity. Most Owners will have a standard deadfreight form to be completed by the Master. This shows the maximum permissible draft for the voyage, which will depend on the controlling port draft or loadline zone. The sum of the bunkers, water, luboils and stores onboard are then deducted from the deadweight corresponding to this draft in order to establish the maximum weight of cargo, which the vessel can load. If this figure is greater than the cargo quantity loaded, the difference is the deadfreight.

However, this calculation on its own may not be sufficient to satisfy the Charterer that he is liable for this amount. The deadfreight calculated this way can be cross-checked by comparison of the mean draft on sailing with the applicable fully loaded mean draft for the voyage. The difference between these two mean drafts, multiplied by the appropriate TPI (tons per inch i.e. the amount which will increase the draft of the vessel by one inch) should correspond to the first deadfreight calculation. It is of course difficult to read draft marks with precision except in daylight and in still water. It is particularly difficult in sea berths, so this method of calculation will only be as accurate as the reading of the draft marks.

The foregoing calculations may establish the deadfreight but still not necessarily the Charterer's deadfreight liability. The available cargo capacity of the vessel's tanks may have limited the deadweight to which the vessel could load. This capacity has to be compared with the volume of the cargo at its specific gravity at the loaded temperature. This will establish how much of the cubic capacity of the cargo tanks was needed to load the cargo in question and how much, if any, remained unused. The lesser of the deadweight calculations and the cubic calculation will be the recoverable deadfreight.

Apart from the involvement of temperature with specific gravity, the requirements of the calculations mentioned so far are the same as those for dry cargo. With tankers there is usually the additional matter of retained tank washings to be taken into consideration. The various load on top clauses differ in the detail and manner in which they deal with this matter. A few Charterers fix on the basis that no freight will be paid on the tank washings and, if there are washings which have to be segregated and there is any additional deadweight as a consequence, it will not be recoverable. Most other Charterers contract to pay freight on retained washings and for any deadfreight caused by their segregation, when a full cargo is to be loaded.

Most charters include a statement of the vessel's capacity for cargo, expressed in tons or tonnes, plus or minus 5%. The maximum quantity so declared limits the quantity of cargo that the Owner can demand as a "full cargo". It therefore also limits the amount of deadfreight the Owner may demand as the Charterer is not obliged to supply cargo in excess of that amount. When declaring the vessel's cargo capacity, the Owner must take into account the voyage length and the possible specific gravity of the agreed cargo. These are relevant to the vessel's capability of loading not less than the minimum and not more than the maximum declared quantity.

In any instance where the ship has to stop the shore loading of further cargo the question of deadfreight in the usual sense does not arise but there may still be a claim by one party or the other. If there is an agreed minimum specific gravity for the cargo which may be loaded and the actual SG is less, so restricting the quantity the vessel could load, the Owner would have a claim for damages for the short loading so caused. If there is no minimum specific gravity stated but the vessel cannot load to the minimum declared capacity, then the Charterer will have a potential claim for damages in respect of the cargo short-loaded and that which he was entitled to anticipate would be shipped and which he may have already sold.

9.2   DEMURRAGE

Demurrage is usually defined as liquidated damages for delay beyond the agreed laytime allowed for loading and discharging. In general usage, the term is employed in a broader and looser sense and this can cause confusion. A notable example is that the term is used to mean the time after laytime has expired, as well as the liquidated damage for such delay time. When reference is made to demurrage being at half rate, this is sometimes construed as meaning that only 50% of the time will count for demurrage payment, as opposed to the full-time counting but being charged at 50% of the full demurrage rate, The difference between the calculation on each of these assumptions can be substantial. The case for the latter construction seems to be the better one. With the exception of one particular aspect, the calculation of demurrage for tankers is more straightforward than is sometimes thought and provided the necessary facts are collected and correctly presented there should be little room for dispute. Apart from the reluctance of the Charterer to make a – perhaps substantial – unanticipated payment in addition to the freight (a payment which he may not be able to recover from his buyer) the answer turns on two points; the first is in the collection and presentation of the facts, the second is in the matter of pumping warranties.

The first problem, the question of facts, is that both the ship and shore will not wish to accept responsibility for any delay if it is possible to attribute it to the other party. Many operations are carried out concurrently and therefore two reasons may be proffered as the cause of the same delay. Usually one reason is clearly the prime cause and what has happened is that the other party simply used that time for some ship or shore purpose, as the case may be. If the ship and shore cannot sort out the true facts at the time on the spot, what chance has someone else at a later date and in an office far removed from the port in question?

A properly authenticated time sheet, port-log or loading or discharging statement, should detail every operation, preferably in chronological order, giving reasons for all waiting time and stoppages and be signed on behalf of both ship and shore. Then, if a properly, rather than optimistically prepared demurrage claim is submitted, together with properly authenticated supporting documents, it is less likely to suffer dispute and thereby delay. There are at any time millions of dollars overdue in outstanding demurrages.

Most charters now contain time bars, which prevent the presentation of demurrage claims after a certain period. Usually in the region of 60/90 days after completion of the voyage. Now that faxed time sheets are usually accepted there is more chance of submitting demurrage claims promptly while the information is fresh and can be more easily checked, as necessary. A demurrage claim submitted six months after the voyage, even if not time barred, is hardly likely to be viewed favourably by the Charterer, who may have thought that all the financial aspects of that voyage had been settled. An Owner is unlikely to avoid the time bar without submitting a full claim and if Charterers Agents are involved he would be wise to make the provision "provided no delay occurs in the presentation of agents time sheets".

The second source of problems is the pumping warranty. The majority of these specify that the vessel will discharge within 24 hours or maintain a back pressure of 100 PSI at the vessel's manifold. With usually only 72 hours allowed for loading and discharging, it is not surprising that the Charterer wants to ensure an efficient discharge, so as to avoid demurrage arising. If the vessel takes longer than 24 hours to discharge, the Charterer often takes the attitude that this was due to the vessel's inefficiency or, if it was not, it is up to the Owner to prove otherwise. All the factors affecting the discharge rate cannot be detailed in this Chapter but it is essential to remember that it is the shore facilities and the ship's facilities jointly which will determine the maximum rate of discharge, not the ship alone.

If the shore receiving capacity is larger than the ship's discharging capacity, then the resistance will be low, the pumps can operate at their design speed and the flow rate will be high. A quick discharge can therefore result. If the shore receiving capacity is smaller than the vessel's pumping capacity then the back pressure against which the vessel has to pump will be high and the flow rate lower. Other things being equal, the vessel will then have maintained the required back pressure. Unfortunately other things are seldom equal. It would require a very complex clause to deal with all the relevant factors but two points need to be remembered

(a) If, as frequently happens, the shore restricts the flow rate or back pressure by express instruction or by the facilities offered, e.g. too few or too small hoses or lines, the ship cannot comply with the warranty. This warranty should always be qualified by the words "if the shore facilities permit" or,

(b) Warranty should refer to 24 hour or 100 PSI because they are alternatives, whereas some Charterers call for the vessel to discharge in 24 hours and to maintain the head.

Small cargo hoses causing slow discharge do not prevent demurrage being payable if the ship maintains the stated 100 PSI pressure.

The pumping warranty time, if pro-rated, is not sufficient for a part cargo or where different grades have to be pumped consecutively, it may not be possible to maintain the back pressure with a very viscous cargo.

9.3   COMMISSIONS

A shipbroking company aims to have knowledge of all business available and concluded on the section of a worldwide market that they intend to cover. For an Owner or a Charterer to operate a department that had the same ability as all the Ship Brokers who could provide such a service to the Principal is quite impossible. For example, one Owner or Charterer would not disclose his actions to a competitor, nor would he secure information on what others are doing. It is far more efficient for Principals to pay a commission to Brokers, only on business concluded (the failure rate can be high), than to attempt to cover the market direct. The only exception to this is where two Principals have an ongoing and *mutually* successful relationship, where they may negotiate direct and appoint a Broker acceptable to both. It has happened often that two Principals imagining they are saving commission by talking direct have ended with a contract well outside current market terms to the embarrassment of one or the other.

The Owner however is the party that pays the commission, although taking commission into account when offering for the business, it is the Charterer who has to agree the cost per ton on the cargo moved.

When there are two Brokers involved it is likely that the Broker quoting the business has a close relationship with the Charterer and may indeed have some Owners he can contact direct. But particularly internationally he is likely to contact other Brokers who have access to foreign tonnage so that one Broker will tend to lean towards the Charterer and the other towards the Owner. However the Owner paying the agreed total commission to his Broker is not concerned with how that commission is shared. Typically a commission clause may read "2½% commission payable to..............on freight deadfreight and demurrage, as and when paid, for division with others". To the general public the word "commission" suggests something close to a bribe, so the more open the commission declaration becomes the better, i.e. to be included in the charter.

A Charterer having a close relationship with a Broker may agree to deduct commission from freight and pay the Broker, but without Owners agreement they have no right to do so. However as the commission is almost certainly payable on payment of freight the Owner has no grounds on which to seek recovery.

Understandably some Owners consider that they should not (rightly or wrongly) pay commission until all outstandings including demurrage are settled. The idea is to put pressure on the Broker to secure settlement. Some Owners pay no commission on demurrage and the reason for this is Brokers failure to do anything to promote settlement. It has, however, happened that a Broker's efforts have resulted in payment of a demurrage commission not due under the fixture terms, so service can promote income. Brokers have requested Charterers to take action to secure unpaid commission, but Charterers do not usually want such complications, making deduction from freight a safer alternative.

If the Charterer should terminate or alter a charter, whether by negotiation directly with the Owner or in any other way, it will very probably affect the Broker's commission. The Charterer does not have an obligation to the Broker in this respect but in such circumstances some Charterers would ask the Owner to take the Broker's commission into account.

So-called address commission can occur particularly with oil traders but where it is due will be deducted from freight on payment. Address commission is usually paid at 1¼%,

9.4   METHODS OF FREIGHT PAYMENT

Having considered how much freight will be paid we will now look at the differences between the different methods which are negotiated for freight payment which are Worldscale, lumpsum freight and $/ton and how they affect the earnings for the voyage.

What are the earnings for the voyage? Freight is an important element but under Worldscale you will recall there is also the possibility of a fixed and a variable differential which is calculated by Worldscale with regard to certain costs with respect to a vessel's call at a port with different cargo types e.g. Rotterdam or various costs due to size e.g. canal dues. Fixing under Worldscale where the expression "WSHTC" is included means that reference is made to the Worldscale conditions as laid down in the preamble to determine what extra monies are earned. Remember unless otherwise agreed the Worldscale schedule applicable is the one in force at the date of loading. Thus, for a voyage from the Mediterranean to India via the Suez Canal the flat rate and the Suez Canal differential would be applied plus any other amounts as laid down in the schedule. There may also be mention of certain items which are for Owner's account or Charterer's account, all of which would be applied to determine total earnings, subject to any alteration in the terms of fixing outside WSHTC.

The determination of earnings on a lumpsum basis should be reasonably easy, that is to say the lumpsum rate agreed e.g. $1 million. However we need to find out what this covers and therefore, we need to look at the charter party. For instance does the rate cover more than one load and one discharge port? Does the rate include canal dues or are they to be paid in addition? Quite often the charter party which includes a lumpsum rate will also include "WSHTC" and confusion can now ensue. It can be argued that WS terms include the canal differential, therefore same would have to be added to the $1 million. The other side could argue that the canal differential is part of the freight. Thus, because the freight agreed is a lumpsum the canal tolls are inclusive. The experienced Broker would spot that such a misunderstanding could ensue and seek clarification in the first offer of the negotiations.

The tanker market sometimes works in very strange ways. Let us take the example of a tanker fixing a cargo from the Mediterranean for various discharge options say, Mediterranean, UK Continent and USA. These rates will usually be negotiated in Worldscale points. However, suppose during negotiations the Charterer says "Can you give us a rate for the Far East, our traders just need the option" such a rate will often be required on a lumpsum basis. If the negotiations are moving quickly it is too easy to forget that a lumpsum may be interpreted as including Suez Canal costs i.e. Charterer has nothing else to pay. The second element is that whereas the WS flat will compensate the Owner for difference in time and distance between, say Singapore and Japan, the lumpsum rate does not. So more than one rate should be given e.g. $1 million for Singapore/Hong Kong range and $1.2 million Hong Kong/Japan range (making sure, of course, that everybody understands which of the two rates will apply if the vessel discharges in Hong Kong). In fact the number of rates should be increased if more than one load and discharge port is required. Perhaps an extra US $40,000 for each additional port. Such an amount has to include not only extra port costs but extra steaming time as well. Basically the Owner must consider the rate per ton needed for loading at a range of ports and discharge at a range of ports converted to lumpsum figures.

Similar problems of interpretation can arise when fixing a rate in currency per ton e.g. USD/TON. However, in this case we also need to be specific as to which currency and which ton is being used, viz: "$/TON" could be understood by one party as "US$PMT" and the other side as "Singapore $PLT". The three types of ton frequently used in shipping are metric ton or tonne, long ton, 2,240 lbs and rarely a short ton, 2,000 lbs. Again, it is important to be specific as to what is included in the rate, how many ports, which ports, canal dues, taxes on freight and/or cargo etc. Today most tanker charters are concluded internationally in US$ per metric tonne.

9.5   ARBITRATION

There are a number of reasons for choosing arbitration rather than the courts for resolving shipping disputes. The parties can make their own choice of arbitrator from a group of arbitrators, who are experienced in the industry. In many arbitration centres, cases can be heard in private or, if the parties agree, just on documents. At the hearing, time can be saved because arbitrators are familiar with the commercial and technical background and because the whole procedure is more informal than the courts. To approach a dispute informally and in privacy often means the parties can carry on doing business together because they have solved their differences in a friendly fashion without upsetting future relationships between them.

The assumption that arbitration is a quicker and cheaper way to deal with maritime disputes has been questioned in recent years. Some commentators claim to have experienced a time lag of one or two years between a request for a hearing and the date set. In London an effort has been made to transform this situation with the introduction of the London Maritime Arbitrators Association (LMAA) Terms (1987). It is now the case that London arbitrators can offer two or three day hearings within six months. Very often the delay occurs more from case preparation than ability to find a competent arbitrator.

Where two or more arbitrators have to match up their diaries, the LMAA terms lay down strict rules that oblige an arbitrator to resign if he cannot match his colleagues dates within a set time limit, but in practice this provision has rarely been used. It has been known for urgent hearings and awards to be made in a very much shorter space of time. Arbitrators can arrange hearings for the evenings or even at weekends and awards can be made within the same day, if the situation and parties require it. To speed up the procedures further parties can agree to submit their dispute to a single arbitrator, the choice is in the hands of the parties.

The LMAA terms set up a procedure whereby a sole arbitrator who is unable to offer a date for a hearing within a reasonable time will offer to retire in order that a substitute may be appointed within that time. Such reasonable time is defined in accordance with the expected duration of the hearing.

	Estimated Duration	**Reasonable Time**
i)	up to 2 days	4 months
ii)	3-5 days	6 months
iii)	6-10 days	10 months

These terms require a booking fee of £250 per day to discourage last minute postponements.

In an effort to reduce costs the LMAA has introduced a small claims procedure. The more costly features of English procedure, discovery, oral evidence and argument, and appeal, are largely eliminated and in consequence there is a fixed fee of £750. In 1994 there were 85 appointments of arbitrators and 70 awards, which is interesting to compare on success ratio with the full LMAA procedure in the same year totalling 3,558 appointment and 377 awards. Thus, the scheme is able to give people the choice of an alternative way of dealing with disputes if they do not wish to embark on a full-scale arbitration.

There are a number of centres where arbitration is carried out throughout the world, the best-known are New York, Paris, New Delhi and Beijing, but London arbitration is by far the most common means of resolving shipping disputes. One of the great strengths of London arbitration is claimed to be that they apply English law. No court in the world has the expertise of England's commercial courts, in which decisions have been made for centuries in all aspects of shipping commerce creating a massive library of case law.

In order to avoid unnecessary high costs it should be emphasised that the correct training of a ship's Master would be useful. It should be standard practice for Master to take photographs in the event of a situation arising, which may lead to a claim or dispute. Such photographs should include the condition of the cargo and the machinery then be labelled and authenticated. The Master should then keep the relevant specimens, for example oil, and be taught how to authenticate such samples. Written reports should be taken as they are more valid than statements taken much later. Telephone calls arising out of the dispute should be followed by a confirming telex, fax or even letter. All relevant documents, including log books should be preserved and made available to the solicitors. It should not be necessary for solicitors to visit clients' offices and search for the relevant documents. It cannot be emphasised enough that records taken at the time of every incident that occurs are absolutely invaluable.

Once an arbitration has been won the same may have to be enforced. It is true that in some jurisdictions it is easier to enforce a court judgement than an arbitration award but in such cases it is possible to convert an award into a judgement. It is true to say that on the other hand there are countries where a London arbitration award may be enforced but not a decision by an English court.

9.6 WARRANTY OF AUTHORITY

The Shipbroker who negotiates as an intermediary between the Shipowner and Charterer is deemed to warrant that he has full authority of the Principal to contract on the terms of an offer which he transmits. If for some reason it transpires that he did not have the necessary full authority, he may be liable in an action brought by the person who receives the offer and accepts it. Consider the following two examples.

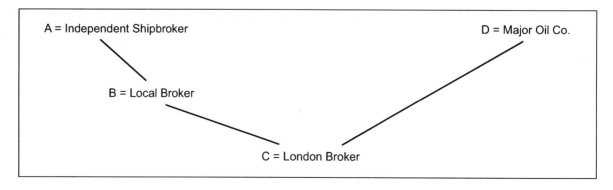

A = Independent Shipbroker   D = Major Oil Co.

B = Local Broker

C = London Broker

Example 1. A offers his ship to B who passes it on correctly to C at Worldscale 110. C mistakenly passes on the offer at Worldscale 100 and D accepts. It is considered that there is no contract between A and D because they were not of the same mind, i.e. agreed, but C could be liable in an action for breach of warranty of authority "with negligence".

Example 2. A offers his ship to B at Worldscale 110 and B mistakenly passes on the offer to C at Worldscale 100. C passes the offer to D exactly as received from B and D accepts. There is no contract between A and D but C could be liable in the first instance in an action for breach of warranty of authority "without negligence".

C may have recourse action against B which B will no doubt satisfy if he is a man of good reputation and financially sound; if he is not, the liability would remain with C The solution is, for Example 1, the exercise of care and an insurance policy. The solution to Example 2 is care to deal with reputable companies and an insurance policy.

A few years ago, prior to the introduction of Professional Indemnity insurance, claims against Brokers were virtually unheard of, but unfortunately it is a fact of life that now this insurance is available Principals are more likely to make a claim against a Broker, saying that "you made a mistake, your insurance company can cover our claim". It is essential, therefore, to ensure that no misunderstandings occur due to slipshod work.

9.7   BILLS OF LADING

These are documents, issued on behalf of the carrier (Shipowner or Charterer as the case may be):

i)   As prima facie evidence that the goods stated therein were actually received from the Shipper, in the condition as stated (i.e. a receipt)

ii)   They act as evidence of contract of carriage between the Shipper and carrier.

iii)   They act, in commercial transactions, as documents of title to the goods stated therein.

These three purposes of the Bill of Lading impose an absolute duty on the person signing them to ensure that they contain true statements. Before signing, the Master, or other official, should verify the following particulars:

(a)   The goods are actually on board, (this he does by sighting the Mate's receipts).

(b)   All Mate's receipt clauses are included on the bills of lading.

(c)   Check the Bill of Lading is correctly dated.

(d)   Freight, if prepaid, is collected before signing, including any other charges such as unpaid demurrage incurred at loading port (rare) or deadfreight and any agreed proportion of advanced freight if the vessel is on charter.

On the face of all Bills of Lading is a statement that a certain number (2, 3 or 4 as stated) have been signed and are equally valid. These are referred to as the original Bills of Lading. For commercial uses, a number of copies of Bill of Lading will be issued. These are not signed and will be over-printed with the statement "copy non negotiable". This statement will be in large capital letters and frequently in red ink to make it more obvious. The reason that these copies are not signed is that the signed Bills of Lading are title to the goods stated thereon. In consequence, the goods may be sold by the transfer of the Bills of Lading to a third party by the named Shipper (or Consignee) endorsing it on the back to some other party.

This will often occur between the time of shipment and the time of discharge of the cargo. To reduce the chance of fraud it is normal that all stated original copies will be similarly endorsed.

The face of the Bill of Lading will contain the description of the cargo, marks, ship's name, date of shipment, number or weight. The details will be obtained from the Mate's receipts as the Shipper delivers the goods to the port or vessel he is given a copy of the Mate's receipt. If the goods are damaged or imperfect the fact should be distinctly noted on the face of the receipt. In the case of liquid bulk cargoes an accurate measurement should be taken because any mistakes will pass from the Mate's receipts to the Bill of Lading. Where the Bill of Lading is considered conclusive evidence of quantity shipped, an inaccurate measurement will make the Shipowner liable for the quantity apparently short delivered but in fact short shipped. Mate's receipts should be exchanged for the Bill of Lading.

Let us consider three circumstances:

(a) **As between Shipowner and Shipper.**

Where the shipper is not a party to any charter (as in the case of a liner service or FOB contract) the Bill of Lading is not itself the contract between the Shipowner and the Shipper as that is made before the bill is issued. It is, however, the evidence of the terms agreed.

(b) **As between Shipowner and indorsee or consignee.**

Once a Bill of Lading has passed to an indorsee or consignee it contains the terms of the contract of carriage. Under English law a Bill of Lading acquires its conclusive character by virtue of the Carriage of Goods by Sea Act 1992 which replaced the Bill of Lading Act of 1855.

(c) **Where a Bill of Lading is issued under a charter party.**

Where the Bill of Lading is issued to a vessel under a charter it is very common for the terms of the Bill of Lading to differ from those of the charter party.

Generally, where a Bill of Lading is issued to the Charterer, the Bill of Lading in law is a mere receipt and not a contractual document. So long as the Bill of Lading remains in the hands of the Charterer the goods are carried under the terms of the charter party.

Once the Bill of Lading is transferred to a third party who is a stranger to the charter party, a new contract springs into existence between the Shipowner and the third party on the terms of the Bill of Lading.

There are then two contracts of carriage, one with the Charterer as set out in the charter party and the other with the holder of the Bill of Lading in terms contained on that document.

It is unusual in the tanker industry for an original Bill of Lading to be available at the discharge port, either the voyage has been short, thus insufficient time has elapsed for the documents to be transmitted to the discharge port or the oil has been purchased against credit advanced by a bank. As a form of security the bank will require all original Bills of Lading to be in their custody until they have received payment for the cargo stated thereon. Thus they will not release the bills of lading in time for the ship to discharge her cargo. This in practice is overcome by Charterers issuing a Letter of Indemnity as covered in our earlier Chapter.

9.8   SELF-ASSESSMENT AND TEST QUESTIONS

1.   How is the cargo quantity established for freight payment purposes?

2.   When is freight earned and payable?

3.   What deductions from freight may be made under the BEEPEEVOY charter party?

4.   Under what circumstances would deadfreight be payable?

5.   In which ways could a freight rate be expressed?

6.   What are the three functions of a Bill of Lading?

Having completed Chapter Nine, attempt the following and submit your essay to your Tutor:
In a voyage charter explain the elements that will contribute to the earnings of a vessel

Chapter 10

ORGANISATIONS IN THE TANKER INDUSTRY

In the shipping world it is often said "it's not what you know but who you know." This is true of people and organisations. A lot of organisations and their initials are used in shipping and the tanker industry and there are occasions when it would be useful, not only to know what the organisations do, but their addresses and contact points. We will now look at the background and, where applicable, reasons for the organisations which the people involved in tanker chartering will most often come across in their daily working life.

Some of the organisations you will know, it will be worthwhile to think about their role and consider whether they are making an effective contribution. With respect to those organisations you have not heard about, try to take the view of an outsider and consider what role and contribution they might provide to a newcomer to the industry.

It is assumed you have understood the earlier Chapters on Worldscale and AFRA.

10.1 AAA

Association of Average Adjusters
The Baltic Exchange
St Mary Axe
London
EC3A 8BH

Tel: +44 (0) 207 623 5501   Fax: +44 (0) 207 623 1623
Website aaa@balticexchange.com

This Association brings together average adjusting firms, organisations in insurance and shipping, Shipowners, underwriters and lawyers with the aim of promoting professional standards in the adjustment of marine insurance claims.

The Association endeavours to ensure that correct principles be applied to adjusting, achieving uniformity of practice, ensure impartiality and independence of the members by imposing a strict code of practice to provide a service to the marine community by giving advice on all aspects of marine insurance claims.

The Association was founded in London in 1869 and now has over 70 members, all of whom are average adjusters, 45 representative members who are appointed by insurance interests worldwide and over 400 subscribers from a variety of marine related businesses and representing most of the main geographical areas of the world.

Full membership of the Association is open only to practising average adjusters who are considered experts in the law and practice of general average and marine insurance who have passed the AAA entrance examination.

The rules of the Association set strict standards of impartiality on members. The Rules of Practice are aimed at a uniformity and have become accepted as the international authority on matters related to adjusting. Policy for the Association is fixed at an Annual General Meeting. Changes to the Rules of Practice passed by the General Meetings are considered by the Association's Advisory Committee. This Committee has the additional duty of reporting on matters on which the advice of the Association has been sought. The opinions of the Committee are circulated to Members and representative members for a valuable source of reference. If there is a specific dispute the Association appoints a panel of referees which rule on these.

10.2   ACOPS

Advisory Committee on Pollution of the Sea
11 Dartmouth Street
London
SW1H 9BN
United Kingdom

Tel: +44 (0) 207 799 3033   Fax: +44 (0) 207 799 2933
Website www.acops.org

This is an international and non-governmental charity organisation based in London. The aims of the Committee is to monitor the international environmental scene, to support policies and legislation aimed at improving the quality of the marine environment and to encourage and initiate related research.

In fact, ACOPS is one of the oldest environmental organisations in existence. The need to clarify whether dead seabirds washed up on beaches was caused by sunken warships or marine transport, led Jim Callaghan, later British Prime Minister, to set up a group to monitor pollution. During the 1960s and 70s damage caused by shipwrecks and dumping at sea caught the public eye and over the years, ACOPS developed into an international network with considerable influence and respect.

Events such as the *'Amoco Cadiz'* and the *'Exxon Valdez!* spill have drawn attention to the current scale of the problem. However, ACOPS is not simply working to keep the seas and beaches clean, it also monitors disposal of poisons. The Committee has consultative status within the United Nations Environment Programme (UNEP), the International Maritime Organization (IMO) and the London Dumping Convention (LDC). As such ACOPS had a leading role at the UNEP Conference on the control of transboundary movements of hazardous wastes, which drew up the Basle Convention and is committed to increasing the public awareness and the gravity of the problem of dumping wastes at sea.

10.3   BIMCO

Bimco
Bagsvaerdvej 161
2880 Bagsvaerd
Denmark

Tel: +45 444 36 6800   Fax: +45 44 36 6868
E-mail mailbox@bimco.dk
Website www.bimco.dk

The Baltic and International Maritime Council claims to be the world's leading shipping organisation as well as the largest. BIMCO's membership comprises Shipowners and managers, Ship Brokers, port and chartering Agents, and clubs such as P&I, freight, demurrage and defence associations, shipping federations, Shipowners' and Ship Brokers' associations. Associate membership is open to entities having a demonstrable interest in the shipping industry. For example, banks, maritime lawyers, port authorities, classification societies. Representing members from more than 120 countries, BIMCO is a focal point for shipping professionals where vital information is collected, collated and made available to all members for the good of the industry.

Ever since its foundation in 1905, Copenhagen-based BIMCO has stressed the international nature both of its membership and of its role within the shipping world. The organisation has emphasised that it is non political and that it acts for the shipping industry as a whole. It is governed by an executive committee and holds a General Meeting every two years. Between 600 and 800 delegates will attend the General Meeting where members fix priorities for BIMCO.

All members have access to a wide range of services which alone, it is claimed, justifies the membership fee. BIMCO is also a respected voice speaking on international affairs with governments and authorities worldwide. The full-time secretariat and expert staff receive over 150 queries and requests for assistance on a daily basis. BIMCO is known for its work on standardising shipping documentation and for its publications.

Efficient communications have always been an essential element in BIMCO's service and philosophy. They achieve this through a wide variety of specialised publications. The range of publications includes:

- The BIMCO News which contains news on port and labour conditions as well as general shipping articles. Available to members through the website.

- The BIMCO Bulletin, featuring arbitration awards, legal decisions, developments affecting the industry.

Over the years BIMCO has accumulated expertise on matters of importance for running successful businesses in shipping. Much of this information has been compiled into practical handbooks. Current titles include:

- Forms of Approved Documents

- Check before Fixing

- Freight Taxes

- Port Costs.

BIMCO Informatique A/S was formed in the summer of 1988, this subsidiary being manned by computer experts specialising in developing software for the shipping industry. They have developed databases covering port information for the tanker trades, port information for dry cargo trades covering European, African and American ports and a voyage estimating package.

Members can consult a company register on known credit risks and BIMCO regularly issues warnings to prevent exposure to credit losses. Though not a collection agency, BIMCO may assist members to collect outstanding receivables and to date is recovering an average of $4 million a year. BIMCO represents its members within international organisations such as IMO and UNCTAD working in close rapport with other shipping bodies, proud to be known as cosmopolitan and impartial.

10.4   FONASBA

The Federation of National Associations of Shipbrokers and Agents
The Baltic Exchange
St Mary Axe
London
EC3A 8BH

Tel: +44 (0)20 7623 1111   Fax: +44 (0)20 7623 3113
E-mail generalmanager@fonasba.com
Website www.fonasba.com

The Federation exists to give Brokers and Agents an authoritative voice in international affairs. Being non-profit making, non-state federation, with full membership limited to **National Associations** of Shipbrokers and ships' agents. Set up in 1969 by the National Associations of eleven European countries it now has members representing 47 countries. In countries where no national association is available, individual companies are able to apply for Associate membership. P&I Clubs and other shipping related bodies may be Club members.

The aims of the Federation are:

i)   To be consulted and to speak with authority on relevant matters concerning Agents and Brokers.

ii)   To maintain an organisation capable of co-operating with other international bodies.

iii) To promote fair and equitable practice amongst Shipbrokers and Agents.

FONASBA provides support services for members, strives to improve and simplify standard shipping documentation and organises courses and conferences on subjects of interest to Ship Brokers and Agents.

The Federation's policy making body is a Council on which all members are represented and meets annually. The Council elects a President, an executive Vice-President and a Vice-President for two-year terms. These officers, along with the immediate Past President and the President Designate form the Executive Committee which governs the Federation and meets as and when required. There are four Standing Committees, the Executive Committee, the Liner and Tramp Committee, the Chartering and Documentary Committee and the Membership Committee.

FONASBA enjoys consultative status at UNCTAD and also maintains close links with BIMCO, INTERTANKO, INTERCARGO, FIATA and other international maritime bodies. It has produced a number of standard documents, guidelines and contracts and assisted in producing others. The General Agency Agreement and the Standard Liner Agency Agreement have received wide acceptance. The International Brokers' Commission Contract is a means of assisting the recovery of unpaid Brokerage.

The Federation has defended its members' interests against attempts to legislate Agents' and Brokers' business and has been successful in putting the Agents' case to both Owners, governments and international bodies.

10.5   ECASBA

European Community Association of Shipbrokers and Agents
Address details as for FONASBA

Has been formed as a separate standing committee of FONASBA specifically to promote and protect the interests of Shipbrokers and Agents within the European Community and in negotiation with the directorates of the Commission. All the maritime member states are represented through their national associations and ECASBA has permanent representation at Brussels.

10.6   IMIF

International Maritime Industries Forum
Secretariat
C/o Baltic Exchange
38 St Mary Axe
London
EC3A 8BH
United Kingdom

Tel: +44(0) 207 929 6429   Fax: +44 (0) 207 929 6430
website imif@btconnect.com

The International Marine Industries Forum is an organisation of Shipowners, shipbuilders, cargo interests and bankers, plus other interested organisations such as classification societies, insurers, accountants and lawyers. Membership is drawn from 23 countries. A number of international organisations maintain observer status.

The IMIF was founded at the end of 1975 following the publication of a report on the problems of the tanker industry commissioned by tanker Owners, banks, Shipowners and oil companies, who were concerned about the effect of surplus tanker capacity. In subsequent years the IMIF has increased its area of influence beyond the tanker industry to include all aspects of shipping and government related activities.

This Forum describes its principal aim as "The re-establishment and subsequent maintenance of a healthy commercial and financial climate for all sectors of the maritime industries." The controlling body for the receipt and dissemination of information is a steering committee which prepares policy statements. The steering committee is fed information for its meetings from reports by committee members or their sub-committee meetings and submissions from members of reports following contact with other industry participants. The Committee visits strategic areas, principally in the Far East, to spread the word and hear at first hand the views of Owners, yards, governments, Shipbrokers and international organisations.

IMIF provides an impartial forum gathering information and informed views from responsible sources within the industry and uses the same to ensure that these sources and other interested parties are made aware of the strategic issues affecting the industry. The objective is to ensure that participants in the industry work in a responsible way to ensure that dramatic swings in the industry are avoided. The key issue is responsibility of actions of participants who must be encouraged to realise that long-term stability is an important an issue as their short-term profits.

The Forum argues that the key to maintaining its credibility is impartiality, topicality, and information sources throughout the industry and the world.

10.7   IMO

International Maritime Organization
4 Albert Embankment
London
SE1 7SR
United Kingdom

Tel +44 (0) 207 735 7611   Fax: +44 (0) 207 587 3210
Website www.imo.org

The International Maritime Organization is a specialised agency of the United Nations dealing with maritime affairs. Its aims are to improve maritime safety, the prevention of marine pollution and the facilitation of marine traffic. Its method of achieving these aims is to co-ordinate the actions of individual countries through the promotion of international conventions, protocols, codes and recommendations. Any member of the United Nations can be a member of IMO and attend any of the main committees. The result of casting the net so wide and restricting the programme to technical concerns, is that IMO has not been politicised so that countries do not speak or vote as political groups at IMO. IMO does not originate legislation or have any executive power. Ideas are started by individual governments with IMO providing a place and means for turning that idea into an international agreement. Individual governments then agree to be bound by that agreement enforcing it themselves through their own legislation procedures.

The member states meet at an assembly every two years and, as the highest governing body votes the budget, approves the work programme and elects members to the Council. The 32 member states of the Council which are elected for a two-year period are divided into three groups. These groups represent interests who provide shipping services and have special interests in maritime transport.

There are four main technical Committees which carry out the work of IMO. The Maritime Safety Committee (MSC) and its sub-committees meet for 12 weeks a year. This Committee has a broad mandate to consider any matter related to maritime safety.

The Marine Environment Protection Committee (MEPC) considers matters to do with controlling or preventing pollution from ships. The Technical Co-operation Committee looks after the technical co-operation of projects which IMO co-ordinates. The Legal Committee deals with IMO's legal concerns. Sub-committees report to the MSC or MEPC on topics such as safety of navigation, carriage of dangerous goods, fire protection and other safety areas.

Funding for the Agency is raised by contributions from members, the size of which is based on the tonnage of the member's merchant fleet. The work is supported by a large secretariat.

IMO co-ordinates a technical co-operation programme which is aimed to help nations upgrade maritime administrations and enable them to implement IMO conventions. Under this heading the biggest project is the World Maritime University based in Malmo, Sweden. Other countries receive direct assistance towards the establishment of maritime training. This assistance takes the form of expert advisers rather than direct funding. The achievement of IMO has been to publish 25 International Conventions as well as other Protocols and many Codes and Recommendations, providing a comprehensive structure for merchant shipping of all types. Acceptance rate is very high, with conventions like SOLAS (Safety of Life at Sea) and Loadline covering 90% of world shipping. In an environment of technical change, together with more states having an interest in shipping, IMO is concentrating on implementing existing standards and assisting countries to implement them, whilst continuing to provide a place of understanding.

10.8 INMARSAT

International Maritime Satellite Organization
99 City Road
London
EC1Y 1AX
United Kingdom

Tel: +44 (0) 207 728 1000   Fax: +44 (0) 207 728 1044
Website www.inmarsat.org

With the increasing need for reliable communications in international shipping, conventional radio has not been able to keep up with the increase in traffic. Satellite communications are further possibilities for clear lines for voice and data and have an almost unlimited capacity. Translating that possibility into reality to cover all the oceans of the world has proved to be beyond the investment abilities of any one country.

INMARSAT is the international organisation charged with meeting the needs of international shipping for all satellite communications. Since its establishment in 1979 INMARSAT today owns or operates a network of satellite communication systems covering the world's major trading areas. INMARSAT'S purpose, as laid down in its founding convention, is to make the provision for a space segment necessary to improve maritime communications. The aim is to improve communications for distress, safety of life, management of ships, public correspondence and radio determination.

There are five components of the system which go to fulfil these aims. The space segment consists of geo-stationary satellites and support systems owned or leased by INMARSAT. Coast Earth Stations, (CES) connect the space segment into land based telecommunications networks. These are owned and operated by individual signatories to INMARSAT agreement rather than by INMARSAT itself. Network Co-ordination Stations (NCS) are leased by INMARSAT in each ocean region to assigned space open segment to CES and SES as required.

Ship Earth Stations (SES) are the satellite communications terminals which are purchased or leased by the individual users of the systems. The operations control centre is located at INMARSAT headquarters, from where it monitors and co-ordinates operational activities in the INMARSAT network.

The network is able to provide a service of telex, telephone and data links to ships and off-shore platforms and compressed video transmissions to some passenger vessels.

The INMARSAT system will form a key part of the global maritime distress and safety system currently being implemented by IMO. The SES currently in use are of a standard A type which give a full service but are bulky and require a sophisticated antenna. The microterminal standard C system now coming into service which will provide data and telex links through portable units with suitable antennae.

INMARSAT was established under an international convention which remains open for signature at the IMO headquarters. It currently has 55 members. A state wishing to become a member of INMARSAT has to ratify the convention then appoint a competent entity known as a signatory, which will sign the INMARSAT operated agreement. The signatory is usually the national telecommunications network. It may also be an organisation designated by the state. The signatory's role is to provide the earth segment services linking the space segment and to participate in the running and financing of INMARSAT. Technical assistance and training is available to members from the multi-lingual INMARSAT staff. INMARSAT has a permanent staff of over 200 people based in London. Since the first satellite communications links became available to civil users in 1982, INMARSAT has grown in size and stature. Satcoms are the main means of communication for the bulk of the higher value part of shipping.

10.9   INTERTANKO

International Association of Independent Tanker Owners

INTERTANKO
PO Box 761
Sentrum
Oslo
Norway

Tel:+47 22 122 640
Fax: +47 22 122 641

INTERTANKO
St Clare House
30-33 Minories
London
EC3N 1DD
United Kingdom

+44(0)207 623 4311

E-mail oslo@intertanko.com or
london@intertanko.com Website www.intertanko.com

The International Association of Independent Tanker Owners represents over 80% of independently owned tanker tonnage and acts as a service association gathering intelligence and dispensing advice and services to members. The INTERTANKO membership covers 33 countries, over 140 million dwt of tanker tonnage within its 280 members. Membership is open to Owners and managing operators of tankers which are independent, excluding tonnage owned by oil companies and governmental agencies. Part of the success of INTERTANKO is that it has shown its usefulness as an information centre, and thus become an effective organ for promoting the interests of the independent Owner.

INTERTANKO gathers information and provides an intelligence centre for members. The Port Information Office publishes monthly bulletins on port conditions and costs. Individual advice is given in cases of over-charging and for matters concerning port costs, agencies and rate taxes.

The freight and demurrage information pool has, since its inception in 1983, become a very useful tool for the industry. So far FDIP has succeeded in collecting or speeding up the settlement of claims in excess of $33 million, exceeding the cost of running the entire organisation.

INTERTANKO has always been particularly interested in documentary work and has pioneered and published forms for all types of tanker chartering. Its experts provide practical advice on chartering problems. The Association has recently stepped up its campaign against imbalanced chartering terms which accords with the INTERTANKO philosophy that the strength and weakness of the market should be reflected in market freight rates not in charter party terms and conditions.

INTERTANKO conducts market research and publishes an independent view of basic trends in the supply and demand for tankers. In addition members receive regular bulletins with information on regulatory developments, port and bunker costs, market trends, charter party news and other operational information.

INTERTANKO uses its collective strength by having consultative status with IMO and UNCTAD where it forcefully represents the independent tanker industry with the aim of promoting freedom of competition in shipping, ensuring safety at sea and protecting the marine environment.

Membership of INTERTANKO is direct without intervening layers of national associations. The members approve policy at the AGM but the defining of policy is in the hands of the Council which is made up of members of different countries according to a scale of entered tonnage. The Association has its permanent secretariat in Oslo where 15 staff work under the Managing Director. Funding is based on membership contributions, sale of publications and advertising revenue. The Association has identified four challenges for the future. Commercially the Association wants Owners to maintain a confident market posture aimed at overcoming the problem of an ageing tanker fleet and freight rates which do not justify newbuildings. INTERTANKO intends to provide Owners with factual information about the tanker market to help them make judicious investment decisions. The Association intends to take the lead in achieving a balanced set of contractual terms between Owner and Charterer and strive to resolve the continuing threat to Owners imposed by the absence of Bills of Lading at the discharge port.

As for policy, INTERTANKO totally opposes cargo-sharing regimes and remains committed to the preservation of the current competitive structure of the tanker market.

10.10   ITF

International Transport Workers Federation
49-60 Borough High Street
London
SE1 1DR
United Kingdom

Tel: +44 (0) 207 403 2733   Fax: +44 (0) 207 357 7871
E-mail mail@itf.org.uk Website www.itf.org.uk

According to its literature, the International Transport Workers Federation is founded on respect for human and trade union rights. The Federation claims that these rights are regularly violated and as a defender of these rights it finds itself in conflict with employers and governments. Its campaign against flags of convenience is the most visible part of that conflict. Behind that conflict there is a study programme of work promoting solidarity between workers in the transport industry and supporting workers in an uneven fight against the worst kind of employers.

The ITF is an independent organisation whose members are organisations with trades union members in the transport industries. The condition of membership is that democratic principles must be upheld and be free of outside control. The ITF brings together the trades unions with transport workers from most of the free economies of the world.

The aims of the ITF are based on the UN Declaration on Human Rights and the rights of freedom of association laid down in the ILO conventions. The ITF's aims are set out in the Constitution as follows.

1.   Promote respect for trade union and human rights worldwide.

2.   To work for peace based on social justice and economic progress.

3. To help its affiliated unions defend the interests of their members.

4. To provide research and information services to its affiliates.

5. To provide general assistance to transport workers in difficulties.

An executive board meets twice a year and is backed up by a management sub-committee for day to day administrative matters with a full-time General Secretary being elected at each Congress.

The basic precept of the ITF is that, to be effective, unions must support each other. Transport being international and the very nature of the industry make it particularly vulnerable to pressure from employers and governments. The ITF brings together all workers involved in transport to provide strength through solidarity. Fishermen, truck drivers, airline pilots, dockers, railway men and seamen can support each other within the ITF.

The Federation was first set up in 1896, as a group of European and US trade unionists in ship and dock work. Two years later it became the ITF Until the end of the Second World War it remained European dominated, but since then has increased its influence in developing countries in particular.

The ITF has an active information section publishing a regular seafarers' bulletin and monthly news and a series of studies and bulletins on labour related matters. The ITF has representation at or co-operation with other major international organisations, in particular with the ILO, IMO, ICAO and the EC Commission.

The best-known aspect of the ITF's work is its campaign against flags of convenience. The campaign is waged jointly by the seafarers' and dockers' affiliates with two main objectives. The first being to establish a link between the flag of a ship and the domicile of the Owners, managers and seafarers. The second is to protect seafarers on flag of convenience ships from exploitation.

The practical symbol of this campaign is that more than 2,000 flag of convenience ships now sail with ITF blue certificates. These certificates are issued by the Federation to the Shipowners who have signed an agreement (employment contract) with the crew which the ITF or its affiliates consider acceptable. Ships without the blue certificate may find themselves subject to industrial action in the ports where ITF inspectors regularly visit ships to check on conditions of employment.

At the moment the point of concern for the ITF is the development of the so-called second registers which the Federation sees as an attempt by employers to enjoy the exploitative benefits of flags of convenience without the attached stigma. The ITF may not be popular with some shipowners but it claims to fight an honest corner and has had some success in its control of the worst abuses of labour.

10.11 ITOPF

The International Tanker Owners Pollution Federation Limited
1 Olivers Yard
55 City Road
London
EC1Y 1HQ

Tel: +44 (0) 207 566 6999   Fax: +44 (0) 207 566 6950
E-mail central@itopf.com
Website www.itopf.com

The International Tanker Owners Pollution Federation is an organisation set up to respond to oil spills. The Federation administers the tanker Owners' voluntary agreement concerning liability for oil pollution and provides expert response to oil spills, damage assessment and claims analysis, contingency planning, advice, training and information services.

Despite the existence of international conventions concerning oil spill claims, ITOPF still has a strong role to play in ensuring that parties have adequate security (normally through P&I Clubs) and to issue certificates to participating vessels.

The response team is primarily available for spills involving members' vessels but both CRISTAL (the oil cargo Owners' voluntary agreement) and IOPC (the inter-governmental counterpart of CRISTAL) also use ITOPF services.

The response involves assessing the seriousness of the spill, and assisting with cost effective clean-up, monitoring and reporting on clean-up, organising equipment and operations on behalf of Owners and investigating harmful effects of the spill. The aim of ITOPF in this sort of work is to co-operate with all parties to reach acceptable solutions to the problems.

ITOPF is aware that a good response to a spill depends on both planning and training. The staff are frequently asked by governments and other organisations to help with contingency planning for oil spills and to provide advice on oil spill response arrangements. One of its largest assignments was an evaluation for the US Navy of response arrangements in ports with abuses.

Contingency plans will not work without trained personnel. ITOPF runs and participates in training courses where the practical expertise gained by its technical staff can be passed on.

In addition to direct training, the Federation has published information on oil spills and response techniques. Twelve technical information papers have been published, the success of these leading to the production of a series of 20 minutes videos covering response to oil spills.

Although ITOPF was conceived as a lobby to administer TOVALOP it has grown by the success of its work into more than that. ITOPF is recognised as a centre of technical expertise on oil pollution in the marine environment and is the principal industry organisation concerned with combating oil spills from tankers.

10.12 OCIMF

Oil Companies International Marine Forum
29 Queen Anne's Gate
London
SW1H 9BU
United Kingdom

Tel: +44 (0) 207 654 1200   Fax: +44 (0) 207 654 1205
E-mail enquiries@ocimf.com Website www.ocimf.com

The Oil Companies International Marine Forum is a voluntary association of oil companies having an interest in the shipment and terminaling of crude oil and oil products. "Our mission is to be the foremost authority on the safe and environmentally responsible operation of oil tankers and terminals, promoting continuous improvement in standards of design and operation."

OCIMF provides a medium whereby its members can formulate their views and present them to inter-governmental bodies, governments and industrial organisations. Formed in 1970 as the oil industry's response to growing public concern over pollution, it now has member companies and groups worldwide.

OCIMF has consultative status at IMO and maintains close liaison with other industrial bodies. It co-ordinates oil industry views at IMO meetings, reviews technical documents circulated by IMO, advises members on legislation which affects them and sponsors research projects, many of which have resulted in the publication of technical guidelines.

OCIMF policy is decided at an Annual General Meeting which elects a Chairman and three vice-Chairmen. Between AGMs, the Association is run by an elected executive committee which normally meets once a year. There are three Standing Committees which deal with general matters, ports and terminals and legal matters and these in turn are supported by sub-committees and working groups made up of industry experts which are set up to deal with specific projects.

There is a full-time secretariat based in London under the charge of a Director. Secretariat members attend all IMO meetings and report to the relevant committees, the costs of the secretariat being shared amongst members on an annual basis in accordance with the quantity of oil received by them each year, subject to a minimum fee.

Guidelines from OCIMF have become accepted as the standard industrial practice. These cover hoses, moorings, offshore terminals, safe mooring of ships and the handling of disabled ships. Having celebrated its 20th anniversary, OCIMF has made a positive and practical contribution to safety at sea and pollution prevention.

10.13   SIGTTO

The Society of International Gas Tanker and Terminal Operators
17 St. Helen's Place
London
EC3
United Kingdom

Tel: +44 (0) 207 628 1124   Fax: +44 (0) 207 628 3163
email: secretariat@sigtto.org

SIGTTO is a non-profit making organisation dedicated to the protection and promotion of the mutual interests of its members and the safe operation of liquefied gas tankers and gas loading and receiving terminals.

Essentially the Society serves as a Forum for the exchange of technical information and expertise on safety and reliability and the conduct of studies relating to safety and the environment for ocean transportation or bulk storage of liquefied gases.

The Society was formed in 1979 and now comprises members from all over the world representing about 80% of the world LNG interests and 40% of the world LPG interests. Membership is open to Operators of shipping or terminals handing gas and membership is assessed annually based on a charge related to the cubic capacity operated by the member.

The Society holds two meetings each year, one in each hemisphere. At the meetings there is a general panel meeting which is open to all members. The panel meetings cover any topics concerning safety and reliability, which members raise and are intended to allow free, non-public discussion of the problems facing the industry. At the same time the General Purposes Committee meets, which is the central technical body and manager of the Society.

SIGTTO has consultative status at IMO and keeps a close liaison with IMS, ICS, OCIMF and other bodies as necessary. The Society publishes a number of authoritative works which have become industry standards, including guides to contingency planning, a review of quantity calculations, a review of gas handling principles and other safety related works.

The ethos of the Society is that the whole industry will be judged by the record of the least safe operator, and it is therefore to the benefit of all to help that operator by sharing technical and safety information as freely as possible.

10.14   OTHER ORGANISATIONS

There are many other national and international nautical and maritime organisations, as well as the great number of purely commercial groupings such as the freight conferences of the liner shipping industry. Almost every maritime discipline and service has its own bodies to regulate, inform or lobby for its members.

There is no self assessment question set for this Chapter but instead find out about three more international organisations which have not been mentioned above. You may prefer to find some based in your own part of the world. To assist here are some suggestions:

Comite Maritime International, Antwerp
CENSA, London
ECSA, Brussels
EMEC, Utrecht
GATT, Geneva
FAO, Rome
International Maritime Bureau, London
IAPH, Tokyo
ICC Commission on Sea Transport, Paris

that is only a sample of some of those from "C" to "I", there are many more!

10.15   TEST QUESTION

Having completed Chapter Ten attempt the following and send your essay to your Tutor:

Take a maritime organisation of your choice, examine the reasons for its establishment and comment on the extent to which it is successful in achieving its aims and objectives.

Appendices

CONTENTS

APPENDIX 1

Introduction to Worldscale Freight Rate Schedules

The concept of freight rate schedules is over 60 years old and originated during the 1939-1945 war.

Before the war, rates of freight for tanker voyage charters were expressed in dollars or shillings and pence per long ton (there were twenty shillings to a pound, 12 pence in a shilling) and this meant that when a charterer required wide loading or discharging options it was necessary to agree many rates of freight.

During the war, first the British Government and later the U.S. Government requisitioned shipping and Owners received compensation on the basis of a daily hire rate.

However, from time to time, the Government were able to make requisitioned tankers available on a voyage basis to the major oil companies for their private use particularly during the period from the end of hostilities until control of shipping was relinquished. On such occasions, the oil companies paid freight to the government concerned and the rate of freight, which was dependent upon the voyage performed, was determined in accordance with a scale or schedule of rates laid down by that government.

The rates were calculated so that, after allowing for port costs, bunker costs and canal expenses, the net daily revenue was the same for all voyages.

Here then was the genesis of the principle for tanker rate schedules, namely the Owners should receive the same net daily revenue irrespective of the voyage performed.

The last schedule of tanker voyage rates to be issued by the British Ministry of Transport gave rates effective 1st January 1946 and this schedule became known simply as "MOT". Similarly, the last rates to be issued by the United States Maritime Commission, which took effect from 1st February 1946, became known as "USMC".

In fact, government control of shipping continued until 1948 and by that time the tanker trade had come to recognise the advantages of freight rate schedules and therefore, in the free market, the system evolved of negotiating in terms of MOT or USMC plus or minus a percentage as dictated by the demand/supply position in the market.

Between 1952 and 1962 a number of different schedules were issued as a service to the tanker trade by non-governmental bodies; Scales Nos. 1, 2 and 3 and then Intascale in London, ATRS in New York.

Then in 1969 there came the joint London/New York production issued to replace both Intascale and ATRS called the "Worldwide Tanker Nominal Freight Scale", more usually know under its code name "Worldscale".

The full name is mentioned because it provides the opportunity to stress the word "nominal" and to emphasize that it was only during the period of government control that the schedule rates were intended to be used as actual rates. Subsequently, it has been freely negotiated percentage adjustments to the scale rates that has determined the actual rate used for the payment of freight.

APPENDIX 1

Incidentally, with the introduction of Worldscale, it became the custom to express market levels of freight in terms of a direct percentage of the scale rates instead of a plus or minus percentage. This method is known as "Points of Scale" and thus Worldscale 100 means 100 points of 100 per cent of the published rate or, in other words, the published rate itself, sometimes referred to as Worldscale flat, while Worldscale 250 means 250 points or 250 per cent of the published rate and Worldscale 30 means 30 points or 30 per cent of the published rate. Under the older method these would have been referred to as plus 150 per cent and minus 70 per cent respectively.

During its life span, from September 1969 until the end of 1988, Worldscale was regularly revised for changes in bunker prices and port costs but the fixed daily hire element of $1,800 remained constant.

Finally, to bring the story up to date, "New Worldscale" was introduced with effect from 1st January 1989. However, in deference to the custom that emerged in the trade, the epithet "new" was soon dropped and now it is generally understood that "Worldscale" refers to the new scale, while the previous scale is called "Old Worldscale".

Until the introduction of Old Worldscale, the various scales issued in London were all based on the old MOT rate of 32/6d (thirty two shillings and six pence) for the voyages Curacao to London. Indeed, the daily hire element of $1,800 used for Old Worldscale was indirectly related to that rate in so far as this, at the rate of exchange of £1/$2.40 (as applied in 1969), was close to the sterling hire rate for its immediate predecessor Intascale.

It was only when a replacement for Old Worldscale was being considered that systematic attempt was made to establish, by a series of lengthy exercises, the size of standard vessel and the relevant daily hire element that would provide the best practicable basis for a scale. It was concluded, from the results of these exercises, that a standard vessel with a carrying capacity of 75,000 tonnes and a daily hire element of $12,000 was likely to provide such a basis for a scale to be used during the 1990s.

Both "Worldscales" are the joint endeavour of two non-profit making organisations know as Worldscale Association (London) Limited and Worldscale Association (NYC) INC. NYC standing of course for New York City. Each company is under the control of a Management Committee, the members of which are senior brokers from leading tanker broking firms in London and New York respectively.

Worldscale is available on a subscription basis and the annual fee entitles the subscriber not only to the Schedule itself but also to notices of all amendments and the right to request rates for any voyage not shown in the Schedule.

APPENDIX 1

1. DEFINITIONS

the Associations	Worldscale Association (London) Limited, a company incorporated in England
	and
	Worldscale Association (NYC) Inc., a company incorporated in the USA
Worldscale	New Worldwide Tanker Nominal Freight Scale – i.e. the entire scale, comprising rates, fixed and variable rate differentials, and terms and conditions, etc. including but not limited to the rates, fixed and variable rate differentials, and terms and conditions contained in the Schedule.
the Schedule	the printed book as issued from time to time by the Associations.
the Preamble	that part of the Schedule, which precedes the rates pages, numbered "Preamble 1, Preamble 2", et seq.
USD	dollar ($), the currency of the United States of America.
tonne	a metric ton, i.e. 1000 kilograms.
USD/MT	dollars per tonne.
standard vessel	a vessel as described in Section 4 of Part A of the Preamble.

2. AREAS

Subscribers are (unless otherwise agreed with a particular Association) required to pay fees to the Association in whose area they are resident as follows:

NEW YORK	if resident in North, Central or South America or the Caribbean Islands (including the Bahamas), Bermuda, Greenland, or Hawaii
LONDON	if resident elsewhere.

Each Association maintains a comprehensive computer record of all rates calculated and enquiries should normally be made to the Association to which fees have been paid. If a rate is urgently required when the office of that Association is closed, an enquiry may be put to the other Association, giving the registered subscriber number.

APPENDIX 1

3. GENERAL

(1) Like its predecessors, the New Worldwide Tanker Nominal Freight Scale (Worldscale) is intended merely as a standard of reference to assist subscribers to conduct business.

It includes a number of "Terms and Conditions", which are set out in Part B of the Preamble.

Any additional "Terms and Conditions" applying to a particular port or trans-shipment area, which is not mentioned in Part D of the Preamble, will be stated when quoting the requested rate for the voyage in question.

Contracting parties are free to vary the "Terms and Conditions" as they see fit.

(2) The responsibility of each of the Associations is limited to providing subscribers with rates for voyages calculated in accordance with the basis of calculation described in Section 4 of Part A of the Preamble and to revising Worldscale in accordance with the procedure described in Section 9 of Part A of the Preamble.

The application of the rates, rate differentials and demurrage rates and the application or interpretation of the "Terms and Conditions" are matters which are solely the concern of the contracting parties and neither of the Associations will undertake to resolve disputes that may arise between subscribers.

(3) The nominal rate for a voyage does not in itself have any significance as representing a fair or reasonable rate for the standard vessel or any other size and/or type of vessel at any particular time.

(4) Market levels of freight are to be expressed in terms of a percentage of the nominal freight rate. Thus Worldscale 100 would mean the rate for the voyage in question as calculated and issued by the Associations, while Worldscale 175 would mean 175 per cent of that rate and Worldscale 75 would mean 75 per cent of that rate.

(5) Rates are calculated and quoted only in USD per tonne. However, freight may of course be payable in any currency and the contracting parties should specify clearly the currency of payment and the method to be used to determine the rate of exchange to apply if the currency of payment is to be other than USD.

(6) Rates are shown in the Schedule under the port or ports of discharge.

For an explanation of how to obtain rates for voyages involving loading at ports in the Arabian Gulf, Black Sea, or Lake Maracaibo, please refer to pages 1, 17 and 19 respectively.

(7) Rates for voyages not shown in the Schedule are available upon application to either of the Associations; as are rates for voyages involving ports and/or trans-shipment areas not mentioned in Part D of the Preamble.

(8) The fixed and variable rate differentials mentioned on pages D-1/D-8 must be taken into consideration when using Worldscale rates.

Any fixed or variable rate differential applying to a particular port or trans-shipment area, which is not mentioned in Part D of the Preamble, will be stated when quoting the requested rate for the voyage in question.

5.   NOTES ON CALCULATIONS

(1)   It is assumed that the standard vessel is able to navigate the selected route to reach and load or discharge at the ports concerned. See Section 6 of Part A of the Preamble for a description of the Route Policy.

(2)   Bunkers are deemed to be available at every port at the bunker price stated in Section 4 of Part A of the Preamble and, for the purposes of calculating cargo quantity, it is assumed that 50 per cent of the total bunkers required for the round voyage are required at the first loading port.

(3)   The port time mentioned under item (b) in Section 4 of Part A of the Preamble is deemed to include the laytime of 72 hours mentioned in Section 2 of Part B of the Preamble.

(4)   Rates are calculated for voyages with loading and discharging ports in whatever order is requested, irrespective of whether that order is consistent with the principle of geographical rotation.

(5)   No allowance is made for any Tax on Freight or Income Tax, nor is there any provision as to whether such Taxes are for Owners' or for Charterers' Account.

(6)   No allowance is made for any additional Marine Insurance on hull or machinery, including War Risk Insurance, which may be incurred when trading to or from certain areas.

(7)   No allowance is made for deviation for any purpose whatsoever.

(8)   No allowance is made for any deballasting expenses, nor is there any provision as to whether such costs are for Owners' or Charterers' Account.

(9)   An allowance has been made for ISPS costs in ports whenever such costs have been advised to the Associations.

(10)   An allowance has been made for all European Union (EU) Ports for the increase in costs of fuel with a sulphur content not exceeding 0.1% for fuel used in EU ports.

6.   ROUTE POLICY/DISTANCES

(1)   The following route indicators are used both in the Schedule and when quoting rates in response to requests from subscribers.

   C   which means via Cape of Good Hope, laden and in ballast.
   CS   which means via Cape of Good Hope, laden, Suez Canal in ballast.
   S   which means via Suez Canal, laden and in ballast.
   P   which means via Panama Canal, laden and in ballast.
   CP   which means via Cape of Good Hope, laden, Panama Canal in ballast.
   H   which means via Cape Horn, laden and in ballast.
   CH   which means via Cape of Good Hope, laden and in ballast, and Cape Horn, laden and in ballast.

(2)   Except as otherwise explained, the route used for a rate shown in the Schedule (for the round voyage from loading port or ports to discharging port or ports and return to first loading port) is that which produces the lowest rate for the voyage in question at Worldscale 100.

   In most cases, such a route is that via the most direct normal shipping route, which usually means via whatever route provides the shortest distance (see Paragraph 8). However, in those cases where, for rate calculation purposes, extra time is allowed for transit of a canal and/or an allowance made for expenses incurred for transit of a canal, waterway or strait, the rate shown may not be via the route with the shortest distance but via a route which, although longer, nevertheless produces the lowest rate. In deciding which route produces the lowest rate, the fixed rate differentials for Panama Canal and/or Suez Canal transits as applicable to the standard vessel are taken into account.

   Rates are shown in the Schedule for both of the following routes whenever they are viable alternatives:

   (a)   Suez Canal, laden and in ballast, (S); and

   (b)   Cape of Good Hope, laden and in ballast, (C);

   also, in some cases, a rate is shown via a third route, namely

   (c)   Cape of Good Hope, laden, Suez Canal in ballast, (CS),

   whenever such a route produces the lowest rate.

   The parties to a contract should agree which one of the two or three rates should apply.

(3)   There are several examples of routes that are not used for rates shown in the Schedule, in spite of the fact that they may produce a lower rate.

   For instance, when calculating routes for voyages which involve passage through Danish waters (Belts and Sound) from Skaw to the Baltic Sea or vice versa it is assumed that the vessel will proceed via the Great Belt when laden (fully or partly) and via the Sound when in ballast, notwithstanding that a route via the Sound, both laden and in ballast, may produce a lower rate.

APPENDIX 1

5. NOTES ON CALCULATIONS

(1)   It is assumed that the standard vessel is able to navigate the selected route to reach and load or discharge at the ports concerned. See Section 6 of Part A of the Preamble for a description of the Route Policy.

(2)   Bunkers are deemed to be available at every port at the bunker price stated in Section 4 of Part A of the Preamble and, for the purposes of calculating cargo quantity, it is assumed that 50 per cent of the total bunkers required for the round voyage are required at the first loading port.

(3)   The port time mentioned under item (b) in Section 4 of Part A of the Preamble is deemed to include the laytime of 72 hours mentioned in Section 2 of Part B of the Preamble.

(4)   Rates are calculated for voyages with loading and discharging ports in whatever order is requested, irrespective of whether that order is consistent with the principle of geographical rotation.

(5)   No allowance is made for any Tax on Freight or Income Tax, nor is there any provision as to whether such Taxes are for Owners' or for Charterers' Account.

(6)   No allowance is made for any additional Marine Insurance on hull or machinery, including War Risk Insurance, which may be incurred when trading to or from certain areas.

(7)   No allowance is made for deviation for any purpose whatsoever.

(8)   No allowance is made for any deballasting expenses, nor is there any provision as to whether such costs are for Owners' or Charterers' Account.

(9)   An allowance has been made for ISPS costs in ports whenever such costs have been advised to the Associations.

(10)   An allowance has been made for all European Union (EU) Ports for the increase in costs of fuel with a sulphur content not exceeding 0.1% for fuel used in EU ports.

6. ROUTE POLICY/DISTANCES

(1)   The following route indicators are used both in the Schedule and when quoting rates in response to requests from subscribers.

    C   which means via Cape of Good Hope, laden and in ballast.
    CS   which means via Cape of Good Hope, laden, Suez Canal in ballast.
    S   which means via Suez Canal, laden and in ballast.
    P   which means via Panama Canal, laden and in ballast.
    CP   which means via Cape of Good Hope, laden, Panama Canal in ballast.
    H   which means via Cape Horn, laden and in ballast.
    CH   which means via Cape of Good Hope, laden and in ballast, and Cape Horn, laden and in ballast.

(2)   Except as otherwise explained, the route used for a rate shown in the Schedule (for the round voyage from loading port or ports to discharging port or ports and return to first loading port) is that which produces the lowest rate for the voyage in question at Worldscale 100.

In most cases, such a route is that via the most direct normal shipping route, which usually means via whatever route provides the shortest distance (see Paragraph 8). However, in those cases where, for rate calculation purposes, extra time is allowed for transit of a canal and/or an allowance made for expenses incurred for transit of a canal, waterway or strait, the rate shown may not be via the route with the shortest distance but via a route which, although longer, nevertheless produces the lowest rate. In deciding which route produces the lowest rate, the fixed rate differentials for Panama Canal and/or Suez Canal transits as applicable to the standard vessel are taken into account.

Rates are shown in the Schedule for both of the following routes whenever they are viable alternatives:

(a)   Suez Canal, laden and in ballast, (S); and

(b)   Cape of Good Hope, laden and in ballast, (C);

also, in some cases, a rate is shown via a third route, namely

(c)   Cape of Good Hope, laden, Suez Canal in ballast, (CS),

whenever such a route produces the lowest rate.

The parties to a contract should agree which one of the two or three rates should apply.

(3)   There are several examples of routes that are not used for rates shown in the Schedule, in spite of the fact that they may produce a lower rate.

For instance, when calculating routes for voyages which involve passage through Danish waters (Belts and Sound) from Skaw to the Baltic Sea or vice versa it is assumed that the vessel will proceed via the Great Belt when laden (fully or partly) and via the Sound when in ballast, notwithstanding that a route via the Sound, both laden and in ballast, may produce a lower rate.

Also, the route used for rates shown in the Schedule for voyages involving ports located within the entrances to the Baltic Sea (the area between the Skaw and a line joining Trelleborg and Cape Arkona) may not be that which produces the lowest rate. Details of the route actually used when calculating such rates will be provided upon request. See also (7) below.

Other examples of routes that are not used, notwithstanding that they may produce lower rates are:

Cape Cod Canal (except for voyages involving Sandwich (Mass.))
Chesapeake and Delaware Canal
Kiel Canal (except for voyages involving Rendsburg).

Passages through the Minches
Passages inside the Great Barrier Reef except for access to Queensland ports.

(4)   It is assumed that the standard vessel is able to navigate unhindered in the Japanese Inland Sea.

(5)   The principles referred to in (2), (3) and (4) above will also be followed when calculating rates for voyages not shown in the Schedule, but see (6) below.

(6)   Rates for voyages via any route nominated by a subscriber are available upon application. However, if the rate calculated on the basis of the nominated route does not conform to the principles referred to in (2), (3) and (4) above, the subscriber will be so informed and the use of such a rate will be dependent upon specific agreement between the contracting parties.

(7)   The actual route used (laden and in ballast) for any rate, whether in the Schedule or not, will be provided upon request.

(8)   Distances used for rate calculation purposes on the basis of the round voyage appear in the Schedule after the rate and are established by reference to the new BP Shipping Marine Distance Tables (2004) produced by AtoBviaC plc as at 30th September 2009 or, if these tables do not include necessary distances, they are obtained from AtoBviaC plc direct, using the basis upon which the new Distance Tables were developed. The distances shown in the Schedule are for rate calculation and no other purpose. We are advised by AtoBviaC plc that the new distance tables, in both electronic and printed formats, show distances, in nautical miles, that are, in most cases, the shortest sea route or the sea route customarily followed by merchant ships, with the following major distinction; the shortest sea route distances in the new Distance Tables now take into account IMO Conventions, littoral state legislation and published official recommendations for environmentally sensitive routeing.

(9)   Also see Section 5 of Part A of the Preamble.

7.   ASSESSMENT OF PORT COSTS

See Section 4 and 5 of Part B of the Preamble.

Although some assumptions have to be made, the objective is to include in the rate calculations realistic allowances for all of those port cost items which are levied against the vessel (i.e. are for Owners' Account) even when they are assessed on the quantity of cargo loaded or discharged or by reference to the time spent in port/alongside a berth.

In general terms, this means that allowances are made for vessel's items such as these:

Light Dues, both National and Local
Pilotage, in and out
Towage, in and out
Terminal Fees/Charges
Mooring and Unmooring expenses
Stand-by Tugs and/or Stand-by Launches, when compulsory
Watchmen
Conservancy Dues
Harbour Dues
Port Dues
Quay Dues
Berth Hire
Tonnage Dues
Wharfage/Dockage/Berthage
Launches
Port Clearance
Quarantine/Free Pratique Fees
Customs Surveillance/Attendance
Customs Overtime
Sundries and Petties
Agency
ISPS Costs

See page Preamble 4, 5. Notes on Calculations (9) regarding ISPS costs.

APPENDIX 1

The above is not a comprehensive list and subscribers may seek clarification from the Associations as to whether or not an allowance has been made for any items that do not fall under one of these broad headings. (Also see Section 4 of Part B of the Preamble.)

Occasionally, it will be necessary to make particular items that are levied upon or against the vessel "For Charterers' Account", which means, there being no allowance for such an item in the rate, that Owners are entitled to obtain reimbursement from Charterers for the cost involved. Such items, together with certain others that are directly "For Charterers' Account", are listed in Section 5 of Part B of the Preamble.

When assessing port costs:

(a)   It is assumed that the standard vessel proceeds direct to the cargo handling place upon arrival at a port.

(b)   The allowance made for an item that is related to time is based upon 48 hours.

(c)   The allowance made for an item that is based upon the quantity of cargo loaded or discharged is always based upon a full cargo for the standard vessel, irrespective of the number of loading or discharging ports on the voyage.

(d)   In cases where a port operates a dual charging system for non segregated and segregated ballast tanks and/or double hulls the port costs have been assessed using the lowest rate.

(e)   For an item that is payable either on a "single-trip" basis or on a reduced "multi-trip" basis the allowance made is on the basis of a "single-trip".

(f)   No allowance is made for any costs that would not be incurred by a vessel of the size of the standard vessel.

(g)   No allowance is made for items or surcharges on items that are incurred only at certain times of the year.

However, in some cases, such items or surcharges are made "For Charterers' Account". See Section 5 of Part B of the Preamble under:

Canada
Denmark
Estonia
Finland
Germany
Norway
Russia
U.S.A.
Former U.S.S.R.

(h)   Also see Section 5 (5) of Part A of the Preamble regarding Tax on Freight and Income Tax.

(i)   Also see Section 5 (8) of Part A of the Preamble regarding deballasting expenses.

8.   VARIOUS TRANSIT/VOYAGE EXPENSES

Apart from the port costs described above it is also necessary to include costs incurred during sea passage, canals, straits etc. Listed below are those areas where expenses are incurred and appropriate cost allowance have been made in either the flat rate calculation or shown as a differential:

ARGENTINA	Pilotage costs & Dredging (when applicable) for passage through the Martin Garcia & Mitre Channels.
AUSTRALIA	Pilotage costs for passages through the Torres Straits pilotage area.
CHILE	Pilotage and Light Dues (when applicable) for transiting the Magellan Straits.
DENMARK	Danish Pilotage costs for passages through Skaw, Kattegat, Great and Little Belts and the Sound to and from the Baltic Sea. Tolls and expenses for transiting the Kiel Canal.
EGYPT	Suez Canal Transit Tolls and expenses are subject to the Fixed Differential shown on page D-2.
ITALY	Pilotage costs for transiting the Messina Straits.
JAPAN	Costs of Pilot/escort boats for transiting the Inland Sea and Osaka Bay.
PANAMA	Panama Canal Transit Tolls are subject to the Fixed Differential on page D-1. Miscellaneous transit expenses are included in the flat rate.

APPENDIX 1

TURKEY	Pilotage, Sanitary Dues, Light Dues, Life Saving/Salvage Dues, Agency fees and petties incurred whilst transiting the Dardanelles and Bosporous Straits.
	In recognition of night navigation restrictions an extra 12 hours has been added to the flat rate calculations for each transit of the Turkish Straits (i.e. a transit of the Dardanelles and the Bosporous Straits equals one transit of the Turkish Straits for Worldscale purposes).
UKRAINE	Pilotage and Channel Dues for transiting the Kertch Straits.
USA	Pilotage costs and expenses for transiting the Cape Cod Canal and Chesapeake and Delaware Canal.

9. REVISION POLICY

Worldscale will be completely recalculated once every twelve months providing revised rates effective as from 1st January of each year that reflect changes in bunker prices and port costs (as per page Preamble 3) and also changes in distances provided by AtoBviaC plc on 30th September each year.

For each revision an average worldwide bunker price between October to September prior to the effective date will be used. This bunker price, which will be assessed by LQM Petroleum Services, Inc., will be stated in Section 4 (d) of Part A of the Preamble to each edition of the Schedule.

Port costs used will be those assessed by the Associations in the light of information available to them up to the end of September prior to the effective date. Port costs will be converted from local currency to USD using the average rate of exchange applicable during September prior to the effective date. For the guidance of subscribers sample exchange rates for selected currencies will be stated in Section 4 (e) of Part A of the Preamble.

Interim revisions will be confined to those thought necessary in the judgement of the Associations because of significant changes in port costs arising from tariff revisions at particular ports.

10. TRANS-SHIPMENT AREAS

List 3 of Part D of the Preamble shows most of those places and their approximate locations that are presently designated by the Associations as being "trans-shipment areas". This list is arranged by geographical area. Elsewhere in the Schedule, trans-shipment areas are identified by means of the letters TSA in brackets after the name.

The Associations define a trans-shipment area as a place at which cargo is transferred that is outside the limits of a port and where there are no mooring facilities.

All rates for voyages which involve a trans-shipment area shown in List 3 of Part D of the Preamble, whether as a sole loading/discharging place or combined with loading/discharging at a port or ports, are incorporated with other rates throughout the Schedule.

Such rates are calculated in accordance with the basis of calculation set out in Section 4 of Part A of the Preamble, a trans-shipment area being deemed to be a "port" for rate calculation purposes.

Places other than those shown in List 3 of Part D of the Preamble may be designated as "trans-shipment areas" by the Associations. Rates for voyages involving such trans-shipment areas as the sole loading/ discharging place are obtainable upon application to the Associations and will be regarded as "official" rates. However, rates for voyages involving partial loading/discharging at any trans-shipment area not shown in List 3 of Section 3 of Part D of the Preamble, combined with a port or ports, will be regarded as "special" rates and their use will be dependent upon agreement between the contracting parties.

List 3 of Part D of the Preamble is subject to revision from time to time.

PREAMBLE PART B
TERMS AND CONDITIONS

1. EFFECTIVE DATE

This edition of Worldscale shall apply for all voyages on which loading is commenced on or after the 1st January 2010, except in the case of amendments that are notified by circulars as being effective from subsequent dates.

2. LAYTIME

The time allowed for loading and discharging shall be 72 hours and shall be subject to whatever qualifications, if any, that are stated in the applicable charter party or contract.

3. PORT AND TERMINAL COMBINATIONS

(1) Any two or more of the places in any one of the combinations shown below are to be regarded, for freight and demurrage purposes, as "berths within a single port".

The first named place (shown in bold print) in the list of such combinations is the port name under which rates are shown in the Schedule and, subject to any fixed or variable rate differential that may apply, the rate shown also applies to any other place in the same group.

(2) There are no terms and conditions under Worldscale relating to the settlement of shifting costs. The settlement of such costs shall be governed by the terms and conditions of the applicable charter party or contract.

(3) This list of port and terminal combinations includes most of those that apply for the purposes of Worldscale; however it should not be regarded as a complete list.

Also, in the case of any particular combination shown, there may be places, in addition to those mentioned, that are designated by the Associations as coming within that combination.

(4) List 1 of Part D of the Preamble includes cross references to places mentioned in this Section of Part B of the Preamble.

CARIBBEAN AREA

ARUBA:	All terminals
BAHAMAS:	(a) **Nassau** and Clifton Pier
	(b) **Freeport** and Boro
COLOMBIA:	(a) **Mamonal** and Cartagena
	(b) **Pozos Colorados** and Santa Marta
COSTA RICA:	**Port Limon**, Moin Bay and Puerto Moin
CUBA:	(a) **Antilla**, Nicaro, Preston and Felton
	(b) **Guantanamo** (US Base), Boqueron and Deseo
	(c) **Nuevitas**, Bufadero, Pastelillo and Tarafa
JAMAICA:	**Port Esquivel** and Escobedo
PUERTO RICO:	(a) **Guayama**, Jobos, Puerto de Las Mareas and Arroyo
	(b) **Guayanilla** and Tallaboa Bay
	(c) **San Juan**, Bayamon and Catano
TRINIDAD:	**Trinidad**, Point Lisas, Pointe a Pierre, Point Fortin and Point D'or
VENEZUELA:	(a) **El Palito**, Moron, Puerto Cabello and Borburta
	(b) **Puerto la Cruz**, Guaraguao Terminal (El Chaure), Jose Monobuoy, Jose Platform (TAECJ), Jose Terminal and Petrozuata
	(c) **Paraguana Refinery Center – CRP**, Amuay Bay, Las Piedras, Punta Cardon and Punta Fijo

MEXICO

	(a) **Coatzacoalcos**, Nanchital, Pajaritos, Rabon Grande and Puerto Mexico
	(b) **Tampico**, Ciudad Madero, Altimira and Tamaulipas
	(c) **Lazaro Cardenas** (Mexico) and Bahia de Petacalco
	(d) **Cantarell Offshore Terminal** and Ta Kuntah

U.S. GULF

BAYTOWN:	**Baytown**, Bayport, Lunchburg and Lynchburg
BEAUMONT:	**Beaumont**, Atreco, Magpetco, Nederland, Orange, Port Arthur, Port Neches, Sabine and Smiths Bluff
BROWNSVILLE:	**Brownsville** and Port Isabel

APPENDIX 1

CORPUS CHRISTI:	**Corpus Christi**, Aransas Pass, Harbor Island and Ingleside
HOUSTON:	All ports and terminals on the Houston Ship Channel, west of Lynchburg, including Galena Park, Deer Park and Pasadena
LAKE CHARLES:	**Lake Charles**, Clifton Ridge and Devil's Elbow
MISSISSIPPI RIVER:	(a) **Ostrica**, Empire, Pilot Town and any port/terminal above South West Pass but below Empire
	(b) **New Orleans**, Alliance, Amesville, Chalmette, Gretna, Marrero, Meraux, Westwego and any ports/terminals above Empire but below Huey Long Bridge in New Orleans
	(c) **Good Hope (La)**, AMA Anchorage, Avondale, Destrehan, Norco, St. Rose, Taft and any ports/terminals above Huey Long Bridge in New Orleans but below Norco
	(d) **Convent**, Garyville, St. James (La.) and any ports/terminals above Norco but below Convent
	(e) **Baton Rouge**, Port Allen and any ports/terminals above Convent but below Port Allen
MOBILE:	**Mobile** and Blakely Island
POINT COMFORT:	**Point Comfort** and Port Lavaca
TAMPA:	**Tampa**, Port Tampa, Port Manatee and St. Petersburg
TEXAS CITY:	**Texas City** and Galveston

U.S.A. AND CANADA–EAST COAST

BALTIMORE:	**Baltimore** and Annopolis Anchorge
BOSTON (Mass.):	**Boston (Mass.)**, Castle Island, Chelsea, East Braintree, Everett, North Weymouth, Quincy and Revere
DELAWARE RIVER:	**Philadelphia**, Claymount, Delair, Eagle Point, Fort Miflin, Mantua, Marcus Hook, Paulsboro, Pennsauken, Point Breeze, Westville and Wilmington
FALL RIVER:	**Fall River**, Brayton Point and Somerset
HALIFAX:	**Halifax**, Darthmouth and Tufts Cove
HUDSON RIVER:	(a) **Peekskill**, Hastings-on-Hudson and any ports/terminals above Yonkers but below Peekskill
	(b) **Kingston (N.Y.)**, Newburgh, Poughkeepsie, Roseton and any ports/terminals above Peekskill but below Kingston
	(c) **Albany (N.Y.)**, Ravena, Rensselaer and any ports/terminals above Kingston but below Albany
MIAMI:	**Miami** and Fisher Island
MOREHEAD CITY:	**Morehead City** and Beaufort
NEW LONDON (Conn.):	**New London (Conn.)** and Groton
NEW YORK:	All terminals in New York Harbor Area, provided not north of Yonkers (Hudson River), not east of Throggs Neck Bridge, not south of Sandy Hook Bay, not west of Edison Bridge
NORFOLK (Va.):	**Norfolk**, Cape Charles, Chesapeake, Craney Island, Newport News, Portsmouth (Va.), Sewell's Point and York town
POINT TUPPER:	**Point Tupper** and Port Hawkesbury
PORT EVERGLADES:	**Port Everglades** and Fort Lauderdale
PORTLAND (Me.):	**Portland (Me.)**, Cousins Island and Yarmouth
PORTSMOUTH (N.H.):	**Portsmouth (N.H.)** and Newington
PROVIDENCE (R.I.):	**Providence (R.I.)** and Kettle Point
SEVEN ISLANDS:	**Seven Islands** and Pointe Noire
SOREL:	**Sorel** and Tracey
ST. JOHN (N.B.):	**St. John (N.B.)** and Canaport
TIVERTON:	**Tiverton** and Melville
VANCOUVER:	**Vancouver** and Nanaimo

APPENDIX 1

U.S.A. AND CANADA–WEST COAST

ALASKA: **Nikishka** and Kenai

COLUMBIA RIVER: **Portland (Ore.)**, Linnton, Longview, St. Helens, Vancouver (Wash.) and Willbridge

LOS ANGELES: **Los Angeles**, Edington Anchorage, Huntington Beach, Long Beach, San Pedro and Wilmington

PUGET SOUND:
(a) **Anacortes**, Bellingham, Cherry Point, Equilon, Ferndale and Oak Harbor
(b) **Seattle**, Bremerton, Edmonds, Everett, Manchester, Mukilteo, Point Wells and Riverton
(c) **Tacoma** and Olympia

SAN FRANCISCO BAY: **San Francisco**, Amorco, Avon, Benicia, Martinez, Oakland, Oleum, Port Costa, Point Orient, Redwood City, Richmond, Rodeo Terminal and Hunters Point

VANCOUVER (B.C.): **Vancouver (B.C.)**, Burnaby, Crofton, Harmac, Ioco, Nanaimo, Port Moody and Shellburn

HAWAIIAN ISLANDS (U.S.A.)

OAHU ISLAND: **Honolulu** and Pearl Harbor

CENTRAL AMERICA

GUATEMALA: **San Jose** and Escuintla

PANAMA:
(a) **Balboa APSA Terminal** and Port Rodman
(b) **Chiriqui Grande** and Rambala
(c) **Puerto Armuelles (PTP)** and Charco Azul
(d) **Taboguilla Terminal** and Decal SA Terminal

SOUTH AMERICA

ARGENTINA:
(a) **Buenos Aires**, Darsena and Dock Sud
(b) **Comodoro Rivadavia**, Caleta Cordova, Caleta Olivares, Caleta Olivia and Golfo San Jorge
(c) **Puerto Galvan** and Bahia Blanca
(d) **Puerto Rosales**, Punta Ancla SBM and Punta Cleguena SBM

BRAZIL:
(a) **Bonito SBM** and Marimbo SBM
(b) **Madre de Deus**, Bahia and Salvador (Brazil)
(c) **Rio de Janeiro** and Manguinhos Terminal
(d) **Sao Luiz de Maranhao**, Italqui and Ponta de Madre
(e) **Tebig Terminal**, Andro SBM, Angra Dos Reis and Ilha Grand Bay
(f) **Tramandai**, Porto alegre and Santa Clara

CHILE:
(a) **Chanaral**, Barquito and Caleta Borquito
(b) **Coquimbo** and Guayacan
(c) **Quintero Bay** and Puerto Ventanas
(d) **Valparaiso** and Las Salenas Terminal

ECUADOR: **Esmeraldas** and Balao

FAR EAST, ETC.

AUSTRALIA:
(a) **Adelaide** and Birkenhead
(b) **Botany Bay** and Kurnell
(c) **Melbourne**, Altona and Williamstown
(d) **Port Walcott**, Cape Lambert and Samson Point

CHINA: **Bohai BZ Terminals** – BZ 28 Terminal and BZ 34 Terminal

INDONESIA:
(a) **Djakarta** and Tandjung Priok
(b) **Pladju**, Palembang and Sungei Gerong
(c) **Tandjung Uban** and Pulo Sambu

JAPAN:
(a) **Chiba**, Anegasaki and Goi
(b) **Funakawa** and Akita
(c) **Kanmon**, Kokura, Moji, Mutsure, Shimonoseki, Tobata, Wakamatsu and Yawata
(d) **Nagoya** and Chita
(e) **Shimotsu**, Kainan and Wakayama
(f) **Tokuyama** and Kudamatsu
(g) **Yokohama**, Kawasaki, Negishi and Tokyo
(h) **Yokosuka** and Koshiba

APPENDIX 1

KOREA – SOUTH:	**Ulsan** and Onsan
MALAYA:	**Penang** and Prai
NEW ZEALAND:	**Whangarei** and Marsden Point
OKINAWA:	**Nakagusuku** and Nishihara
PAPUA NEW GUINEA:	**Port Moresby** and Napa Napa
PHILIPPINES:	**Batangas Bay** – Batangas and Tabangao
SINGAPORE:	**Singapore**, Jurong, Pasir Panjang, Pulau Ayer Chawan, Pulau Merimau, Pulo Bukom, Pulo Busing, Pulo Sebarok, Tanjong Pagar, Tanjong Penjuru and Woodlands
THAILAND:	**Map Ta Phut** and Rayong
VIETNAM:	**Bach ho** and Rong Field

RED SEA

SAUDI ARABIA:	**Yanbu**, Al Muajjiz Terminal and King Fahd Industrial Port (Yanbu)

U.A.E.

FUJAIRAH:	**Port of Fujairah**, Vopak Terminal and Fujairah Refining Co.

MEDITERRANEAN

ALGERIA:	**Arzew** and Bethioua
CROATIA:	(a) **Rijeka**, Bakar, Susak and Urinj (b) **Split** and Solin
FRANCE:	**Lavera**, Fos and St. Louis Du Rhone
GREECE:	(a) **Megara** and Pachi
ITALY:	(a) **Ancona** and Falconara (b) **Augusta** Priolo ERG/ISAB (North Site) (c) **Cagliari**, Porto Foxi and Sarroch (d) **Santa Panagia Bay**, Magnisi and Priolo ERG/ISAB (South Site) (e) **Savona** and Vado (f) **Trieste** and Monfalcone (g) **Venice** and Porto Marghera
MALTA:	**Malta**, Marsaxlokk Bay and Valletta
SPAIN:	**Cartagena** and Escombreras
TURKEY:	(a) **Aliaga** and Nemrut Bay (b) **Gulf of Izmit** – Derince, Izmit and Tutunciftlik (c) **Istanbul**, Ambarli, Cekmece, Haramidere (or Thrace), Haydarpasa, Kartal and Serviburnu

WEST AFRICA

ANGOLA:	(a) **Cabinda**, Malongo Terminal and Takula (b) **Xikomba Terminal**, Kizomba A FPSO, Kizomba B FPSO and Kizomba C FPSO
GABON:	**Port Gentil** and Cap Lopez
NIGERIA:	(a) **Bonny**, Bonny Anchorage and Inshore Bonny (b) **Lagos**, Apapa, Atlas Cove and Lagos SBM (c) **Port Harcourt** and Okrika

U.K./CONTINENT AND SCANDINAVIA

BELGIUM:	(a) **Antwerp** and Hemixem (b) **Ghent**, Doornzelle and Ertvelde
DENMARK:	(a) **Aabenraa** and Ensted (b) **Aalborg** and Norresundby (c) **Gulfhavn** and Stignaes
FRANCE:	(a) **Bordeaux**, Bec D'Ambes and Pauillac (b) **Dunkirk** and Gravelines (c) **Havre**, Antifer, Berville and Gonfreville (d) **Loire River** – Cordemais, Donges, Nantes and St. Nazaire (e) **Rouen**, Gravenchon, Petit Couronne, Port Jerome and Honfleur

APPENDIX 1

GERMANY:	(a) **Bremen**, Blexen, Brake, Bremerhaven, Einswarden, Farge and Nordenham
	(b) **Brunsbuttel** and Ostermoor
	(c) **Hamburg**, Harburg, Hoheschaar, Stade, Stadersand and Wilhelmsburg
ICELAND:	**Reykjavik**, Hafnarfjordur, Hvalfjordur, Laugarnes, Orfirisey, Skerjafjordur and Akureyri
NETHERLANDS:	**Rotterdam**. Botlek, Dordrecht, Europoort, Pernis and Vlaardingen
NORWAY:	(a) **Heroya** and Porsgrunn
	(b) **Oslo**, Ekeberg, Fagerstrand, Halvorshavn, Lysaker, Sjursoya, Slemmestad and Steilene
SWEDEN:	(a) **Gothenburg**, Hjartholmen, Rhyahamen and Skarvikshamnen
	(b) **Malmo** and Limhamn
	(c) **Norrkoping**, Affarsverken, Gastgivarehagen and Ramshall
	(d) **Ornskoldsvik**, Domsjo, Husum and Kopmanholmen
	(e) **Skredsvik**, Lysekil and Munkedal
	(f) **Stockholm**, Bergs Oljehamn, Flaxenvik, Gashaga, Kvarnholmen, Loudden, Rasta, Resaro, St. Hoggarn, Telegrafberget and Vartan
	(g) **Sundsvall**, Essvik, Fagervik, Johannedal, Ortviken, Ostrand, Svartvik and Wifstavarf
	(h) **Umea**, Holmsund and Obbola
UNITED KINGDOM:	(a) **Avonmouth** and Bristol
	(b) **Humber River** – All terminals
	(c) **London**, Canvey Island, Cliffe, Coryton, Dagenham, Grays, Holehaven, Littlebrook, Northfleet, Purfleet, Shellhaven and Thameshaven
	(d) **Manchester Ship Canal** –Eastham, Stanlow, Ellesmere Port and Ince
	(e) **Medway River** – Isle of Grain and Kingsnorth
	(f) **Milford Haven**, Angle Bay and Pembroke Dock
	(g) **Tees River** – All terminals
	(h) **Tyne River** – Jarrow and Newcastle

4. OWNERS' ACCOUNT

Dues and other charges which are levied upon or against the vessel, even when assessed on the quantity of cargo loaded or discharged, shall be paid by Owners and shall be for Owners' Account. However, Owners shall be reimbursed by Charterers for costs they have incurred in respect of items specified as being "For Charterers' Account" in Section 5 of Part B of the Preamble.
See page Preamble 4, 5. Notes on Calculations (9) regarding ISPS costs.

5. CHARTERERS' ACCOUNT

Dues and other charges which are levied upon or against the cargo shall be paid by the Charterers and shall be for Charterers' Account.

Without prejudice to the generality of the foregoing, the following particular items shall be for Charterers' Account, even when such an item is levied upon or against the vessel and is payable in the first instance by Owners.

ALGERIA:	(a) Dues (i.e. Droits de Quai, Redevances, Portuaires) assessed on the vessel's GT and on the quantity of cargo loaded or discharged
	(b) Standby Tugs at the **SPM's** of Arzew, Skikda and Bejaia
ANGOLA:	(a) Pipeline charges
	(b) Mooring charges
ARGENTINA:	(a) Standby Tugs at Puerto Rosales SBM
	(b) O.R.S.O Oil Pollution charges
AUSTRALIA:	(a) "Emergency Response Tug Service" charges, or Hazardous Cargo Fee at Fremantle and Kwinana
	(b) Draft surcharge on Tonnage/Channel dues at Geelong
	(c) Port enhancement charge assessed on the quantity of cargo loaded or discharged at Geraldton
BAHAMAS:	(a) Additional Launch Hire
	(b) Tug hire for other than berthing/unberthing
	(c) Wharfage at Nassau
BERMUDA:	Wharfage assessed on the quantity of cargo discharged at St. George's (Bermuda).
BRAZIL:	Port Dues which includes wharfage (Port/Canal Utilization Taxes/Inframar Tax/Protection and Access to the Port)

APPENDIX 1

Charterers' Account (contd.)

CAMEROUN:	Tonnage Dues/Cargo Dues assessed on the quantity of cargo loaded or discharged
CANADA:	(a) Berthage and Wharfage
	(b) Escort tugs at Come by Chance
	(c) Extra Towage and Pilotage costs during the Winter Season
	(d) Standby launches and Standby tugs at Canaport, St. John (N.B.)
	(e) Escort tugs at all ports in British Columbia
	(f) Escort tugs at Halifax
	(g) BOCF costs assessed on the quantity of cargo loaded or discharged and administration fees
	(h) Marine Service Fees
	(i) Canadian Ice Breaking Fee during the Winter Season
CANARY ISLANDS:	J.O.P. (Junta del Obras del Puerto) dues assessed on the quantity of cargo loaded or discharged at Las Palmas
CARIBBEAN ISLANDS:	(a) Cargo dues assessed on the quantity of cargo loaded or discharged at Georgetown (Gd. Cayman)
	(b) Towage costs at St. Lucia
CHILE:	Dockage/Wharfage
CHINA – PEOPLE'S REPUBLIC OF:	(a) Superintendency fee
	(b) Sea Channel Maintenance charge
	(c) Towage at Huizhou (Shore Terminals)
CROATIA:	Port Dues assessed on the quantity of cargo loaded or discharged
DENMARK:	(a) Ice Dues
	(b) Surcharge on Towage during the Winter Season
ECUADOR:	(a) Lighthouse and Buoy Dues
	(b) Port Dues (Derechos Portuarios) assessed on the quantity of cargo loaded or discharged
	(c) Standby Tugs and Tugs for Mooring and Unmooring at the OCP, Tempre Terminal, and Sote Terminals Esmeraldas
ESTONIA:	(a) Surcharges on Navigation Dues during the Winter Season
	(b) Surcharge on Towage during the Winter Season
FIJI:	Dock Dues at Lautoka
FINLAND:	(a) Surcharge on Harbour Dues during the Winter Season
	(b) Surcharge on Towage during the Winter Season
	(c) Fairway Dues
	(d) Standby/Escort Tugs at Porvoo and Naantali
FRANCE:	(a) CIM and SHMPP Dues (Basin Taxes) at Havre and Antifer
	(b) Charge for boatmen placing anti-pollution belt whilst discharging at APF Terminal, Dunkirk
	(c) Jetty Dues (Taxes d'Appontement) assessed on the quantity of cargo loaded or discharged at Dunkirk
	(d) Petroleum Tax at Sete
	(e) Harbour Dues at Loire River
GAMBIA:	Harbour Dues assessed on the quantity of cargo loaded or discharged at Banjul
GERMANY:	(a) Ice Surcharges
	(b) Surcharge on Mooring during the Winter Season
	(c) Surcharge on Towage during the Winter Season
GHANA:	Port Dues of any description assessed on the quantity of cargo loaded or discharged
GUATEMALA:	Terminal Fees based on cost per barrel at Puma Energy Terminal, San Jose
GUINEA REPUBLIC:	(a) Side and Top Wharfage and Channel Maintenance Surcharge assessed on the quantity of cargo loaded or discharged at Kamsar
	(b) Armatorial Dues/SNG Tax/Shipping Royalty
HAITI:	Dockage/Wharfage/Berthage
HAWAIIAN ISLANDS (U.S.A.):	(a) Dockage and Wharfage, Pipeline Charges
	(b) Additional tug from Honolulu for Hilo and Kahului
INDIA:	Pull Back Tugs and Launch Hire charges at Jamnagar SPM's'
ITALY:	Standby Tugs at Genoa
IRAN:	Side Wharfage Fee
IVORY COAST:	Port Operation Fee based on quantity of cargo loaded or discharged

APPENDIX 1

KOREA SOUTH:	(a) Standby, Mooring and Unmooring Tugs at the Dae San SBM (b) Standby Tugs and Tailing Tugs at Keoje
MALAYSIA:	Charges of any description that are assessed on the quantity of cargo loaded or discharged
MALTA:	Wharfage assessed on the quantity of cargo loaded or discharged at Oiltanking Terminal, Marsaxlokk
MEXICO:	(a) Dockage/Wharfage
MOROCCO:	(a) Peage Dues assessed on the quantity of cargo loaded or discharged
NETHERLANDS:	Quay Dues
NETHERLANDS ANTILLES:	(a) Wharfage at Bullen Bay and Emmastad Terminal (b) Additional Tugs in excess of 2 in/2 out at St. Eustatius Island
NICARAGUA:	(a) Wharfage
NIGERIA:	(a) Cargo Dues (Bulk Liquid/ton and/or Bulk Liquid Offshore/Barrel) including VAT (b) Nigerian Maritime Administration and Safety Agency or (NIMASA) levy including VAT
NORWAY:	(a) Ice Dues (b) Tax on NOx emissions
PAKISTAN:	Swing around expenses at Karachi
PANAMA:	(a) Tug Service for Docking and Undocking at Puerto Armuelles (b) Mandatory Boom Fee at Rodman Terminal (c) Lightering, lightening, transhipment costs per barrel at Chiriqui Grande and Puerto Armuelles (d) Oil boom and oil spill mobilisation at Chiriqui Grande and Puerto Armuelles
PAPUA NEW GUINEA:	Wharfage
PERU:	Navigation License Fee
PORTUGAL:	(a) Cost of tugs brought from other ports to assist vessels loading or discharging at Leixoes (b) Port (harbour) dues at Aveiro
PUERTO RICO:	Dockage and Wharfage
QATAR:	QP Dues based on vessel's NRT/cargo type at Mesaieed
RUSSIA:	(a) Ice Dues (b) Towage expenses at Vysotsk (c) Surcharge on towage during the Winter season (d) Terminal Dues at Moknatkina Pakhta Terminal, Murmansk (e) Port expenses incurred at either Murmansk, Archangel or Kandalaksha for obtaining inward/outward clearance for calling at Vitino
SAMOA (AMERICAN):	Wharfage Tax and Tonnage Tax assessed on the quantity of cargo discharged at Pago Pago
SAMOA (WESTERN):	Cargo Dues and Wharfage charges assessed on the quantity of cargo discharged at Apia
SENEGAL:	Standby tugs at Dakar
SIERRA LEONE:	(a) Charges of any description that are assessed on the quantity of cargo loaded or discharged at Freetown (b) Shipping Policy Charge (Government Freight Levy) assessed on the quantity of cargo loaded or discharged at Freetown
SINGAPORE:	Dockage and Wharfage at PSA berths
SLOVENIA:	Port Dues assessed on the quantity of cargo loaded or discharged
SOUTH AFRICA:	(a) Standby Tugs/Tanker watch at Mossel Bay (b) Support tug costs at the Durban SBM terminal
SPAIN:	J.O.P. (Junta del Obras del Puerto) dues assessed on the quantity of cargo loaded or discharged at Las Palmas, Canary Islands
SRI LANKA:	Stevedoring charges assessed on the quantity of cargo loaded or discharged
SUDAN:	Royalty Fee assessed on the quantity of cargo loaded or discharged at Port Sudan
SWEDEN:	(a) Escort Tugs at Brofjorden and Gothenburg (b) Ice Dues (c) Surcharge on Harbour Dues during the Winter Season (d) Surcharge on Towage during the Winter Season (e) Costs of tugs brought in from other ports to assist vessels at Karlshamn (f) Standby Tugs at Stenungsund

APPENDIX 1

Charterers' Account (contd.)

TAIWAN:	Stern Tug Assistance Fee at Kaohsiung and Sha Lung
TANZANIA:	TCFB Fee assessed on the quantity of cargo loaded or discharged at Tanzanian ports
THAILAND:	(a) Channel Dues at Map Ta Phut (b) Standby Tugs at Map Ta Phut
UNITED KINGDOM:	(a) Charges levied upon the vessel (Ship Dues/Dock Dues/Jetty Tonnage Rates) at Hull, Immingham (East and West Jetties) and Saltend, Humber River (b) Berthing Charge at the SEM Logistics installation, Milford Haven (c) Mob/Demob towage charges at Nigg Terminal
U.S.A.:	(a) Dockage and Wharfage at U.S.A. and U.S.A. controlled ports (b) Extra Towage during the Winter Season at ports on the St. Lawrence River (c) Supplemental Harbor Fee assessed on the quantity of cargo loaded or discharged at ports within the Plaquemines Port, Harbor and Terminal District, Mississippi River (d) Mooring Master, Cargo Master and divers fees for inspecting underwater hoses at Huntington Beach (Los Angeles) (e) Fire Protection Service Fee assessed on cargo outturned at Port Everglades (f) Additional tugs required for turning when proceeding stern first from ConocoPhillips Berth, Boston (g) Standby Tugs at Selby Terminal and the Valero Terminal Bernicia, San Francisco
UNITED ARAB EMIRATES:	Government Loading Dues/Port Dues/Oil Tax at Ruwais
VENEZUELA:	(a) Orinoco River Tolls (b) Lake Maracaibo Bar Tolls/Channel dues
YUGOSLAVIA:	Port Dues assessed on the quantity of cargo loaded or discharged

APPENDIX 1

PREAMBLE PART C

TABLE OF DEMURRAGE RATES

SIZE RANGES sdw. in tonnes	RATES USD per day
15,000/ 19,999	3000
20,000/ 24,999	3750
25,000/ 29,999	5000
30,000/ 34,999	6000
35,000/ 39,999	7000
40,000/ 44,999	8000
45,000/ 49,999	9500
50,000/ 59,999	11000
60,000/ 69,999	13750
70,000/ 79,999	16250
80,000/ 89,999	18500
90,000/ 99,999	21000
100,000/109,999	23000
110,000/119,999	25750
120,000/129,999	28000
130,000/139,999	31000
140,000/149,999	33250
150,000/174,999	38000
175,000/199,999	44000
200,000/224,999	50000
225,000/249,999	57000
250,000/274,999	63750
275,000/299,999	68500
300,000/324,999	75000
325,000/349,999	81500
350,000/399,999	91000
400,000/449,999	103000
450,000/499,999	117000
500,000 and over	134000

NB (1) In calculating these demurrage rates an allowance has been made for one day's consumption of bunkers in port with engines at standby.

NB (2) No allowance is made in the demurrage rates for port costs incurred when the vessel is on demurrage, nor is any allowance made for the cost of cargo heating when on demurrage.

APPENDIX 1

PREAMBLE PART D

LIST 1

A list of ports (including trans-shipment areas) mentioned in the Schedule and/or website, cross references to ports and terminals mentioned in Section 3 of Part B of the Preamble, and ports for which alternative names are commonly used – arranged alphabetically. Rates for ports not shown in the book may show on the website. If not shown in either the book or website please contact the Associations.

Aabenraa – DENMARK
Aalborg – DENMARK
Aalesund – NORWAY
Aarhus – DENMARK
Aberdeen – UNITED KINGDOM
Abidjan – IVORY COAST
Abo FPSO Terminal – NIGERIA
Acajutla – EL SALVADOR
Adelaide – AUSTRALIA
Aden – YEMEN – REPUBLIC OF
Affarsverken (Norrkoping rates apply) – SWEDEN
Agadir – MOROCCO
Agbami Terminal – NIGERIA
Agia Trias (Megara rates apply) – GREECE
Agioi Theodoroi – GREECE
Aichi (Nagoya rates apply) – JAPAN
Ain Sukhna – EGYPT
Akita (Funakawa rates apply) – JAPAN
Akrotiri – CYPRUS
Akureyri (Reykjavik rates apply) – ICELAND
Al Jurf (Farwah Terminal rates apply) – LIBYA
Al Rayyan Marine Terminal (See page 1) – QATAR
Al Shaheen Terminal (See Page 1) – QATAR
Alba Field – NORTH SEA INSTALLATIONS (UK)
Albacora (S.B.M.) – BRAZIL
Albany (N.Y.) – U.S.A.
Albany (W.A.) – AUSTRALIA
Alexandria – EGYPT
Algeciras – SPAIN
Algiers – ALGERIA
Aliaga – TURKEY
Alicante – SPAIN
Alicante Bay (TSA) – SPAIN
Alliance (New Orleans rates apply) – U.S.A.
Alpha Zone (TSA) – ARGENTINA
Altamira (Tampico rates apply) – MEXICO
Altona (Melbourne rates apply) – AUSTRALIA
AMA Anchorage (Good Hope (La.) rates apply) – U.S.A.
Amagasaki (Osaka rates apply) – JAPAN
Ambarli (Istanbul rates apply) – TURKEY
Amberes (Antwerp rates apply) – BELGIUM
Ambes (See Bec D'Ambes) – FRANCE
Amesville (New Orleans rates apply) – U.S.A.
Amorco (San Francisco rates apply) – U.S.A.
Amoy (See Xiamen) – CHINESE REPUBLIC
Amsterdam – NETHERLANDS
Amuay Bay (Paraguana Refinery Center-CRP rates apply) – VENEZUELA
Anacortes – U.S.A.
Anchorage – U.S.A.
Ancona – ITALY
Andro SBM (Tebig Terminal rates apply) – BRAZIL
Anegasaki (Chiba rates apply) – JAPAN
Angle Bay (Milford Haven rates apply) – UNITED KINGDOM

Ango Ango – ZAIRE
Angra Dos Reis (See Tebig Terminal) – BRAZIL
Angsi Marine Terminal – MALAYSIA
Annapolis Anchorage (Baltimore rates apply) – U.S.A.
Anoa Natuna – INDONESIA
Antalya – TURKEY
Antan Terminal – NIGERIA
Antifer (Havre rates apply) – FRANCE
Antigua – CARIBBEAN SUNDRY ISLANDS
Antilla – CUBA
Antofagasta – CHILE
Antsirinana (See Diego Suarez) – MADAGASCAR
Antwerp – BELGIUM
Anvers (See Antwerp) – BELGIUM
Anyer Kidul (Tanjung Gerem rates apply) – INDONESIA
Aokata – JAPAN
Apapa (Lagos rates apply) – NIGERIA
Apia – PACIFIC OCEAN SUNDRY ISLANDS
APSA Terminal (Balboa Rates apply) – PANAMA REPUBLIC
Aqaba – JORDAN
Aracaju – BRAZIL
Aransas Pass (Corpus Christi rates apply) – U.S.A.
Aratu – BRAZIL
Archangel – RUSSIA
Ardmore Field – NORTH SEA INSTALLATIONS (UK)
Arendal – NORWAY
Arica – CHILE
Arroyo (P.R.) (See Guayama) – PUERTO RICO
Aruba – NETHERLANDS ANTILLES
Arun (See Blang Lancang) – INDONESIA
Arzew – ALGERIA
Ascension Island – S.E. ATLANTIC SUNDRY ISLANDS
Ash Shihr – YEMEN – REPUBLIC OF
Ashdod – ISRAEL
Ashkelon – ISRAEL
Ashtart – TUNISIA
Asnaes (Kalundborg rates apply) – DENMARK
Aspra Spitia – GREECE
Aspropyrgos – GREECE
Assab – ETHIOPIA
Assaluyeh SBM (See page 1) – IRAN
Astoria (Queens) (New York rates apply) – U.S.A.
Atas Terminal (Mersin rates apply) – TURKEY
Atherinolakkos – GREECE
Atlas Cove (Lagos rates apply) – NIGERIA
Atreco (Beaumont rates apply) – U.S.A.
Atsumi – JAPAN
Attaka Terminal (Santan rates apply) – INDONESIA
Auckland – NEW ZEALAND
Augusta – ITALY
Auk Field – NORTH SEA INSTALLATIONS (UK)
Aviero – PORTUGAL
Aviles – SPAIN
Avon (Calif.) (San Francisco rates apply) – U.S.A.

APPENDIX 1

PREAMBLE PART D

LIST 3

PLEASE REFER TO SECTION 10 OF PART A OF THE PREAMBLE FOR DEFINITION.

A list of trans-shipment areas arranged by geographical area; the names used for these trans-shipment areas have been assigned by the Associations for identification purposes only.

	Approx. Position	
Arabian Gulf		
Offshore Mesaieed	25 16N 51 46E	Offshore Qatar
Gulf of Oman		
*Offshore Fujairah	25 15N 56 40E	Gulf of Oman
Offshore Khor Fakkan	25 35N 56 40E	Gulf of Oman
Red Sea/Gulf of Suez		
Offshore Ain Sukhna	29 46N 32 36E	Gulf of Suez
Offshore Jeddah	21 23N 39 06E	Red Sea
Caribbean Area		
Offshore Curacao	12 10N 69 10W	Netherlands Antilles
Offshore Freeport (Bahamas)	26 10N 78 30W	Bahamas
Offshore Great Isaac Island	26 15N 79 05W	Bahamas
U.S. Gulf		
Gulfmex No. 1	28 00N 89 30W	Offshore Mississippi
Offshore Corpus Christi No. 1	27 28N 96 49W	Offshore Texas
Offshore Corpus Christi No. 2	27 48N 95 31W	Offshore Texas
Offshore Freeport (Texas)	28 45N 95 03W	Offshore Texas
Offshore Galveston No. 1	28 27N 94 30W	Offshore Texas
Offshore Galveston No. 2	28 40N 94 08W	Offshore Texas
Offshore Pascagoula No. 1	29 27N 88 13W	Offshore Mississippi
South Sabine Point No. 1	28 30N 93 40W	Offshore Sabine, Texas
South Sabine Point No. 2	28 37N 93 22W	Offshore Sabine, Texas
South West Point	28 27N 90 42W	Offshore Louisiana
U.S.A. – East Coast		
Big Stone Beach	38 59N 75 12W	Delaware Bay
Jamestown Anchorage	41 31N 71 21W	Narragansett Bay
Offshore Ambrose Light	40 12N 72 00W	Offshore New York
Offshore Delaware No. 1	38 30N 74 30W	Offshore Delaware
Offshore Delaware No. 2	38 20N 73 45W	Offshore Delaware
U.S.A. –West Coast		
Santa Catalina Gulf	32 56N 118 00W	Offshore Los Angeles/San Diego
South America – East Coast		
Alpha Zone	35 06S 56 00W	River Plate
Bravo Zone	35 32S 56 33W	River Plate
Cabo San Antonio/Charlie Zone	36 15S 56 30W	River Plate
Delta Zone	35 04S 55 11W	River Plate
Golfo San Matias	41 58S 65 00W	Offshore Argentina
La Plata Roads/Zona Comun	34 45S 57 47W	River Plate
Talcuhauano Bay	36 40S 73 01W	Offshore Chile

*Rates for this position do not apply for Fujairah Offshore Anchorage Area 'S', rates for which are quoted upon application to the Associations.

APPENDIX 1

Far East

Offshore Kaohsiung	22 32N 120 13E	West Coast of Taiwan
Offshore Karimun Besar	1 04N 103 30E	Singapore Strait
Offshore Singapore No. 1	1 14N 103 33E	Singapore Strait
Offshore Singapore No. 2	1 40N 104 30E	Singapore Strait

India

Offshore Bombay	19 00N 72 25E	West Coast of India
Offshore Kakinada	16 58N 82 27E	East Coast of India
Offshore Cochin	10 00N 76 00E	West Coast of India
Offshore Sikka	22 34N 69 42E	Gulf of Kutch
Sandheads	20 52N 88 20E	Offshore Haldia

Mediterranean

Alicante Bay	38 30N 01 00E	Offshore Alicante, Spain
Offshore Malta	35 54N 14 46E	Hurd Bank

West Africa

Offshore Dakar	14 15N 17 25E	Cap Vert
Zaire Estuary	06 04S 12 17E	River Zaire

Northern Europe

Lyme Bay	50 31N 03 09W	Offshore Portland (U.K.)
Scapa Flow	58 55N 03 02W	Orkney Islands
Seine Bay	49 36N 01 07W	Offshore Havre
Southwold	52 16N 01 57E	Offshore East Coast U.K.

APPENDIX 2

Braemar Seascope

Thursday, 10 March 2011

Market Indicator

Wet		09-Mar-11	Feb Avg	Avg YTD	2010 Avg
		TCE (US$/Day)	TCE (US$/Day)	TCE (US$/Day)	TCE (US$/Day)
260,000 NHC AG/EAST	TD3	31,500	24,000	17,500	40,500
130,000 NHC WAFR/USAC	TD5	28,500	13,500	10,500	24,000
80,000 NHC UK/CONT	TD7	38,500	15,500	10,500	19,000
55,000 CLN AG/JAPAN	TC5	4,500	3,500	5,000	9,500
37,000 CLN CONT/USAC	TC2	17,500	11,000	10,500	12,000
38,000 CLN CARIB/USAC	TC3	17,500	4,500	6,500	8,500

Dry	09-Mar-11	Feb Avg	Avg YTD	2010 Avg
BDI	1,472	1,401	1,290	2,758
BCI	1,699	1,626	1,492	3,480
BPI	2,095	1,732	1,709	3,115
BSI	1,512	1,361	1,289	1,365

Container	07-Mar-11	Feb Avg	Avg YTD	2010 Avg
B O X i	98.28	91.70	85.18	63.83

Financial	09-Mar-11	Feb Avg	Avg YTD	2010 Avg
BRENT CRUDE US$/bbl	115.04	105.52	101.17	79.49
IFO 380 ROTT US$/mt	606.50	569.73	542.42	449.24
YEN/US$	82.78	82.54	82.59	87.70
WON/US$	1,115	1,118	1,117	1,155
US$/EURO	1.38	1.37	1.35	1.33
US$/STERLING	1.61	1.62	1.60	1.55
GOLD /USUS$	1,427	1,381	1,370	1,224

Weekly Chartering Report

All details given in good faith but without guarantee
Deep Sea Tankers   +44 (0)20 7535 2626
Dry Cargo Chartering   +44 (0)20 7535 2666
Container Chartering   +44 (0)20 7535 2867

APPENDIX 2

10/03/2011

VLCC

Crude Chartering

The situation in Libya remains unresolved and today we saw a change of tactics, as inevitably the oil producing installations were attacked directly. There are also reports of vessels presenting themselves to load cargo and nothing being available. Every cloud has a silver lining, and there is much speculation that Saudi Arabia may increase their output to cover the lack of Libyan production, but there has been no official confirmation of this yet. Owners have retained the

upper hand, and have been able slowly and steadily to build the rates up from ws60.0 to ws70.0 over the course of the week. This is counter to the adequate tonnage list, and proves that solidarity can produce increased freight rates. The hope of increased Saudi Arabian output has encouraged owners to hold the line at the ws70.0 level, although replacement and early deals have been completed higher. Owners' ideas remain firm for the moment. The last three months have produced consecutively 120, 112, 110 spot fixtures, and if this month produces the same number of fixtures, the volume of upcoming cargoes will push rates upwards again. Should demand slacken, it is possible that we are looking at the top of the rates curve for the moment. In reaction to owners' increasing ideas, AG/West fixing levels crept up again from ws42.5 to a last-done level of ws47.5 and, although charterers are trying to convince owners the rates should be less than this, it remains to be seen if they will triumph.

The lack of available VLCC tonnage in the Atlantic means that W African rates have maintained their firmness from last week, supported by a busy and tight suezmax market keeping levels around ws80.0 for W Africa/US Gulf and slightly less for east. The Indian charterers have been less busy this week: IOC covered only one W Africa stem for discharge WC India at US$4.6m, slightly below the TD15 rate at the time of fixing. In addition, for the first time we saw IOC lift a cargo out of storage at Saldanha Bay for WC India discharge at US$3.1m. We can expect more cargo liftings from this area in the future. A VLCC was concluded from Rotterdam with fuel oil destined for Singapore at US$4.8m today, proving that although the freight demand has increased, the arbitrage can support just above US$17/tonne.

The 30 day availability of VLCCs arriving at Fujairah shows 58 double hulls and eight single hulls, compared to 62 double hull and nine single hull vessels last week. So far for the month of March, we have seen a total of 89 cargoes and, with 37 double hulls which can theoretically make cancelling within March, there should be more than enough vessels. However, owners' ideas remain firm for the moment. Also worth bearing in mind is that, with Saudi Arabian stem date confirmation next week, charterers could potentially start to look for April dates before March is complete.

The freight rate for 280,000tonne AG/US Gulf is ws47.5, up ws5.0pts from last week, and with bunkers at US$640/tonne, down US$1/tonne from last week, owners' theoretical earnings are:

Double hull TCE: US$11,700/day (US$3,800/day last week)

The freight rate for 270,000tonne AG/S Korea is ws70.0, up ws7.5pts from last week, making owners earnings of:

Double Hull TCE: US$35,700/day (US$25,000/day last week)

Route	Size	Load	Discharge	Today's Assessment	Last Week's Average
TD1	280,000	Ras Tanura	LOOP	ws45.0	ws45.0
TD2	265,000	Ras Tanura	Singapore	ws70.0	ws68.0
TD3	265,000	Ras Tanura	Chiba	ws70.0	ws68.0
TD4	260,000	Bonny	LOOP	ws80.0	ws78.5
TD15	260,000	West Africa	China	ws74.0	ws73.5

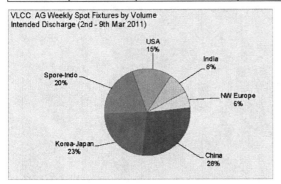

VLCC AG Weekly Spot Fixtures by Volume
Intended Discharge (2nd - 9th Mar 2011)

USA 15%
India 8%
NW Europe 6%
China 28%
Korea-Japan 23%
Spore-Indo 20%

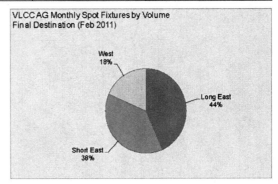

VLCC AG Monthly Spot Fixtures by Volume
Final Destination (Feb 2011)

West 18%
Long East 44%
Short East 38%

APPENDIX 2

10/03/2011

Suezmax

Crude Chartering

W Africa started very disappointingly this week, with the rates dropping from ws110.0 to ws102.5 in the first fixture of the week. There was a clear disparity between owners in the market, and while some looked to push the rates, others decided that happiness is a fixture in the one hundreds. As expected, this week we saw the 25-31 window starting to fix as charterers looked to complete March fixing. The fixture at ws102.5 led some other owners to believe that the rates may have been coming off, and in the middle of the week rates had drifted briefly to ws97.5 and then back up to ws100.0. Charterers coming into the market at this point met some stiff resistance from the owners, as all the cheaper ships had been snapped up, leaving traditionally expensive owners and lower quality vessels to fight it out over the remaining cargoes. The List has certainly thinned, and there is not huge availability for the end of March. It looks as if charterers will push into April dates at the end of this week, and with last done reported to be ws107.5 to the USAC, any fresh enquiry is likely to encourage the owners further.

The Med/Black Sea market has continued down the same path it was on last week. Rates from the Black Sea started the week at ws117.5, but a couple of 20-25 cargoes pulled the market through ws120.0 up to ws140.0 for UKC/Med discharge. When a replacement off mid-month came back, the rates jumped further to ws150.0. This was due mainly to a fixed ship not being replaced on the list, uncertainty in Libya and flexible delays in the Turkish straits. The delays in the straits increased to four days, due to some bad weather in Turkey. The replacements also helped drive the rates. With the Black Sea and W Africa showing signs of life, any cargo out of the Med going US Gulf or east fixed at good rates, with a couple of Med/US Gulf cargoes attracting ws110.0. Surprisingly, this resulted in a premium on W Africa/US Gulf. The uncertainty in Libya seems mainly to be reducing the amount of cargoes in the Med, but with some owners refusing to load there, the uncertainty about the situation seems to be building owners' confidence. There should be a pause in Black Sea fixing after the two remaining March stems get covered, which will bring some relief to the charterers. However, any sort of activity in the Med or Black Sea will continue the trend of rising rates. A sustained period of quiet will let the list replenish and the rates soften, but at the moment the strength appears to be with the owners.

The Eastern suezmax market was relatively busy this week, with a number of AG/East, AG/India and AG/West cargoes being fixed. The rates did not move a huge amount, AG/East stayed at ws85.0, AG/India recovered to ws95.0 and AG/West was done at ws60.0 to the US Gulf. The VLCC market moved approximately ten points this week, which was pleasing to see. This increase probably knocked-on to the suezmaxes and raised levels of activity. It is doubtful that this suezmax market can kick on into three figures, as the West has, while the VLCCs remain stable, as they did at the end of this week. There is the usual split in the tonnage list with AG/East and West cargoes taking out the good quality doubles, and AG/India taking the lower quality units. If the West were to rocket skywards then we would certainly see the better units ballasting westbound, but at the moment the differential was not sufficient to pull the ships round.

Route	Size	Load	Discharge	Today's Assessment	Last Week's Average
TD5	130,000	Bonny	Philadelphia	ws107.5	ws106.0
TD6	135,000	Novorossiysk	Augusta	ws145.0	ws142.0
	135,000	Mediterranean	UK Cont	ws140.0	ws127.5
	135,000	North Sea	US Gulf	ws110.0	ws105.0
	135,000	Ras Tanura	South East Asia	ws85.0	ws85.0

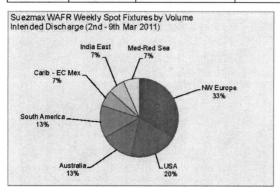

Suezmax WAFR Weekly Spot Fixtures by Volume
Intended Discharge (2nd - 9th Mar 2011)

- Med-Red Sea 7%
- India East 7%
- Carib - EC Mex 7%
- NW Europe 33%
- South America 13%
- Australia 13%
- USA 20%

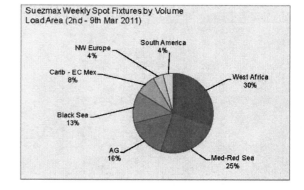

Suezmax Weekly Spot Fixtures by Volume
Load Area (2nd - 9th Mar 2011)

- South America 4%
- NW Europe 4%
- Carib - EC Mex 8%
- West Africa 30%
- Black Sea 13%
- AG 16%
- Med-Red Sea 25%

10/03/2011

Aframax

In the North Sea and Baltic aframax markets, we are seeing the difference in rate levels increase further and further daily. Due to the worsening ice conditions in the Baltic, many ships have been stuck in the ice, unable to proceed into Primorsk. This has caused ships to run late for their cargoes, which has inevitably thrown the stems list out the window. The lack of available ice breakers to free stranded ships has also meant charterers have not been able to fix on, since there have been no workable ships. In some cases, owners were talking in excess of ws300.0 to fix their ship. It wouldn't be a surprise if this eventually happened, if the current situation worsens, which it seems it will. We have started to see some charterers come into the market in an attempt to cover end month stems. We have seen cargoes currently up until the 27 March, which is well in advance, especially as the majority of ice class ships have an uncertain itinerary. At the time of writing, last done is currently ws240.0, however, we would rate the market around the ws260.0 level. Non-ice rates from the Baltic have softened this week in line with North Sea market. Very little has been done in the North Sea, which really needs to be tested to see where the market is. The number of prompt and available ships has grown day by day this week in this region. We anticipate that the market will crash, and that rate levels will soften significantly.

Moving down south, it's all over in the Med and Black Sea as a relatively quiet week and an over-tonnaged market has caused rates to come crashing down. We do however still have a two-tiered market, with Libyan loadings having substantial premiums. In some cases, oil majors are now refusing to call at Libyan ports or even take Libyan owned vessels on charter. At the start of the week, activity was slow and ws125.0 was fixed. The majority of activity was being being kept under wraps, but come mid-week, a Greek charterer fixed three cargoes of similar dates to the same owners at ws100.0, a ws100.0 point's deficit from this time last week. As the week progressed, activity started to pick up as charterers began to take advantage of the softening market. An Italian charterer quoted a cargo today (Thursday) which was reported to have received ten offers, rumoured to have been put on subs at ws97.5. At the time of writing, this remains unconfirmed, however. Black Sea activity has been fairly steady and currently, last done is ws110.0. Reports came out in the news this week that the Kirkuk-Ceyhan pipeline has been the target of sabotage by Kurdish rebels and blown up. The pipeline which carries Iraqi crude from the northern Kirkuk fields to Ceyhan, cut shipments by about 590,000bbl/day. However, it is too early to tell what impact, if any, it will have on the Mediterranean markets.

Much the same as the Mediterranean, owners in the Caribbean have seen their earnings come crashing down. Tonnage which has recently been delayed and held up in poor weather conditions in the US Gulf has since replenished the tonnage list, leaving ample of options for charterers. From Monday to Tuesday this week, rates softened a massive ws35 points in one day, which was just the start of the decline. By Wednesday that had dropped a further ws45.0 points to ws120.0 which, at the time of writing, is last done. We expect further decreases in rates today and tomorrow as the week comes to an end.

It has been a busy week for aframaxes east of the Suez Canal, with rates rising sharply to around ws130.0 on TD8, and around ws102.5 on TD14. These rises are on the back of heightened piracy concerns, expensive bunkers and owners' preference to trade west. We have seen at total of 25 fixtures out of the AG and Red Sea, with one unit fixed off tight dates at ws130.0 east with a west option at US$2.2m. 31 units were fixed in the Far East, with rates firming in line with the AG.

Crude Chartering

Route	Size	Load	Discharge	Today's Assessment	Last Week's Average
TD7	80,000	Sullom Voe	Wilhelmshaven	ws125.0	ws142.0
TD8	80,000	Mina Al Ahmadi	Singapore	ws105.0	ws105.0
TD9	70,000	Puerto La Cruz	Corpus Christi	ws120.0	ws174.5
TD11	80,000	Banias	Lavera	ws97.5	ws135.0
TD14	80,000	Seria	Sydney	ws97.5	ws95.5
TD17	100,000	Primorsk	Wilhelmshaven	ws260.0	ws242.0

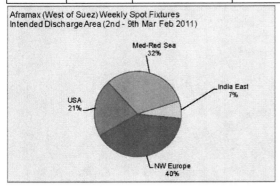

Aframax (West of Suez) Weekly Spot Fixtures Intended Discharge Area (2nd - 9th Mar Feb 2011)

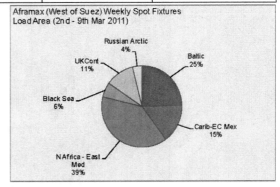

Aframax (West of Suez) Weekly Spot Fixtures Load Area (2nd - 9th Mar 2011)

Braemar Seascope Weekly Chartering Report

4

APPENDIX 2

10/03/2011

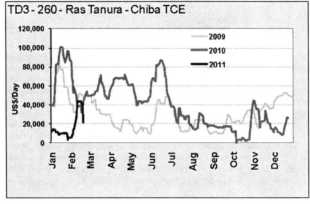

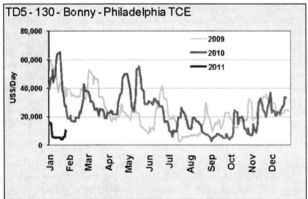

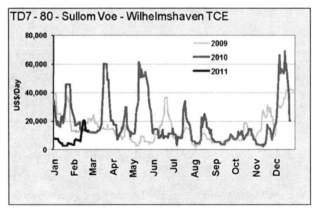

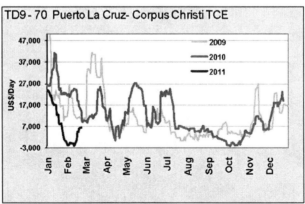

Crude Tanker Summary

APPENDIX 2

10/03/2011

Clean Products - East

LR2s have been busy with a burst of activity mid-week, which has reportedly seen rates lift up to ws105.0 to Japan, although this remains unconfirmed. Tonnage is quite tight for the remainder of March and throughout April, despite some prompt tonnage looking for coverage. Western positions continue to fail to make any sense of the ballast to the AG, so the draw on eastern available ships continues and must take effect at some stage.

LR1s have watched activity greatly increase this week as ships are fixed up to the end of March. TC5 rates again saw slight gains to ws119.0 to Japan, however sufficient tonnage remains to undermine any bullish sentiment in the region. Rates to the West are capped by weak sentiment, as owners eye the much better returns for the western markets and discount their pricing to fix into that region. Again, this gradual but inexorable draw of tonnage should at some point start to impact the tonnage lists, but newbuildings continue to deliver.

At the end of last week, rates for WC India/Japan settled at around ws130.0 and the market has remained flat at this level. Despite bunker prices slightly dropping, their relatively high price still provides a floor to the rates owners are willing to accept for this voyage. Cross-AG and Cross-Red Sea cargoes continue to provide better TCE equivalents than WC India/Japan voyages, with Cross-Red Sea currently trading at the US$300,000 lumpsum level. WC India/S Africa has also been active, with a rate equivalent to ws192.0.

CPP Chartering

Route	Size	Load	Discharge	Today's Assessment	Last Week's Average
TC1	75,000	Ras Tanura	Yokohama	ws105.0	ws102.0
TC5	55,000	Ras Tanura	Yokohama	ws117.5	ws118.0
TC4	30,000	Singapore	Chiba	ws127.5	ws129.5

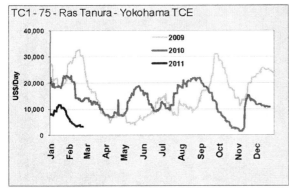

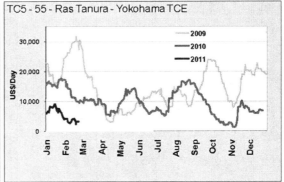

189

APPENDIX 2

10/03/2011

Clean Products - West

Cont

TC2 has remained largely steady at reasonable levels for owners all week, despite a slightly longer than desirable position list, and helped by a stronger Caribbean and back haul market and stock figures that were more bullish than expected. TC2 started the week at nervous ws205.0 levels and with tonnage looking long beyond 17 March and several chemical vessels and ships with palm oil backgrounds, it was looking like the week would belong to the charterers. There were a couple who weren't long tonnage, predicting rates in the ws180s by mid-week. As it turns out, the headline rate has softened, but only to the mid-ws190s, where it's currently ended up. Stock figures stateside showed a draw of 5.5mbbls against an expected 1.5mbbls. Furthermore, a resurgent Caribbean market which has seen Caribbean/USAC rates as high as ws195.0, and backhaul up to ws110.0, has given stateside tonnage a valid alternative to simply ballasting back. This in turn has bolstered confidence on the Continent, despite a quiet end to the week. Looking forward into the month, the list is looking tight up to 16 March; reasonably balanced in the 16/23 March window; and then pretty long in the 24/31 March period. However, the bulk of those are projected positions, so it's probably a bit too early to read anything significant into this. Meanwhile, earnings on the TC2 round are solidly in the mid-teens, despite bunkers nudging US$600/tonne in Rotterdam, providing welcome respite for beleaguered owners.

Med

Med trading has remained largely flat this week despite the unrest in Libya, which has had a far more significant impact on crude oil trade than the product trade, which has been largely unaffected so far. Rates have softened slightly to ws200.0 Cross-Med and ws210.0 Med/UKC.

Caribbean

A resurgent Caribbean market has helped the Atlantic basin this week, with rates peaking at ws195.0, before falling back slightly to ws187.5 levels. This still shows returns better than TC2, without exposing a vessel to the vicissitudes of a North Atlantic winter, albeit for a shorter period. Back haul levels have remained firm at ws110.0, providing owners who are lucky or are able to triangulate with the opportunity of significantly enhancing their earnings.

CPP Chartering

Route	Size	Load	Discharge	Today's Assessment	Last Week's Average
TC2	37,000	Rotterdam	New York	ws195.0	ws199.5
TC3	38,000	Aruba	New York	ws190.0	ws184.0
TC6	30,000	Skikda	Lavera	ws190.0	ws195.0

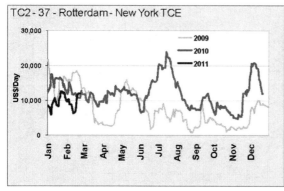

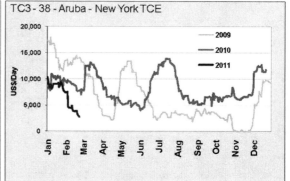

Braemar Seascope Weekly Chartering Report

7

APPENDIX 2

10/03/2011

Tanker Freight Futures

TD3   VLCC   260kmt   Ras Tanura - Chiba

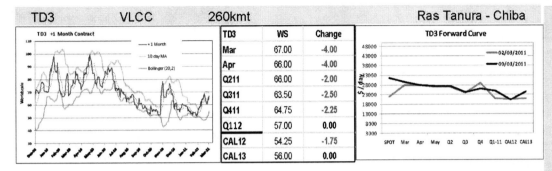

TD3	WS	Change
Mar	67.00	-4.00
Apr	66.00	-4.00
Q211	66.00	-2.00
Q311	63.50	-2.50
Q411	64.75	-2.25
Q112	57.00	0.00
CAL12	54.25	-1.75
CAL13	56.00	0.00

TD5   Suezmax   130kmt   Bonny - Philadelphia

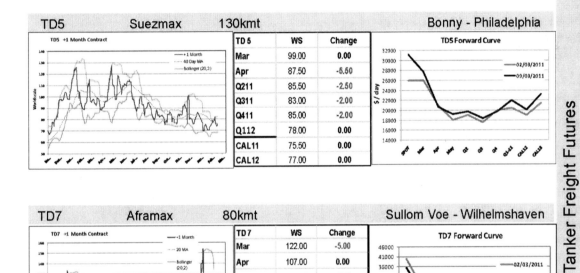

TD 5	WS	Change
Mar	99.00	0.00
Apr	87.50	-6.50
Q211	85.50	-2.50
Q311	83.00	-2.00
Q411	85.00	-2.00
Q112	78.00	0.00
CAL11	75.50	0.00
CAL12	77.00	0.00

TD7   Aframax   80kmt   Sullom Voe - Wilhelmshaven

TD 7	WS	Change
Mar	122.00	-5.00
Apr	107.00	0.00
Q211	105.00	-1.00
Q311	103.00	1.00
Q411	110.00	0.00
Q112	105.00	0.00
CAL11	104.00	0.00
CAL12	104.00	0.00

TC2   MR   37kmt   Continent - USAC

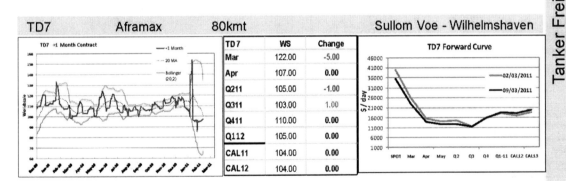

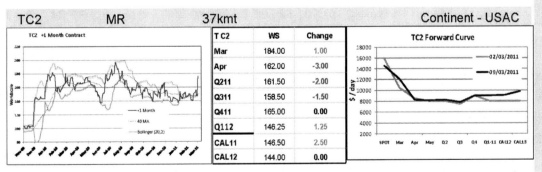

T C2	WS	Change
Mar	184.00	1.00
Apr	162.00	-3.00
Q211	161.50	-2.00
Q311	158.50	-1.50
Q411	165.00	0.00
Q112	146.25	1.25
CAL11	146.50	2.50
CAL12	144.00	0.00

These indicative numbers do not reflect the annual flat rate change.

Braemar Seascope Weekly Chartering Report

8

Tanker Freight Futures

APPENDIX 3

VOYAGE ESTIMATE
Ras Tanura/London/Suez/Ras Tanura

Charterer		Broker			DATE

VESSEL	WALRUS	SPEED +	13.5 Knots		
		CONS	58 IFO		0 MDO
PORT CONS	70 IFO		0 MDO		0

VOYAGE LEGS

		MILES	0	FUEL	MDO
LOAD PORT	Ras Tanura				
LOAD PORT	London	11246	34.71	2013.17	0.00
DISCH PORT	Ras Tanura	6416	19.80	1148.54	0.00
BAD WEATHER			4.49	260.42	0.00
TOTALS AT SEA			59.00	3422.14	0.00
BUNKER PORT					
HEATING				0	
CLEANING					
CANAL TRANSIT			1	20	0
WAITING TIME			0	0	0
PORT TIME			4.00	280.00	0.00
		TOTALS	64.00	3722.14	0.00

VOYAGE EXPENSES

BUNKERS

FUEL OIL	3722.14	PRICE	$620.00		$2,307,724.35
DIESEL OIL	0.00	PRICE	$0.00		$0.00
BUNKER TOTALS					$960,366.17
LOAD PORT				$70,000	
DISCH PORT				$200,000	
BUNKER PORT				$0	
CANAL TRANSIT				$265,000	
DAILY COSTS	$10,000.00			$640,000	
WRAP	plus crew war bonus 5,000			$23,000	
				$1,198,000	$1,198,000.00
					$3,505,724.35

EARNINGS	WS RATE	$30.17			COMM	
CARGO QTTY			WS FRT	GR FRT	2.5	NETT FRT
260000	65.00	$19.6105	$5,098,730.00	$5,098,730.00	$127,468.25	$4,971,261.75
FXD DIFF	0.00			$0.00		
	62.50	$18.8563	$4,902,625.00	$4,902,625.00	$122,565.63	$4,780,059.38
FXD DIFF				$0.00		
VOY		DAILY SURPLUS				
SURPLUS						
$1,465,537.40		$22,898.18		2.5 PTS	$2,987	
$1,274,335.02		$19,910.76		ON	PER	
				RATE	DAY	

To calculate breakeven at $10,000/day

	260,000	$30.17		$7,844,200.00	$196,105.00	$7,648,095.00
WS Break	COSTS	$2,128,489.63				
even =	EARNINGS	$7,648,095.00		0.4584		W 45.84

APPENDIX 4

VOYAGE ESTIMATE
RASTANURA/LONDON

Charterer		Broker			DATE

VESSEL	WALRUS	SPEED +	14 Knots		
		CONS	58 IFO		0 MDO
PORT CONS	70 IFO		0 MDO		0

VOYAGE LEGS

		MILES	0	FUEL	MDO
LOAD PORT	Ras Tanura				
DISCH PORT	London	11246	33.47	1941.27	0.00
LOAD PORT	Ras Tanura	6416	19.10	1107.52	0.00
BAD WEATHER			4.43	256.94	0.00
TOTALS AT SEA			57.00	3305.74	0.00
BUNKER PORT					
HEATING				0	
CLEANING					
CANAL TRANSIT			1	10	0
WAITING TIME			0	0	0
PORT TIME			4.00	280.00	0.00
		TOTALS	62.00	3605.74	0.00

VOYAGE EXPENSES

BUNKERS

FUEL OIL	3605.74	PRICE	$620.00		$2,235,557.32
DIESEL OIL	0.00	PRICE	$0.00		$0.00
BUNKER TOTALS					$2,235,557.32
LOAD PORT				$70,000	
DISCH PORT				$200,000	
BUNKER PORT				$0	
CANAL TRANSIT				$265,000	
DAILY COSTS	$10,000.00			$640.955	
WRAP	plus crew war bonus 5,000			$23,000	
				$1,198,000	$1,198,000.00
					$3,433,557.32

EARNINGS	WS RATE	$21.45			COMM	
CARGO QTTY			WS FRT	GR FRT	2.5	NETT FRT
260000	65.00	$19.6105	$5,098,730.00	$5,098,730.00	$127,468.25	$4,971,261.75
FXD DIFF	0.00			$0.00		
	62.50	$18.8563	$4,902,625.00	$4,902,625.00	$122,565.63	$4,780,059.38
FXD DIFF				$0.00		
VOY SURPLUS		DAILY SURPLUS				
$2,287,293.46		$24,803.49		2.5 PTS	$3,084	
$2,015,414.71		$21,719.36		ON	PER	
				RATE	DAY	

To calculate breakeven at $10,000/day

	260,000	$30.17		$7,844,200.00	$196,105.00	$7,648,095.00
WS Break	COSTS	$3,433,557.32				
even =	EARNINGS	$7,648,095.00		0.4489		W 45.84

APPENDIX 5

Three Types of Ships

<u>Ship Details for Voyage Estimating</u>

M.T. WALRUS Blt 2000 insured value (I.V.) $60 million
278,000 mt SDWT on 20.47 m
326.24 m LOA/56.6 m BM
Capacity 318,000 m³ @ 98%   TPC 155 mt.
Speed/Consumption: 14 kts on 62 mt (380 CST) ODO
(Average laden/ballast):   13.5 kts on 58 mt (380 CST) ODO

<u>M.T. DOLPHIN Blt 2000 I.V. $45 million</u>

139,000 mt SDWT on 16.3 m
274.3 m LOA/43.2 BM
164,200 m³ @ 98% TPC 100 mt.
Speed/Consumption: 15 kts on 47.5 mt)
(Average laden/ballast):   14 kts on 38 mt) 380 est + ODO
                                    13 KTS on 31.5 mt)

M.T. OTTER blt 2000 I.V. $26 million
40,000 mt. SDWT on 11.2 m
176 m LOA/32 m BM
43,620 m³ TPC 41 mt
Speed/Consumption: 14.5 kts on 33)
(Average laden/ballast):   14   kts on 28)
                                    14   kts on 26) 380 cst + ODO
                                    13   kts on 20)
                                    12.5 kts on 17)

APPENDIX 6

Worldscale Extracts – Flat Rates / Distances

Disport	Load Port	USD/mt	Miles
Ain Sukhna	Quoin Island	7.72	5,495
Genoa	Mina al Fahal	28.43C	20894
Genoa	Mina al Fahal	13.36S	8012
Genoa	Port Harcourt	13.76	8554
Loop	Bonny	16.69	12,021
Loop	Quoin Island	30.56C	23,927
Loop	Quoin Island	24.55S	18,513
Singapore	Mina al Fahal	9.37	6,337
Fawley	Augusta	8.98	4580
Yokohama	Quoin Island	17.35	12,529

APPENDIX 7

Data Sheet

War Risk Premium	North of 26° N	0.03%
Gulf of Oman	North of 24° N	0.01%
Crew War Bonus	$5,000	

Port Expenses:-

Yokohama	$90,000
Ain Sukhna	$20,000
Loop	$40,000
Genoa	$70,000
Genoa	$40,000 (Walrus)
Singapore	$20,000 (Other)
Mina al Fahal	$10,000
Bonny	$60,000
Port Harcourt	$30,000
Augusta	$40,000
Southampton	$50,000
London	$200,000 (Walrus)

Bunker Prices $620 380cst

APPENDIX 8

Recommended Principles for the Use of Parties
Engaged in Chartering and Ship's Agency Procedures

(As supported by the Executive Committee of BIMCO at its Meeting held in Munich in May, 1969)

1. In the conduct of his profession a broker shall exercise great care to avoid misrepresentation and shall be guided by the principles of honesty and fair dealing.

2. Under no circumstances may a broker avail himself of, or make use of an authority, if he does not actually hold it, neither can he alter the terms of an authority without the approval of Principals concerned.

3. A broker, when requested to do so, must make it quite clear to others who wish to make him an offer that he has already received one or several firm offers for the particular order or vessel concerned.

4. No broker has authority to quote a vessel or a cargo unless duly authorized by Principals or their brokers.

5. Each party has to respect the channel through which a vessel or a cargo has been quoted to the broker in reply to a request from the party concerned.

6. An unsolicited offer or proposal does not in any way bind the party which receives it, unless this party such unsolicited offer or proposal.

7. Each party must describe honesty the conditions of availability of a vessel or cargo, namely in specifying whether, according to his knowledge, some reservations are attached to the vessel or the cargo. In such cases reservations should be made quite clear.

8. The commissions due to the brokers are to be paid in accordance with the terms of the charterparty and must not be retained by either party pending final settlement of accounts or eventually of a dispute in which the brokers have no liability.

9. Restrictions:

    A – The restriction "subject stem" can only apply to shippers' and/or suppliers' agreement to make a cargo available for specified dates, to the exclusion of any other meaning. In case of stem not granted as required, no other ship can be fixed by Charterers before the one initially fixed "subject stem" has received the first refusal to accept the amended dates and/ or quantity, provided they are reasonably near.

    B – The restriction "subject open" or "subject unfixed" can only apply when a vessel or a cargo is already under offer, once only, for a limited time, and the "subject open" offer must be made with the same time limit. No extension can be granted, no further negotiation can take place until the time limit has expired or until both offers have been answered.

    C – Any other "subject" to be clearly stipulated and limited and to be eventually properly justified.

10. The Chartering Conditions are hereunder described:

    A – Dry Cargo: Names and Domicile of contracting parties.
    - Name of the vessel, flag, class and specifications,
    - Ports and berths of loading and discharging,
    - Laydays/Cancelling dates.

APPENDIX 8

- ○ Accurate description of the cargo.
- ○ Rates and conditions of loading and discharging.
- ○ Rate of demurrage and despatch, if any.
- ○ Rate of freight, basis of payment.
- ○ Commissions.
- ○ Type of charterparty with main amendments.
- ○ Clauses of calculation of time, winch clause, etc.
- ○ Special clauses for the trade concerned.

B – Oil Charterparty:
- ○ Same as for dry cargo except:
- ○ Rate of freight (plus or minus "WORLDSCALE" or any other Internationally recognized scale).

C – Time Charter: Names and domicile of contracted parties.
- ○ Name of vessel, flag, class and main specifications.
- ○ Place of delivery and re-delivery.
- ○ Date of re-delivery or period.
- ○ Intended trade and trading limits including exclusions.
- ○ Quantity and type of bunkers on board on delivery and re-delivery.
- ○ Price of bunkers.
- ○ Rate of hire, basis of payment.
- ○ Commissions.
- ○ Type of charterparty with main amendments.

The details of a fixture consist of all terms which are not described above, and in some cases can refer to a considerable number of typewritten clauses attached to printed charterparty, or to alterations in the printed text of charterparty.

If a fixture is confirmed, or an offer made or confirmed "subject approval of details" or "subject details" or "subject arranging details" such negotiations can only be suspended if one party cannot agree and other party maintains one or more of such "details" ... and the above proviso cannot be taken as an excuse to break off negotiations for some other reason.

A broker shall not negotiate for or fix any vessel or any cargo on behalf of Shipowners or Charterers while he is interested directly or indirectly as Charterer or Shipowner or otherwise as Principal, without the fact of such interest being previously disclosed to the Shipowners or Charterers.

Where a Broker Acts as Ship's Agent

11. Duties.

The protection of the vessel's interests at all times should be the aim and duty of a ship's agent, especially with regard to the quickest turnround of a ship in port at lowest possible expense.

12. Attendance to Time Chartered Vessels.

The agents appointed by the time charterers must perform all the normal services to the ship and her master as would have been performed if the vessel called under a voyage charter and the agent was appointed by the owners. All normal agency fees for ordinary agency services shall be charged against the time charterers.

13. Attendance as Agents Appointed by Charterers.

If a vessel by the charterparty is considered to agents nominated by the charterers, the agents so appointed must perform all the normal services to the ship and her master as if the agent had been appointed direct by the owners, the agent charging the normal fees for his work, such fees not exceeding what would have been charged under direct appointment by the owners.

14. Agency Fees.

The broker's agency fee should be clearly advised to shipowner and should be according to the Scale of Agency Fees customary applying in respective ports and countries. Such agency fee should represent the base of all ship's agency negotiations.

15. Ship's Disbursements.

A ship's agent should not retain more freight than actually required for ship's disbursements, and should remit any balance promptly to owners.

Should the agent not collect any freight he should advise owners in good time the approximate amount required for ship's disbursements and owners should remit such funds to the agent in advance of ship's arrival in port.

Other General Chartering Principles
Supported by The Baltic and International Maritime Conference (BIMCO)

Ship Agents.

Shipowners should always have full liberty to select and appoint their own agents at port of loading as well as at port of discharge to look after the business of the vessels and assist the captains. Any provisions in charterparties to the contrary are most objectionable and should not be tolerated.

If, when shipping a cargo by a tramp vessel, a merchant needs somebody in the port of loading or discharge to attend to the transhipment or forwarding, he should appoint a separate agent but should not try to prevent owners from having their own agents to look after vessel's interests.

Cargo Handling.

If it is desired that the shipowners should pay for the loading and discharge of the cargoes, they should have liberty to select and appoint their own stevedores.

If it is desired that the charterers, shippers or receivers should appoint the stevedores, it should be agreed that the cargo should be loaded and/or discharged.

a) free of any costs whatsoever to the vessel, or

b) at a reasonable fixed price to include all "extras" whatsoever.

Loading and Discharging Time.

Loading and discharging time should be as close as possible to the average capacity actually established in a particular port or trade. If a certain type of cargo is normally loaded or discharged at a port of range of ports, the daily loading or discharging quantity to be inserted in the charterparty should be as near the normal figure as possible. Loading or discharging should commence soon after the vessel has arrived, time counting from commencement of cargo operations.

APPENDIX 9

FIRM OFFER SHEET

Charterers: **Brokers:**   **Date:**

Description of Ship:

Name: Blt: Flag:

SDWT: on SDWFT

LOA: BM:

CARGO CAPACITY: 98% (inc slops?)

BCM: TPC: DERRICKS: SCNRT:

IGS/COW/SBT/COILED/COATED

LAST THREE CARGOES: -

TO BEST OF OWNER'S KNOWLEDGE (TBOOK) VESSEL IS ACCEPTABLE

TO:

CARGO DESCR:

LOAD RANGE:

DISCH RANGE:

LAYDAYS:

ASBATANKVOY

Owners option to Slow Steam down to about...kts Weather and safe navigation

permitting

FREIGHT PAYMENT:

GA + ARB LDN, ENGLISH LAW/NY AMERICAN LAW

YA 94

CONOCO WEATHER CLAUSE

FMC/USCG

ITOPF

WSHTC + Special Rates to Apply

R E W S

Demurrage

CHEVRON WRISK CLAUSE:

COMMISSION

Reply Time:

(Refer P.12/14)

APPENDIX 10

VOYAGE CHECKLIST

1. FIRM OFFER / FIRM INDICATION	2 SUBJECT: WHEN DECLARABLE:
3. REPLY TIME:	4. BROKER A.O.H.:
5. PLACE AND DATE:	

6. CHARTERERS:
7. OWNERS:
8. VESSEL: LPG/C "

9. DETAILS	
	CAPACITY:
LOA:	BEAM:
SUMMER LOAD DRAFT:	CLASS:
BUILT:	FLAG:

10. CARGO   (AWVNS)
11. LOADPORT / LIGHTERAGE
12. DISCHARGE PORT / LIGHTERAGE
13. FREIGHT RATE: (PMT / LUMPSUM)
14. LAY/CAN: LAY TIME:
15. DEMURRAGE: (PER DAY AND PRO RATA)
16. LAST CARGO:
17. PRESENTATION:
18. TEMPERATURE CLAUSE   (LOAD, CARRY, DISCHARGE)
19. NOTICES:
20. SHORTAGE CLAUSE:

21. C/P:	22. G.A./ARB LAW Y/A 74

23. AGENTS:
24. INSPECTORS:

APPENDIX 10

25. LIGHTERAGE CLAUSE:

26. WIND / SWELL CLAUSE:

27. IMCO / FCM / USCG / RINA, ETC., JAPANESE CUSTOMS CALIBRATION:

28. PAYMENT TERMS & BANK:

29. COMMISSION:

30. SLACK TANKS: YES / NO

31. SYSTEMS NO.:   COMPOSITION:

32. SLOW STEAM:

33. WAR RISK INSURANCE:

APPENDIX 11

TIME CHARTER CHECKLIST ☐IN ☐OUT

1. FIRM OFFER / INDICS:	2. SUBJECT: WHEN DECLARABLE:
3. REPLY TIME:	4. BROKER: A.O.H.:
5. PLACE & DATE:	

6. CHARTERERS:

7. OWNERS:

8. VESSEL: LPG/C "

9. DETAILS:

10. PERIOD OF CHARTER:

11. RATE OF HIRE: (INCLUDING O.T.)

12. LAY / CAN:

13. PLACE OF DELIVERY:

14. PLACE OF RE-DELIVERY:

15. PRODUCTS TO BE CARRIED:

16. NUMBER OF GRADES / SEGREGATION

17. PRESENTATION ON DELIVERY:

18. PRESENTATION ON RE-DELIVERY:

APPENDIX 11

19. TRADING LIMITS AND EXCLUSIONS:

20. CHARTER PARTY:
    LIGHTERAGE CLAUSE: AGREE ATTACHED NOTICE

21. SPEED AND BUNKER CONSUMPTION (WARRANTED / GUARANTEED):

22. VESSEL'S PUMPING CAPACITY:

23. HEATERS / BOOSTERS: TYPE / RATING:

24. RE-DELIVERY CLAUSE:

25. BUNKERS ON DELIVERY / PRICES:

    BUNKERS ON RE-DELIVERY / PRICES:

26. DRYDOCKING (INTERVAL, NOTICE AND D.D. RANGE):

27. LAW: 28. GA / ARB:

29. OVERALL MAINTENANCE (NO. OF HOURS AGREED):

30. WAR RISK INSURANCES / BLOCKING:

31. BOYCOTT CLAUSE:

32. USCG / FMC / RINA / IMCO / JAPANESE CUSTOMS-CALIBRATION:

33. PAYMENT:

34. COMMISSION:

APPENDIX 12

**Association of Ship Brokers
& Agents (U.S.A.), Inc.
October 1977**

**CODE WORD FOR THIS
CHARTER PARTY:
ASBATANKVOY**

TANKER VOYAGE CHARTER PARTY

PREAMBLE

_____ _____

Place   Date

ITISTHISDAYAGREEDbetween_____

chartered owner/owner (hereinafter called the "Owner") of the _____

SS/MS_____(hereinafter called the "Vessel")

and_____ (hereinafter called the "Charterer") that the

transportation herein provided for will be performed subject to the terms and conditions of this Charter Party, which includes this

Preamble and Part I and Part II. In the event of a conflict, the provisions of Part I will prevail over those contained in Part II.

PART I

A. Description and Position of Vessel:

    Deadweight: tons (2240 lbs.)   Classed:

    Loaded draft of Vessel on assigned summer freeboard   ft.   in. in salt water.

    Capacity for cargo: tons (of 2240 lbs. each)   % more or less, Vessel's option.

    Coated: □ Yes   □ No

    Coiled: □ Yes   □ No   Last two cargoes:

    Now: Expected Ready:

B. Laydays:

    Commencing: Cancelling:

C. Loading Port(s)

                                                                Charterer's Option

D. Discharging Port(s):

                                                                Charterer's Option

E. Cargo:

                                                                Charterer's Option

F. Freight Rate: per ton (of 2240 lbs. each).

G. Freight Payable to:

APPENDIX 12

H.   Total Laytime in Running Hours:

I.   Demurrage per day:

J.   Commission of   % is payable by Owner to

  on the actual amount freight, when and as freight is paid.

K.   The place of General Average and arbitration proceedings to be London/New York (strike out one).

L.   Tovalop: Owner warrants vessel to be a member of TOVALOP scheme and will be so maintained throughout duration of this charter.

M.   Special Provisions:

IN WITNESS WHEREOF, the parties have caused this Charter, consisting of a Preamble, Parts I and II, to be executed in duplicate as of the day and year first above written.

Witness the signature of:

  By: _____

Witness the Signature of:

  By: _____

APPENDIX 12

Part II

1. WARRANTY—VOYAGE—CARGO. The vessel, classed as specified in Part I hereof, and to be so maintained during the currency of this Charter, shall, with all convenient dispatch, proceed as ordered to Loading Port(s) named in accordance with Clause 4 hereof, or so near thereunto as she may safely get (always afloat), and being seaworthy, and having all pipes, pumps and heater coils in good working order, and being in every respect fitted for the voyage, so far as the foregoing conditions can be attained by the exercise of due diligence, perils of the sea and any other cause of whatsoever kind beyond the Owner's and/or Master's control excepted, shall load (always afloat) from the factors of the Charterer a full end complete cargo of petroleum and/or its products in bulk, not exceeding what she can reasonably stow and carry over and above her bunker fuel, consumable stores, boiler feed, culinary end drinking water, and complement and their effects (sufficient space to be left in the tanks to provide for the expansion of the cargo), and being so loaded shall forthwith proceed, as ordered on signing Bills of Lading, direct to the Discharging Port(s), or so near thereunto as she may safely get (always afloat), end deliver said cargo. If heating of the cargo is requested by the Charterer, the Owner shall exercise due diligence to maintain the temperatures requested.

2. FREIGHT. Freight shall be at the rate stipulated in Part I and shall be computed on intake quantity (except deadfreight as per Clause 3) as shown on the Inspector's Certificate of Inspection. Payment of freight shall be made by Charterer without discount upon delivery of cargo at destination, less any disbursements or advances made to the Master or Owner's agents at ports of loading and/or discharge and cost of insurance thereon. No deduction of freight shall be made for water and/or sediment contained in the cargo. The services of the Petroleum Inspector shall be arranged and paid for by the Charterer who shall furnish the Owner with a copy of the Inspector's Certificate.

3. DEADFREIGHT. Should the Charterer fail to supply a full cargo, the Vessel may, at the Master's option, and shall, upon request of the Charterer, proceed on her voyage, provided that the tanks in which cargo is loaded are sufficiently filled to put her in seaworthy condition. In that event, however, deadweight shall be paid at the rate specified in Part I hereof on the difference between the intake quantity and the quantity the Vessel would have carried if loaded to her minimum permissible freeboard for the voyage.

4. NAMING LOADING AND DISCHARGE PORTS.

(a) The Charterer shall name the loading port or ports at least twenty-four (24) hours prior to the Vessel's readiness to sail from the last previous port of discharge, or from bunkering port for the voyage, or upon signing this Charter if the Vessel has already sailed. However, Charterer shall have the option of ordering the Vessel to the following destinations for wireless orders:

	On a voyage to a port or ports in:
ST. KITTS	Caribbean or U.S. Gulf loading port(s)
PORT SAID	Eastern Mediterranean or Persian Gulf loading port(s) (from ports west of Port Said.)

(b) If lawful and consistent with Part I and with the Bills of Lading, the Charterer shall have the option of nominating a discharging port or ports by radio to the Master on or before the Vessel's arrival at or off the following places:

Place	*On a voyage to a port or ports in:*
LAND'S END	United Kingdom/Continent (Bordeaux/Hamburg range) or Scandinavia (including Denmark)
SUEZ	Mediterranean (from Persian Gulf)
GIBRALTER	Mediterranean (from Western Hemisphere).

(c) Any extra expense incurred in connection with any change in loading or discharging ports (so named) shall be paid for by the Charterer and any time thereby lost to the Vessel snail count as used laytime.

5. LAYDAYS. Laytime shall not commence before the date stipulated in Part I, except with the Charterer's sanction. Should the Vessel not be ready to load by 4:00 o'clock P.M. (local time) on the cancelling date stipulated in Part I, the Charterer shall have the option of cancelling this Charter by giving Owner notice of such cancellation within twenty-four (24) hours after such cancellation date; otherwise this Charter to remain in full force and effect.

6. NOTICE OF READINESS. Upon arrival at customary anchorage at each port of loading or discharge, the Master or his agent shall give the Charterer or his agent notice by letter, telegraph, wireless or telephone that the Vessel is ready to load or discharge cargo, berth or no berth, and laytime, as hereinafter provided, shall commence upon the expiration of six (6) hours after receipt of such notice, or upon the Vessel's arrival in berth (i.e., finished mooring when at a sealoading or discharging terminal and all fast when loading or discharging alongside a wharf), whichever first occurs. However, where delay is caused to Vessel getting into berth after giving notice of readiness for any reason over which Charterer has no control, such delay shall not count as used laytime.

7. HOURS FOR LOADING AND DISCHARGING. The number of running hours specified as laytime in Part I shall be permitted the Charterer as laytime for loading and discharging cargo; but any delay due to the Vessel's condition or breakdown or inability of the Vessel's facilities to load or discharge cargo within the time allowed shall not count as used laytime. If regulations of the Owner or port authorities prohibit loading or discharging of the cargo at night, time so lost shall not count as used laytime; if the Charterer, shipper or consignee prohibits loading or discharging at night, time so lost shall count as used laytime, Time consumed by the vessel in moving from loading or discharge port anchorage to her loading or discharge berth, discharging ballast water or slops, will not count as used laytime.

8. DEMURRAGE. Charterer shall pay demurrage per running hour and pro rata for a part thereof at the rate specified in Part I for ell time that loading and discharging and used laytime as elsewhere herein provided exceeds the allowed laytime elsewhere herein specified. If, however, demurrage shall be incurred at ports of loading and/or discharge by reason of fire, explosion, storm or by a strike, lockout, stoppage or restraint of labor or by breakdown of machinery or equipment in or about the plant of the Charterer, supplier, shipper or consignee of the cargo, the rate of demurrage shall be reduced one-half of the amount stated in Part I per running hour or pro rata for part of an hour for demurrage so incurred. The Charterer shall not be liable for any demurrage for delay caused by strike, lockout, stoppage or restraint of labor for Master, officers and crew of the Vessel or tugboat or pilots.

9. SAFE BERTHING—SHIFTING. The vessel shall load and discharge at any safe place or wharf, or alongside vessels or lighters reachable on her arrival, which shall be designated and procured by the Charterer, provided the Vessel can proceed thereto, lie at, and depart therefrom always safely afloat, any lighterage being at the expense, risk and peril of the Charterer. The Charterer shall have the right of shifting the Vessel at ports of loading and/or discharge from one safe berth to another on payment of all towage and pilotage shifting to next berth, charges for running lines on arrival at and leaving that berth, additional agency charges and expense, customs overtime and fees, and any other extra port charges or port expenses incurred by reason of using more than one berth. Time consumed on account of shirting shall count as used laytime except as otherwise provided in Clause 15.

10. PUMPING IN AND OUT. The cargo shall be pumped into the Vessel at the expense, risk and peril of the Charterer, and shall be pumped out of the Vessel at the expense of the Vessel, but at the risk and peril of the Vessel only to far as the Vessel's permanent hose connections, where delivery of the cargo shall be taken by the Charterer or its consignee. If required by Charterer, Vessel after discharging is to clear shore pipe lines of cargo by pumping water through them and time consumed for this purpose shall apply against allowed laytime. The Vessel shall supply her pumps and the necessary power for discharging in all ports, as well as necessary hands. However, should the Vessel be prevented from supplying such power by reason of regulations prohibiting fires on board, the Charterer or consignee shall supply, at its expense, all power necessary for discharging as well as loading, but the Owner shall pay for power supplied to the Veasel for other purposes. If cargo is loaded from lighters, the Vessel shall furnish steam at Charterer's expense for pumping cargo into its Vessel, if requested by the Charterer, providing the Vessel has facilities for generating steam and is permitted to have fires on board. All overtime of officers and crew incurred in loading and/or discharging shall be for account of the Vessel.

11. HOSES: MOORING AT SEA TERMINALS. Hoses for loading and discharging shall be furnished by the Charterer and shall be connected and disconnected by the Charterer, or, at the option of the Owner, by the Owner at the Charterer's risk and expense. Laytime shall continue until the hoses have been disconnected. When Vessel loads or discharges at a sea terminal, the Vessel shall be properly equipped at Owner's expense for loading or discharging at such place, including suitable ground tackle, mooring lines and equipment for handling submarine hoses.

12. DUES—TAXES—WHARFAGE. The Charterer shall pay all taxes, dues and other charges on the cargo, including but not limited to Customs overtime on the cargo, Venezuelan Habilitation Tax, C.I.M. Taxes at Le Havre and Portuguese Imposto de Comercio Maritime. The Charterer shall also pay all taxes on freight at loading or discharging ports and any unusual taxes, assessments and governmental charges which are not presently in effect but which may be imposed in the future on the Veasel or freight. The Owner shall pay all dues and other charges on the Vessel (whether or not such dues or charges are assessed on the basis of quantity of cargo), including but not limited to French droits de quai and Spanish derramas taxes. The Vessel shall be free of charges for the use of any wharf, dock, place or mooring facility arranged by the Charterer for the purpose of loading or discharging cargo: however, the Owner shall be responsible for charges for such berth when used solely for Vessel's purposes, such as awaiting Owner's orders, tank cleaning, repairs, etc. before, during or after wading or discharging.

13. (a). CARGOES EXCLUDED VAPOR PRESSURE. Cargo shall not be shipped which has a vapor pressure at one hundred degrees Fahrenheit (100°F.) in excess of thirteen and one-half pounds (13.5 lbs.) as determined by the current A.S.T.M. Method (Reid) D-323.

(b) FLASH POINT. Cargo having a flash point under one hundred and fifteen degrees Fahrenheit (115°F.) (closed cup) A.S.T.M. Method D-56 shall not be loaded from lighters but this clause shall not restrict the Charterer from loading or topping off Crude Oil from vessels or barges inside or outside the bar at any port or place where bar conditions exist.

14. (a). ICE. In case port of loading or discharge should be inaccessible owing to ice, the Vessel shall direct her course according to Master's judgment, notifying by telegraph or radio, if available, the Charterers, shipper or consignee, who is bound to telegraph or radio orders for another port, which is free from ice and where there are facilities for the loading or reception of the cargo in bulk. The whole of the time occupied from the time the Vessel is diverted by reason of the ice until her arrival at an ice-free port of loading or discharge, as the case may be, shall be paid for by the Charterer at the demurrage rate stipulated in Part I.

(b) If on account of ice the Master considers it dangerous to enter or remain at any loading or discharging place for fear of the Vessel being frozen in or damaged, the Master shall communicate by telegraph or radio, if available, with the Charterer, shipper or consignee of the cargo, who shall telegraph or radio him in reply, giving orders to proceed to another port as per Clause 14 (a) where, there is no danger of ice and where there are the necessary facilities for the loading or reception of the cargo in bulk, or to remain at the original port at their risk, and in either case Charterer to pay for the time that the Vessel may be delayed, at the demurrage rate stipulated in Part I.

15. TWO OR MORE PORTS COUNTING AS ONE. To the extent that the freight rate standard of reference specified in Part IF hereof provides for special groupings or combinations of ports or terminals, any two or more ports or terminals within each such grouping or combination shall count as one port for purposes of calculating freight and demurrage only, subject to the following conditions:

(a) Charterer shall pay freight at the highest rate payable under Part I F hereof for a voyage between the loading and discharge ports used by Charterer.

(b) All charges normally incurred by reason of using more than one berth shall be for Charterer's account as provided in Clause 9 hereof.

(c) Time consumed shifting between the ports or terminals within the particular grouping or combination shall not count as used laytime.

(d) Time consumed shifting between berths within one of the ports or terminals of the particular grouping or combination shall count as used laytime.

16. GENERAL CARGO. The Charterer shall not be permitted to ship any packaged Roods or non-liquid bulk cargo of any description; the cargo the Vessel is to load under this Charter is to consist only of liquid bulk cargo as specified m Clause I.

17. (a). QUARANTINE. Should the Charterer send the Vessel to any port or place where a quarantine exists, any delay thereby caused to the Vessel shall count as used laytime; but should the quarantine not be declared until the Vessel is on passage to such port, the Charterer shall not be liable for any resulting delay.

(b) FUMIGATION. If the Vessel, prior to or after entering upon this Charter, has docked or docks at any wharf which is not rat-free or stegomyia-free, she shall, before proceeding to a rat-free or stegomyia-free wharf, be fumigated by the Owner at his expense, except that if the Charterer ordered the Vessel to an infected wharf the Charterer shall bear the expense of fumigation.

18. CLEANING. The Owner shall clean the tanks, pipes and pumps of the Vessel to the satisfaction of the Charterer's Inspector. The Vessel shall not be responsible for any admixture if more than one quality of oil is shipped, nor for leakage, contamination or deterioration in quality of the cargo unless the admixture, leakage, contamination or deterioration results from (a) unseaworthiness existing at the time of loading or at the inception of the voyage which was discoverable by the exercise of due diligence, or (b) error or fault of the servants of the Owner in the loading, care or discharge of the cargo.

19. GENERAL EXCEPTIONS CLAUSE. The Vessel, her Master and Owner shall not, unless otherwise in this Charter expressly provided, be responsible for any loss or damage, or delay or failure in performing hereunder, arising or resulting from:—any act, neglect, default or barratry of the Master, pilots, mariners or other servants of the Owner in the navigation or management of the Vessel; fire, unless caused by the personal design or neglect of the Owner collision, stranding or peril, danger or accident of the sea or other navigable waters; saving or attempting to save life or property: wastage in weight or bulk, or any other loss or damage arising from inherent defect, quality or vice of the cargo; any act or omission of the Charterer or Owner, shipper or consignee of the cargo, their agents or representatives; insufficiency of packing; insufficiency or inadequacy or marks; explosion, bursting of boilers, breakage of shafts or any latent defect in bull, equipment or machinery; unseaworthiness of the Vessel unless caused by want of due diligence on the par t of the Owner to make the Vessel sea worthy or to have her properly manned, equipped and supplied; or from any other cause of whatsoever kind arising without the actual fault or privity of the Owner. And neither the Vessel nor Master or Owner nor the Charterer, shall, unless otherwise in this Charter expressly provided, be responsible for any loss of damage or delay or failure in performing hereunder, arising or resulting from:—Act of God; act of war; perils of the seas; act of public enemies, pirates or assailing thieves; arrest or restraint of princes, rulers or people; or seizure under legal process provided bond is promptly furnished to release the Vessel or cargo; strike or lockout or stoppage, or restraint of labor from whatever cause, either partial or general; or riot or civil commotion.

20. ISSUANCE AND TERMS OF BILLS OF LADING

(a) The Master shall, upon request, sign Bills of Lading in the form appearing below for all cargo shipped but without prejudice to the rights of the Owner and Charterer under the terms of this Charter. The Master shall not be required to sign Bills of Lading for any port which, the Vessel cannot enter, remain at and leave in safety and always afloat nor for any blockaded port.

(b) The carriage of cargo under this Charter Party and under all Bills of Lading issued for the cargo shall be subject to the statutory provisions and other terms set forth or specified in sub-paragraphs (i) through (vii) of this clause and such terms shall be incorporated verbatim or be deemed incorporated by the reference in any such Bill of Lading. In such sub-paragraphs and in any Act referred to therein, the word "carrier" shall include the Owner and the Chartered Owner of the Vessel.

(i) CLAUSE PARAMOUNT. This Bill of Lading shall have effect subject to the provisions of the Carriage of Goods by Sea Acts of the United States, approved April 16, 1936, except that if this Bill of Lading is issued at a place where any other Act, ordinance or legislation gives statutory effect to the International Convention for the Unification of Certain Rules relating to Bills of Lading at Brussels, August 1924, then this Bill of Lading shall have effect, subject to the provisions of such Act, ordinance or legislation. The applicable Act, ordinance or legislation (hereinafter called the "Act") shall be deemed to be incorporated herein and nothing herein contained shall be deemed a surrender by the Owner of any of its rights or immunities or an increase of any of its responsibilities or liabilities under the Act. If any term of this Bill of Lading be repugnant to the Act to any extent, such term shall be void to the extent but no further.

(ii) JASON CLAUSE. In the event of accident, danger, damage or disaster before or after the commencement of the voyage, resulting from any cause whatsoever, whether due to negligence or not, for which, or for the consequence of which, the Owner is not responsible, by statute, contract or otherwise, the cargo shippers, consignees or owners of the cargo snail contribute with the Owner in General Average to the payment of any sacrifices, losses or expenses of a General Average nature that may be made or incurred and shall pay salvage and special charges incurred in respect of the cargo. If a salving ship is owned or operated by the Owner, salvage shall be paid – for as fully as if the said salving ship or ships belonged to strangers. Such deposit as the Owner or his agents may deem sufficient to cover the estimated contribution of the cargo and any salvage and special charges theron shall, if required, be made by the cargo, shippers, consignees or owners of the cargo to the carrier before delivery.

(iii) GENERAL AVERAGE. General Average shall be adjusted, stated and settled according to York/Antwerp Rules 1950 and, as to matters not provided for by those rules, according to the laws and usages at the port of New York or at the port of London, whichever place is specified in Part I of this Charter. If a General Average statement is required, it shall be prepared at such port or place in the United States or United Kingdom, whichever country is specified in Part I of this Charter, as may be selected

APPENDIX 12

by the Owner, unless otherwise mutually agreed, by an Adjuster appointed by the Owner and approved by the Charterer. Such Adjuster shall attend to the settlement and the collection of the General Average, subject to customary charges, General Average Agreements and/or security shall be furnished by Owner and/or Charterer, and/or Owner and/or Consignee of cargo, if requested. Any cash deposit being made as security to pay General Average and/or salvage shall be remitted to the Average Adjuster and shall be held by him at his risk in a special account in a duly authorized and licensed bank at the place where the General Average statement is prepared.

(iv) BOTH TO BLAME. If the Vessel comes into collision with another ship as a result of the negligence of the other shin and any act, neglect or default of the Master, maringer, pilot or the servants of the Owner in the navigation or in the management of the Vessel, the owners of the cargo carried hereunder shall indemnify the Owner against all loss or liability to the other or non-carrying ship or her owners in so far as such loss or liability represents loss of, or damage to, or any claim whatsoever of the owners of said cargo, paid or payable by the other or recovered by the other or non-carrying ship or her owners as part of their claim against the carrying ship or Owner. The foregoing provisions shall also apply where the owners, operators or those in charge of any ships or objects other than, or in addition to, the colliding ships or object are at fault in respect of a collision or contact.

(v) LIMITATION OF LIABILITY. Any provision of this Charter to the contrary notwithstanding, the Owner shall have the benefit of all limitations of, and exemptions from, liability accorded to the owner or chartered owner of vessels by any statute or rule of law for the time being in force.

(vi) WAR RISKS, (a) If any port of loading or of discharge named in this Charter Party or to which the Vessel may properly be ordered pursuant to the terms of the Bills of Lading be blockaded, or

(b) If owing to any war, hostilities, warlike operations, civil war, civil commotions, revolutions or the operation of international the (a) entry to any such port of loading or of discharge or the loading or discharge of cargo at any such port be considered by the Master or Owners in his or their discretion dangerous or prohibited or (b) it be considered by the Master or Owners in his or their discretion dangerous or impossible for the Vessel to reach any such port of loading or discharge—the Charterers shall have the right to order the cargo or such part of it as may be affected to be loaded or discharged at any other safe port of loading or of discharge within the range of loading or discharging ports respectively established under the provisions of the Charter Party (provided such other port is not blockaded or that entry thereto or loading or discharge of cargo thereat is not in the Master's or Owner's discretion dangerous or prohibited). If in respect of a port of discharge no orders be received from the Charterers within 48 hours after they or their agents have received from the Owners a request for the nomination of a substitute port, the Owners shall then be at liberty to discharge the cargo at any safe port which they or the Master may in their or his discretion decide on (whether within the range of discharging ports established under the provisions of the Charter Party or not) and such discharge shall be deemed to be due fulfillment of the contract or contracts of affreightment so far as cargo so discharged is concerned. In the event of the cargo being loaded or discharged at any such other port within the respective range of loading or discharging ports established under the provisions of the Charter Party, the Charter Party shall be read in respect of freight and all other conditions whatsoever as if the voyage performed were that originally designated. In the event, however, that the Vessel discharges the cargo at a port outside the range of discharging ports established under the provisions of the Charter Party, freight shall be paid as for the voyage originally designated and all extra expenses involved in reaching the actual port of discharge and or discharging the cargo thereat snail be paid by the Charterers or Cargo Owners. In the latter event the Owners shall have a hen on the cargo for all such extra expenses.

(c) The Vessel shall have liberty to comply with any directions or recommendations as to departure, arrival, routes, ports of call, stoppages, destinations, zones, waters, delivery or in any otherwise whatsoever given by the government of the nations under whose flag the Vessel sails or any other government or local authority including any de facto government or local authority or by any person or body acting or purporting to act as or with the authority of any such government or authority or by any committee or person having under the terms of the war risks insurance on the vessel the right to give any such directions or recommendations. If by reason of or in compliance with any such directions or recommendations, anything is done or is not done such shall not be deemed a deviation.

If by reason of or in compliance with any such direction or recommendation the Vessel does not proceed to the port or ports of discharge originally designated or to which she may have been ordered pursuant to the terms of the Bills of Lading, the Vessel may proceed to any safe port of discharge which the Master or Owners in his or their discretion may decide on and there discharge the cargo. Such discharge shall be deemed to be due fulfillment of the contract or contracts of affreightment and the Owners shall be entitled to freight as if discharge has been effected at the port or ports originally designated or to which the vessel may have been ordered pursuant to the terms of the Bills of Lading. All extra expenses involved in reaching and discharging the cargo at any such other port of discharge shall be paid by the Charterers and/or Cargo Owners and the Owners shall have a lien on the cargo for freight and all such expenses.

(vii) DEVIATION CLAUSE. The Vessel shall have liberty to call at any ports in any order, to sail with or without pilots, to tow or to be towed, to go to the assistance of vessels in distress, to deviate for the purpose of saving life or property or of landing any ill or injured person on board, and to call for fuel at any port or ports in or out of the regular course of the voyage. Any salvage shall be for the sole benefit of the Owner

21. LIEN. The Owner shall have an absolute lien on the cargo for all freight, deadfreight, demurrage and costs, including attorney fees, of recovering the same, which lien shall continue after delivery of the cargo into the possession of the Charterer, or of the holders of any Bills of Lading covering the same or of any storageman.

22. AGENTS. The Owner shall appoint Vessel's agents at all ports.

23. BREACH. Damages for breach of this Charter shall include all provable damages, and all costs of suit and attorney fees incurred in any action hereunder.

24. ARBITRATION. Any and all differences and disputes of whatsoever nature arising out of this Charter shall be put to arbitration in the City of New York or in the City of London whichever place is specified in Part I of this charter pursuant to the laws relating to arbitration there in force, before a board of three persons, consisting of one arbitrator to be appointed by the Owner, one by the Charterer, and one by the two so chosen. The decision of any two of the three on any point or points shall be final. Either party hereto may call for such arbitration by service upon any officer of the other, wherever he may be found, of a written notice specifying the name and address of the arbitrator chosen by the first moving party and a brief description of the disputes or differences which such party desires to put to arbitration. If the other party shall not, by notice served upon an officer of the first moving party within twenty days of the service of such first notice, appoint its arbitrator to arbitrate the dispute or differences specified, then the first moving party shall have the right without further notice to appoint a second arbitrator, who shall be a disinterested person with precisely the same force and effect as if said second arbitrator has been appointed by the other party. In the event that the two abritrators fail to appoint a third arbitrator within twenty days of the appointment of the second arbitrator, either arbitrator may apply to a Judge of any court of maritime jurisdiction in the city above-mentioned for the appointment of a third arbitrator, and the appointment of such arbitrator by such Judge on such application shall have precisely the same force and effect as if such arbitrator had been appointed by the two arbitrators. Until such time as the arbitrators finally close the hearings either party shall have the right by written notice served on the arbitrators and on an officer of the other party to specify further disputes or differences under this Charter for hearing and determination. Awards made in pursuance to this clause may include costs, including a reasonable allowance for attorney's fees, and judgement may be entered upon any award made hereunder in any Court having jurisdiction in the premises.

25. SUBLET. Charterer shall have the right to sublet the Vessel. However, Charterer shall always remain responsible for the fulfillment of this Charter in all its terms and conditions.

26. OIL POLLUTION CLAUSE, Owner agrees to participate in Charterer's program covering oil pollution avoidance. Such program prohibits discharge overboard of all oily water, oily ballast or oil in any form of a persistent nature, except under extreme circumstances whereby the safety of the vessel, cargo or life at sea would be imperiled.

Upon notice being given to the Owner that Oil Pollution Avoidance controls are required, the Owner will instruct the Master to retain on board the vessel all oily residues from consolidated tank washings, dirty ballast, etc., in one compartment, after separation of all possible water has taken place. All water separated to be discharged overboard.

If the Charterer requires that demulsifiers shall be used for the separation of oil/water, such demulsifiers shall be obtained by the Owner and paid for by Charterer.

The oil residues will be pumped ashore at the loading or discharging terminal, either as segregated oil, dirty ballast or co-mingled with cargo as it is possible for Charterers to arrange. If it is necessary to retain the residue on board co-mingled with or segregated from the cargo to be loaded, Charterers shall pay for any deadfreight so incurred.

Should it be determined that the residue is to be co-mingled or segregated on board, the Master shall arrange that the quantity of tank washings be measured in conjunction with cargo suppliers and a note of the quantity measured made in the vessel's ullage record.

The Charterer agrees to pay freight as per the terms of the Charter Party on any consolidated tank washings, dirty ballast, etc., retained on board under Charterer's instructions during the loaded portion of the voyage up to a maximum of 1% of the total deadweight of the vessel that could be legally carried for such voyage. Any extra expenses incurred by the vessel at loading or discharging port in pumping ashore oil residues shall be for Charterer's account, and extra time, if any, consumed for this operation shall count as used laytime.

BILL OF LADING

Shipped in apparent good order and condition by ______________________________

on board the ______________________________ Steamship / Motorship ______________________________

whereof ______________________________ is Master, at the port of ______________________________

____

____

____

____

____

to be delivered at the port of ______________________________

or so near thereto as the Vessel can safely get, always afloat, unto ______________________________

____

or order on payment of freight at the rate of ______________________________

This shipment is carried under and pursuant to the terms of the contract / charter dated New York/London ______________________________

between ______________________________ and ______________________________, as

Charterer, and all the terms whatsoever of the said contract / charter except the rate and payment of freight specified therein apply to and govern the rights of the parties concerned in this shipment.

In witness whereof the Master has signed ______________________________ Bills of Lading of this tenor and date, one of which being accomplished, the others will be void.

Dated at ______________________________ this ______________ day of ______________________________

____

Master

Form 30-165 Printed and Sold by UNACO 190 Baldwin Ave., Jersey City, NJ 07308 • (800) 631-3098 • (201) 795-5400

APPENDIX 13

SHELL ITOPF CLAUSE

Owners warrant that throughout the duration of this Charter the vessel will be:

i) *owned or demise chartered by a member of the < International Tanker Owners= Pollution Federation Limited=, and*

ii) *entered in the Protection and Indemnity (P&I) Club stated in Part 1(A) 1 (xii) of SHELLVOY 5, as amended December 1996.*

APPENDIX 14

BPVOY 4 CLAUSE 43 (CLAUSE PARAMOUNT)

All Bills of Lading issued under this Charter shall contain the following Clause Paramount.

(1) *This Bill of Lading shall have effect subject to any national law making the International Convention for the Unification of certain rules of law relating to Bills of Lading signed at Brussels on 25th August 1924 (The Hague Rules) or the Hague Rules as amended by the Protocol signed at Brussels on 23rd February 1968 (The Hague/Visby Rules) compulsorily applicable to this Bill of Lading. If any item of this Bill of Lading be repugnant to that legislation to any extent, such term shall be void to that extent but no further. Neither the Hague Rules nor the Hague/Visby Rules shall apply to this contract where the goods carried hereunder consist of live animals or cargo which by this contract is stated as being carried on deck and is so carried.*

(2) *Save where the Hague or Hague/Visby Rules apply by reason of (1) above, this Bill of Lading shall take effect subject to any national law in force at the port of shipment or place of issue of the Bill of Lading making the United Nations Convention on the Carriage of Goods by Sea 1978 (the Hamburg Rules) compulsorily applicable to this Bill of Lading in which case this Bill of Lading shall have effect subject to the Hamburg Rules which shall nullify any stipulation derogating therefrom to the detriment of the shipper or consignee.*

(3) *Where the Hague, Hague/Visby or Hamburg Rides are not compulsorily applicable to this Bill of Lading, the carrier shall be entitled to the benefits of all privileges, rights and immunities contained in Articles I to VIII of the Hague Rules.*

(4) *Nothing in this Bill of Lading shall be construed as in any way restricting, excluding or waiving the right of any relevant party or person to limit his liability under any available legislation and/or law.*

APPENDIX 15

tanker voyage charter party

ExxonMobil VOY2005

PREAMBLE

_____	_____
PLACE	DATE

IT IS THIS DAY AGREED between_____Owner/Chartered Owner (hereinafter called "Owner") of the _____Flag MS/SS_____ (hereinafter called "Vessel") and_____(hereinafter called "Charterer") that the transportation herein provided for shall be performed subject to the terms and conditions of this Charter, which includes this Preamble and Part I and II. In the event of a conflict, the provisions of Part I will prevail over those contained in Part II to the extent of such conflict.

PART I

(A)   VESSEL DESCRIPTION AND POSITION:

Year built: Classed: IMO#:

Hull Type (as per IOPPC):   P&I Club: H&M value:

Summer Deadweight: Metric tons on   feet/meters in salt water on assigned summer freeboard.

Maximum Cargo Capacity: Metric tons   % more or less. Vessel's option.

Cubic capacity for cargo (at 98%):   cubic meters/barrels.

Length overall: feet/meters   Beam: feet/meters

Inert Gas System: ❏ Yes   ❏ No

Crude Oil Wash System: ❏ Yes   ❏ No. If Crude Oil Wash is required, the allowed pumping hours specified in Part II, Clause 18 (g) shall be increased by a maximum of   hours pursuant to Part II, Clause 18 (g).

Vessel has full segregated ballast tanks (SBT): ❏ Yes   ❏ No

Vessel has clean ballast tanks (CBT): ❏ Yes   ❏ No

Cargo Tanks Coated: ❏ Yes   ❏ No   Type:

Cargo Tanks Coiled: ❏ Yes   ❏ No   Type:

Last cargo: Next to last cargo:

Vessel onboard quantity (gross standard volume) on date of Charter:

Vessel location on date of Charter:

Expected ready to load:

Charter speed in all weather: knots laden.

(B)   LAYDAYS: Commencing: Cancelling:

(C)   LOADING RANGE(S) / PORT(S) / PLACE(S): One (1) or   safe

APPENDIX 15

(D) DISCHARGING RANGE(S) / PORT(S) / PLACE(S): One (1) or   safe

(E) CARGO QUANTITY:

Full Cargo as defined in Part II, Clause 1 subject to the Maximum Cargo Capacity limits specified in Part I (A): ❑ Yes ❑ No
or
Part Cargo Minimum Metric tons with Charterer's option to load up to Full Cargo as described in this Paragraph (E); provided Part Cargo Minimum is supplied by Charterer, no deadfreight for Charterer's account whether option exercised or not.

(F) CARGO DESCRIPTION:

(G) FREIGHT RATE:

Freight rate for Full Cargo or Part Cargo Minimum (hereinafter called "Base Freight Rate"):

Freight rate for quantity above Part Cargo Minimum (hereinafter called "Overage Freight Rate"):

(H) BILLING:

Freight, deadfreight, demurrage and any other monies payable to Owner pursuant to this Charter shall be payable in United States dollars and invoiced to Charterer at:

and paid to Owner at:

(I) LAYTIME: Total Laytime in running hours:

(J) DEMURRAGE / DEVIATION PER DAY:

In accordance with Part II, Clause 8, demurrage and/or deviation per day shall be based on:

Summer deadweight of Metric tons
or
Part Cargo Minimum plus Metric tons totalling Metric tons
or
United States dollars per day pro rata

(K) SPECIAL PROVISIONS:

(L) INCORPORATED CLAUSE(S):

The following specified Clause(s), the text(s) of which are attached hereto, shall be deemed incorporated in and made a part of this Part I.

IN WITNESS WHEREOF, the parties have caused this Charter, consisting of a Preamble, Parts I and II, to be executed in duplicate as of the day and year first above written.

WITNESS:

                  _____
                     Owner

_____   By: _____

WITNESS:

                  _____
                     Charterer

_____   By: _____

APPENDIX 15

1. **DEFINITIONS.** In this Charter: 1
    (a) "place" shall mean any berth, dock, anchorage, sea terminal, submarine line, alongside vessel and/or lighter, whether at anchor or   2
    underway, and/or any other place to which Charterer is entitled to order Vessel hereunder.   3
    (b) "ILL Convention" shall mean the International Load Line Convention, 1966, or any amendment thereof as may be applicable to the   4
    voyage(s) to be performed hereunder.   5
    (c) "Full Cargo" shall mean a cargo which fills Vessel to its minimum freeboard, as permitted by the ILL Convention, or fills the cubic capacity   6
    of Vessel's available cargo spaces, whichever occurs first, after leaving appropriate space in the tanks for the expansion of cargo.   7
    (d) "Arrival in Berth" shall mean the completion of mooring of the Vessel when loading or discharging at a sea terminal, Vessel being all fast   8
    with gangway down and secure when loading or discharging alongside a wharf/berth or Vessel being all fast alongside a barge, lighter or other   9
    vessel when loading from or discharging to a barge, lighter or other vessel.   10
    (e) Where it is stipulated herein that the Vessel shall meet some "requirement", such stipulation shall be taken to include any requirement that   11
    might be placed upon the Owner, operator, and/or personnel of the Vessel.   12
    (f) "Affiliate" shall mean any company which is directly or indirectly owned or controlled, in whole or in part, by Exxon Mobil Corporation.   13
    (g) Where it is stipulated herein that notices, advices, consents, approvals and other communications be given, same may, unless otherwise   14
    specified herein, be given by electronic mail, telex, facsimile, telephone or radio (if telephone or radio, subsequently confirmed in writing).   15
2. **VESSEL.**   16
    (a) **DESCRIPTION / CONDITION.** Owner warrants that, from the time when the obligation to proceed to the loading port(s) or place(s)   17
    attaches and throughout Vessel's service under this Charter, Vessel shall be as described in Part I (A). Owner further warrants that, during   18
    the period just described, Owner shall exercise due diligence to ensure that Vessel and its hull, machinery, boilers, all tanks and all other   19
    equipment including, but not limited to, pipes, pumps, valves, inert gas and crude oil wash systems (if Vessel is so equipped), navigational   20
    equipment, heating coils and facilities, shall be fully functional and in good working order and condition and in every way seaworthy and fit to   21
    carry cargo and perform the voyage(s) required under this Charter.   22
    (b) **COMPLEMENT.** Owner warrants that, during the period described in Paragraph (a) of this Clause, Vessel shall have a full and efficient   23
    complement of Master, officers and crew, with adequate training and experience in operating all Vessel's equipment, including, but not limited   24
    to, inert gas and crude oil wash systems (if Vessel is so equipped), and that Master and all officers shall possess valid and current certificates/   25
    documents issued or approved by the country of Vessel's registry. Owner further warrants the conversational English language proficiency of   26
    Master and officer(s) in charge of cargo and bunker oil handling.   27
    (c) **COMPLIANCE.** Owner warrants that Vessel shall, during the period described in Paragraph (a) of this Clause, be in full compliance with   28
    all applicable international conventions, all applicable laws, regulations and/or other requirements of the country of Vessel registry and of   29
    the countries of the port(s) and/or place(s) to which Vessel may be ordered hereunder and all applicable regulations and/or requirements of   30
    any terminals or facilities in such port(s) or place(s) where Vessel shall load or discharge. Owner further warrants that Vessel shall have on   31
    board, during the subject period, all certificates, records or other documents required by the aforesaid conventions, laws, regulations and/or   32
    requirements.   33
    (d) **BREACH.** If any of the warranties stipulated in this Clause are breached, any delay resulting therefrom shall not count as laytime or, if   34
    Vessel is on demurrage, as time on demurrage, and any expense attributable to such delay shall be for Owner's account.   35
    (e) **SALE.** Owner warrants that the Vessel has not been sold, is not on offer to be sold, and will not be offered for sale during the period of   36
    this Charter.   37
3. **CLEANING.**   38
    (a) Owner shall clean the tanks, pipes and pumps of Vessel at its expense to the satisfaction of Charterer's representative(s). If the cargo   39
    specified in Part I (F) is clean product and inspection of the tanks is required. Owner shall gasfree the tanks as necessary. Any time used for   40
    tank inspection and any re-inerting of Vessel shall count as laytime or, if Vessel is on demurrage, as time on demurrage. Any time required for   41
    cleaning and gasfreeing shall not count as laytime or, if Vessel is on demurrage, as time on demurrage. Compliance with this Clause shall not   42
    be deemed compliance with Owner's obligations under Clause 2, which are in no way lessened by this Clause.   43
    (b) Vessel shall not be responsible for any admixture, if more than one quality of cargo is shipped, nor for contamination or deterioration in   44
    quality of the cargo unless the admixture, contamination or deterioration results from (i) unseaworthiness existing at the inception of loading   45
    which was discoverable by the exercise of due diligence or (ii) error or fault of the servants of Owner in the loading, care or discharging of   46
    the cargo.   47
    (c) In performing its obligations under this Clause 3, Owner shall comply with the latest ISGOTT guidelines.   48
4. **VOYAGE(S).**   49
    (a) Vessel shall proceed with utmost dispatch to any port(s) or place(s) as ordered by Charterer in accordance with Part I (C) and there load   50
    a cargo as specified in Part I (E) and (F). On completion of loading, Vessel shall then with utmost dispatch proceed to any port(s) or place(s)   51
    as ordered by Charterer in accordance with Part I (D) and there deliver said cargo. Except when required by reason of Vessel fault, lightering   52
    within port limits shall be at Charterer's expense.   53
    (b) Owner shall timely transmit Charterer's voyage instructions in their entirety to the Vessel for Master's implementation. Owner shall ensure   54
    that Charterer is promptly advised of all accidents to, and/or pollutions involving, the Vessel and of any Vessel system failure. Notwithstanding   55
    anything contained in this Charter or in the voyage instructions, the Master and Owner shall continue to be fully and solely responsible for the   56
    operation, management and navigation of the Vessel throughout the Vessel's service under this Charter.   57
    (c) Owner warrants that, throughout Vessel's service under this Charter, Owner shall have full and valid Protection and Indemnity Insurance   58
    ("P&I Insurance") for the Vessel, as described herein, with the P&I Insurance placed with a P&I Club which is a Member of the International   59
    Group of P&I Clubs. This P&I Insurance shall be at no cost to Charterer. The P&I Insurance must include full coverage against liability for   60
    cargo loss/damage and coverage against liability for pollution for an amount not less than US $1,000 Million (One Billion Dollars) per incident.   61
    If requested by Charterer, Owner shall promptly furnish to the Charterer proper evidence of such P&I Insurance upon signing this Charter   62
    or at any time during the Charter term. The above warranty is to be regarded as an essential part of this Charter, which is conditional on its   63
    truth or performance, so that its breach entitles the Charterer, in Charterer's option, to terminate the Charter and/or to recover any damages   64
    allowable in law.   65
5. **MAXIMUM CARGO.** In no event shall Charterer be required to provide, nor shall Vessel load, a cargo quantity in excess of a Full Cargo.   66
    In addition, Charterer shall not be required to provide a cargo quantity in excess of the maximum cargo capacity specified in Part I (A). All time   67
    lost and expense incurred by reason of Vessel loading a quantity of cargo which puts Vessel, at any stage of the voyage(s) hereunder, below   68
    the marks permissible under the ILL Convention shall be for Owner's sole account.   69
6. **FREIGHT.**   70
    (a) Freight shall be paid at the rate stipulated in Part I (G) and shall be computed on gross quantity as stated on the Bill of Lading and on   71
    quantity of documented tank washings if freight thereon is payable in accordance with Clause 33 (a); provided, however, that no freight   72
    shall be payable on any quantity of cargo which puts Vessel, at any stage of the voyage(s) hereunder, below the marks permissible under   73
    the ILL Convention. Deadfreight shall be paid in accordance with Clause 7. Except as provided in Clause 18 (h), no deduction from freight   74

APPENDIX 15

shall be made for water and/or sediment contained in the cargo, nor for any claim Charterer or cargo interests may have against Owner 75
or Vessel arising under this Charter or Bills of Lading issued for the cargo. Payment of freight shall be made by Charterer without 76
discount upon Charterer's receipt of notice of completion of discharge of cargo at last discharging place less any disbursements 77
made to Master or Owner's agent(s) at port(s) or place(s) of loading and/or discharging plus cost of insurance, commissions 78
and expenses on said disbursements and any other costs incurred by Charterer on Owner's behalf pursuant to this Charter. 79
(b) **WORLDSCALE.** Unless otherwise stipulated herein, all rates, hours, terms and conditions in the Worldwide Tanker Nominal Freight 80
Scale current on the date of this Charter (hereinafter called "WORLDSCALE") shall apply to this Charter regardless of when Vessel loads. 81
(c) If cargo is carried between places and/or by a route for which no rate is expressed in WORLDSCALE, then, in the absence of agreement 82
as to the freight rate, the parties hereto will apply to either of the publishers of WORLDSCALE for a binding determination of an appropriate 83
WORLDSCALE rate. 84
(d) Regardless of whether or not the freight specified in Part I (G) is lumpsum, for the purposes of Section 4(5) of the Carriage of Goods 85
by Sea Act of the United States, or the corresponding provisions of any international regime that may otherwise apply in accordance with 86
Clause 27, Owner and Charterer agree that the customary freight unit, shipping unit or unit (as the case may be) of the cargo is Metric ton. 87
(e) Owner shall deduct in favor of Charterer an address commission of one point two five percent (1.25%) from freight, deadfreight, and 88
demurrage payable under this Charter. Owner shall clearly identify such deduction on the freight, deadfreight and/or demurrage invoice. 89
7. **DEADFREIGHT.** Should the entire cargo quantity specified in Part I (E) not be supplied, Master shall give immediate notice to Charterer 90
that such cargo quantity has not been furnished, indicating shortage, and shall then await Charterer's instructions. Should Charterer fail 91
to provide further cargo. Vessel, upon request of Charterer, shall then proceed on its voyage provided that the tanks in which the cargo is 92
loaded are sufficiently filled to put it in a seaworthy condition. If any delay is caused to Vessel by reason of Master waiting for Charterer's 93
instructions as aforesaid, such delay shall count as laytime or, if Vessel is on demurrage, as time on demurrage and any expense incurred by 94
Vessel attributable solely to such delay shall be for Charterer's account. Deadfreight shall be paid at the Base Freight Rate on the shortage 95
(being the difference between the cargo quantity specified in Part I (E) and the quantity loaded as shown on the Bills of Lading) provided 96
such deadfreight charge is fully documented by cable advice from Master or by deadfreight certificate. Charterer shall be credited with any 97
freight on residues earned by Owner in accordance with Clause 33(a)(iii). 98
8. **DEMURRAGE / DEVIATION RATE.** The rate for demurrage and/or deviation shall be the fixed dollar figure specified in Part I (J) or the rate 99
derived by determining the applicable rate from the WORLDSCALE Demurrage Table for tonnage specified in Part I (J) and multiplying that 100
rate by the Base Freight Rate. If a Part Cargo Minimum basis is specified in Part I (E) and Charterer exercises its option to load additional 101
cargo, any demurrage and/or deviation shall, nevertheless, remain payable at either the aforesaid fixed dollar rate or at the aforesaid rate 102
based on the tonnage specified in Part I (J), whichever is applicable. The applicable rate under this Clause shall hereinafter be called 103
"Demurrage Rate" or "Deviation Rate" as is appropriate. 104
9. **LOADING AND DISCHARGING PORT(S) / PLACE(S).** 105
(a) Charterer shall nominate loading or discharging port(s) and/or place(s) or order Vessel to a destination for orders. If Vessel is ordered to 106
a destination for orders, Charterer shall thereafter nominate loading or discharging port(s) and/or place(s). All such nominations or orders 107
shall be made in sufficient time to avoid delay to Vessel. 108
(b) **CHANGE OF DESTINATION.** After nominating loading and/or discharging port(s) or place(s) pursuant to Paragraph (a) of this Clause, 109
Charterer may nominate new port(s) or place(s), whether or not they are within the range of the previously nominated port(s) or place(s) 110
and/or vary the rotation of any nominated port(s) or place(s) and Owner shall issue instructions necessary to make such change(s). It is 111
understood and agreed, however, that the aforesaid option to nominate new loading port(s) or place(s) in different ranges shall lapse on 112
Vessel tendering Notice of Readiness at a nominated loading port or place and that aforesaid option to nominate new discharging port(s) or 113
place(s) in different ranges shall lapse on Vessel tendering Notice of Readiness at a nominated discharging port or place. If a change to, or 114
varying the rotation of, nominated port(s) or place(s) occurs or if Vessel is sent to a destination for orders, any time by which the steaming 115
time to the port(s) or place(s) to which Vessel is finally ordered exceeds that which would have been taken if Vessel had been ordered to 116
proceed to such port(s) or place(s) in the first instance shall be compensated at the Deviation Rate per running day and pro rata for a part 117
thereof. In addition, Charterer shall pay for extra bunkers consumed during such excess time at Owner's documented actual replacement 118
cost at the port where bunkers are next taken. 119
(c) Any order of Vessel to a destination for orders, all nominations and any renominations pursuant to this Clause shall be consistent with 120
Part I (C) and (D). 121
10. **ESTIMATED TIME OF ARRIVAL (ETA).** 122
(a) Unless otherwise instructed, the following Estimated Time of Arrival (ETA) notifications shall be given. As soon as commencing the 123
voyage to the nominated loading port(s) or place(s), but in no event later than seventy-two (72) hours prior to the commencement of laydays 124
specified in Part I (B), Master shall advise Charterer and Vessel's agent and terminal of Vessel's estimated date and time of arrival at the 125
nominated loading port(s) or place(s). Further, provided the length of the voyage permits, Master shall confirm or amend such advice 126
seventy-two (72), forty-eight (48) and twenty-four (24) hours prior to Vessel's arrival at the loading port(s) or place(s). On leaving the final 127
loading port or place, Master shall advise Charterer and Vessel's agent of Vessel's estimated date and hour of arrival at the nominated 128
discharging port(s) or place(s). Further, provided the length of the voyage permits, Master shall confirm or amend such advice seventy-two 129
(72), forty-eight (48) and twenty-four (24) hours prior to Vessel's arrival at the discharging port(s) or place(s). In addition, on leaving the final 130
loading port or place, Master shall advise Charterer of expected maximum draft at arrival and, provided the length of voyage permits, shall 131
confirm or amend such advice no later than seventy-two (72) hours prior to Vessel's arrival at the discharging port(s) or place(s). 132
(b) An alteration of more than three (3) hours in the twenty-four (24) hour notice or an alteration of more than twelve (12) hours in any other 133
advice given pursuant to Paragraph (a) of this Clause shall be advised by Master to Charterer and Vessel's agent. 134
(c) If, for any reason, Vessel is unable to trim to even keel for arrival at the discharging port(s) or place(s), Master shall give notice of this 135
to Charterer as soon as possible after receiving such loading instructions but no later than sailing from the final loading port or place. Such 136
notice shall include Vessel's estimated arrival draft forward and aft. 137
(d) If Master fails to comply with the requirements of Paragraphs (a), (b) and/or (c) of this Clause, any delay resulting therefrom at loading 138
and/or discharging port(s) or place(s) shall not count as laytime or, if Vessel is on demurrage, as time on demurrage. 139
(e) At each loading and discharging port or place, Master or Vessel's agent shall promptly notify Charterer of the dates and times the 140
following events occurred: 141
Notice of Readiness to load/discharge tendered; 142
- All fast; 143
- Hoses connected; 144
- Hoses disconnected; 145
- All cargo documents on board; and 146
- Vessel sailed. 147
11. **NOTICE OF READINESS.** Upon arrival at customary anchorage or waiting place at each loading and discharging port or place, Master or 148
Vessel's agent shall give Charterer or its representative notice that Vessel is in all respects ready to load or discharge cargo, berth or no 149

berth. At each load port or place, the Vessel shall be fully bunkered for the intended voyage and the Notice of Readiness shall, without limitation, confirm such bunkering. [150][151]

12. **CANCELLATION OF CHARTER.** If Vessel has not tendered a valid Notice of Readiness ("NOR") by 1600 hours local time on the Cancelling Date specified in Part I (B) ("Cancelling Date"), Charterer shall have the right to cancel this Charter by notifying Owner or Owner's agent of such cancellation within forty-eight (48) hours local time after expiration of the said Cancelling Date, failing which this Charter shall remain in full force and effect; in which case, laytime shall commence no earlier than forty-eight (48) hours after the tender of NOR or on the commencement of loading, whichever occurs first. Charterer's cancellation option shall continue to apply even if Vessel tenders NOR within the forty-eight (48) hour period after expiration of the Cancelling Date. However, if Vessel is delayed by reason of Charterer's change of orders pursuant to Clause 9 and/or by ice risks as stipulated in Clause 21, the Cancelling Date shall be extended, with the option of cancellation as aforesaid, by any time so directly lost. Cancellation or failure to cancel shall be without prejudice to any claims for damages Charterer may have for late tender of Vessel's services. [152][153][154][155][156][157][158][159][160]

13. **LAYTIME / DEMURRAGE.** [161]

   (a) **COMMENCEMENT / RESUMPTION.** Laytime or time on demurrage, as herein provided, shall commence or resume upon the expiration of six (6) hours after receipt by Charterer or its representative of Notice of Readiness or upon Vessel's Arrival in Berth, whichever occurs first. Laytime shall not commence before 0600 hours local time on the Commencing Date specified in Part I (B) unless Charterer shall otherwise agree, in which case laytime shall commence upon commencement of loading. [162][163][164][165]

   (b) **EARLY LOADING.** In the event Charterer agrees to load Vessel prior to commencement of laydays, laytime will begin at commencement of loading and the amount of time from commencement of loading until 0600 hours local time on the commencing date specified in Part I (B), shall be added to the laytime specified in Part I (I). [166][167][168]

   (c) **DURATION.** The laytime specified in Part I (I) shall be allowed free of expense to Charterer for the purpose of loading and discharging cargo and all other Charterer's purposes. Laytime or, if Vessel is on demurrage, time on demurrage, shall continue until all cargo hoses have been completely disconnected upon the final termination of the loading or discharging operation. Disconnection of all cargo hoses shall be promptly effected. If Vessel is delayed in excess of two (2) hours after such disconnection of cargo hoses solely for Charterer's purpose, laytime or, if Vessel is on demurrage, time on demurrage shall resume upon the expiration of said two (2)-hour period and shall continue from that point until the termination of such delay. [169][170][171][172][173][174]

   (d) **PAYMENT.** Charterer shall pay demurrage per running day and pro rata for a part thereof for all time by which the allowed laytime specified in Part I (I) is exceeded by the time taken for loading and discharging and for all other Charterer's purposes and which, under this Charter, counts as laytime or as time on demurrage. [175][176][177]

14. **LAYTIME / DEMURRAGE CONSEQUENCES.** [178]

   (a) **SPECIFIED.** Any delay to Vessel after the expiration of six (6) hours from Charterer's receipt of Notice of Readiness before Arrival in Berth or any delay to Vessel after Arrival in Berth, due to unavailability of berth (prior to Arrival in Berth), unavailability of cargo, or solely for Charterer or terminal purposes, shall count as laytime or, if Vessel is on demurrage, as time on demurrage. [179][180][181]

   (b) **HALF-RATE DEMURRAGE.** If demurrage is incurred and the Vessel has been delayed in berthing, loading and/or discharging (hereinafter in this Paragraph (b) called "Delay") due to: weather and/or sea conditions; fire; explosion; strike, picketing, lockout, slowdown, stoppage or restraint of labor; breakdown of machinery or equipment in or about the facilities of Charterer, supplier, shipper or consignee of the cargo (hereinafter in this Paragraph (b) separately and jointly called "Listed Conditions"), be the Delay prior to or after the expiration of laytime, that span of time on demurrage equal to the period or periods of Delay as just described shall be paid at half of the Demurrage Rate. If, during a period of Delay, Listed Conditions co-existed, along with any of the other conditions described in Paragraph (a) of this Clause 14, the Listed Conditions shall conclusively be deemed to be sole cause of the Delay, either if they caused the Delay independently of the other conditions or could have caused the Delay if the other conditions had not so co-existed. Weather and/or sea conditions shall include, but not be limited to, lightning, restricted visibility (the term "restricted visibility" shall mean any condition in which visibility is restricted by fog, mist, falling snow, ice, heavy rainstorms, sandstorms and any other similar causes), storm, wind, waves and/or swells. The provisions of Paragraph 14(b) shall apply irrespective of any option given in Part I (C) and (D). The foregoing provisions as to payment of half the Demurrage Rate in respect to weather and/or sea conditions shall not apply where the Vessel is lightered or discharged at sea. [182][183][184][185][186][187][188][189][190][191][192][193][194]

   (c) *EXCLUSIONS. Notwithstanding the provisions of any other Paragraph of this Clause or any other Clause of this Charter to the contrary, time shall not count as laytime or, if Vessel is on demurrage, as time on demurrage, if such time is spent or lost:* [195][196]

   (i) As a result of labor dispute, strike, go slow, work to rule, lockout, stoppage or restraint of labor involving Master, officers or crew of Vessel or tugboats or pilots unless, in the case where Charterer has load/discharge port options, a labor dispute, strike, go slow, work to rule, lockout, stoppage or restraint of labor of tug boats or pilots, is in force at the port at the time Charterer nominated such port; [197][198][199]

   (ii) On an inward passage, including, but not limited to, awaiting daylight, tide, tugs or pilot, and moving from anchorage or other waiting place, even if lightering has taken place at the anchorage or other waiting place, until Vessel's Arrival in Berth; [200][201]

   (iii) Due to overflow, breakdown, inefficiency, repairs, or any other conditions whatsoever attributable to Vessel, Master, officers, crew and/or Owner, including inability to load or discharge the cargo within the time allowed and/or failure to meet Vessel warranties stipulated in this Charter; [202][203][204]

   (iv) Due to Owner or port authority prohibiting loading or discharging; [205]

   (v) By reason of local law or regulations, action or inaction by local authorities (including, but not limited to, Port, Coast Guard, Naval. Customs, Immigration and/or Health authorities), with the exception, however, of port closure due to weather and/or sea conditions; [206][207]

   (vi) In ballasting or deballasting, lining up and/or draining of pumps/pipelines, cleaning of tanks, pumps, pipelines, bunkering or for any other purposes of the Vessel only, unless same is carried out concurrent with loading and/or discharging so that no loss of time is involved; or [208][209][210]

   (vii) Due to an escape or discharge of cargo and/or pollutant substances (herein after called "pollutants") or the threat of an escape or discharge of pollutants on or from Vessel. (The phrase "threat of an escape or discharge of pollutants" shall for the purposes of this paragraph (vii) mean a grave and imminent danger of the escape or discharge of pollutants which, if it occurred, would create a serious danger of pollution damage). [211][212][213][214]

   (d) **OTHER REFERENCES.** Laytime and demurrage references are also contained in the following Clauses: [215]

Clause: 2 (d)	Vessel-Breach	
3 (a)	Cleaning	[216]
5	Maximum Cargo	[217]
7	Deadfreight	[218]
8	Demurrage/Deviation Rate	[219]
10 (d)	Estimated Time of Arrival (ETA)	[220]
13	Laytime/Demurrage	[221]
15 (b) and (c)	Lightering/Cargo Advisor	[222]
16 (c) and (d)	Shifting and Off Berth	[223]
		[224]

APPENDIX 15

(e) **UNSPECIFIED.** Any delays for which laytime/demurrage consequences are not specifically allocated in this or any other Clause of this Charter and which are beyond the reasonable control of Owner or Charterer shall count as laytime or, if Vessel is on demurrage, as time on demurrage. If demurrage is incurred, on account of such delays, it shall be paid at half the Demurrage Rate.

15. **LIGHTERING / CARGO ADVISOR.**

(a) Any partial lightering or lightering to extinction, at sea or at a place outside a port, shall be conducted in accordance with the latest OCIMF guidelines for ship-to-ship transfers and with port authority approval, if applicable. The Vessel shall not lighter, either partially or to extinction, as just described, without prior consent or specific request from Charterer.

(b) Where lightering is requested by Owner or required by reason of fault attributable to Vessel, all expense and time related to the lightering shall be for the account of the Owner, irrespective of any consent from Charterer.

(c) Any lightering, at sea or at a place outside a port, except as described in subparagraph (b), shall be at the expense of Charterer and, notwithstanding Clauses 11, 13 (a) and 14 (a) and (b), time used for such lightering shall count as laytime or as time on demurrage, as provided below:

(i) If Vessel is partially lightered at sea or at a place outside a port, laytime or, if Vessel is on demurrage, time on demurrage shall commence when Vessel arrives at the lightering site designated by Charterer and shall end when disconnecting of the cargo hoses from the last cargo receiving vessel has been completed.

(ii) If Vessel is lightered to extinction at sea or at a place outside a port, laytime or, if Vessel is on demurrage, time on demurrage shall commence upon the expiration of six (6) hours after Vessel arrives at the lightering site designated by Charterer or when Vessel is all fast alongside the first cargo receiving vessel, whichever occurs first, and end when disconnection of the cargo hoses from the last cargo receiving vessel has been completed.

(d) If Vessel is lightered to extinction at sea, freight payment shall, in the absence of agreement as to the appropriate freight rate, be based on the freight rate stipulated in Part I (G) multiplied by a flat rate which shall be obtained from the Worldscale Association (London) Limited or the Worldscale Association (NYC) Inc. If Vessel is partially lightered at sea, the lightering site shall not constitute a port or place additional to those specified in Part I (D) and the freight rate for the voyage shall be the same as if the lightering had not taken place. Charterer, however, shall reimburse Owner for any time by which the steaming time to the final discharging port or place exceeds that which would have been taken if Vessel had not lightered at the Deviation Rate per day or pro rata for a part thereof. In addition, Charterer shall pay for extra bunkers consumed by Vessel during such excess time at Owner's documented actual replacement cost at the port where bunkers are next taken.

(e) With respect to any loading or discharging in port or at sea, Charterer may, at its option and cost, place on the Vessel one or more cargo advisors to monitor the loading, lightering and/or discharge of cargo and, if applicable, the inert gas and/or crude oil washing. It is understood and agreed however, that the Master and Owner shall continue to be fully and solely responsible for the operation, management and navigation of Vessel during the entire loading, lightering and/or discharging operation.

16. **LOADING / DISCHARGING PLACE.**

(a) Vessel shall not be required to berth where the maximum draft of Vessel is greater than the depth of water at low tide. In such cases, Charterer undertakes to discharge sufficient cargo into vessels and/or lighters within port limits to enable Vessel to safely reach and lie at berth always afloat.

(b) **SAFE LOCATION(S).** Charterer shall exercise due diligence to order Vessel to port(s) or place(s) which are safe for Vessel and where it can lie always safely afloat. Notwithstanding anything contained in this or any other Clause in this Charter to the contrary, Charterer shall not be deemed to warrant the safety of any such port(s) or place(s) and shall not be liable for any loss, damage, injury or delay resulting from any unsafe condition at such port(s) or place(s) which could have been avoided by the exercise of reasonable care on the part of the Master or Owner. The term "safe", as used in Part I (C) and (D), shall be construed to be consistent with Charterer's obligation as set forth in this Paragraph (b).

(c) **SHIFTING.** Charterer shall have the right to shift Vessel within any port of loading and/or discharging from one loading or discharging place back to the same or to another such place once or more often. In the event that Charterer exercises this right, Charterer shall pay all additional expenses properly incurred, including additional Bunkers. Time spent shifting shall count as laytime or, if Vessel is on demurrage, as time on demurrage. For purposes of freight payment, the places grouped in port and terminal combinations in WORLDSCALE are to be considered as berths within a single port, with Charterer paying shifting expenses in accordance with the foregoing.

(d) **OFF BERTH.** Charterer or terminal operator shall have the right to shift Vessel from a loading and/or discharging place if Vessel fails to meet the pumping and/or heating warranties stipulated in Clauses 18 and 25 so as to avoid delay to other vessels waiting to use such place. Charterer or terminal operator shall also have the right to shift Vessel from a loading and/or discharging place due to an unsafe condition of Vessel or failure of Vessel to meet the warranties of Clauses 2(a), (b) and/or (c). In such situation(s), Charterer shall not be obliged to provide an alternative loading or discharging place to the place from which Vessel was shifted. However, Charterer shall exercise due diligence to arrange prompt reberthing and commencement of loading or discharging once Vessel has corrected deficiency(ies). All expenses related to this shifting and any reberthing shall be for Owner's account and all time lost by reason of the foregoing shall not count as laytime or, if Vessel is on demurrage, as time on demurrage. An Off Berth reference is also contained in Clause 24 (b).

17. **CARGO MEASUREMENT.**

(a) Prior to loading, Master shall measure the on board quantities of cargo, water and sediment residues which are segregated in all holding tanks and slop tanks and those which remain in cargo tanks and, if requested, shall advise supplier(s) and Charterer of such quantities. After loading, Master shall determine the cargo quantities loaded, expressing these cargo quantities in barrels at standard temperature (60°F), using for such calculations the latest Manual of Petroleum Measurement Standards issued by the American Petroleum Institute (API MPMS) or similar standards issued by the American Society for Testing and Materials. A written tank-by-tank ullage report containing all measurements of oil, water and sediment residues on board prior to loading and quantities of cargo loaded shall be prepared and promptly submitted by Master to Charterer.

(b) If Master's calculations of cargo loaded (oil, water and sediment residues on board excluded), after applying the Vessel's Experience Factor (VEF), show any deficiency from the Bill of Lading figures, Master shall, if investigation and recalculation verify such deficiency, issue a Letter of Protest to supptier(s) (which should, if practical, be acknowledged) and shall advise Charterer of such deficiency immediately and thereafter shall send a copy of the Letter of Protest to Charterer. Vessel shall have on board sufficient historical information for the calculation of a VEF using the latest edition of the API MPMS. Master shall calculate and apply the VEF as so determined during all loadings.

(c) Prior to discharging. Master shall measure the quantity of each grade of cargo on board, expressing these quantities in barrels at standard temperature (60°F), using the same calculation procedures specified in Paragraph (a) of this Clause. Before and after discharging, Master shall cooperate with shore staff to ascertain discharged quantities. Vessel shall be obliged to discharge all liquid cargo and, if ordered by Charterer, any residues of cargo, water and sediment. Vessel's just-mentioned obligation shall not in any way be qualified or limited by any purported custom of the trade which is based on a stated in-transit loss or which otherwise would excuse Vessel from discharging all liquid cargo and residues.

(d) An inspector may be employed by Charterer at its expense to verify quantities and qualities of cargo and residues on board Vessel at both loading and discharging port(s) and/or place(s). If Vessel is equipped with an Inert Gas System, depressurization of tanks to permit ullage measurements shall be allowed in accordance with the provisions of the most recent Inert Gas Systems for Oil Tankers publication issued by the International Maritime Organization (IMO). Any time used solely for such inspections and/or measurements shall count as laytime or, if Vessel is on demurrage, as time on demurrage.

18. **PUMPING IN AND OUT.**

(a) Hoses for loading and discharging shall be furnished by Charterer and shall be connected and disconnected by Charterer or by Owner, at Charterer's option. When Vessel loads and/or discharges at sea terminal(s), Vessel shall be properly equipped, at Owner's expense, for operations at such terminal(s), including suitable anchors, ground tackle, mooring lines and equipment for handling submarine hoses. Vessel shall also be properly equipped with a sufficient number of cargo manifold reducing pieces of steel or comparable material (excluding aluminum and gray cast iron) which meet the most recent Oil Companies International Marine Forum (OCIMF) standards, to make available appropriate flanges for cargo hoses/arms at all manifold connections on one side of Vessel. If Vessel is not properly equipped as required in this Paragraph (a), any time thereby lost shall not count as laytime or, if Vessel is on demurrage, as time on demurrage.

(b) The cargo shall be pumped into Vessel at the expense and risk of Charterer only up to Vessel's permanent hose connections. The cargo shall be discharged from Vessel at the expense and risk of Owner only up to Vessel's permanent hose connections. Vessel shall provide all necessary pumps, power, and hands required on board for mooring and unmooring, connecting and disconnecting of hoses and loading and discharging. If requested by Charterer, Vessel shall load and/or discharge more than one grade simultaneously if Vessel is technically capable of doing so.

(c) Owner warrants that Vessel shall arrive at the loading place(s) with cargo tanks properly inerted and that such tanks shall so remain inerted throughout the loading of the cargo, the voyage and the subsequent discharging of the cargo. In case of an Inert Gas System failure during loading and/or discharging, cargo operations shall be suspended immediately until the System becomes fully operational, any deficiency in inerting is fully corrected and the terminal (or other loading and/or discharging facility) has given permission to resume operations. Time used from cessation to resumption of cargo operations shall not count as laytime or, if Vessel is on demurrage, as time on demurrage.

(d) If required by Charterer, Vessel, after loading or discharging, shall clear shore pipelines of cargo by pumping water through them and the time thereby consumed shall count as laytime or, if Vessel is on demurrage, as time on demurrage.

(e) All overtime incurred by officers and crew in loading and/or discharging shall be for the account of Owner.

(f) Vessel shall load at rates requested by Charterer having due regard for the safety of Vessel. Owner warrants that Vessel shall discharge entire cargo (be it one or more grades) within twenty-four (24) hours pumping time or maintain the maximum safe psi pressure at Vessel's rail that the Vessel can discharge at, but always at a minimum of 100 psi, during the entire period of discharge provided shore facilities permit. All time lost as a result of Vessel being unable to discharge its cargo in accordance with the pumping warranty above shall not count as laytime or, if Vessel is on demurrage, as time on demurrage. If the terminal or place of discharging does not allow or permit Vessel to meet the above warranty or requires discharging grades consecutively, Master shall forthwith issue a Letter of Protest (which should, if practical, be acknowledged) to such terminal or place and shall immediately advise Charterer. If Master fails to issue the Letter of Protest, Owner shall be deemed to waive any rights to contest that time was lost as a result of Vessel's failure to comply with the above pumping warranty. Any pumping time lost solely due to restrictions imposed by the terminal or place of discharging shall count as laytime or, if Vessel is on demurrage, as time on demurrage.

(g) Charterer shall have the right to require Vessel, if it is so equipped, to Crude Oil Wash the cargo tanks and, in such case, the allowed pumping hours (i.e. the twenty-four (24) hours of pumping time specified in Paragraph (f) of this Clause or the number of pumping hours taken to discharge the entire cargo when Vessel maintains the applicable rail pressure in accordance with Paragraph (f) of this Clause, whichever is applicable) shall be increased by the maximum hours specified in Part I (A) for Crude Oil Wash operations. If less than all of the tanks are washed, the said maximum hours shall be prorated on the basis of the number of tanks washed to the total number of cargo tanks and the hours resulting from such proration shall be added to the allowed pumping hours. If Crude Oil Wash is not conducted, Charterer shall have the right to require Vessel to remain at berth for clingage rundown or other cargo recovery technique. The time for such clingage rundown or other cargo recovery technique shall not exceed ten (10) hours and the time so used shall count as laytime or, if Vessel is on demurrage, as time on demurrage.

(h) In the event that any liquid cargo remains on board at completion of discharge for the final voyage under this Charter, then Charterer shall have the right to deduct from freight an amount equal to the Free On Board (FOB) port of loading value of such cargo plus freight due with respect thereto. The quantity and quality of such liquid hydrocarbon material shall be determined by a mutually agreeable independent cargo inspector. The quantity of Remaining On Board (ROB) material shall be measured using the Vessel's wedge tables, if available, or otherwise by wedge formula.

19. **BACK LOADING.** Charterer shall have the option of loading Vessel with a part cargo at any discharging port or place to which Vessel may have been ordered, provided that such part cargo is as described in Part I (F) and is compatible with cargo then on board. Owner shall discharge such part cargo at any other discharging port(s) or place(s) previously nominated, provided such port(s) or place(s) lie within the rotation of the discharging ports or places previously nominated. If this option is exercised, additional time consumed awaiting berth and/or cargo and/or tank preparation and/or loading and discharging such part cargo shall count as laytime or, if Vessel is on demurrage, as time on demurrage. Any additional expenses, including port charges, incurred as sole result of loading and discharging such part cargo shall be for Charterer's account.

20. **DUES, TAXES AND OTHER CHARGES.**

(a) Unless otherwise specified in WORLDSCALE and to the extent not prohibited by law, dues, taxes and other charges upon Vessel (including those assessed on the quantity of cargo loaded or discharged or on the freight) shall be paid by Owner and dues, taxes and other charges on the cargo shall be paid by Charterer. Vessel shall be free of charges for the use of any place(s) arranged by Charterer solely for the purpose of loading or discharging cargo. However, Owner shall be responsible for charges for any such place(s) when used solely for Vessel's purposes, such as, but not limited to, awaiting Owner's orders, tank cleaning, repairs, before, during or after loading and/or discharging.

APPENDIX 15

(b) Notwithstanding the provisions of Clause 20(a), dockage and wharfage shall be deemed included in the freight rate specified in Part I (G). 379

21. **ICE.** 380

(a) **DURING VOYAGE.** In case a nominated port or place of loading or discharging should be inaccessible due to ice, Master shall immediately 381
notify Charterer, requesting revised orders and shall remain safely outside the ice-bound area. Charterer shall give orders for another port 382
or place which is free from ice and where there are facilities for the loading or discharging of the cargo in bulk. In this event, freight shall be 383
paid at the rate stipulated in Part I (G) from or to such alternate port or place and any time by which the steaming time from or to such port or 384
place exceeds that which would have been taken if the Vessel had been ordered to proceed from or to such port or place in the first instance 385
shall be compensated at the Deviation Rate per running day and pro rata thereof. In addition, Charterer shall pay for extra bunkers consumed 386
during such excess time at Owner's documented actual replacement cost for such bunkers at the port where bunkers are next taken. 387

(b) **AT PORT.** If, on or after Vessel's arrival at the loading or discharging port or place, it is dangerous to remain at such port or place for fear 388
of Vessel being frozen-in or damaged, Master shall notify Charterer who shall give orders for Vessel either to proceed to another port or place 389
where there is no danger of ice and where there are facilities for the loading or discharging of the cargo in bulk or to remain at such original 390
port or place at Charterer's risk. If Vessel is ordered to proceed to another port or place, the sum in respect of freight and delay to be paid by 391
Charterer shall be as stipulated in Paragraph (a) of this Clause. If Vessel remains at such original port or place, any time so lost on account 392
of ice shall count as laytime or, if Vessel is on demurrage, as time on demurrage. 393

22. **DRY CARGO.** Charterer has the option of shipping packaged and/or general cargo (including oils and bitumen in drums) in the available 394
dry cargo space. Freight shall be payable on such cargo in accordance with Clause 6 at the Base Freight Rate and Charterer shall pay, in 395
addition, all expenses, including port dues, incurred solely as a result of the packaged and/or general cargo being carried. The time used 396
loading and discharging such dry cargo shall count as laytime or, if Vessel is on demurrage, as time on demurrage, but only to the extent 397
that such time is not concurrent with time used loading and/or discharging the liquid cargo carried hereunder. 398

23. **QUARANTINE.** Time lost at any port or place due to quarantine shall not count as laytime or, if Vessel is on demurrage, as time on 399
demurrage unless such quarantine was in force at the time when such port or place was nominated by Charterer. 400

24. **INSPECTION.** 401

(a) **OPERATIONS/INCIDENTS.** Charterer's representative(s) shall have the right at loading and/or discharging port(s) or place(s) to 402
inspect Vessel and observe operations. Charterer's representatives shall also have the right to attend on board the Vessel to ascertain the 403
circumstances of any incident involving cargo carried hereunder. Owner shall instruct Master to give every assistance so as to enable said 404
representative(s) to properly observe operations throughout Vessel and to ascertain any incident circumstances. 405

(b) **BUNKER SAMPLING.** Charterer's representative(s) shall have the right to survey and take samples of all Vessel's bunker tanks and non- 406
cargo spaces. Refusal by Master to permit such bunker surveying and sampling shall give Charterer or terminal operator the right to order 407
Vessel off berth. All time lost by reason of such refusal, including any time used in shifting Vessel off and back to berth, shall not count as 408
laytime or, if Vessel is on demurrage, as time on demurrage. Further, all expenses related to such refusal, including Vessel shifting expenses, 409
shall be for Owner's account. Any delay to Vessel caused solely by bunker surveying and sampling shall count as laytime or, if Vessel is on 410
demurrage, as time on demurrage. 411

25. **HEAT.** If Vessel is described as coiled in Part I (A), Owner warrants that Vessel is capable of heating the cargo up to and maintaining 412
it at a maximum temperature of 135°F/57°C. However, unless otherwise requested by Charterer, Vessel shall only be required to 413
maintain the cargo at the temperature loaded (up to a maximum of 135°F/57°C) throughout the voyage and the entire discharge. 414
If requested by Charterer and if the length of the voyage allows, Vessel shall increase and maintain the temperature of the cargo 415
from the loaded temperature to a temperature specified by Charterer, up to a maximum of 135°F/57°F), and Charterer shall pay for 416
extra bunkers consumed solely in increasing the temperature as aforesaid at Owner's documented actual replacement cost for such 417
bunkers at the port where bunkers are next taken. If Vessel fails to maintain the loaded temperature or to increase and maintain 418
the temperature of the cargo, as requested by Charterer, Charterer shall have the option to hold Vessel off berth and/or to suspend 419
discharging, all until the cargo is properly heated, all time and expense in connection with the foregoing being for Owner's account. 420

26. **BUNKERS.** When, in connection with the performance of any voyage provided for in this Charter, Owner plans to purchase bunkers at any 421
port(s) outside the United States or its territories, Owner shall purchase the bunkers from Charterer or its designated Affiliate(s) whenever 422
they are so available at competitive prices. In the event lower prices are quoted to Owner by any supplier at the port(s) in question, Owner 423
shall give Charterer or its designated Affiliate(s) the opportunity to meet such quotation. 424

27. **BILLS OF LADING.** 425

(a) Bills of Lading shall be signed by Master as presented, Master attending daily, if required, at the offices of Charterer or its agents. 426
However, at Charterer's option, Charterer or its agents may sign Bills of Lading on behalf of Master. All Bills of Lading shall be without 427
prejudice to this Charter and Charterer shall indemnify Owner against all consequences or liabilities which may arise from any inconsistency 428
between this Charter and any Bills of Lading or other documents signed by Charterer or its agents or by Master at their request or which may 429
arise from an irregularity in papers supplied by Charterer or its agents. 430

(b) Notwithstanding anything in this Charter to the contrary, the carriage of cargo under this Charter and under all Bills of Lading issued for 431
the cargo shall be subject to the statutory provisions and other terms set forth or specified in sub-paragraphs (i) through (vi) of this Clause 432
and such terms shall be incorporated verbatim or be deemed incorporated by reference in any such Bill of Lading. In such sub-paragraphs 433
and in any Act referred to therein, the word "Carrier" shall include Owner and Chartered Owner of Vessel. 434

(i) **CLAUSE PARAMOUNT.** This Bill of Lading shall have effect subject to the provisions of the Carriage of Goods By Sea Act of the 435
United States, approved April 16, 1936, except that if this Bill of Lading is issued at a place where any other Act, ordinance or legislation 436
gives statutory effect to: (i) the International Convention for the Unification of certain Rules relating to Bills of Lading at Brussels, August 437
1924 ("Hague Rules"), or (ii) the Hague Rules as amended by the Protocol signed at Brussels, February 1968 ("Hague/Visby Rules"), or (iii) 438
the United Nations Convention on the Carriage of Goods by Sea 1978 ("Hamburg Rules"), then this Bill of Lading shall have effect subject 439
to the provisions of such Act, ordinance or legislation. The applicable Act, ordinance or legislation (hereinafter called "Act") shall be deemed 440
to be incorporated herein and nothing herein contained shall be deemed a surrender by the Carrier of any of its rights or immunities or an 441
increase of any of its responsibilities or liabilities under the Act. If any term of this Bill of Lading be repugnant to the Act to any extent, such 442
term shall be void to that extent but no further. 443

(ii) **JASON CLAUSE.** In the event of accident, danger, damage or disaster before or after the commencement of the voyage, resulting 444
from any cause whatsoever, whether due to negligence or not, for which, or for the consequence of which, the Carrier is not responsible, by 445
statute, contract or otherwise, the cargo shippers, consignees or owners of the cargo shall contribute with the Carrier in General Average 446
to the payment of any sacrifices, losses or expenses of a General Average nature that may be made or incurred and shall pay salvage and 447
special charges incurred in respect of the cargo. If a salving ship is owned or operated by the Carrier, salvage shall be paid for as fully as if 448
the said salving ship or ships belonged to strangers. Such deposit as the Carrier or his Agents may deem sufficient to cover the estimated 449
contribution of the cargo and any salvage and special charges thereon shall, if required, be made by the cargo shippers, consignees or 450
owners of the cargo to the Carrier before delivery. 451

452

(iii) **GENERAL AVERAGE.** General Average shall be adjusted, stated, and settled according to the York Antwerp Rules 2004 ("Rules") and, as to matters not provided for by those Rules, according to the laws and usages at the port of New York; provided that, when there is an actual escape or release of oil or pollutant substances from the Vessel (irrespective of Vessel location), the cost of any measures, continued or undertaken on that account, to prevent or minimize pollution or environmental damage shall not be allowable in General Average; and, provided further, that any payment for pollution damage (as defined in Article I 6.(a) of the 1992 Protocol to the International Convention on Civil Liability for Oil Pollution Damage) shall also not be allowable in General Average. It is understood and agreed, however, that the cost of measures to prevent pollution or environmental damage, undertaken in respect of oil or pollutant substances which have not escaped or been released from the Vessel, shall be included in General Average to the extent permitted by the Rules. If a General Average statement is required, it shall be prepared at such port by an Adjuster from the port of New York appointed by the Carrier and approved by Charterer of Vessel. Such Adjuster shall attend to the settlement and the collection of the General Average, subject to customary charges. General Average Agreements and/or security shall be furnished by Carrier and/or Charterer, and/or Owner, and/or Consignee of cargo, if requested. Any cash deposit being made as security to pay General Average and/or salvage shall be remitted to the Average Adjuster and shall be held by the Adjuster at the Adjuster's risk in a special account in a duly authorized and licensed bank at the place where the General Average statement is prepared.

(iv) **BOTH TO BLAME.** If Vessel comes into collision with another ship as a result of the negligence of the other ship and any act, neglect or default of Master, mariner, pilot or the servants of the Carrier in the navigation or in the management of Vessel, the owners of the cargo carried hereunder shall indemnify the Carrier against all loss or liability to the other or non-carrying ship or its owners insofar as such loss or liability represents loss of or damage to or any claim whatsoever of the owners of said cargo, paid or payable by the other or recovered by the other or non-carrying ship or its owners as part of their claim against the carrying ship or Carrier. The foregoing provisions shall also apply where the owners, operators or those in charge of any ships or objects other than, or in addition to, the colliding ships or objects are at fault in respect of a collision or contact. The provisions in this subparagraph (iv) shall only apply if the Owner shall have exercised due diligence to make the Vessel seaworthy, and properly manned, equipped, and supplied, with the burden of proof in this regard resting solely on Owner.

(v) **LIMITATION OF LIABILITY.** Any provision of this Charter to the contrary notwithstanding, the Carrier shall have the benefit of all limitations of, and exemptions from, liability accorded to owner or chartered owner of vessels by any statute or rule of law for the time being in effect.

(vi) **DEVIATION.** Vessel shall have liberty to sail with or without pilots, to tow or be towed, to go to the assistance of vessels in distress, to deviate for the purpose of saving life or property or of landing any ill or injured person on board, and to call for fuel at any port or ports in or out of the regular course of the voyage.

(c) Except as provided in Paragraph (d) of this Clause, Owner and Vessel shall not be required to deliver cargo at a discharging port or place nominated by Charterer unless the party claiming right to such delivery shall first surrender to Vessel at such port or place one of the original Bills of Lading issued for the cargo, duly endorsed; provided however that, if the Bills of Lading name specific port(s) or place(s) of discharging and the nominated port or place is different or if the Bills of Lading provide for discharge at port(s) or place(s) as ordered, Owner and Vessel shall not be required to deliver the cargo unless the party claiming right to such delivery first surrenders to Vessel all the original Bills of Lading, duly endorsed. The foregoing shall apply even in the situation where one but not all of the original Bills of Lading have been placed on board Vessel at loading but, in such case, only the original Bill(s) of Lading not on board Vessel need first to be surrendered to Vessel in accordance with the foregoing requirements. Any delay to Vessel at the nominated port or place due to the unavailability at such port or place of original Bill(s) of Lading and/or the failure to timely surrender such Bill(s) of Lading to Vessel in accordance with the foregoing requirements shall count as laytime or, if Vessel is on demurrage, as time on demurrage.

(d) If original Bill(s) of Lading are not available at the discharging port or place for timely surrender to Vessel as provided in Paragraph (c) of this Clause, Vessel shall deliver the cargo to a party and at a facility at the discharging port or place as directed by Charterer in writing, if Charterer first executes a written indemnity in connection with such delivery in favor of Owner, Vessel, any Chartered Owner(s) of Vessel, Master, Vessel operators, agents and underwriters and delivers such indemnity to Owner or Owner's designee. The subject indemnity shall meet the requirements of Paragraph (e) of this Clause, and shall be limited in value to 200 per cent of the CIF value of the cargo.

(e) The indemnity referred to in Paragraph (d) of this Clause shall be a short form indemnity document incorporating the terms and conditions set forth in Clause 27(f) of this Charter. This document (which must be properly filled in) shall be given to Owner by telex, electronic mail, letter or facsimile as requested by Owner and be in the exact form quoted below, which document, when transmitted, shall be deemed to have been signed by person acting on behalf of Charterer.

"VOYAGE CHARTER OF

DATED _____

BETWEEN_____ , AS OWNER
                        AND
              _____ , AS CHARTERER

Reference is made to the cargo ('Cargo') now laden aboard the above Vessel ('Vessel'). Pursuant to Clause 27(e) of the above captioned Charter ('Charter'), the undersigned requests that Owner(s) of the Vessel deliver the Cargo at _____ unto _____without prior discharge site presentation to the Vessel of all original bills of lading issued for the Cargo appropriately endorsed for such delivery and/or at a discharge port or site other than one specifically named in said bills of lading. In consideration of such delivery, the undersigned hereby gives an indemnity containing the terms and conditions set forth in Clause 27(f) of the Charter ('Indemnity Terms And Conditions'). The Indemnity Terms And Conditions are deemed incorporated in and made a part of this document. The term 'Indemnifier' in the Indemnity Terms And Conditions shall be deemed to refer to the undersigned. The term 'Cargo' and the phrase 'Requested Delivery' in the Indemnity Terms And Conditions shall be deemed to, respectively, mean the Cargo and the delivery request set forth in the preceding paragraph of this document. The term 'Ship' as used in the Indemnity Terms And Conditions shall be deemed to refer to the Vessel. Print the following information:

Name of Charterer   _____

Name of Person Acting on Behalf of Charterer   _____

Authority/Title of Above Person   _____

Date Indemnity Given   _____ "

APPENDIX 15

(f) Indemnity Terms and Conditions. 521

"1. Indemnifier shall indemnify and hold harmless the Owner of the Ship, any chartered Owner of the Ship, the Ship operator, the Ship 522 Master, the Ship underwriters and the Ship agents (hereinafter jointly and individually called 'Indemnitees') in respect of any liability, loss, 523 damage, costs (including, but not limited, to Attorney/Client costs) and other expense of whatever nature which the Indemnitees may sustain 524 or incur by reason of the Requested Delivery. 525

2. In the event of any legal action or proceedings being commenced against the Indemnitees in connection with the Requested Delivery, 526 Indemnifier shall provide Indemnitees from time to time, on the Indemnitees' demand, with sufficient funds to defend same. 527

3. If the Ship or any other vessel or other property belonging to the Indemnitees should be arrested or detained or if the arrest or detention 528 thereof should be threatened for any claim in connection with the Requested Delivery, the Indemnifier shall provide, upon demand of the 529 Indemnitees, such bail or other security as may be required to prevent such arrest(s) or detention(s) or to secure the release of the Ship or 530 such vessel or other property from arrest or detention, and shall indemnify and hold harmless the Indemnitees against and from any loss, 531 damage, costs (including but not limited to Attorney/Client costs) and other expense resulting from such arrest or detention or threatened 532 arrest or detention, whether or not same may be justified and to pay to the Indemnitees, on the Indemnitees' demand, the amount of such 533 loss, damages, costs and/or expense. 534

4. This Indemnity shall automatically become null and void, and Charterer's liability hereunder shall cease, upon presentation of all original 535 Bills of Lading duly endorsed to reflect delivery of Cargo in accordance with the Requested Delivery, or upon the expiration of 36 months after 536 completion of discharge, whichever occurs first; provided that no legal proceedings arising from delivery of the Cargo in accordance with the 537 Requested Delivery have been instituted against the Indemnitees and/or Vessel within such 36-month period. Owner shall advise Charterer 538 with reasonable dispatch in writing if any proceedings are instituted. 539

5. The within Indemnity shall be governed and construed in accordance with the internal substantive laws of the State of New York, USA. 540 The Indemnitees may, but shall not be obligated to, bring any legal action or proceeding with respect to such Indemnity in the Courts of the 541 State of New York, USA or in the U.S. Federal Court situated therein and the Indemnifier unconditionally and generally accepts in regard to 542 such legal action or proceeding, for itself and its property, the jurisdiction and venue of the aforesaid courts." 543

28. **WAR.** 544

(a) No contraband of war shall be shipped, but petroleum and/or its products shall not be deemed contraband of war for the purposes of 545 this Clause. Vessel shall not, however, be required, without the consent of Owner, which shall not be unreasonably withheld, to enter any 546 port, place, or zone which is involved in a state of war, warlike operations or hostilities, civil strife, terrorism and other politically or religiously 547 motivated activities, or piracy, whether there be a declaration of war or not, where it might reasonably be expected to be subject to capture, 548 seizure or arrest, or to a hostile act by a belligerent power (the term "power" meaning any de jure or de facto authority or any other purported 549 governmental organization maintaining naval, military or air forces or any terrorist group or organization). 550

(b) For the purposes of this Clause, it shall be unreasonable for Owner to withhold consent to any voyage, route, or port or place of loading 551 or discharging if insurance against all risks defined in Paragraph (a) of this Clause is then available commercially or under a government 552 program in respect of such voyage, route or port/place of loading or discharging. If such consent is given by Owner, Charterer shall pay 553 any provable additional cost of insuring Vessel against Hull war risks over and above such costs in effect on the date of this Charter in an 554 amount equal to the insured value stipulated in its ordinary marine policy as of the date of this Charter. If such insurance is not obtainable 555 commercially or through a government program, Vessel shall not be required to enter or remain at any such port, place or zone and, in such 556 case, Charterer shall have the right to order Vessel to load or discharge, as the case may be, at any other port(s) or place(s) consistent with 557 Part I (C) and (D). 558

(c) In the event of the existence of the conditions described in Paragraph (a) of this Clause subsequent to the date of this Charter, Charterer 559 shall, in respect of a voyage to any such port, place or zone, assume any provable additional cost of wages and insurance properly incurred 560 in connection with Master, officers and crew as a consequence of such war, warlike operations or hostilities over and above such costs in 561 effect on the date of this Charter. 562

29. **EXCEPTIONS.** 563

(a) Vessel, Master and Owner shall not, unless otherwise expressly provided in this Charter, be responsible for any loss or damage to 564 cargo arising or resulting from: any act, neglect, default or barratry of Master, pilots, mariners or other servants of Owner in the navigation 565 or management of Vessel; fire, unless caused by the personal design or neglect of Owner; collision, stranding, or peril, danger or accident 566 of the sea or other navigable waters; or from explosion, bursting of boilers, breakage of shafts, or any latent defect in hull, equipment or 567 machinery. Neither Vessel, Master or Owner, nor Charterer, shall, unless otherwise expressly provided in this Charter, be responsible for 568 any loss or damage or delay or failure in performing hereunder arising or resulting from: act of God; act of war; perils of the sea; act of public 569 enemies, pirates or assailing thieves; arrest or restraint of princes, rulers or people, or seizure under legal process provided bond is promptly 570 furnished to release Vessel or cargo; strike or lockout or stoppage or restraint of labor from whatever cause, either partial or general; or riot 571 or civil commotion. 572

(b) The exceptions stated in Paragraph (a) of this Clause shall not affect Owner's warranties and undertakings herein with respect to the 573 condition of Vessel, the obligations of Owner in respect of the loading, handling, stowage, carriage, custody, care and discharge of the 574 cargo and/or the rights or obligations of either Owner or Charterer with respect to laytime or demurrage as elsewhere provided in this 575 Charter. 576

30. **LIEN.** Owner shall have a lien on all cargoes and subfreights for all amounts due under this Charter, and Charterer shall have a lien on 577 Vessel for all monies paid in advance and not earned, and all disbursements for Owner's account, including commissions, cost of insurance 578 and expenses thereon and for any damages sustained by Charterer as a result of the breach of this Charter by Owner. 579

31. **AGENTS.** Unless otherwise agreed, Charterer shall nominate Vessel's agents at all port(s) and place(s). Such agents shall be appointed, 580 instructed and paid for by Owner and represent solely the Owner and Vessel. 581

32. **ASSIGNMENT / SUBLET.** Charterer shall have the option of assigning this Charter or of subletting Vessel, but in either case, Charterer shall 582 always remain responsible for the due fulfillment of this Charter in all terms and conditions. 583

33. **CLEAN SEAS.** 584

(a) **HANDLING OF TANK WASHINGS.** Owner agrees to participate in Charterer's program covering oil pollution avoidance. Such 585 Program requires compliance with latest IMO and Port State regulations. The Program prohibits discharge overboard of all oil and all oily 586 water, oily ballast or cargo in any form unless in compliance with IMO and Port State local regulations or under extreme circumstances 587 whereby the safety of Vessel, cargo or life at sea would be imperiled. Owner shall ensure that Vessel's personnel comply with the 588 following: 589

(i) Subsequent to the date of this Charter and in the course of the ballast passage before presenting for loading hereunder, any oily 590 residues remaining in Vessel from its previous cargoes shall be retained on board and shall be handled according to Charterer's instructions. 591

(ii) During tank washing, the tank washings shall be collected into one cargo compartment and, after maximum separation of free water, 592 such free water shall be discharged overboard to the extent permitted by applicable international regulations. 593

(iii) Thereafter, Charterer shall be notified promptly of the estimated quantity of the segregated tank washings and the type and source 594 of such washings. If Charterer requires that demulsifiers shall be used for the separation of oil/water, such demulsifiers shall be obtained 595

by Owner and paid for by Charterer. Any additional Canal dues incurred on the ballast passage by reason of Vessel having tank washings 596
on board shall be for the sole account of Owner. Owner shall ensure that Master, on Vessel's arrival at the loading port(s) or place(s), does 597
the following: 598
- arranges for the measurement of the segregated tank washings in conjunction with the cargo supplier(s); 599
- records the quantity of tank washings so measured in Vessel's ullage record; 600
- issues a Slop Certificate; and 601
- arranges that the Slop Certificate and/or Vessel's ullage record be duly signed by the cargo supplier(s) and promptly sent to Charterer. 602
The segregated tank washings and any other oily residues on board (hereinafter called "residues") shall, at Charterer's option, be pumped 603
ashore into slop facilities at the loading port(s) or place(s), commingled with the cargo to be loaded or segregated from the cargo to be 604
loaded. 605
If Charterer requires Master to discharge the residues at facilities at loading port(s) or place(s), no freight shall be payable on same but the 606
time involved in accomplishing such discharge shall count as laytime or, if Vessel is on demurrage, as time on demurrage, including, but 607
not limited to, waiting for availability of, or for berthing at, the slop receiving facility and shifting to and from such facility. Further, the cost 608
of such facilities and the ultimate disposal of the residues shall be for Charterer's sole account. If Charterer requires residues to be kept 609
separate from the cargo to be loaded, same shall, at Charterer's option, be discharged at the discharging port(s) or place(s) in accordance 610
with Charterer's instructions. 611
If Charterer requires that the cargo be loaded on top of residues or that such residues be kept separate from the cargo to be loaded, in either 612
case freight shall be payable in accordance with Clause 6 on the quantity of residues at the Overage Rate, if such rate exists, or otherwise 613
at the Base Freight Rate, up to a maximum tonnage equivalent to one percent (1.0%) of Vessel's deadweight as specified in Part I (A), with 614
the exception that, in the case of a Part Cargo Minimum, no freight shall be paid if the residues are kept separate and not discharged. In no 615
event shall Charterer hold any liability for deadfreight in connection with residues, except where the Vessel is ordered to load a full cargo 616
and is required to keep residues segregated, in which case deadfreight shall be due. Nothing in Charterer's instruction shall be construed as 617
permission to contravene any applicable laws or regulations by the discharging of oily residues. 618
(b) **CLEAN BALLAST.** Owner warrants that Vessel will arrive at load port(s) with clean ballast. 619
(c) **ITOPF.** Owner warrants that it is a Member of the International Tanker Owners Pollution Federation ("ITOPF") and that Owner will retain 620
such membership during the entire period of the services of the Vessel under this Charter. 621
34. **DRUG AND ALCOHOL POLICY.** Owner warrants that it has a policy on Drug and Alcohol Abuse ("Policy") applicable to the Vessel which 622
meets or exceeds the standards in the Oil Companies International Marine Forum Guidelines For the Control of Drugs and Alcohol Onboard 623
Ship. Under the Policy, alcohol impairment shall be defined as a blood alcohol content of 40 mg/100 ml or greater; the appropriate seafarers 624
to be tested shall be all Vessel officers and the drug/alcohol testing and screening shall include unannounced testing in addition to routine 625
medical examinations. An objective of the Policy should be that the frequency of the unannounced testing be adequate to act as an effective 626
abuse deterrent, and that all officers be tested at least once a year through a combined program of unannounced testing and routine medical 627
examinations. Owner further warrants that the Policy will remain in effect during the term of this Charter and that Owner shall exercise due 628
diligence to ensure that the Policy is complied with. It is understood that an actual impairment or any test finding of impairment shall not in 629
and of itself mean the Owner has failed to exercise due diligence. 630
35. **ARBITRATION.** 631
(a) Any and all differences and disputes of whatsoever nature arising out of this Charter shall be put to arbitration in the City of New York, 632
pursuant to the laws relating to arbitration there in force, before a board of three persons, consisting of one arbitrator to be appointed by 633
Owner, one by Charterer and one by the two so chosen. The decision of any two of the three on any point or points shall be final. Until 634
such time as the arbitrators finally close the hearings either party shall have the right by written notice served on the arbitrators and on the 635
other party to specify further disputes or differences under this Charter for hearing and determination. The arbitrators may grant any relief 636
which they, or a majority of them, deem just and equitable and within the scope of the agreement of the parties, including, but not limited to, 637
specific performance. Awards made in pursuance to this Clause may include costs, including a reasonable allowance for attorney's fees, and 638
judgment may be entered upon any award made hereunder in any Court having jurisdiction in the premises. 639
(b) Where cargo carried pursuant to this Charter is owned by an Affiliate, any claim related to the carriage of such cargo hereunder shall be subject to this 640
Clause 35, said Affiliate having authorized Charterer to so agree on Affiliate's behalf. If this subparagraph (b) applies, the term "Charterer" in 641
subparagraph (a) of this Clause 35 shall be taken to mean the aforementioned Affiliate. 642
36. **WAIVER OF CLAIMS.** Any claim for freight, deadfreight, demurrage and/or charges or expenses under this Charter shall be deemed 643
waived, extinguished and absolutely barred if such claim is not received by Charterer or Owner, as the case may be, in writing with 644
supporting documentation within 90 days from the date of final discharge of the cargo on the voyage with respect to which said claim arises. 645
This Clause shall not apply with respect to claims for damage, loss or shortage of cargo. 646
37. **BUSINESS POLICY.** Owner agrees to comply with all laws and lawful regulations applicable to any activities carried out in the name, or 647
otherwise on behalf, of Charterer under the provisions of this Charter. Owner agrees that all financial settlements, billings and reports 648
rendered by Owner to Charterer, as provided for in this Charter, shall, in reasonable detail, accurately and fairly reflect the facts about all 649
activities and transactions handled for the account of Charterer. 650
38. **INTERPRETATION.** The interpretation of this Charter and the rights and obligations of the parties thereto shall be governed by the Federal 651
Maritime Law of the United States and where applicable by the Law of the State of New York, without taking into consideration any conflict 652
of laws principles. The heading of Clauses and Paragraphs are for convenience of reference only and shall not affect the interpretation of 653
this Charter. No modification, waiver or discharge of any term of this Charter shall be valid unless in writing and signed by the party to be 654
charged therewith. Notwithstanding anything in this Charter to the contrary, this Charter shall not be interpreted or applied so as to require 655
Owner or Charterer to do, or to refrain from doing, anything which would constitute a violation of, or result in a loss of economic benefit under, 656
United States anti-boycott laws and regulations. 657
39. **CHARTER ADMINISTRATION.** All Charter terms and conditions finally agreed to by the parties shall be evidenced by a fixture confirmation 658
notice approved by Owner and Charterer. Charterer shall cause the fixture confirmation notice to be transmitted to both Owner and Charterer 659
and each party shall give approval of the fixture confirmation notice one to the other no later than three (3) business days after transmission 660
of the notice. Failure of either party to respond within the said three (3) days shall be conclusively deemed to constitute that party's 661
unqualified acceptance of the fixture confirmation notice. Except as requested in writing by either Owner or Charterer, there shall be no 662
formal written and signed Charter Party. 663
664

APPENDIX 15

INDEX OF CLAUSES
PART I

(A) VESSEL DESCRIPTION AND POSITION
(B) LAYDAYS
(C) LOADING RANGE(S) / PORT(S) / PLACES(S)
(D) DISCHARGING RANGE(S) / PORT(S) / PLACE(S)
(E) CARGO QUANTITY
(F) CARGO DESCRIPTION
(G) FREIGHT RATE
(H) BILLING
(I) LAYTIME
(J) DEMURRAGE / DEVIATION PER DAY
(K) SPECIAL PROVISIONS
(L) INCORPORATED CLAUSE(S)

PART II

1. DEFINITIONS
2. VESSEL
3. CLEANING
4. VOYAGE(S)
5. MAXIMUM CARGO
6. FREIGHT
7. DEADFREIGHT
8. DEMURRAGE/DEVIATION RATE
9. LOADING AND DISCHARGING PORT(S) / PLACE(S)
10. ESTIMATED TIME OF ARRIVAL (ETA)
11. NOTICE OF READINESS
12. CANCELLATION OF CHARTER
13. LAYTIME / DEMURRAGE
14. LAYTIME / DEMURRAGE CONSEQUENCES
15. LIGHTERING / CARGO ADVISOR
16. LOADING / DISCHARGING PLACE
17. CARGO MEASUREMENT
18. PUMPING IN AND OUT
19. BACK LOADING
20. DUES, TAXES AND OTHER CHARGES
21. ICE
22. DRY CARGO
23. QUARANTINE
24. INSPECTION
25. HEAT
26. BUNKERS
27. BILLS OF LADING
28. WAR
29. EXCEPTIONS
30. LIEN
31. AGENTS
32. ASSIGNMENT / SUBLET
33. CLEAN SEAS
34. DRUG AND ALCOHOL POLICY
35. ARBITRATION
36. WAIVER OF CLAIMS
37. BUSINESS POLICY
38. INTERPRETATION
39. CHARTER ADMINISTRATION

APPENDIX 16

Code word for this Charter Party

Issued March 2005   **"SHELLVOY 6"**

VOYAGE CHARTER PARTY

LONDON,   20

PREAMBLE	1

IT IS THIS DAY AGREED between	2
of (hereinafter referred to as "Owners"), being owners/disponent owners of the	3
motor/steam tank vessel called with an IMO number of	4
(hereinafter referred to as "the vessel")	5
and of	6
(hereinafter referred to as "Charterers"):	7
that the service for which provision is herein made shall be subject to the terms and conditions of this Charter which includes Part I, Part II and Part	8
III. In the event of any conflict between the provisions of Part I, Part II and Part III hereof the provisions of Part I shall prevail.	9

PART I	10

(A) Description of vessel	(I)	Owners wan-ant that at the date hereof, and from the time when the obligation to proceed to the loadport(s) attaches, the	11
	vessel		12
	(i)	Is classed	13
	(ii) (a)	Has a deadweight of tonnes (1000 kg) on a salt-water draft on assigned summer freeboard of m. and if	14
		applicable,	15
	(b)	Has on board documentation showing the following additional drafts and deadweights	16
	(iii)	Has capacity for cargo of m³	17
	(iv)	Is fully fitted with heating systems for all cargo tanks capable of maintaining cargo at a temperature of up to	18
		degrees Celsius and can accept a cargo temperature on loading of up to a maximum of degrees Celcius.	19
	(v)	Has tanks coated as follows:	20
	(vi)	Is equipped with cranes/derricks capable of lifting to and supporting at the vessel's port and starboard manifolds submarine	21
		hoses of up to tonnes (1000 kg) in weight	22
	(vii)	Can discharge a full cargo (whether homogenous or multi grade) either within 24 hours, or can maintain a back pressure of 100 PSI at the	23
		vessel's manifold and Owners warrant such minimum performance provided receiving facilities permit and subject always to the obligation	24
		of utmost despatch set out in Part II, clause 3(1).	25
		The discharge warranty shall only be applicable provided the kinematic viscosity does not exceed 600 centistokes at the discharge	26
		temperature required by Charterers. If the kinematic viscosity only exceeds 600 centistokes on part of the cargo or particular grade(s) then	27
		the discharge warranty shall continue to apply to all Other cargo/grades.	28
	(viii)	Has or will have carried, for the named Charterers, the following three cargoes (all grades to be identified) immediately prior to loading	29
		under this Charter:-	30
		Last Cargo/charterer	31
		2nd Last Cargo/charterer	32
		3rd Last Cargo/charterer	33
	(ix)	Has a crude oil washing system complying with the requirements of the International Convention for the Prevention of Pollution from	34
		Ships 1973 as modified by the Protocol of 1978 ("MARPOL 73/78").	35
	(x)	Has an operational inert gas system and is equipped for and able to carry out closed sampling/ullaging/loading and discharging operations	36
		in full compliance with the International Safety Guide for Oil Tankers and Terminal ("ISGOTT") guidelines current at the date of this	37
		Charter.	38
	(xi)	Has on board all papers and certificates required by any applicable law, in force as at the date of this Charter, to enable the vessel to	39
		perform the charter service without any delay.	40

APPENDIX 16

Issued March 2005   **"SHELLVOY 6"**

(xii)	Is entered in the	P&I Club, being a member of the International Group of P&I Clubs.	41

(xiii)   Has in full force and effect Hull and Machinery insurance placed through reputable Brokers on Institute Time   42
Clauses-Hull dated   for the value of   43

(xiv)   Complies with the latest edition of the Oil Companies International Marine Forum ("OCIMF") standards for oil tankers'   44
manifolds and associated equipment applicable to its size for cargo manifolds and vapour recovery systems.   45

(xv)   Is equipped to comply with, and is operated in accordance with, and has on board, the latest edition of the International   46
Chamber of Shipping ("ICS") and/or OCIMF guidelines / publications covering: 47
     (a)   Ship to Ship Operations   48
     (b)   ISGOTT   49
     (c)   Clean Seas Guide for Oil Tankers   50
     (d)   Bridge Procedure Guide   51

(II)   Throughout the charter service. Owners shall ensure that the vessel shall be maintained, or that they take all steps necessary   52
to promptly restore vessel to be, within the description in <u>Part I clause (A)(I)</u> and any questionnaires requested by Charterers or   53
within information provided by Owners.   54

(III)   Owners warrant that any information provided on any Questionnaire(s) requested by Charterers or any other vessel   55
information/details provided by Owners to Charterers is always complete and correct as at the date hereof, and from the time   56
when the obligation to proceed to the loadport attaches and throughout the charter service. This information is an integral part of   57
this Charter but if there is any conflict between the contents of the Questionnaire(s), or information provided by Owners, and any   58
other provisions of this Charter then such other provisions shall govern.   59

(B) Position/
Readlines   Now   Expected ready to load   60

In addition to the above details on the position of the vessel Owners will advise Charterers of the known programme, including   61
any contractual options available to the Charterers in <u>Part I clause (A)(I)</u> (viii) above between current position up to expected   62
ready to load date at Charterers nominated or indicated first load port/area. Owners will not, unless with Charterers' prior consent,   63
negotiate or enter into any business or give current Charterers any further options that may affect or alter the programme of the   64
vessel as given in this clause.   65

(C) Laydays   Commencing Noon Local Time on   (Commencement Date)   66

Terminating Noon Local Time on   (Termination Date)   67

(D) Loading
port(s)/
Range   68

(E) Discharging
Port(s)/
Range   69

(F) Cargo
description   Charterers' option   70

Owners wan-ant that where different grades of cargo are carried pursuant to this Part I clause (F), they will be kept in complete   71
segregation from each other during loading, transit, and discharge, to include the use of different pumps/lines for each grade. If,   72
however. Charterers so require it, the vessel may be required to: 73

(a) co-mingle different grades of cargo providing such grades fall within the cargo description set out in this Part I clause (F);   74
(b) otherwise breach the vessel's natural segregation;   75
(c) add dye to the cargo after loading, and/or   76
(d) carry out such other cargo operations as Charterers may reasonably require as long as the vessel is capable of such operations   77

provided that the Charterers will indemnify Owners for any loss damage delay or expense caused by following Charterers'   78
instructions, except to the extent that such loss damage delay or expense could have been avoided by the exercise of due diligence   79
by Owners.   80

(G) Freight   At   % of the rate for the voyage as provided for in the New Worldwide Tanker Nominal Freight Scale current at the date of   81
commencement of loading (hereinafter referred to as "Worldscale") per ton (2240 lbs)/tonne (1000 Kg) or, if agreed, the following   82
lumpsum amount(s)/or freight per tonne for named load and discharge area(s)/port(s) combinations   83

APPENDIX 16

Issued March 2005   **"SHELLVOY 6"**

(H) Freight payable to		84
(I) Laytime	running hours	85
(J) Demurrage per day (or pro rata)		86
(K)ETAs	All radio/telex/e-mail messages sent by the master to Charterers shall be addressed to	87
	All telexes must begin with the vessel name at the start of the subject line (no inverted commas, or use of MT / SS preceding the vessel name)	88
		89

(L) Speed

The vessel shall perform the ballast passage with utmost despatch and the laden passage at   knots weather and safe navigation   90
permitting at a consumption of   tonnes of Fueloil (state grade   ) per day.   91
Charterers shall have the option to instruct the vessel to increase speed with Charterers reimbursing Owners for the additional   92
bunkers consumed, at replacement cost.   93
Charterers shall also have the option to instruct the vessel to reduce speed on laden passage. Additional voyage time caused by   94
such instructions shall count against laytime or demurrage, if on demurrage, and the value of any bunkers saved shall be deducted   95
from any demurrage claim Owners may have under this Charter with the value being calculated at original purchase price.   96
Owners shall provide documentation to fully support the claims and calculations under this clause.   97

(M) Worldscale

Worldscale Terms and Conditions **apply do not apply** to this Charter, [delete as applicable]   98

(N) Casualty/ Accident contacts

In the event of an accident/marine casualty involving the vessel, Owners' technical managers can be contacted on a 24 hour basis   99
as follows: 100
Company Full Name: 101
Contact Person: 102
Full Address: 103
Telephone Number: 104
Fax Number: 105
Telex Number: 106
Email Address: 107
24 Hour Emergency Telephone number: 108

(O) Special provisions   109

Signatures

IN WITNESS WHEREOF, the parties have caused this Charter consisting of the Preamble, Parts I, II and III to be executed as of   110
the day and year first above written.   111

By   112

By   113

Printed by BIMCO's idea

APPENDIX 16

Issued March 2005 **"SHELLVOY 6"**

Part II

Condition of vessel	1. Owners shall exercise clue diligence to ensure that from the time when the obligation to proceed to the loading port(s) attaches and throughout the charter service -	1 2

      (a) the vessel and her hull, machinery, boilers, tanks, equipment and facilities are in good order and condition and in every way equipped and fit for the service required; and   3, 4

      (b) the vessel has a full and efficient complement of master, officers and crew and the senior officers shall be fully conversant in spoken and written English language   5, 6

and to ensure that before and at the commencement of any laden voyage the vessel is in all respects fit to carry the cargo specified in Part I clause (F). For the avoidance of doubt, references to equipment in this Charter shall include but not be limited to computers and computer systems, and such equipment shall (inter alia) be required to continue to function, and not suffer a loss of functionality and accuracy (whether logical or mathematical) as a result of the run date or dates being processed.   7–10

Cleanliness of tanks

2. Whilst loading, carrying and discharging the cargo the master shall at all times keep the tanks, lines and pumps of the vessel always clean for the cargo. Unless otherwise agreed between Owners and Charterers the vessel shall present for loading with cargo tanks ready and, subject to the following paragraphs, if vessel is fitted with Inert Gas System ("IGS"), fully inerted.   11–13

Charterers shall have the right to inspect vessel's tanks prior to loading and the vessel shall abide by Charterers' instructions with regard to tank or tanks which the vessel is required to present ready for entry and inspection. If Charterer's inspector is not satisfied with the cleanliness of the vessel's tanks. Owners shall clean them in their time and at their expense to the satisfaction of Charterers' inspector, provided that nothing herein shall affect the responsibilities and obligations of the master and Owners in respect of the loading, carriage and care of cargo under this Charter nor prejudice the rights of Charterers, should any contamination or damage subsequently be found, to contend that the same was caused by inadequate cleaning and or some breach of this or any other clause of this Charter.   14–20

Notwithstanding that the vessel, if equipped with IGS, shall present for loading with all cargo tanks fully inerted, any time used for de-inerting (provided that such de-inerting takes place after laytime or demurrage time has commenced or would, but for this clause, have commenced) and/or re-inerting those tanks that at Charterers' specific request were gas freed for inspection, shall count as laytime or if on demurrage as demurrage, provided the tank or tanks inspected are found to be suitable. In such case Charterers will reimburse Owners for bunkers consumed for de-inerting/re-inerting, at replacement cost.   21–25

If the vessel's tanks are inspected and rejected, time used for de-inerting shall not count towards laytime or demurrage, and laytime or demurrage time shall not commence or recommence, as the case may be, until the tanks have been re-inspected, approved by Charterers' inspector, and re-inerted.   26–28

Voyage

3. (1) Subject to the provisions of this Charter the vessel shall perform her service with utmost despatch and shall proceed to such berths as Charterers may specify, in any port or ports within Part I clause (D) nominated by Charterers, or so near thereunto as she may safely get and there, always safely afloat, load the cargo specified in Part I clause (F) of this Charter, but not in excess of the maximum quantity consistent with the International Load Line Convention for the time being in force and, being so loaded, proceed as ordered on signing bills of lading to such berths as Charterers may specify, in any port or ports within Part I clause (E) nominated by Charterers, or so near thereunto as she may safely get and there, always safely afloat, discharge the cargo.   29–34

Charterers shall nominate loading and discharging ports, and shall specify loading and discharging berths and. where loading or discharging is interrupted, shall provide fresh orders in relation thereto.   35, 36

In addition Charterers shall have the option at any time of ordering the vessel to safe areas at sea for wireless orders. Any delay or deviation arising as a result of the exercise of such option shall be compensated by Charterers in accordance with the terms of Part II clause 26 (1).   37–39

(2) Owners shall be responsible for and indemnify Charterers for any time, costs, delays or loss including but not limited to use of laytime, demurrage, deviation expenses, replacement tonnage, lightening costs and associated fees and expenses due to any failure whatsoever to comply fully with Charterers' voyage instructions and clauses in this Charter which specify requirements concerning Voyage Instructions and/or Owners'/masters' duties including, without limitation to the generality of the foregoing, loading more cargo than permitted under the International Load Line Convention, for the time being in force, or for not leaving sufficient space for expansion of cargo or loading more or less cargo than Charterers specified or for not loading/discharging in accordance with Charterers' instructions regarding the cargo quantity or draft requirements.   40–46

This clause 3(2) shall have effect notwithstanding the provision of Part II clause 32 (a) of this Charter or Owners' defences under the Hague-Visby Rules.   47, 48

(3) Owners shall always employ pilots for berthing and unberthing of vessels at all ports and/or berths under this Charter unless prior exemption is given by correct and authorised personnel. Owners to confirm in writing if they have been exempt from using a pilot and provide Charterers with the details, including but not limited to, the authorising organisation with person's name.   49–51

(4) Without prejudice to the provisions of sub-clause (2) of this clause, and unless a specific prior agreement exists, if a conflict arises between terminal orders and Charterers' voyage instructions, the master shall stop cargo operations, and/or other operations under dispute, and contact Charterers immediately. Terminal orders shall never supersede Charterers' voyage   52–54

APPENDIX 16

Issued March 2005   **"SHELLVOY 6"**

Part II

instructions and any conflict shall be resolved prior to resumption of cargo, or other, operations in dispute. Where such a conflict 55
arises the vessel shall not sail from the port or resume cargo operations, and/or other operations under dispute, until Charterers 56
have directed the vessel to do so. 57
Time spent resolving the vessel/terminal conflict will count as laytime or demurrage except that failure of Owners/master to 58
comply with the procedure set forth above shall result in the deduction from laytime or demurrage time of the time used in 59
resolving the vessel/terminal instruction conflict 60
    (5) In this Charter, "berth" means any berth, wharf, dock, anchorage, submarine line, a position alongside any vessel or 61
lighter or any other loading or discharging point whatsoever to which Charterers are entitled to order the vessel hereunder, and 62
"port" means any port or location at sea to which the vessel may proceed in accordance with the terms of this Charter. 63

Safe berth   4. Charterers shall exercise due diligence to order the vessel only to ports and berths which are safe for the vessel and to 64
ensure that transhipment operations conform to standards not less than those set out in the latest edition of ICS/OCIMF Ship-to- 65
Ship Transfer Guide (Petroleum). Notwithstanding anything contained in this Charter, Charterers do not warrant the safety of any 66
port, berth or transhipment operation and Charterers shall not be liable for loss or damage arising from any unsafely if they can 67
prove that due diligence was exercised in the giving of the order or if such loss or damage was caused by an act of war or civil 68
commotion within the trading areas defined in Part I clauses (D/E). 69

Freight   5. (1) Freight shall be earned concurrently with delivery of cargo at the nominated discharging port or ports and shall be 70
paid by Charterers to Owners without any deductions, except as may be required in the Singapore Income Tax Act and/or under 71
Part II clause 48 and/or under clause 55 and/or under Part III clause 4(a), in United States Dollars at the rate(s) specified in Part I 72
clause (G) on the gross bill of lading quantity as furnished by the shipper (subject to Part II clauses 8 and 40). upon receipt by 73
Charterers of notice of completion of final discharge of cargo, provided that no freight shall be payable on any quantity in excess 74
of the maximum quantity consistent with the International Load Line Convention for the time being in force. 75
If the vessel is ordered to proceed on a voyage for which a fixed differential is provided in Worldscale, such fixed differential 76
shall be payable without applying the percentage referred to in Part I clause (G). 77
If cargo is carried between ports and/or by an agreed route for which no freight rate is expressly quoted in Worldscale, 78
then the parties shall, in the absence of agreement as to the appropriate freight rate, apply to Worldscale Association (London) 79
Ltd., or Worldscale Association (NYC) Inc., for the determination of an appropriate Worldscale freight rate. If Owners or master 80
unilaterally elect to proceed by a route that is different to that specified in Worldscale, or different to a route agreed between 81
Owners and Charterers, freight shall always be paid in accordance with the Worldscale rate as published or in accordance with any 82
special rate applicable for the agreed route. 83
Save in respect of the time when freight is earned, the location of any transhipment at sea pursuant to Part II clause 26(2) 84
shall not be an additional nominated port, unless otherwise agreed, for the purposes of this Charter (including this clause 5) and 85
the freight rate for the voyage shall be the same as if such transhipment had not taken place. 86
(2) If the freight in Part I clause (G) is a lumpsum amount and such lumpsum freight is connected with a specific number of 87
load and discharge ports given in Part I clause (L) and Owners agree that Charterers may order the vessel to additional load and/or 88
discharge ports not covered by the agreed lumpsum freight, the following shall apply: 89
    (a)   the first load port and the final discharge port shall be deemed to be the port(s) that form the voyage and on 90
        which the lumpsum freight included in Part I clause (G) refers to; 91
    (b)   freight for such additional ports shall be calculated on basis of deviation. Deviation shall be calculated on 92
        the difference in distance between the specified voyage (for which freight is agreed) and the voyage actually 93
        performed. 94
BP Shipping Marine Distance Tables (2004). produced by AtoBriac shall be used in both cases. Deviation time/bunker 95
consumption shall be calculated using the charter speed and bunker consumption as per the speed and consumptions given in 96
Part I clause(L) of this Charter. 97
Deviation time and time spent in port shall be charged at the demurrage rate in Part I clause (J) of this Charter except that time 98
used in port which would otherwise qualify' for half rate laytime and/or demurrage under Part II clause (15) (2) of this Charter 99
will be charged at half rate. 100
Additional bunkers consumed shall be paid at replacement cost, and actual port costs shall be paid as incurred. Such deviation 101
costs shall be paid against Owners' fully documented claim. 102

Claims, due   6. (1) Dues and other charges upon the vessel, including those assessed by reference to the quantity of cargo loaded or 103
and other   discharged, and any taxes on freight whatsoever shall be paid by Owners, and dues and other charges upon the cargo shall be paid 104
charges   by Charterers. However, notwithstanding the foregoing, where under a provision of Worldscale a due or charge is expressly for 105
the account of Owners or Charterers then such due or charge shall be payable in accordance with such provision. 106
    (2) Any costs including those itemised under applicable "Worldscale" as being for Charterers' account shall, unless otherwise 107
instructed by Charterers, be paid by Owners and reimbursed by Charterers against Owners' fully documented claim. 108

APPENDIX 16

Issued March 2005   **"SHELLVOY 6"**

Part II

(3) Charterers shall be discharged and released from all liability in respect of any charges/claims (other than demurrage and   109
Worldscale charges/dues and indemnity claims) including but not limited to additional bunkers, detention, deviation, shifting,   110
heating, deadweight, speed up, slow down, drifting, port costs, additional freight, insurance. Owner may send to Charterers under   111
this Charter unless any such charges/claims have been received by Charterer in writing, fully and correctly documented, within   112
ninety (90) days from completion of discharge of the cargo concerned under this Charter. Part II clause 15 (3) of this Charter   113
covers the notification and fully documented claim procedure for demurrage.   114

(4) If, after disconnection of hoses, the vessel remains at berth for vessel's purposes. Owners shall be responsible for   115
all direct and indirect costs whether advised to Owners in advance or not, and including charges by Terminal Suppliers/   116
Receivers.   117

Loading and discharging cargo	7. The cargo shall be loaded into the vessel at the expense of Charterers and, up to the vessel's permanent hose connections, at Charterers' risk. The cargo shall be discharged from the vessel at the expense of Owners and, up to the vessel's permanent hose connections, at Owners' risk. Owners shall, unless otherwise notified by Charterers or their agents, supply at Owners' expense all hands, equipment and facilities required on board for mooring and unmooring and connecting and disconnecting hoses for loading and discharging.

Loading and   7. The cargo shall be loaded into the vessel at the expense of Charterers and, up to the vessel's permanent hose connections,   118
discharging   at Charterers' risk. The cargo shall be discharged from the vessel at the expense of Owners and, up to the vessel's permanent hose   119
cargo   connections, at Owners' risk. Owners shall, unless otherwise notified by Charterers or their agents, supply at Owners' expense   120
                all hands, equipment and facilities required on board for mooring and unmooring and connecting and disconnecting hoses for   121
                loading and discharging.   122

Deadfreight   8. Charterers need not supply a full cargo, but if they do not freight shall nevertheless be paid as if the vessel had been loaded   123
                with a full cargo.   124
                The term "full cargo" as used throughout this Charter means a cargo which, together with any collected washings (as defined   125
                in Part II clause 40) retained on board pursuant to the requirements of MARPOL 73/78, tills the vessel to either her applicable   126
                deadweight or her capacity stated in Part I clause (A) (I) (iii), whichever is less, while leaving sufficient space in the tanks for   127
                the expansion of cargo. If under Part I clause (F) vessel is chartered for a minimum quantity and the vessel is unable to load such   128
                quantity due to having reached her capacity as stated in Part I clause (A) (I) (iii), always leaving sufficient space for expansion   129
                of cargo, then without prejudice to any claims which Charterers may have against Owners, no deadweight between the quantity   130
                loaded and the quantity shown in Part I clause (F) shall be due.   131

Shifting   9. Charterers shall have the right to require the vessel to shift at ports of loading and/or discharging from a loading or   132
                discharging berth within port limits and/or to a waiting place inside or outside port limits and back to the same or to another   133
                such berth/place once or more often on payment of all additional expenses incurred. For the purposes of freight payment and   134
                shifting the places grouped in Port and Terminal Combinations in Worldscale are to be considered as berths within a single   135
                port. If at any time before cargo operations are completed it becomes dangerous for the vessel to remain at the specified berth   136
                as a result of wind or water conditions, Charterers shall pay all additional expenses of shifting from any such berth and back   137
                to that or any other specified berth within port limits (except to the extent that any fault of the vessel contributed to such   138
                danger).   139
                Subject to Part II clause 14(a) and (c) time spent shifting shall count against laytime or if the vessel is on demurrage for   140
                demurrage.   141

Charterers'   10. If the vessel is delayed due to Charterers' breach of Part II clause 3 Charterers shall, subject to the terms hereof,   142
failure to   compensate Owners in accordance with Part II clause 15(1) and (2) as if such delay were time exceeding the laytime. Such   143
give order   compensation shall be Owners' sole remedy in respect of such delay.   144
                The period of such delay shall be calculated: 145
                  (i) from 6 hours after Owners notify Charterers that the vessel is delayed awaiting nomination of loading or   146
                       discharging port until such nomination has been received by Owners, or   147
                  (ii) from 6 hours after the vessel gives notice of readiness at the loading or discharging port until commencement of   148
                       loading or discharging,   149
                as the case may be, subject always to the same exceptions as those set out in Part II clause 14. Any period of delay in respect   150
                of which Charterers pay compensation pursuant to this clause 10 shall be excluded from any calculation of time for laytime   151
                or demurrage made under any other clause of this Charter.   152
                Periods of delay hereunder shall be cumulative for each port, and Owners may demand compensation after the vessel   153
                has been delayed for a total of 20 running days, and thereafter after each succeeding 5 running days of delay and at the   154
                end of any delay. Each such demand shall show the period in respect of which compensation is claimed and the amount   155
                due. Charterers shall pay the full amount due within 14 days after receipt of Owners' demand. Should Charterers fail to   156
                make any such payments Owners shall have the right to terminate this Charter by giving written notice to Charterers or   157
                their agents, without prejudice to any claims which Charterers or Owners may have against each other under this Charter   158
                or otherwise.   159

Laydays/   11. Should the vessel not be ready to load by noon local time on the termination date set out in Part I clause (C) Charterers   160
Termination   shall have the option of terminating this Charter unless the vessel has been delayed due to Charterers' change of orders pursuant   161
                to Part II clause 26, in which case the laydays shall be extended by the period of such delay.   162

APPENDIX 16

Issued March 2005 **"SHELLVOY 6"**

Part II

As soon as Owners become aware that the vessel will not be ready to load by noon on the termination date, Owners will give 163
notice to Charterers declaring a new readiness date and ask Charterers to elect whether or not to terminate this Charter. 164
Within 4 days after such notice, Charterers shall either: 165

    (i) declare this Charter terminated or 166

    (ii) confirm a revised set of laydays which shall be amended such that the new readiness date stated shall be the 167
        commencement date and the second day thereafter shall be the termination date or, 168

    (iii) agree a new set of laydays or an extension to the laydays mutually acceptable to Owners and Charterers 169

The provisions of this clause and the exercise or non-exercise by Charterers of their option to terminate shall not prejudice 170
any claims which Charterers or Owners may have against each other. 171

Laytime   12. (1) The laytime for loading, discharging and all other Charterers' purposes whatsoever shall be the number of running 172
hours specified in Part I clause (I). Charterers shall have the right to load and discharge at all times, including night, provided that 173
they shall pay for all extra expenses incurred ashore. 174

    (2) If vessel is able to, and Charterers so instruct, the vessel shall load earlier than the commencement of laydays and 175
Charterers shall have the benefit of such time saved by way of offset from any demurrage incured. Such benefit shall be the time 176
between commencement of loading until the commencement of the original laydays. 177

Notice of   13. (1) Subject to the provisions of Part II clauses 13(3) and 14, 178
readiness/   (a) Time at each loading or discharging port shall commence to run 6 hours after the vessel is in all respects ready to 179
Running time   load or discharge and written notice thereof has been tendered by the master or Owners' agents to Charterers or their 180
         agents and the vessel is securely moored at the specified loading or discharging berth. However, if the vessel does 181
         not proceed immediately to such berth time shall commence to run 6 hours after (i) the vessel is lying in the area 182
         where she was ordered to wait or, in the absence of any such specific order, in a usual waiting area and (ii) written 183
         notice of readiness has been tendered and (iii) the specified berth is accessible. A loading or discharging berth shall 184
         be deemed inaccessible only for so long as the vessel is or would be prevented from proceeding to it by bad weather, 185
         tidal conditions, ice, awaiting daylight, pilot or tugs, or port traffic control requirements (except those requirements 186
         resulting from the unavailability of such berth or of the cargo). If Charterers fail to specify a berth at any port, the first 187
         berth at which the vessel loads or discharges the cargo or any part thereof shall be deemed to be the specified berth at 188
         such port for the purposes of this clause. 189
         Notice shall not be tendered before commencement of laydays and notice tendered by radio shall qualify as written 190
         notice provided it is confirmed in writing as soon as reasonably possible. 191
         Time shall never commence before six hours after commencement of laydays unless loading commences prior to this 192
         time as provided in clause 13 (3). 193
         If Owners fail; 194
         (i) to obtain Customs clearance; and/or 195
         (ii) to obtain free pratique unless this is not customary prior to berthing; and/or 196
         (iii) to have on board all papers/certificates required to perform this Charter, either within the 6 hours after notice 197
              of readiness originally tendered or when time would otherwise normally commence under this Charter, then 198
              the original notice of readiness shall not be valid. A new notice of readiness may only be tendered when 199
              Customs clearance and or free pratique has been granted and/or all papers/certificates required are in order 200
              in accordance with relevant authorities' requirements. Laytime or demurrage, if on demurrage, would then 201
              commence in accordance with the terms of this Charter. All time, costs and expenses as a result of delays due 202
              to any of the foregoing shall be for Owners' account. 203
     (b) Time shall: 204
         (i) continue to run until the cargo hoses have been disconnected. 205
         (ii) recommence two hours after disconnection of hoses if the vessel is delayed for Charterers' purposes and shall 206
              continue until the termination of such delay provided that if the vessel waits at any place other than the berth, 207
              any time or part of the time on passage to such other place that occurs after two hours from disconnection of 208
              hoses shall not count. 209

(2) If the vessel loads or discharges cargo by transhipment at sea time shall commence in accordance with Part II clause 13 210
(1) (a), and run until transhipment has been completed and the vessels have separated, always subject to Part II clause 14. 211

(3) Notwithstanding anything else in this clause 13, if Charterers start loading or discharging the vessel before time would 212
otherwise start to run under this Charter, time shall run from commencement of such loading or discharging. 213

(4) For the purposes of this clause 13 and of Part II clause 14 and Part II clause 15 "time" shall mean laytime or time 214
counting for demurrage, as the case may be. 215

APPENDIX 16

Issued March 2005   **"SHELLVOY 6"**

Part II

Suspension of time	14. Time shall not count when.	216
	(a) spent on inward passage from the vessel's waiting area to the loading or discharging berth specified by Charterers,	217
	even if lightening occurred at such waiting area; or	218
	(b) spent in carrying out vessel operations, including but not limited to bunkering, discharging slops and tank washings,	219
	and handling ballast, except to the extent that cargo operations are carried on concurrently and are not delayed	220
	thereby; or	221
	(c) lost as a result of:	222
	(i) breach of this Charter by Owners; or	223
	(ii) any cause attributable to the vessel, (including but not limited to the warranties in Part I (A) of this Charter)	224
	including breakdown or inefficiency of the vessel; or	225
	(iii) strike, lock-out, stoppage or restraint of labour of master, officers or crew of the vessel or tug boats or pilot.	226

Demurrage	15. (1) Charterers shall pay demurrage at the rate specified in Part I clause (J).	227

If the demurrage rate specified in Part I clause (J) is expressed as a percentage of Worldscale such percentage shall be applied 228
to the demurrage rate applicable to vessels of a similar size to the vessel as provided in Worldscale or, for the purpose of clause 10 229
and/or if this Charter is terminated prior to the commencement of loading, in Worldscale current at the termination date specified 230
in Part I clause (C). 231

Demurrage shall be paid per running day or pro rata for part thereof for all time which, under the provisions of this Charter, 232
counts against laytime or for demurrage and which exceeds the laytime specified in Part I clause (1). Charterers' liability for 233
exceeding the laytime shall be absolute and shall not in any case be subject to the provisions of Part II clause 32. 234

(2) If, however, all or part of such demurrage arises out of or results from fire or explosion or strike or failure/breakdown of 235
plant and/or machinery at ports of loading and/or discharging in or about the plant of Charterers, shippers or consignees of the 236
cargo (not being a fire or explosion caused by the negligence or wilful act or omission of Charterers, shippers or consignees of the 237
cargo or their respective servants or agents), act of God, act of war, riot, civil commotion, or arrest or restraint of princes, rulers or 238
peoples, the laytime used and/or the rate of demurrage shall be reduced by half for such laytime used and/or for such demurrage or 239
such parts thereof. 240

(3) Owners shall notify Charterers within 60 days after completion of discharge if demurrage has been incurred and any 241
demurrage claim shall be fully and correctly documented, and received by Charterers, within 90 days after completion of 242
discharge. If Owners fail to give notice of or to submit any such claim with documentation, as required herein, within the limits 243
aforesaid. Charterers' liability for such demurrage shall be extinguished. 244

(4) If any part cargo for other charterers, shippers or consignees (as the case may be) is loaded or discharged at the same 245
berth, then any time used by the vessel waiting at or for such berth and in loading or discharging which would otherwise count 246
as laytime or if the vessel is on demurrage for demurrage, shall be pro-rated in the proportion that Charterers' cargo bears to the 247
total cargo to be loaded or discharged at such berth. If however, the running of laytime or demurrage, if on demurrage, is solely 248
attributable to other parties' cargo operations then such time shall not count in calculating laytime or demurrage, if on demurrage, 249
against Charterers under this Charter. 250

Vessel inspection	16. Charterers shall have the right, but no duty, to have a representative attend on board the vessel at any loading and/or	251

discharging ports and the master and Owners shall co-operate to facilitate his inspection of the vessel and observation of cargo 252
operations. However, such right, and the exercise or non-exercise thereof, shall in no way reduce the master's or Owners' 253
authority over, or responsibility to Charterers and third parties for, the vessel and every aspect of her operation, nor increase 254
Charterers' responsibilities to Owners or third parties for the same. 255

Cargo inspection	17. This clause 17 is without prejudice to Part II clause 2 hereof. Charterers shall have the right to require inspection of the	256

vessel's tanks at loading and/or discharging ports to ascertain the quantity and quality of the cargo, water and residues on board. 257
Depressurisation of the tanks to permit inspection and/or ullaging shall be carried out in accordance with the recommendations in 258
the latest edition of the ISGOTT guidelines. Charterers shall also have the right to inspect and take samples from the bunker tanks 259
and other non-cargo spaces. Any delay to the vessel caused by such inspection and measurement or associated depressurising/ 260
repressurising of tanks shall count against laytime, or if the vessel is on demurrage, for demurrage. 261

Cargo measurement	18. The master shall ascertain the contents of all tanks before and after loading and before and after discharging, and shall	262

prepare tank-by-tank ullage reports of the cargo, water and residues on board which shall be promptly made available to 263
Charterers or their representative if requested. Each such ullage report shall show actual ullage/dips, and densities at observed 264
and standard temperature (15° Celsius). All quantities shall be expressed in cubic metres at both observed and standard 265
temperature. 266

Insert gas	19. The vessel's inert gas system (if any) shall comply with Regulation 62. Chapter II-2 of the 1974 Safety of Life at	267

Sea Convention as modified by the Protocol of 1978, and any subsequent amendments, and Owners warrant that such system 268
shall be operated (subject to the provisions of Part II clause 2), during loading, throughout the voyage and during discharge, 269

APPENDIX 16

Issued March 2005

"SHELLVOY 6"

Part II

	and in accordance with the guidance given in the IMO publication "Inert Gas System (1983)". Should the inert gas system fail.	270
	Section 8 (Emergency Procedures) of the said IMO publication shall be strictly adhered to and time lost as a consequence of such	271
	failure shall not count against laytime or, if the vessel is on demurrage, for demurrage.	272

Crude oil washing   20. If the vessel is equipped for crude oil washing Charterers shall have the right to require the vessel to crude oil 273
wash, concurrently with discharge, those tanks in which Charterers' cargo is carried. If crude oil washing is required by 274
Charterers any additional discharge time thereby incurred, always subject to the next succeeding sentences, shall count 275
against laytime or, if the vessel is on demurrage, for demurrage. The number of hours specified in Part I clause (A) (I) 276
(vii) shall be increased by 0.6 hours per cargo tank washed, always subject to a maximum increase of 8 hours. If vessel 277
fails to maintain 100 PSI throughout the discharge then any time over 24 hours, plus the additional discharge performance 278
allowance under this clause, shall not count as laytime or demurrage, if on demurrage. This clause 20 docs not reduce 279
Owners' liability for the vessel to perform her service with utmost despatch as setout in Part II, Clause 3(1). The master 280
shall provide Charterers with a crude oil washing log identifying each tank washed, and stating whether such tank has been 281
washed to the MARPOL minimum standard or has been the subject of additional crude oil washing and whether requested 282
by Charterers or otherwise. 283

Overage insurance   21. Any additional insurance on the cargo required because of the age of the vessel shall be for Owners' account. 284

Ice   22. The vessel shall not be required to force ice or to follow icebreakers. If the master finds that a nominated port is 285
inaccessible due to ice, the master shall immediately notify Charterers requesting revised orders and shall remain outside the 286
ice-bound area; and if after arrival at a nominated port there is danger of the vessel being frozen in, the vessel shall proceed to the 287
nearest safe and ice free position and at the same time request Charterers to give revised orders. 288
    In either ease if the affected port is: 289

(i)   the first or only loading port and no cargo has been loaded. Charterers shall either nominate another port, or 290
give notice cancelling this Charter in which case they shall pay at the demurrage rate in Part I clause (J) for the 291
time from the master's notification aforesaid or from notice of readiness on arrival, as the case may be, until 292
the time such cancellation notice is given; 293

(ii)   a loading port and part of the cargo has been loaded. Charterers shall either nominate another port, or order 294
the vessel to proceed on the voyage without completing loading in which case Charterers shall pay for any 295
deadweight arising therefrom; 296

(iii)   a discharging port, Charterers shall either nominate another port or order the vessel to proceed to or return 297
to and discharge at the nominated port. If the vessel is ordered to proceed to or return to a nominated port, 298
Charterers shall bear the risk of the vessel being damaged whilst proceeding to or returning to or at such port, 299
and the whole period from the time when the master's request for revised orders is received by Charterers until 300
the vessel can safely depart after completion of discharge shall count against laytime or, if the vessel is on 301
demurrage, for demurrage. 302

    If, as a consequence of Charterers revising orders pursuant to this clause, the nominated port(s) or the number or rotation 303
of ports is changed, freight shall nevertheless be paid for the voyage which the vessel would otherwise have performed had 304
the orders not been so revised, such freight to be increased or reduced by the amount by which, as a result of such revision of 305
orders. 306

(a)   the time used including any time awaiting revised orders (which shall be valued at the demurrage rate in Part I 307
clause (J)), and 308

(b)   the bunkers consumed, at replacement cost and 309

(c)   the port charges 310
for the voyage actually performed are greater or less than those that would have been incurred on the voyage 311
which, but for the revised orders under this clause, the vessel would have performed. 312

Quarantine   23. Time lost due to quarantine shall not count against laytime or for demurrage unless such quarantine was in force at the 313
time when the affected port was nominated by Charterers. 314

Agency   24. The vessel's agents shall be nominated by Charterers at nominated ports of loading and discharging. Such agents, 315
although nominated by Charterers, shall be employed and paid by Owners. 316

Charterers' obligation at shallow draft port/ Lightening in port   25. (1) If the vessel, with the quantity of cargo then on board, is unable due to inadequate depth of water in the port safely to reach 317
any specified discharging berth and discharge the cargo there always safely afloat, Charterers shall specify a location within 318
port limits where the vessel can discharge sufficient cargo into vessels or lighters to enable the vessel safely to reach and 319
discharge cargo at such discharging berth, and the vessel shall lighten at such location. 320
    (2) If the vessel is lightened pursuant to clause 25(1) then, for the purposes of the calculation of laytime and demurrage, the 321
lightening place shall be treated as the first discharging berth within the port where such lightening occurs. 322

APPENDIX 16

Issued March 2005   "SHELLVOY 6"

Part II

Charterers' orders/change of orders/Part cargo transhipment	26. (1) If, after loading and or discharging ports have been nominated. Charterers wish to vary such nominations or their rotation. Charterers may give revised orders subject to Part I clause (D) and/or (E), as the case may be. Charterers shall reimburse Owners at the demurrage rate provided in Part I clause (J) for any deviation or delay which may result therefrom and shall pay at replacement cost for any extra bunkers consumed. Charterers shall not be liable for any other loss or expense which is caused by such variation.	323 324 325 326 327

(2) Subject to Part II clause 33(6), Charterers may order the vessel to load and/or discharge any part of the cargo by transhipment at sea in the vicinity of any nominated port or en route between two nominated ports, in which case unless Charterers elect, (which they may do at any time) to treat the place of such transhipment as a load or discharge port (subject to the number of ports and ranges in Part I clauses (D) and (E) of this Charter). Charterers shall reimburse Owners at the demurrage rate specified in Part I clause (J) for any additional steaming time and/or delay which may be incurred as a consequence of proceeding to and from the location at sea of such transhipment and. in addition. Charterers shall pay at replacement cost for any extra bunkers consumed.

328
329
330
331
332
333
334

(3) Owners warrant that the vessel, master, officers and crew are, and shall remain during this Charter, capable of safely carrying out all the procedures in the current edition of the ICS/OCIMF Ship to Ship Transfer Guide (Petroleum). Owners further warrant that when instructed to perform a ship to ship transfer the master Officers and crew shall, at all times, comply with such procedures. Charterers shall provide, and pay for, the necessary equipment and, if necessary, mooring master, for such ship to ship operation.

335
336
337
338
339

Heating of cargo

27. If Charterers require cargo heating the vessel shall, on passage to and whilst at discharging port(s), Maintain the cargo at the loaded temperature or at the temperature stated in Part I clause (A) (I) (iv), whichever is the lower. Charterers may request that the temperature of the cargo be raised above or lowered below that at which it was loaded, in which event Owners shall use their best endeavours to comply with such request and Charterers shall pay at replacement cost for any additional bunkers consumed and any consequential delay to the vessel shall count against laytime or, if the vessel is on demurrage, for demurrage.

340
341
342
343
344
345

ETA

28. (1) Owners shall give Charterers a time and date of expected arrival at the first load port or if the loading range is in the Arabian Gulf, the time of her expected arrival off Quoin Island (hereinafter called "load port" in this clause) at the date of this Charter. Owners shall further advise Charterers at any time between the Charter date and arrival at load port of any variation of 6 hours or more in vessel's expected arrival time/date at the load port.

346
347
348
349

(2) Owners undertake that, unless Charterers require otherwise, the master shall:

350

(a) advise Charterers immediately on leaving the final port of call on the previous voyage of the time and date of the vessel's expected arrival at the first loading port and shall further advise Charterers 72, 48, 36, and 24 hours before the expected arrival time/date.

351
352
353

(b) advise Charterers immediately after departure from the final loading port, of the vessel's expected time of arrival at the first discharging port or the area at sea to which the vessel has been instructed to proceed for wireless orders, and confirm or amend such advice not later than 72, 48, 36 and 24 hours before the vessel is due at such port or area;

354
355
356
357

(c) advise Charterers immediately of any variation of more than six hours from expected times of arrival at loading or discharging ports, Quoin Island or such area at sea to Charterers;

358
359

(d) address all messages as specified in Part I clause (K).

360

Owners shall be responsible for any consequences or additional expenses arising as a result of non-compliance with this clause.

361

(3) If at any time prior to the tender of notice of readiness at the first load port, the vessel ceases to comply with the description set out in Part I clause (A) and in any questionnaire(s), the Owners shall immediately notify Charterers of the same, providing full particulars, and explaining what steps Owners are taking to ensure that the vessel will so comply. Any silence or failure on the part of Charterers to respond to or any inaction taken in respect of any such notice shall not amount to a waiver of any rights or remedies which Charterers may have in respect of the mailers notified by Owners.

362
363
364
365
366

Packed cargo

29. Charterers have the option of shipping products and/or general cargo in available dry cargo space, the Quantity being subject to the master's discretion. Freight shall be payable at the bulk rate in accordance with Part II clause 5 and Charterers shall pay in addition all expenses incurred solely as a result of the packed cargo being carried. Delay occasioned to the vessel by the exercise of such option shall count against laytime or, if the vessel is on demurrage, for demurrage.

367
368
369
370

Subletting Assignment

30. Charterers shall have the option of sub-chartering the vessel and/or of assigning this Charter to any person or persons, but Charterers shall always remain responsible for the due fulfilment of all the terms and conditions of this Charter. Additionally Charterers may novate this charter to any company of the Royal Dutch/ Shell Group of Companies.

371
372
373

APPENDIX 16

Issued March 2005

"SHELLVOY 6"

Part II

| Liberty | 31. The vessel shall be at liberty to tow or be towed, to assist vessels in all positions of distress and to deviate for the purpose | 374 |

Liberty
31. The vessel shall be at liberty to tow or be towed, to assist vessels in all positions of distress and to deviate for the purpose of saving life or property. On the laden voyage the vessel shall not take on bunkers or deviate or stop, except as allowed in this clause 31, without prior permission of Charterers, Cargo Insurers, and Owners' P&I Club.

Exceptions
32. (1) The vessel, her master and Owners shall not, unless otherwise in this Charter expressly provided, be liable for any loss or damage or delay or failure arising or resulting from any act, neglect or default of the master, pilots, mariners or other servants of Owners in the navigation or management of the vessel; fire, unless caused by the actual fault or privity of Owners; collision or stranding; dangers and accidents of the sea: explosion, Bursting of boilers, breakage of shafts or any latent defect in hull, equipment or machinery; provided, however, that Part I clause (A) and Part II clauses 1 and 2 hereof shall be unaffected by the foregoing. Further, neither the vessel, her master or Owners, nor Charterers shall, unless otherwise in this Charter expressly provided, be liable for any loss or damage or delay or failure in performance hereunder arising or resulting from act of God, act of war, act of public enemies, seizure under legal process, quarantine restrictions, strikes, lock-outs, restraints of labour, riots, civil commotions or arrest or restraint of princes, rulers or people.

(2) Nothing in this Charter shall be construed as in any way restricting, excluding or waiving the right of Owners or of any other relevant persons to limit their liability under any available legislation or law.

(3) Clause 32(1) shall not apply to or affect any liability of Owners or the vessel or any other relevant person in respect of

(a) loss or damage caused to any berth, jetty, dock, dolphin, buoy, mooring line, pipe or crane or other works or equipment whatsoever at or near any port to which the vessels may proceed under this Charter, whether or not such works or equipment belong to Charterers, or

(b) any claim (whether brought by Charterers or any other person) arising out of any loss of or damage to or in connection with the cargo. Any such claim shall be subject to the Hague-Visby Rules or the Hague Rules, or the Hamburg Rules as the case may be, which ought pursuant to Part II clause 37 hereof to have been incorporated in the relevant bill of lading (whether or not such Rules were so incorporated) or, if no such bill of lading is issued, to the Hague-Visby rules unless the Hamburg Rules compulsory apply in which case to the Hamburg Rules.

Bills of lading
33. (1) Subject to the provisions of this clause Charterers may require the master to sign lawful bills of lading for any cargo in such form as Charterers direct.

(2) The signing of bills of lading shall be without prejudice to this Charter and Charterers hereby indemnify Owners against all liabilities that may arise from signing bills of lading to the extent that the same impose liabilities upon Owners in excess of or beyond those imposed by this Charter.

(3) All bills of lading presented to the master for signature, in addition to complying with the Requirements of Part II clauses 35, 36 and 37, shall include or effectively incorporate clauses substantially similar to the terms of Part II clauses 22, 33(7) and 34.

(4) All bills of lading presented for signature hereunder shall show a named port of discharge. If when bills of lading are presented for signature discharging port(s) have been nominated hereunder, the discharging port(s) shown on such bills of lading shall be in conformity with the nominated port(s). If at the time of such presentation no such nomination has been made hereunder, the discharging port(s) shown on such bills of lading must be within Part I clause (E) and shall be deemed to have been nominated hereunder by virtue of such presentation.

(5) Article III Rules 3 and 5 of the Hague-Visby Rules shall apply to the particulars included in the bills of lading as if Charterers were the shippers, and the guarantee and indemnity therein contained shall apply to the description of the cargo furnished by or on behalf of Charterers.

(6) Notwithstanding any other provisions of this Charter, Owners shall be obliged to comply with any orders from Charterers to discharge all or part of the cargo provided that they have received from Charterers written confirmation of such orders.

If Charterers by telex, facsimile or other form of written communication that specifically refers to this clause request Owners to discharge a quantity of cargo either:

(a) without bills of lading and/or

(b) at a discharge place other than that named in a bill of lading and/or

(c) that is different from the bill of lading quantity

then Owners shall discharge such cargo in accordance with Charterers' instructions in consideration of receiving the Following indemnity which shall be deemed to be given by Charterers on each and every such occasion and which is limited in value to 200 per cent of the C.I.F. value of the cargo on board:

(i) Charterers shall indemnify Owners, and Owners' servants and agents in respect of any liability loss or damage of whatsoever nature (including legal costs as between attorney or solicitor and client and associated expenses) which Owners may sustain by reason of delivering such cargo in accordance with Charterers' request.

(ii) If any proceeding is commenced against Owners or any of Owners' servants or agents in connection with the vessel having delivered cargo in accordance with such request. Charterers shall provide Owners or any of Owners' servants or agents from time to time on demand with sufficient funds to defend the said proceedings.

APPENDIX 16

Part II

(iii) If the vessel or any other vessel or property belonging to Owners should be arrested or detained, or if the arrest 431
or detention thereof should be threatened, by reason of discharge in accordance with Charterers' instruction as 432
aforesaid, Charterers shall provide on demand such bail or other security as may be required to prevent such arrest 433
or detention or to secure the release of such vessel or property and Charterers shall indemnify Owners in respect of 434
any loss, damage or expenses caused by such arrest or detention whether or not the same may be justified. 435

(iv) Charterers shall, if called upon to do so at any time while such cargo is in Charterers' possession, custody or 436
control, redeliver the same to Owners. 437

(v) As soon as all original bills of lading for the above cargo which name as discharge port the place where 438
delivery actually occurred shall have arrived and/or come into Charterers' possession. Charterers shall produce 439
and deliver the same to Owners, whereupon Charterers' liability hereunder shall cease. Provided however, if 440
Charterers have not received all such original bills of lading by 24.00 hours on the day 36 calendar months after 441
the date of discharge, then this indemnity shall terminate at that time unless before that time Charterers have 442
received from Owners written notice that: 443

    (a) some person is making a claim in connection with Owners delivering cargo pursuant to Charterers' request or 444

    (b) legal proceedings have been commenced against Owners and/or carriers and/Charterers and/or any of their 445
respective servants or agents and/or the vessel for the same reason. 446

When Charterers have received such a notice, then this indemnity shall continue in force until such claim or legal proceedings are 447
settled. Termination of this indemnity shall not prejudice any legal rights a party may have outside this indemnity. 448

(vi) Owners shall promptly notify Charterers if any person (other than a person to whom Charterers ordered cargo to 449
be delivered) claims to be entitled to such cargo and/or if the vessel or any other property belonging to Owners 450
is arrested by reason of any such discharge of cargo. 451

(vii) This indemnity shall be governed and construed in accordance with the English law and each and any dispute arising 452
out of or in connection with this indemnity shall be subject to the jurisdiction of the High Court of Justice of England. 453

(7) The master shall not be required or bound to sign bills of lading for any blockaded port or for any port which the master 454
or Owners in his or their discretion consider dangerous or impossible to enter or reach. 455

(8) Charterers hereby warrant that on each and every occasion that they issue orders under Part II clauses 22, 26, 34 or 456
38 they will have the authority of the holders of the bills of lading to give such orders, and that such bills of lading will not be 457
transferred to any person who does not concur therein. 458

(9) Owners hereby agree that original bill(s) of lading, if available, will be allowed to be placed on board. If original bill(s) 459
of lading are placed on board. Owners agree that vessel will discharge cargo against such bill(s) of lading carried on board, on 460
receipt of receivers' proof of identity. 461

War risks   34.(1) If 462

    (a) any loading or discharging port to which the vessel may properly be ordered under the provisions of this Charter 463
or bills of lading issued pursuant to this Charter be blockaded, or 464

    (b) owing to any war, hostilities, warlike operation, civil commotions, revolutions, or the operation of international 465
law (i) entry to any such loading or discharging port or the loading or discharging of cargo at any such port be 466
considered by the master or Owners in his or their discretion dangerous or prohibited or (ii) it be considered by 467
the master or Owners in his or their discretion dangerous or impossible or prohibited for the vessel to reach any 468
such loading or discharging port, 469

Charterers shall have the right to order the cargo or such part of it as may be affected to be loaded or discharged at any other 470
loading or discharging port within the ranges specified in Part I clause (D) or (E) respectively (provided such other port is not 471
blockaded and that entry thereto or loading or discharging of cargo thereat or reaching the same is not in the master's or Owners' 472
opinion dangerous or impossible or prohibited). 473

(2) If no orders be received from Charterers within 48 hours after they or their agents have received from Owners a request 474
for the nomination of a substitute port, then 475

    (a) if the affected port is the first or only loading port and no cargo has been loaded, this Charter shall terminate forthwith; 476

    (b) if the affected port is a loading port and part of the cargo has already been loaded, the vessel may proceed on 477
passage and Charterers shall pay for any deadfreight so incurred; 478

    (c) if the affected port is a discharging port. Owners shall be at liberty to discharge the cargo at any port which they 479
or the master may in their or his discretion decide on (whether within the range specified in Part I clause (E) or 480
not) and such discharging shall be deemed to be due fulfilment of the contract or contracts of affreightment so 481
far as cargo so discharged is concerned. 482

(3) If in accordance with clause 34(1) or (2) cargo is loaded or discharged at any such other port, freight shall be paid as 483
for the voyage originally nominated, such freight to be increased or reduced by the amount by which, as a result of loading or 484
discharging at such other port, 485

    (a) the time on voyage including any time awaiting revised orders (which shall be valued at the demurrage rate in 486
Part I clause (J)), and 487

APPENDIX 16

"SHELLVOY 6"

Part II

(b)	the bunkers consumed, at replacement cost, and	488
(c)	the port charges	489

for the voyage actually performed are greater or less than those which would have been incurred on the voyage originally nominated save 490
as aforesaid, the voyage actually performed shall be treated for the purpose of this Charter as if it were the voyage originally nominated. 491

(4) The vessel shall have liberty to comply with any directions or recommendations as to departure, arrival, routes, ports of call, 492
stoppages, destinations, zones, waters, delivery or in any otherwise whatsoever given by the government of the nation under whose 493
flag the vessel sails or any other government or local authority including any dc facto government or local authority or by any person 494
or body acting or purporting to act as or with the authority of any such government or authority or by any committee or person having 495
under the terms of the war risks insurance on the vessel the right to give any such directions or recommendations. If by reason of or 496
in compliance with any such directions or recommendations anything is done or is not done, such shall not be deemed a deviation. 497
If, by reason of or in compliance with any such directions or recommendations as are mentioned in clause 34 (4), the vessel does 498
not proceed to the discharging port or ports originally nominated or to which she may have been properly ordered under the 499
provisions of this Charter or bills of lading issued pursuant to this Charter, the vessel may proceed to any discharging port on 500
which the master or Owners in his or their discretion may decide and there discharge the cargo. Such discharging shall be deemed 501
to be due fulfilment of the contract or contracts of affreightment and Owners shall be entitled to freight as if discharging had been 502
effected at the port or ports originally nominated or to which the vessel may have been properly ordered under the provisions of 503
this Charter or bills of lading issued pursuant to this Charter. All extra expenses involved in reaching and discharging the cargo at 504
any such other discharging port shall be paid by Charterers and Owners shall have a lien on the cargo for all such extra expenses. 505

(5) Owners shall pay for all additional war risk insurance premiums, both for annual periods and also for the specific performance of 506
this Charter, on the Hull and Machinery value, as per Part I clause (A) (1) (xiii) applicable at the date of this Charter, or the date the vessel 507
was fixed "on subjects" (whichever is the earlier), and all reasonable crew war bonus. The period of voyage additional war risks premium 508
shall commence when the vessel enters a war risk zone as designated by the London insurance market and cease when the vessel leaves 509
such zone. If the vessel is already in such a zone the period shall commence on tendering notice of readiness under this Charter. 510
Any increase or decrease in voyage additional war risk premium and any period in excess of the first fourteen days shall be for Charterers' 511
account and payable against proven documentation. Any discount or rebate refunded to Owners for whatever reason shall be passed on to 512
Charterers. Any premiums, and increase thereto, attributable to closure insurance (i.e. blocking and trapping) shall be for Owners' account. 513

Both to
blame clause
35. If the liability for any collision in which the vessel is involved while performing this Charter falls to be determined in 514
accordance with the laws of the United States of America, the following clause, which shall be included in all bills of lading 515
issued pursuant to this Charter shall apply: 516
"If the vessel comes into collision with another vessel as a result of the negligence of the other vessel and any act, neglect or 517
default of the master, mariner, pilot or the servants of the Carrier in the navigation or in the management of the vessel, the owners 518
of the cargo carried hereunder will indemnify the Carrier against all loss or liability to the other or non-carrying vessel or her 519
owners in so far as such loss or liability represents loss of, or damage to, or any claim whatsoever of the owners of the said 520
cargo, paid or payable by the other or non-carrying vessel or her owners to the owners of the said cargo and set off, recouped or 521
recovered by the other or non-carrying vessel or her owners as part of their claim against the carrying vessel or the Carrier. 522

The foregoing provisions shall also apply where the owners, operators or those in charge of any vessel or vessels or objects 523
other than, or in addition to, the colliding vessels or objects are at fault in respect of a collision or contact." 524

General
average/
New Jason
clause
36. General average shall be payable according to the York/Antwerp Rules 1994, as amended from time to time, and shall be 525
adjusted in London. All disputes relating to General Average shall be resolved in London in accordance with English Law. Without 526
prejudice to the foregoing, should the adjustment be made in accordance with the Law and practice of the United States of 527
America, the following clause, which shall be included in all bills of lading issued pursuant to this Charter, shall apply: 528
"In the event of accident, danger, damage or disaster before or after the commencement of the voyage, resulting from any 529
cause whatsoever, whether due to negligence or not, for which, or for the consequence of which, the Carrier is not responsible, by 530
statute, contract or otherwise, the cargo, shippers, consignees or owners of the cargo shall contribute with the Carrier in general 531
average to the payment of any sacrifices, losses or expenses of a general average nature that may be made or incurred and shall 532
pay salvage and special charges incurred in respect of the cargo. 533

If a salving vessel is owned or operated by the Carrier, salvage shall be paid for as fully as if the said salving vessel or vessels 534
belonged to strangers. Such deposit as the Carrier or its agents may deem sufficient to cover the estimated contribution of the 535
cargo and any salvage and special charges thereon shall, if required, be made by the cargo, shippers, consignees or owners of the 536
cargo to the Carrier before delivery." 537

Clause Paramount
37. The following clause shall be included in all bills of lading issued pursuant to this Charter: 538
(1) Subject to sub-clauses (2) or (3) hereof, this bill of lading shall be governed by, and have effect subject to the rules 539
contained in the International Convention for the Unification of Certain Rules relating to bills of lading signed at Brussels on 540
25th August 1924 (hereafter the "Hague Rules") as amended by the Protocol signed at Brussels on 23rd February 1968 (hereafter 541
the "Hague-Visby Rules"). Nothing contained herein shall be deemed to be either a surrender by the carrier of any of his rights or 542
immunities or any increase of any of his responsibilities or liabilities under the Hague-Visby Rules. 543

APPENDIX 16

Part II

(2) If there is governing legislation which applies the Hague Rules compulsorily to this bill of lading, to the exclusion of the Hague-Visby Rules, then this bill of lading shall have effect subject to the Hague Rules. Nothing herein contained shall he deemed to be either a surrender by the carrier of any of his rights or immunities or an increase of any of his responsibilities or liabilities under the Hague Rules. 544 545 546

(3) If there is governing legislation which applies the United Nations Convention on the Carriage of Goods By Sea 1978 (hereafter the "Hamburg Rules") compulsorily to this bill of lading to the exclusion of the Hague-Visby Rules, then this bill of lading shall have effect subject to the Hamburg Rules. Nothing herein contained shall be deemed to be either a surrender by the carrier of any of his rights or immunities or an increase of any of his responsibilities or liabilities under the Hamburg Rules. 547 548 549 550

(4) If any term of this bill of lading is repugnant to the Hague-Visby Rules, or Hague Rules or Hamburg Rules, if applicable, such term shall be void to that extent but no further. 551 552

(5) Nothing in this bill of lading shall be construed as in any way restricting, excluding or waiving the right of any relevant party or person to limit his liability under any available legislation and/or law. 553 554

Back loading 38. Charterers may order the vessel to discharge and/or backload a part or full cargo at any nominated port within the loading/discharging ranges specified within Part I clauses (D/E) and within the rotation of the ports previously nominated, provided that any cargo loaded is of the description specified in Part I clause (F) and that the master in his reasonable discretion determines that the cargo can be loaded, segregated and discharged without risk of contamination by, or of any other cargo. 555 556 557 558

Charterers shall pay in respect of loading, carrying and discharging such cargo as follows: 559

(a) a lumpsum freight calculated at the demurrage rate specified in Part I clause (J) on any additional port time used by the vessel; and 560 561

(b) any additional expenses, including bunkers consumed (at replacement cost) over above those required to load and discharge one full cargo and port costs which included additional agency costs: and 562 563

(c) if the vessel is fixed on a Worldscale rate in Part I clause (G) then freight shall always be paid for the whole voyage at the rate(s) specified in Part I clause (G) on the largest cargo quantity carried on any ocean leg. 564 565

Bunkers 39. Owners shall give Charterers or any other company in the Royal Dutch/Shell Group of Companies first option to quote for the supply of bunker requirements for the performance of this Charter. 566 567

Oil pollution 40.(1) Owners shall ensure that the master shall: 568
prevention/
Ballast   (a) comply with MARPOL 73/78 including any amendments thereof; 569
management
(b) collect the drainings and any tank washings into a suitable tank or tanks and, after maximum separation of free water, discharge the bulk of such water overboard, consistent with the above regulations; and 570 571

(c) thereafter notify Charterers promptly of the amounts of oil and free water so retained on board and details of any other washings retained on board from earlier voyages (together called the "collected washings"). 572 573

(d) not to load on top of such 'collected washings' without specific instructions from Charterers. 574

(e) provide Charterers with a slops certificate to be made up and signed by the master and an independent surveyor/terminal representative. The certificate shall indicate: 575 576

Origin and composition of slops. Volume, Free water and API measured in barrels at 60 deg F. 577

(2) On being so notified. Charterers, in accordance with their rights under this clause (which shall include without limitation the right to determine the disposal of the collected washings), shall before the vessel's arrival at the loading berth (or if already arrived as soon as possible thereafter) give instructions as to how the collected washings shall be dealt with. Owners shall ensure that the master on the vessel's arrival at the loading berth (or if already arrived as soon as possible thereafter) shall arrange in conjunction with the cargo suppliers for the measurement of the quantity of the collected washings and shall record the same in the vessel's ullage record. 578 579 580 581 582

(3) Charterers may require the collected washings to be discharged ashore at the loading port, in which case no freight shall be payable on them. 583 584

(4) Alternatively Charterers may require either that the cargo be loaded on top of the collected washings and the collected washings be discharged with the cargo, or that they be kept separate from the cargo in which case Charterers shall pay for any deadweight incurred thereby in accordance with Part II clause 8 and shall, if practicable, accept discharge of the collected washings at the discharging port or ports. 585 586 587 588

In either case, provided that the master has reduced the free water in the collected washings to a minimum consistent with the retention on board of the oil residues in them and consistent with sub-clause (I) (a) above, freight in accordance with Part II clause 5 shall be payable on the quantity of the collected washings as if such quantity were included in a bill of lading and the figure therefore furnished by the shipper provided, however, that 589 590 591 592

(i) if there is a provision in this Charter for a lower freight rate to apply to cargo in excess of an agreed quantity, freight on the collected washings shall be paid at such lower rate (provided such agreed quantity of cargo has been loaded) and 593 594 595

(ii) if there is provision in this Charter for a minimum cargo quantity which is less than a full cargo, then whether or not such minimum cargo quantity is furnished, freight on the collected washings shall be paid as if such minimum cargo quantity had been furnished, provided that no freight shall be payable in respect of any collected washings which are kept separate from the cargo and not discharged at the discharge port. 596 597 598 599

APPENDIX 16

Issued March 2005   **"SHELLVOY 6"**

Part II

(5)   Whenever Charterers require the collected washings to be discharged ashore pursuant to this clause. Charterers shall provide 600
and pay for the reception facilities, and the cost of any shifting there for shall be for Charterers' account. Any time lost discharging 601
the collected washings and/or shifting therefore shall count against laytime or, if the vessel is on demurrage, for demurrage. 602

(6) Owners warrant that the vessel will arrive at the load port with segregated/ clean ballast as defined by Annex 1 of 603
MARPOL 73/78 including any amendments thereof. 604

Oil response pollution and insurance	41.(1) Owners warrant that throughout the duration of this Charter the vessel will be: 605

        (i)   owned or demise chartered by a member of the 'International Tanker Owners Pollution Federation Limited, and 606
        (ii)   entered in the Protection and Indemnity (P&I) Club slated in Part I clause (A) 1 (xii). 607

(2) It is a condition of this Charter that Owners have in place insurance cover for oil pollution for the maximum on offer 608
through the International Group of P&I Clubs but always a minimum of United States Dollars 1,000,000,000 (one thousand 609
million). If requested by Charterers, Owners shall immediately furnish to Charterers full and proper evidence of the coverage. 610

(3) Owners warrant that the vessel carries on board a certificate of insurance as required by the Civil Liability Convention for Oil 611
Pollution damage. Owners further warrant that said certificate will be maintained effective throughout the duration of performance under 612
this Charter. All time, costs and expense as a result of Owners'' failure to comply with the foregoing shall be for Owners' account. 613

(4) Owners warrant that where the vessel is a "Relevant Ship", they are a "Participating Owner", both as defined in the Small 614
Tanker Oil Pollution Indemnification Agreement ("STOPIA") and that the vessel is entered in STOPIA, and shall so remain during 615
the currency of this Charter, provided always that STOPIA is not terminated in accordance with Clause VIII of its provisions. 616

Lien   42. Owners shall have an absolute lien upon the cargo and all subfreights for all amounts due under this charter and the cost 617
of recovery thereof including any expenses whatsoever arising from the exercise of such lien. 618

Drugs and alcohol   43. Owners are aware of the problem of drug and alcohol abuse and warrant that they have a written policy in force, covering 619
the vessel, which meets or exceeds the standards set out in the "Guidelines for the Control of Drugs and Alcohol on board Ship" 620
as published by OCIMF dated June 1995. 621
Owners further warrant that this policy shall remain in force during the period of this Charter and such policy shall be adhered to 622
throughout this Charter. 623

ITWF   44. Owners warrant that the terms of employment of the vessel's staff and crew will always remain acceptable to the 624
International Transport Workers Federation on a worldwide basis. All time, costs and expenses incurred as a result of Owners' 625
failure to comply with foregoing shall be for Owners' account. 626

Letters of protest/ Deficiencies   45. It is a condition of this Charter that from the time the vessel sails to the first load port there will be no Letter(s) of Protest 627
("LOP"s) or deficiencies outstanding against the vessel. This refers to LOP's or deficiencies issued by Terminal Inspectorate or 628
similar Port or Terminal or Governmental Authorities. 629

Documentation   46. Owners shall ensure that the master and agents produce documentation and provide Charterers with copies of all such 630
documentation relevant to each port and berth call and all transhipments at sea, including but not limited to: 631
Notice of Readiness/ Statement of Facts/ Shell Form 19x (if Charterers nominate agents under Part II clause 24)/Time sheet(s) / 632
LOPs/ Hourly pumping logs /COW performance logs by facsimile (to the number advised in the voyage instructions). These 633
documents to be faxed within 48 hours from sailing from each load or discharge port or transhipment area. If the vessel does not 634
have a facsimile machine on board the master shall advise Charterers, within 48 hours from sailing from each port under this 635
Charter, of the documents he has available and ensure copies of such documents are faxed by agents to Charterers from the relevant 636
port of call or at latest from the next port of call. Complying with this clause does not affect the terms of Part II clause 15(3) with 637
regard to notification and submission of a fully documented claim for demurrage or a claim described in Part II clause 6(3) of this 638
Charter. Any documents to be faxed under this clause may be, alternatively, scanned and e-mailed to Charterers. If any actions 639
or facilities of Suppliers/Receivers/Terminal/Transhipment vessels or Charterers, as applicable, impinge on the vessel's ability 640
to perform the warranties and/or guarantees of performance under this Charter the master must issue a LOP to such effect. If the 641
master fails to issue such LOP then Owners shall be deemed to have waived any rights to claim. Master and agents shall ensure 642
that all documents concerning port berth and cargo activities at all ports/berths and transhipment at sea places are signed by both an 643
officer of the vessel and a representative of either Suppliers/Receivers/Terminal/Transhipment vessels or Charterers, as applicable. 644
If such a signature from Suppliers/Receivers/Terminal/Transhipment vessels or Charterers, as applicable, is not obtainable the 645
master or his agents should issue a LOP to such effect. All LOP's issued by master or his agents or received by master or his 646
agents must be forwarded to Charterers as per the terms of this clause. 647

Administration   47. The agreed terms and conditions of this Charter shall be recorded and evidenced by the production of a fixture note sent 648
to both Charterers and Owners within 24 hours of the fixture being concluded. This fixture note shall state the name and date of 649
the standard pre-printed Charter Party Form, on which the Charter is based, along with all amendments/additions/deletions to such 650
charter party form. All further additional clauses agreed shall be reproduced in the fixture note with full wording. This fixture 651
note shall be approved and acknowledged as correct by both Owners and Charterers to either the Ship Broker through whom they 652
negotiated or, if no Ship Broker was involved, to each other within two working days after fixture concluded. 653

APPENDIX 16

Issued March 2005

Part II

No formal written and signed Charter Party will be produced unless specifically requested by Charterers or Owners or is required 654
by additional clauses of this Charter. 655

Cargo
retention

48. If on completion of discharge any liquid cargo of a pumpable nature remains on board (the presence and quantity of such 656
cargo having been established, by application of the wedge formula in respect of any tank the contents of which do not reach the 657
forward bulkhead, by an independent surveyor, appointed by Charterers and paid jointly by Owners and Charterers), Charterers 658
shall have the right to deduct from freight an amount equal to the FOB loading port value of such cargo, cargo insurance plus 659
freight thereon; provided, however, that any action or lack of action hereunder shall be without prejudice to any other rights or 660
obligations of Charterers, under this Charter or otherwise, and provided further that if Owners are liable to any third party in 661
respect of failure to discharge such pumpable cargo, or any part thereof, Charterers shall indemnify Owners against such liability 662
up to the total amount deducted under this clause, 663

Hydrogen
sulphide

49. Owners shall comply with the requirements in ISGOTT (as amended from time to time) concerning Hydrogen Sulphide 664
and shall ensure that prior to arrival at the load port the Hydrogen Sulphide (ppm by volume in vapour) level in all bunker, 665
ballast and empty cargo spaces is below the Threshold Limit Value ("TLV") – Time Weighted Average ("TWA"). If on arrival 666
at the loading terminal, the loading authorities, inspectors or other authorised and qualified personnel declare that the Hydrogen 667
Sulphide levels in the vessels' tanks exceed the TLV- TWA and request the vessel to reduce the said level to within the TLV-TWA 668
then the original notice of readiness shall not be valid. A valid notice of readiness can only be tendered and laytime, or demurrage 669
time, if on demurrage, to the relevant authorities can only start to run in accordance with Part II clause 13 when the TLV-TWA is 670
acceptable. 671
If the vessel is unable to reduce the levels of Hydrogen Sulphide within a reasonable time Charterers shall have the option of 672
cancelling this Charter without penalty and without prejudice to any claims which Charterers may have against Owners under this 673
Charter. 674

Port
regulations

50. Owners warrant that the vessel will fully comply with all port and terminal regulations at any named port in this Charter, 675
and any ports to which Charterers may order the vessel to under this Charter in accordance with Part I clauses (D/E) provided that 676
Owners have a reasonable opportunity to acquaint themselves with the regulations at such ports. 677

Single Point/
Buoy and
Jetty
mooring

51. (1) Owners warrant that: 678
    (a)   the vessel complies with the OCIMF recommendations, current at the date of this Charter. for equipment 679
          employed in the mooring of ships at single point moorings in particular for tongue type or hinged bar type 680
          chain stoppers and that the messenger from the Chain Stopper(s) is secured on a winch drum (not a drum end) 681
          and that the operation is totally hands free. 682
    (b)   the vessel complies and operates in accordance with the recommendations, current at the date of this Charter, 683
          contained in the latest edition of OCIMF's "Mooring Equipment Procedures" 684
(2) If requested by Charterers, or in the event of an emergency situation arising whilst the vessel is at a Single Buoy Mooring 685
("SBM"), the vessel shall pump sea water, either directly from the sea or from vessel's clean ballast tanks, to flush SBMs floating 686
hoses prior to, during or/after loading and/or discharge of the cargo; this operation to be carried out at Charterers' expense and 687
with time counting against laytime, or demurrage, if on demurrage. Subject to Owners exercising due diligence in carrying out 688
such an operation Charterers hereby indemnify Owners for any cargo loss or contamination directly resulting from this request. 689
if master or Owners are approached by Suppliers/Receivers or Terminal Operators to undertake such an operation Owners shall 690
obtain Charterers' agreement before proceeding. 691

ISPS/MTSA

52. (1) (a) From the date of coming into force of the International Code for the Security of Ships and of Port Facilities 692
and the relevant amendments to Chapter XI of SOLAS ("ISPS Code") and the US Maritime Transportation Security Act 2002 693
("MTSA") in relation to the vessel, and thereafter during the currency of this Charter, Owners shall procure that both the vessel 694
and "the Company" (as defined by the ISPS Code) and the "owner" (as defined by the MTSA) shall comply with the requirements 695
of the ISPS Code relating to the vessel and "the Company" and the requirements of MTSA relating to the vessel and the "owner". 696
Upon request Owners shall provide a copy of the relevant International Ship Security Certificate to Charterers. Owners shall 697
provide documentary evidence of compliance with this clause 52 (1) (a). 698
(b) Except as otherwise provided in this Charter, loss, damage, expense or delay caused by failure on the part of Owners or "the 699
Company"/"owner" to comply with the requirements of the ISPS Code/MTSA or this clause shall be for Owners' account. 700
(2) (a) Charterers shall provide the Owners with their full style contact details and other relevant information reasonably 701
required by Owners to comply with the requirements of the ISPS Code/MTSA. Additionally, Charterers shall ensure that the 702
contact details of any sub-charterers are likewise provided to Owners. Furthermore, Charterers shall ensure that all sub-charter 703
parties they enter into shall contain the following provision: 704
"The Charterers shall provide the Owners with their full style contact details and, where sub-letting is permitted under the terms of 705
the charter party, shall ensure that contact details of all sub-charterers are likewise provided to the Owners". 706
(b) Except as otherwise provided in this Charter, loss, damage, expense or delay caused by failure on the part of Charterers to 707
comply with this sub clause (2) shall be for Charterers' account. 708

APPENDIX 16

Issued March 2005   **"SHELLVOY 6"**

Part II

(3) (a) Without prejudice to the foregoing. Owners right to tender notice of readiness and Charterers' liability for 709
demurrage in respect of any time delays caused by breaches of this clause 52 shall be dealt with in accordance with Part II 710
clauses 13, (Notice of readiness/Running time), 14, (Suspension of Time), and 15, (Demurrage), of the charter. 711
(b) Except where the delay is caused by Owners and/or Charterers failure to comply, respectively, with clauses (1) and (2) of this 712
clause 52, then any delay arising or resulting from measures imposed by a port facility or by any relevant authority, under the 713
ISPS Code/MTSA, shall count as half rate laytime, or, if the vessel is on demurrage, half rate demurrage. 714
(4) Except where the same are imposed as a cause of Owners and/or Charterers failure to comply, respectively, with clauses 715
(1) and (2) of this clause 52, then any costs or expenses related to security regulations or measures required by the port facility or 716
any relevant authority in accordance with the ISPS Code/MTSA including, but not limited to, security guards, launch services, tug 717
escorts, port security fees or taxes and inspections, shall be shared equally between Owners and Charterers. All measures required 718
by the Owners to comply with the Ship Security Plan shall be for Owners' account. 719
(5) If either party makes any payment which is for the other party's account according to this clause, the other party shall 720
indemnify the paying party. 721

Bussiness principles	53. Owners will co-operate with Charterers to ensure that the "Business Principles", as amended from time to time, of the Royal Dutch/Shell Group of Companies, which are posted on the Shell Worldwide Web (www.Shell.com), are complied with.	722 723

Law and
litigation
Arbitration

54. (a)   This Charter shall be construed and the relations between the parties determined in accordance with the laws of 724
England. 725

(b)   All disputes arising out of this Charter shall be referred to Arbitration in London in accordance with the Arbitration 726
Act 1996 (or any re-enactment or modification thereof for the time being in force) subject to the following 727
appointment procedure: 728

(i)   The parties shall jointly appoint a sole arbitrator not later than 28 days after service of a request in writing by either 729
party to do so. 730

(ii)   If the parties are unable or unwilling to agree the appointment of a sole arbitrator in accordance with (i) then each 731
party shall appoint one arbitrator, in any event not later than 14 days after receipt of a further request in writing by 732
either party to do so. The two arbitrators so appointed shall appoint a third arbitrator before any substantive hearing 733
or forthwith if they cannot agree on a matter relating to the arbitration. 734

(iii)   If a party fails to appoint an arbitrator within the time specified in (ii) (the "Party in Default"), the party who has 735
duly appointed his arbitrator shall give notice in writing to the Party in Default that he proposes to appoint his 736
arbitrator to act as sole arbitrator. 737

(iv)   If the Party in Default does not within 7 days of the notice given pursuant to (iii) make the required appointment 738
and notify the other party that he has done so the other party may appoint his arbitrator as sole arbitrator whose 739
award shall be binding on both parties as if he had been so appointed by agreement. 740

(v)   Any award of the arbitrator(s) shall be final and binding and not subject to appeal. 741

(vi)   For the purposes of this clause 54 any requests or notices in writing shall be sent by fax, e-mail or telex and shall 742
be deemed received on the day of transmission. 743

(c)   It shall be a condition precedent to the right of any party to a stay of any legal proceedings in which maritime 744
property has been, or may be, arrested in connection with a dispute under this Charter, that that party furnishes to 745
the other party security to which that other party would have been entitled in such legal proceedings in the absence 746
of a stay. 747

Small claims   (d)   In cases where neither the claim nor any counterclaim exceeds the sum of United States Dollars 50,000 (or such 748
other sum as Owners/Charterers may agree) the arbitration shall be conducted in accordance with the London 749
Maritime Arbitrators' Association Small Claims Procedure current at the time when the arbitration proceedings are 750
commenced. 751

Address
commission

55. Charterers shall deduct address commission of 1.25% from all payments under this Charter. 752
753

Construction   56. The side headings have been included in this Charter for convenience of reference and shall in no way affect the 754
construction hereof. 755

APPENDIX 16

Issued March 2005   **"SHELLVOY 6"**

Part III

Australia	(1)(a)	The vessel shall not transit the Great Barrier Reef Inner Passage, whether in ballast en route to a loadport or laden,	1
		between the Torres Strait and Cairns. Australia. If the vessel transits the Torres Strait, the vessel shall use the outer reef	2
		passage as approved by the Australian Hydrographer. Owners shall always employ a pilot, when transiting the Torres	3
		Strait and for entry and departure through the Reef for ports North of Brisbane.	4
	(b)	The vessel shall discharge all ballast water on board the vessel and take on fresh ballast water, always in accordance	5
		with safe operational procedures, prior to entering Australian waters.	6
	(c)	On entering, whilst within and whilst departing from the port of Sydney Owners and master shall ensure that the water	7
		line to highest fixed point distance does not exceed 51.8 (fifty one point eight) metres.	8
	(d)	If Charterers or Terminal Operators instruct the vessel to slow the cargo operations down or stop entirely the cargo	9
		operations in Sydney during the hours of darkness due to excessive noise caused by the vessel then all additional time	10
		shall be for Owners' account.	11

Goods Service Tax	(e)(i)	Goods Services Tax ("GST") imposed in Australia has application to any supply made under this Charter, the parties	12
		agree that the Charterer shall account for GST in accordance with Division 83 of the GST Act even if the Owner	13
		becomes registered. The Owner acknowledges that it will not recover from the Charterer an additional amount on	14
		account of GST.	15
	(ii)	The Owner acknowledges that it is a non-resident and that it does not make supplies through an enterprise carried on in	16
		Australia as defined in section 995-1 of the Income Tax Assessment Act 1997.	17
	(iii)	The Charterer acknowledges that it is registered. Where appropriate, terms in this clause have the meaning set out in	18
		section 195-1 of the GST Act.	19

Brazil	(2)(a)	Owners acknowledge the vessel will have, if Charterers so require, to enter a port or place of clearance within mainland	20
		Brazil, to obtain necessary clearance from the Brazilian authorities and/or to pick-up personnel required to be on board	21
		during the loading of the cargo at Fluminense FPSO. The vessel then proceeds to the fluminense FPSO where she can	22
		tender her notice of readiness. Time at the port of clearance, taken from arrival at pilot station to dropping outward pilot	23
		to be for Charterers' account and payable at the agreed demurrage rate together with freight.	24
		However this time not to count as laytime or demurrage if on demurrage.	25
	(b)	freight payment under Part II clause 5 of this Charter shall be made within 5 banking days of receipt by Charterers of	26
		notice of completion of final discharge	27

Canada	(3) Owners warrant that the vessel complies with all the Canadian Oil Spill response regulations currently in force and that the	28
	Owner is a member of a certified oil spill response organisation and that the Owners/vessel shall continue to be members of such	29
	organisation and comply with the regulations and requirements of such organisation throughout the period of this Charter.	30

Egypt	(4)(a)	Any costs incurred by Charterers for vessel garbage or in vessel deballasting at Sidi Kerir shall be for Owners' account	31
		and Charterers shall deduct such costs from freight	32
	(b)	Charterers shall have the option for the discharge range Euromed and/or United Kingdom. Continent (Gibraltar	33
		Hamburg range) to instruct the vessel to transit via Suez Canal. In the event that Charterers exercise this option the	34
		following shall apply:	35
		Charterers option to part discharge Ain Sukhna and reload Sidi Kerir.	36
		Charterers will pay the following with freight against Owners' fully documented claim:	37
	(c)	time incurred at the demurrage rate on the passage from the point at which the vessel deviates from the direct sailing	38
		route between last loadport and Port Suez, till the tendering of notice of readiness at Ain Sukhna, less any time lost by	39
		reason of delay beyond Charterers' reasonable control;	40
	(d)	time incurred at the demurrage rate on the passage from disconnection of hoses at Sidi Kerir to the point at which the	41
		vessel rejoins the direct sailing route between Port Said and the first discharge port UK Continent or Mediterranean,	42
		less any time lost by reason of delay beyond Charterers' reasonable control;	43
	(e)	time incurred at the demurrage rate between tendering of notice of readiness at Ain Sukhna and disconnection of hoses	44
		there;	45
	(f)	time incurred at the demurrage rate between tendering of notice of readiness at Sidi Kerir and disconnection of hoses there:	46
	(g)	all bunkers consumed during the periods (c) to (f) above at replacement cost;	47
	(h)	all port charges incurred at Ain Sukhna and Sidi Kerir.	48
		Freight rate via Suez shall be based on the Suez/Suez flat rate without the fixed Suez rate differential, other than as	49
		described below (the Worldscale rates in Part I clause (G) of this Charter to apply). All canal dues related to Suez laden	50
		transit, including Suez Canal port costs, agency fees and expenses, including but not limited to escort tugs and other	51
		expenses for canal laden transit, to be for Charterers' account and to be settled directly by them. Charterers' to pay	52
		Owners the 'ballast transit only' fixed rate differential as per Worldscale together with freight.	53

India	(5)(a)	In assessing the pumping efficiency under this Charter at ports in India, Owners agree to accept the record of pressure	54
		maintained as stated in receiver's statement of facts signed by the ship's representative.	55

APPENDIX 16

Issued March 2005

"SHELLVOY 6"

Part III

(b) Owners shall be aware of and comply with the mooring requirements of Indian ports. All time, costs and expenses as a result of Owners' failure to comply with the foregoing shall be for Owners' account. 56, 57

(c) Charterers shall not be liable for demurrage unless the following conditions are satisfied: 58

   (i)   the requirements of Part II clause 15 (3) are met in full; and 59

   (ii) a copy of this Charter signed by Owners is received by Charterers at least 2 (two) working days prior to the vessel's arrival in an Indian port. 60, 61

Charterers undertake to pay agreed demurrage liabilities promptly if the above conditions have been satisfied. 62

Japan   (6) (a) Owners shall supply Charterers with copies of:- 63

   (i)   General Arrangement/Capacity plan; and 64

   (ii) Piping/Fire Fighting Diagrams 65

as soon as possible, but always within 4 working days after subjects lifted on this Charter. 66

(b) If requested by Charterers, Owners shall ensure a Superintendent, fully authorised by Owners to act on Owners' and/ or master's behalf, is available at all ports within Japan to attend safety meetings prior to vessel's arrival at the port(s) and be in attendance throughout the time in each port and during each cargo operation. 67, 68, 69

(c) Vessel to record and print out the position with date/time by Global Positioning System when vessel enters Japanese Territorial Waters ("JTW") in order to perform vessel's declaration of entering JTW for crude oil stock piling purpose. 70, 71

(d) If under Part I clause (E) of this Charter Japan, or in particular ports or berths in Tokyo Bay and or the SBM at UBE Refinery, are discharge options and if the vessel is over 220,000 metric tons deadweight and has not previously discharged in Tokyo Bay or the SBM at UBE Refinery then: 72, 73, 74

   (i)   Owners shall submit an application of Safety Pledge Letter confirming that all safety measures will be complied with: and 75, 76

   (ii) Present relevant ship data to the Japanese Maritime Safety Agency. 77

Owners shall comply with the above requirements as soon as possible but always within 4 working days after subjects lifted on this Charter. 78, 79

(e) If Charterers instruct the vessel to make adjustment to vessel's arrival date/time at discharge port(s) in Japan, any adjustments shall be compensated in accordance with Part I clause (L) of this Charter. 80, 81

If vessel is ordered to drift off Japan, at a location in Owners'/master's option, then the following shall apply:- 82

   (i)   Time from vessel's arrival at drifting location to the time vessel departs, on receipt of Charterers' instructions, from such location shall be for Charterers' account at the demurrage rate stipulated in Part I clause (J) of this Charter. 83, 84, 85

   (ii) Bunkers consumed whilst drifting as defined in sub clause (e)(i) above shall be for Charterers' account at replacement cost. 86, 87

Owners shall provide full documentation to support any claim under this clause. 88

New Zealand   (7) (a) Owners of vessels carrying Persistent Oil – as defined by the International Group of P&I Clubs – which shall always incorporate Crude and Fuel Oil, Non Persistent Oil as defined by the International Group of P&I Clubs – which shall always incorporate Petroleum Products; and Chemicals, warrant that the vessel shall comply at all times with the Maritime Safely Authority of New Zealand's Voluntary Routeing Code for Shipping whilst transiting the New Zealand coast and ' or en route to or from ports in New Zealand and whether laden or in ballast. 89, 90, 91, 92, 93

(b) the following voyage routing will apply: 94

   (i)   vessel is to keep a minimum of 5 miles off the New Zealand coast (and outlying islands) until approaching the port's pilot station, with the following exceptions: 95, 96

     a) to pass a minimum of 4 miles off the coast when transiting Cook Strait; 97

     b) to pass a minimum of 5 miles to the east of Poor Knights Islands and High Peaks Rocks; 98

     c) to pass a minimum of 3 miles from land when transiting the Colville or Jellicoe Channels. 99

If due to safe navigation and or other weather related reasons the vessel proceeds on a different route to those set out above, the Owners and master shall immediately advise Charterers and Owner's agents in New Zealand of the route being followed and the reasons for such deviation from the above warranted route. 100, 101, 102

Thailand   (8) If Part I clause (E) of this Charter includes option to discharge at a port/berth in Thailand then the following, which is consistent with industry practice for ships discharging in Thailand, shall apply over and above any other terms contained within this Charter:- 103, 104, 105

   (a) Laytime shall be 96 running hours 106

   (b) Freight payment under Part II clause 5 of this Charter shall be made within 15 days of receipt by Charterers of notice of completion of final discharge of cargo. 107, 108

   (c) Cargo quantity and quality measurements shall be carried out at load and discharge ports by mutually appointed independent surveyors, with costs to be shared equally between Owners and Charterers. 109, 110

APPENDIX 16

Issued March 2005   **"SHELLVOY 6"**

Part III

| | This is additional to any independent surveyors used for the Cargo Retention clause 48 in Part II of this Charter. | 111 |

United
Kingdom

(9) (a) It is a condition of this Charter that Owners ensure that the vessel fully complies with the latest Sullom Voe regulations, including but not limited to:- | 112 / 113

    i) current minimum bulk loading rates; and | 114

    ii) pilot boarding ladder arrangements. | 115

Owners shall also comply with Charterers' instructions regarding the disposal of ballast from the vessel. Charterers shall accept any deadfreight claim that may arise by complying with such instructions. | 116 / 117

(b) It is also a condition of this Charter that Owners ensure that the vessel fully complies with the latest Tranmere and Shellhaven regulations, including but not limited to:- | 118 / 119

    i) being able to ballast concurrently with discharge; or | 120

    ii) maintaining double valve segregation at all times between cargo and ballast if the vessel has to part discharge, stop to ballast, then resume discharge. | 121 / 122

(c) In the event of loading or discharge at Tranmere, Shell U.K. Ltd. shall appoint lugs, pilots and boatmen on behalf of Owners. The co-ordinator of these services shall be OBC, who will submit all bills to Owners direct, irrespective of whether OBC are appointed agents or not. Owners warrant they will put OBC in funds accordingly. | 123 / 124 / 125

United
States of
America

(10) (a) It is a condition of this Charter that in accordance with U.S. Customs Regulations, 19 CFR 4.7a and 178.2 as amended. Owners have obtained a Standard Carrier Alpha Code (SCAC) and shall include same in the Unique Identifier which they shall enter, in the form set out in the above Customs Regulations, on all the bills of lading. Cargo manifest. Cargo declarations and other cargo documents issued under this Charter allowing carriage of goods to ports in the U.S. | 126 / 127 / 128 / 129

Owners shall be liable for all time, costs and expenses and shall indemnify Charterers against all consequences whatsoever arising directly or indirectly from Owners' failure to comply with the above provisions of this clause. | 130 / 131

Owners warrant that they are aware of the requirements of the U.S Bureau of Customs and Border Protection ruling issued on December 5th 2003 under Federal Register Part II Department of Homeland Security 19 CFR Parts 4, 103, et al. and will comply fully with these requirements for entering U.S ports. | 132 / 133 / 134

Coastgurard
compliance

(b) Owners warrant that during the term of this Charter the vessel will comply with all applicable U.S. Coast Guard (USCG) Regulations in effect as of the date the vessel is tendered for first loading hereunder. If waivers are held to any USCG regulation Owners to advise Charterers of such waivers, including period of validation and reason(s) for waiver. All time costs and expense as a result of Owners' failure to comply with the foregoing shall be for Owners' account. | 135 / 136 / 137 / 138

(c) Owners warrant that they will | 139

    (i) comply with the U.S. Federal Water Pollution Control Act as amended, and any amendments or successors to said Act | 140 / 141

Law and
regulation

    (ii) comply with all U.S. State Laws and regulations applicable during this Charter, as they apply to the U.S. States that Charterers may order vessel to under Part I clauses (D/E) of this Charter. | 142 / 143

    (iii) have secured, carry aboard the vessel, and keep current any certificates or other evidence of financial responsibility required under applicable U.S. Federal or State Laws and regulations and documentation recording compliance with the requirements of OPA 90, any amendments or succeeding legislation, and any regulations promulgated thereunder. Owners shall confirm that these documents will be valid throughout this Charter. | 144 / 145 / 146 / 147 / 148

W-8BEN

(d) If the recipient of the freight due under this Charter does not file taxes within the US, then such recipient shall complete an IRS Form W-8BEN and forward the original by mail to Charterers, attention "Freight Payments". Should this not be received in a timely manner, then Charterers shall not be liable for interest on late payment of freight, or be in default of this Charter for such late payment. | 149 / 150 / 151 / 152

Vapour Recovery Owners warrant that the vessel's vapour recovery system complies with the requirements of the United States Coastguard. | 153

Vietnam

(11) If required by Charterers, when loading Bach Ho crude oil. Owners will instruct the master to start the cargo heating system(s) prior to loading commencing. | 154 / 155

BPVOY4

VOYAGE CHARTER PARTY

APPENDIX 17

INDEX TO CLAUSES – BPVOY4

APPENDIX 17

Codeword for this Charterparty
"BPVOY4"

VOYAGE CHARTER PARTY

1   Date _____

2   *It is this day agreed between* _____

3   of _____

4   _____

5   ("Owners") being owners/disponent owners of the motor/steam tank vessel (delete as

6   applicable) called _____ ("Vessel")

7   and _____

8   of _____

9   _____

10   ("Charterers") that the service for which provision is herein made shall be subject to the
11   terms and conditions of this Charter which comprises PART 1 and PART 2 and the "BP
12   Shipping Questionnaire" (which term shall mean the document attached as Appendix 1
13   of this Charter or such subsequent editions of the BP Shipping Questionnaire as may
14   be correct as at the date of this Charter).

15   *Unless the context otherwise requires, words denoting the singular include the plural*
16   *and vice versa.*

17   *In the event of any conflict between the provisions of PART 1 and PART 2 of this*
18   *Charter, the provisions of PART 1 shall prevail.*

19   *In the event of any conflict between the provisions of PART 1 or PART 2 of this Charter*
20   *and any provisions in the BP Shipping Questionnaire, the provisions of PART 1 or*
21   *PART 2 of this Charter shall prevail.*

APPENDIX 17

22		**PART 1**		

A. Name of Vessel _____

B. Description of Vessel

Owners undertake that the Vessel conforms to the following description:-

26	(1)	Summer Deadweight (SDWT) on assigned summer freeboard	_____	Tonnes
27	(2)	Salt Water draught (on SDWT)	_____	Metres
28	(3)	Flag	_____	
29	(4)	Year Built	_____	
30	(5)	Length Overall	_____	Metres
31	(6)	Beam	_____	Metres
32	(7)	Cargo tank capacity at 98% excluding slop tanks	_____	Cu. Metres
33	(8)	Capacity of slop tanks at 98%	_____	Cu. Metres
34	(9)	The Vessel is (delete as applicable) _____ Segregated Ballast Tanker (SBT)/Clean Ballast Tanker (CBT)		
35	(10)	Crude Oil Washing (COW) (delete as applicable)	_____	YES/NO
36	(11)	Inert Gas System (IGS) (delete as applicable)	_____	YES/NO
37	(12)	Closed Cargo Operations (delete as applicable)	_____	YES/NO
38	(13)	The Vessel has (delete as applicable) _____		Double Bottom/Double Sides
39	(14)	Tonnes Per Centimetre Immersion (TPC)	_____	Tonnes
40	(15)	Bow to Centre of Manifold (BCM)	_____	Metres
41	(16)	Derricks/Cranes – Number and Capacity	_____	
42		_____		
43		_____		
44	(17)	Tongue Type Bow Chain Stoppers:-		
45		(a) Number	_____	
46		(b) Safe Working Load	_____	Tonnes
47		(c) Nominal Diameter of Chain	_____	Millimetres
48	(18)	Keel to Top of Mast (KTM)	_____	Metres
49	(19)	Tank Coatings (Type)	_____	
50	(20)	Heating Coils (Type)	_____	
51	(21)	Classification Society and Class Notation	_____	
52	(22)	Gross Tonnage (GT)	_____	Tonnes
53	(23)	Suez Canal Net Registered Tonnage (SCNRT)	_____	Tonnes
54	(24)	Panama Canal Net Registered Tonnage (PCNRT)	_____	Tonnes
55	(25)	Charter Speed (weather and safe navigation permitting) _____ Knots ("Charter Speed")		
56	(26)	Maximum Speed (weather and safe navigation permitting) _____ Knots ("Maximum Speed")		
57	(27)	Last Cargoes:- (a) Last	_____	
58		(b) Second Last	_____	
59		(c) Third Last	_____	

C. Cargo Quantity _____

_____

APPENDIX 17

62 **D. Cargo Description** _____

63 _____

64 _____

65 **E. Loading Port(s)/Range(s) at Charterers' option** _____

66 _____

67 _____

68 **F. Discharge Port(s)/Range(s) at Charterers' option** _____

69 _____

70 _____

71 _____

72 _____

73 **G. Laydays** _____

74 Commencing: 0001 hours local time on _____ ("Commencement Date")

75 Cancelling: 1600 hours local time on _____ ("Cancelling Date")

76 Vessel expected ready to load _____ hours local time on _____ based

77 on following current itinerary _____

78 _____

79 **H. Freight Rate** _____

80 _____ ("Freight Rate")

81 **Increase of Freight Rate applicable to increased speed per knot, or pro rata, between Charter Speed and**

82 **Maximum Speed:**

83 _____

84 **Overage (if any) at 50% of Freight Rate**

85 **I. Laytime** _____ running hours

86 **J. Demurrage** _____ US $ per day or pro rata

87 **K. Owners' Payment Details** _____

88 _____

89 _____

90 _____

91 _____

92 **L. Additional Clauses** _____

93 _____

94 _____

95 _____

96 _____

97 **M. The "BP Shipping Questionnaire"** was last completed and submitted to Charterers on _____

98 _____ and, where applicable, was confirmed as accurate on _____

APPENDIX 17

99	**PART 2**
100	**1. CONDITION OF VESSEL**

101 Owners shall, before, at the commencement of, and throughout the voyage carried out
102 hereunder, exercise due diligence to make and maintain the Vessel, her tanks, pumps,
103 valves and pipelines tight, staunch, strong, in good order and condition, in every way fit
104 for the voyage and fit to carry the cargo stated in Sections C and D of PART 1, with the
105 Vessel's machinery, boilers and hull in a fully efficient state, and with a full complement of
106 Master, officers and crew who are fully qualified (as evidenced by internationally recognised
107 certification and, where applicable, endorsements), and are experienced and competent to
108 serve in the capacity for which they are hired. Owners undertake that the Vessel shall be
109 operated in accordance with the recommendations set out in the 1996 Edition of ISGOTT,
110 as amended from time to time.

111 **2. CHARTERING QUESTIONNAIRE**

112 2.1 Prior to agreement being reached between Owners and Charterers on the terms and
113   conditions of this Charter, Owners have either:-

114   2.1.1 completed and submitted, or have authorised their brokers to complete and
115   submit, the BP Shipping Questionnaire; or

116   2.1.2 confirmed, or have authorised their brokers to confirm, in writing to
117   Charterers that each and every response given by Owners in the BP Shipping
118   Questionnaire last completed and submitted to Charterers in respect of the
119   Vessel remains correct and accurate in every particular;

120   in each case on the date stated in Section M of PART 1.

121 2.2 Notwithstanding the date on which the BP Shipping Questionnaire was last completed
122   by Owners and submitted to Charterers in respect of the Vessel, it is a condition of
123   this Charter that the responses in the BP Shipping Questionnaire are correct as at the
124   date hereof. If any response proves to be incorrect, and as a consequence Charterers
125   are likely to, or do, suffer prejudice or are likely to, or do, incur loss, damage, cost or
126   expense, Charterers shall be entitled either:-

127   2.2.1 to cancel this Charter forthwith without prejudice to any other rights available
128   to them under this Charter or otherwise under English law; or

129   2.2.2 to recover, by deduction from freight or otherwise, the said loss, damage, cost
130   and expense.

131 **3. LOADING/COMPLIANCE WITH CHARTERERS' VOYAGE ORDERS**

132 3.1 Subject to the provisions of this Charter the Vessel shall proceed to the loading
133   port (the term "port" shall include any port, berth, dock, loading or discharging
134   anchorage or offshore location, submarine line, single point or single buoy mooring
135   facility, alongside vessels or lighters, or any other place whatsoever as the context
136   requires) stated in Section E of PART 1, or to such other port (always within the
137   Ranges stated in Section E of PART 1) as is separately or subsequently identified
138   in Charterers' Voyage Orders (which term shall mean any written instruction issued
139   by Charterers in respect of the Vessel at any time during the period of this Charter,
140   including any amendments, corrections or revisions thereto), or so near thereto as
141   she may safely reach and there load the cargo stated in Sections C and D of PART
142   1 subject to any clarification of cargo loading instructions as may be provided in
143   Charterers' Voyage Orders.

144 3.2 Owners undertake that the Vessel is able to load, carry and discharge the quantities,
145   grades and segregations of cargo stated in Sections C and D of PART 1, without loading

146 on top of tank washings ("slops"). Charterers shall not be liable for any loss, damage
147 (including deadfreight), cost or expense incurred by Owners by reason of the Vessel
148 being unable to load in accordance with this undertaking. Loading on top of slops shall
149 not be permitted without Charterers' prior agreement in writing.

150 The cargo loaded on board the Vessel shall not exceed the quantity which she can
151 reasonably stow and carry over and above her equipment and provisions and shall in
152 any case not exceed the quantity permitted by the International Load Line Convention,
153 1966, or any modification or amendment thereof as may be applicable to the voyage to
154 be performed hereunder.

155 3.3 Owners undertake that the Vessel shall, upon completion of loading the cargo,
156 proceed at the speed stated in Section B.25 of PART 1 ("Charter Speed"), or at such
157 other speed, not exceeding the speed stated in Section B.26 of PART 1 ("Maximum
158 Speed"), as may be stated in Charterers' Voyage Orders, to the discharge port stated
159 in Section F of PART 1, or to such other port or location permitted under this Charter,
160 in accordance with Charterers' Voyage Orders, or so near thereto as she may safely
161 reach, and deliver the cargo in consideration of the payment of freight as provided in
 Clause 31.
162

163 3.4 Charterers shall have the right at any time during the voyage to instruct Owners to
164 adjust the Vessel's speed. Charterers shall not instruct Owners to increase the Vessel's
165 speed such as to require the Vessel to proceed in excess of the Maximum Speed. If
166 Owners increase the speed of the Vessel in accordance with Charterers' Voyage Orders,
167 any increase in the freight rate consequent thereon shall be calculated in accordance
 with the Example set out in Clause 31
168

169 3.5 If the Vessel fails to maintain Charter Speed, or Owners fail to comply with any
170 instructions in Charterers' Voyage Orders requiring an increase of speed pursuant to
171 this Clause 3, Owners shall, subject to Clause 38, be liable for all loss, damage, cost
172 and expense arising as a direct consequence thereof save to the extent that Owners
173 can prove that such failure was attributable either to adverse weather conditions
174 and sea state or to the requirements for the safe navigation of the Vessel. Charterers
175 shall be entitled to deduct any such loss, damage, cost and expense from any
176 demurrage due to Owners hereunder without prejudice to any other rights available
177 to Charterers under this Charter or otherwise under English law.

178 **4. ESTIMATED TIMES OF ARRIVAL**

179 4.1 If the Master fails to comply with any of the following provisions any delay resulting
180 therefrom, either at the loading or discharge port, shall not count as laytime or, if
181 the Vessel is on demurrage, as demurrage and Owners shall be responsible for any
182 additional loss, damage, cost and expense incurred by Charterers arising from such
183 non-compliance.

184 4.2 The Master shall send messages by telex to Charterers, the Agents (which term
185 wherever used in this Charter shall mean the Vessel's agents under Clause 15) and
186 to any other parties as required by Charterers (hereafter referred to collectively
187 as the "ETA Notify Parties"), advising the dale and estimated time of the Vessel's
188 arrival ("ETA"). Such messages shall be sent upon the Vessel's sailing from the
189 last discharge port and seven (7) days and seventy-two (72), forty-eight (48) and
190 twenty-four (24) hours prior to the Vessel's ETA at each loading port. If the Vessel is
191 at sea or elsewhere when ordered by Owners to proceed to a loading port the Master
192 shall, if the Vessel is less than seven (7) days or seventy-two (72), forty-eight (48)
193 or twenty-four (24) hours from that loading port, immediately notify the ETA Notify
194 Parties of the Vessel's ETA at that loading port. Thereafter, the Master shall advise
195 the ETA Notify Parties of the Vessel's ETA at such of the times as aforesaid as are
196 applicable or immediately provide them with such other ETAs as Charterers may
197 require.

APPENDIX 17

198
199
200
201
202
203
204

4.3 The Master shall send messages by telex to the ETA Notify Parties advising the Vessel's ETA at each discharge port, together with information as to the Vessel's expected arrival draught on even keel, immediately upon the Vessel leaving the final loading port and thereafter, where applicable, seven (7) days, seventy-two (72), forty-eight (48) and twenty-four (24) hours prior to the Vessel's ETA at each discharge port or immediately provide the ETA Notify Parties with such other ETAs as Charterers may require.

205
206
207

4.4 The Master shall also advise the ETA Notify Parties by telex of any variation of more than six (6) hours in estimated times of arrival at the loading and/or discharge ports.

208
209
210

4.5 Charterers may require Owners to provide them with copies of all telexes (showing answerbacks) to be sent under this Clause 4 and Owners shall promptly comply with such requirement.

211

5. LOADING AND DISCHARGE PORT/SHIFTING

212
213
214
215
216
217

5.1 The Vessel shall be loaded and discharged at any port in accordance with Charterers' Voyage Orders. Before instructing Owners to direct the Vessel to any port, Charterers shall exercise due diligence, to ascertain that the Vessel can always lie safely afloat at such port, but Charterers do not warrant the safety of any port and shall be under no liability in respect thereof except for loss or damage caused by Charterers' failure to exercise due diligence.

218
219
220
221

5.2 Charterers shall have the option of instructing Owners to load the Vessel at more than one berth at each loading port and to discharge at more than one berth at each discharge port in which event Owners shall, in the first instance, pay expenses arising from any of the following movements of the Vessel:-

222

5.2.1 unmooring at, and pilotage and towage off, the first loading or discharge berth;

223
224

5.2.2 mooring and unmooring at, and pilotage and towage on to and off, any intermediate loading or discharge berth; and

225

5.2.3 mooring at, and pilotage and towage on to, the last loading or discharge berth.

226
227
228

Charterers shall reimburse Owners in respect of expenses properly incurred, arising from any of the aforementioned movements, upon presentation by Owners of all supporting invoices evidencing prior payment by Owners.

229
230
231
232
233
234

5.3 Charterers shall reimburse Owners in respect of any dues and/or other charges incurred in excess of those which would have been incurred if all the cargo required to be loaded or discharged at the particular port had been loaded or discharged at the first berth only. Time used on account of shifting shall count as laytime or, if the Vessel is on demurrage, as demurrage, except as otherwise provided in Clauses 17 and 18.2.

235
236
237
238
239

5.4 For the purpose of the payment of freight, the places grouped in the section "Port and Terminal Combinations", in the "New Worldwide Tanker Nominal Freight Scale" as amended from time to time ("Worldscale"), shall be considered as berths within a single port and Charterers shall pay shifting expenses in accordance with the provisions of this Clause 5.

240

6. NOTICE OF READINESS ("NOR")

241
242
243
244

6.1 Upon arrival of the Vessel at each loading or discharge port the Master or Agents shall tender NOR to Charterers or to their order when the Vessel is ready in all respects to carry out Charterers' orders in accordance with the provisions of this Charter. Such NOR may be tendered either by letter, telex, facsimile or

245
246
247
248
telephone (but if NOR is tendered by facsimile or telephone it shall subsequently be confirmed promptly by telex). Owners shall provide Charterers with an NOR Certificate signed by the Master and a Terminal representative in respect of each port at which the Vessel loads or discharges.

249
250
251
6.2 NOR shall not be tendered, nor shall the Vessel proceed to berth, prior to the Commencement Date stated in Section G of PART 1 without Charterers' prior agreement in writing.

252
253
254
6.3 Notwithstanding tender of a valid NOR by the Vessel such NOR shall not be effective, or become effective, for the purposes of calculating laytime, or if the Vessel is on demurrage, demurrage unless and until the following conditions have been met:-

255
256
6.3.1 in the case of the Vessel proceeding directly to the loading or discharging place, she is securely moored and her gangway, if it is to be used, is in place; or

257
258
259
260
261
6.3.2 in the case of the Vessel not berthing upon arrival and being instructed to anchor, she has completed anchoring at an anchorage where vessels of her type customarily anchor at the port or, if she has been instructed to wait, she has reached the area within the port where vessels of her type customarily wait; and

262
263
264
265
266
267
268
6.3.3 free pratique has been granted or is granted within six (6) hours of the Master tendering NOR. If free pratique is not granted within six (6) hours of the Master tendering NOR, through no fault of Owners, Agents, or those on board the Vessel, the Master shall issue a protest in writing ("NOP") to the port authority and the facility at the port ("Terminal") failing which laytime or, if the Vessel is on demurrage, demurrage shall only commence when free pratique has been granted; and

269
270
271
272
6.3.4 in the case of calls at US ports, a US Coast Guard Tanker Vessel Examination Letter ("TVEL") has been issued, or in the case of calls at non-US ports where any similar certificate is required to be issued by a state authority at those ports prior to loading or discharging of cargo, such certificate has been issued.

273
7. LAYTIME/DEMURRAGE

274
275
276
277
7.1 Charterers shall be allowed the number of hours stated in Section 1 of PART 1, together with any period of additional laytime arising under Clause 7.3.1, as laytime for loading and discharging and for any other purposes of Charterers in accordance with the provisions of this Charter.

278
279
280
281
282
283
7.2 Sundays and holidays shall be included in respect of laytime for loading and discharging, unless loading or discharging on the Sunday or holiday in question is prohibited by law or regulation at the loading or discharge port. Charterers shall have the right to require the Vessel to load and discharge during the night, unless loading or discharging at night is prohibited by law or regulation at the loading or discharge port.

284
7.3 Subject as provided elsewhere in this Charter:-

285
286
287
288
289
290
291
292
7.3.1 laytime for the purposes of loading shall not commence before 0600 hours local time on the Commencement Date stated in Section G of PART 1, unless with Charterers' prior agreement in writing, in which event laytime shall commence when the Vessel commences loading. If the Vessel, with Charterers' prior agreement in writing, has commenced loading prior to 0600 hours local time on the Commencement Date, then the time from the commencement of loading to 0600 hours local time on the Commencement Date shall constitute additional laytime.

APPENDIX 17

293		7.3.2	Laytime or, if the Vessel is on demurrage, demurrage shall commence, at
294			each loading and each discharge port, upon the expiry of six (6) hours after a
295			valid NOR has become effective as determined under Clause 6.3, berth or no
296			berth, or when the Vessel commences loading, or discharging, whichever first
297			occurs.

297   7.3.2   Laytime or, if the Vessel is on demurrage, demurrage shall commence, at each loading and each discharge port, upon the expiry of six (6) hours after a valid NOR has become effective as determined under Clause 6.3, berth or no berth, or when the Vessel commences loading, or discharging, whichever first occurs.

298   7.3.3   Laytime or, if the Vessel is on demurrage, demurrage shall run until the cargo hoses have been finally disconnected upon completion of loading or discharging, and the Master shall procure that hose disconnection is effected promptly; provided always that if the Vessel is detained solely for the purposes of awaiting cargo documents at loadport for more than three (3) hours beyond the final disconnection of cargo hoses, laytime or it the Vessel is on demurrage, demurrage shall recommence after such period of three (3) hours and terminate upon the completion of cargo documentation. If, after completion of loading or discharging, the Vessel is required to proceed to an anchorage for Charterers' purposes, then the time spent moving from the berth to the anchorage shall not count as part of the period of three (3) hours referred to above or as laytime or, if the Vessel is on demurrage, as demurrage.

311   7.4   Charterers shall pay demurrage at the rate staled in Section J of PART 1 per running day, and pro rata for part of a running day, for all time that loading and discharging and any other time counting as laytime exceeds laytime under this Clause 7. If, however, demurrage is incurred by reason of the causes specified in Clause 17, the rate of demurrage shall be reduced to one-half of the rate stated in Section J of PART 1 per running day, or pro rata for part of a running day, for demurrage so incurred.

317   **8.   CARGO TRANSFERS**

318   8.1   Charterers shall have the option of transferring the whole or part of the cargo (which shall include topping-off and lightening) to or from any other vessel including, but not limited to, an ocean-going vessel, barge and/or lighter (the "Transfer Vessel"). Such transfers may take place at an In-port Transfer Position, an Additional Port Transfer Position and/or a Transshipment Area, which terms shall have the following meanings when used in this Charter:-

324   8.1.1   "In-port Transfer Position":-
325   A position within a nominated loading or discharge port within the Ranges stated in Sections E and F of PART 1 where part of the cargo is transferred to or from a Transfer Vessel, provided that cargo operations other than transfers to or from Transfer Vessels also take place within this port.

329   8.1.2   "Additional Port Transfer Position":-
330   A position at a port in the Ranges stated in Sections E and F of PART 1, or en route thereto, where part of the cargo is transferred to or from a Transfer Vessel, provided that the only cargo operations taking place at this port are transfers to or from Transfer Vessels, but the position is not the first or sole loading position or last or sole discharge position under this Charter.

335   8.1.3   "Transshipment Area":-
336   A position at a port in the Ranges stated in Sections E and F of PART 1, where the whole or part of the cargo is transferred to or from a Transfer Vessel, provided that the only cargo operations taking place at this port are transfers to or from Transfer Vessels, and the position is the first or sole loading position or last or sole discharge position under this Charter.

341   All transfers of cargo to or from Transfer Vessels shall be carried out in accordance with the recommendations set out in the latest edition of the "ICS/OCIMF Ship to

343 Ship Transfer Guide (Petroleum)". Owners undertake that the Vessel and her crew
344 shall comply with such recommendations, and similarly Charterers undertake that the
345 Transfer Vessel and her crew shall comply with such recommendations. Charterers
346 shall provide and pay for all necessary equipment including suitable fenders and cargo
347 hoses. Charterers shall have the right, at their expense, to appoint supervisory personnel
348 to attend on board the Vessel, including a mooring master, to assist in such transfers of
349 cargo.

350 8.2 **In-port Transfer Position.**
351 An In-port Transfer Position shall not constitute an additional loading or discharge port
352 for the purposes of calculating freight and the freight rate for the voyage shall be the
353 same as if no cargo transfer at such In-port Transfer Position had taken place. If the
354 Vessel moves from an in-port Transfer Position to berth, or vice versa, such movement
355 shall not be deemed to constitute shifting under Clause 5. Charterers shall reimburse
356 Owners for any additional port costs incurred by Owners in complying with Charterers'
357 instructions under this Clause 8.2.

358 Subject to the exceptions and exclusions of laytime and/or demurrage found
359 elsewhere in this Charter, including but not limited to those under Clauses 17 and 18,
360 the time used at an In-port Transfer Position shall count as laytime or, if the Vessel
361 is on demurrage, as demurrage. If an in-port Transfer Position is the first position at
362 which loading or discharge takes place within that port then laytime shall commence
363 in accordance with Clauses 7.3.1 and 7.3.2. If an In-port Transfer Position is the last
364 position at which loading or discharge takes place within that port then laytime shall
365 end when unmooring has been completed and fenders have been removed from the
366 Vessel.

367 8.3 **Additional Port Transfer Position.**
368 Except for the purposes of calculating laytime and/or demurrage, the Additional Port
369 Transfer Position shall not constitute an additional loading or discharge port and the
370 freight rate for the voyage shall be the same as if no cargo transfer at such Additional
371 Port Transfer Position had taken place.

372 Subject to the exceptions and exclusions of laytime and/or demurrage found
373 elsewhere in this Charter (save that the provisions of Clause 18.1 shall not apply to
374 this Clause 8.3), the time used at an Additional Port Transfer Position shall count
375 as laytime or, if the Vessel is on demurrage, as demurrage. Laytime or, if the Vessel
376 is on demurrage, demurrage, shall commence when a valid NOR has been tendered
377 at the Additional Port Transfer Position and has become effective as determined
378 under Clause 6.3, and shall end when unmooring has been completed and fenders
379 have been removed from the Vessel. For this purpose Charterers shall not have the
380 benefit of the period of six (6) hours provided in Clause 7.3.2.

381 Any additional period by which the steaming time taken to reach the next loading or
382 discharge port via an Additional Port Transfer Position exceeds the time that should
383 have been taken had the Vessel proceeded to the next port directly shall count as laytime
384 or, if the Vessel is on demurrage, as demurrage. Such additional period shall be the time
385 required for the Vessel to steam the additional distance at the average speed actually
386 achieved by the Vessel during the voyage or the Charter Speed as stated in Section B.25
387 of PART 1, whichever is the higher.

388 Charterers shall pay Owners for additional bunkers consumed for steaming the
389 additional distance at the price paid by Owners, net of all discounts and rebates, for the
390 last bunkers lifted.

391 Charterers shall reimburse Owners for any additional port costs incurred by Owners in
392 complying with Charterers' instructions under this Clause 8.3.

APPENDIX 17

393
394 **8.4 Transshipment Area.**
395 A Transshipment Area shall be deemed to be a port for the purposes of calculating
396 freight and the freight rate for the voyage shall be the rate as published in Worldscale
397 for the relevant Transshipment Area. If a rate is not already published for the relevant
398 Transshipment Area the rate shall be the rate determined by Worldscale on the
application of either party.

399 Subject to the exceptions and exclusions of laytime and/or demurrage found elsewhere
400 in this Charter, including but not limited to those under Clauses 17 and 18, the time
401 used at a Transshipment Area shall count as laytime or, if the Vessel is on demurrage, as
402 demurrage. Laytime or, if the Vessel is on demurrage, demurrage, shall commence and
403 end in accordance with Clause 7.3.

404 **9. DOCUMENTATION**

405 9.1 Owners undertake that for the duration of this Charter the Vessel shall have on board all
406 such valid documentation as may, from time to time, be required to enable the Vessel to
407 enter, carry out all required operations at, and leave, without let or hindrance, all ports
408 to which the Vessel may be directed under the terms of this Charter and Owners hereby
409 expressly undertake that:-

410 9.1.1 they shall be responsible for any loss, damage, delay, cost or expense; and

411 9.1.2 time shall not count as laytime or, if the Vessel is on demurrage, as demurrage,
412 during any period in which the Vessel is not fully and freely available to
413 Charterers,

414 as a result of action, or the threat thereof, taken against her by any government,
415 government organisation, competent authority, person or organisation, owing to her
416 flag, failure to have on board valid documentation as aforesaid or any dispute relating
417 to the wages, or crew employment policy of Owners or to the condition of the Vessel or
418 her equipment.

419 **10. DRUGS AND ALCOHOL POLICY**

420 10.1 Owners undertake that they have, and shall maintain for the duration of this Charter, a
421 policy on Drugs and Alcohol Abuse applicable to the Vessel (the "D & A Policy") that
422 meets or exceeds the standards in the OCIMF Guidelines for the Control of Drugs and
423 Alcohol Onboard Ship 1995 as amended from time to time.

424 10.2 Owners shall exercise due diligence to ensure that the D & A Policy is understood and
425 complied with on and about the Vessel. An actual impairment, or any test finding of
426 impairment, shall not in and of itself mean that Owners have failed to exercise due
427 diligence.

428 10.3 Owners undertake that to the best of their knowledge, information and belief, having
429 made due inquiry, neither the Master, nor any officer or crew member has any un-spent
430 convictions whatsoever concerning drug or alcohol abuse.

431 **11. CLEANING OF VESSEL'S TANKS, PUMPS AND PIPELINES**

432 Without prejudice to Clause 1, Owners shall exercise due diligence to ensure that the
433 Vessel presents for loading with her tanks, pumps and pipelines properly cleaned to the
434 satisfaction of any inspector appointed by or on behalf of Charterers and ready for loading
435 the cargo described in Sections C and D of PART 1. Any time used to clean tanks, pumps
436 and pipelines to Charterers' inspector's satisfaction shall not count as laytime or, if the
437 Vessel is on demurrage, as demurrage and shall, together with any costs incurred in the
438 foregoing operations, be for Owners' account.

439 **12. INERT GAS SYSTEM ("IGS")**

440 12.1 Owners undertake that the Vessel is equipped with a fully functional IGS which
441 is in full working order, and is or is capable of being fully operational on the date
442 hereof and that they shall so maintain the IGS for the duration of this Charter,
443 and that the Master, officers and crew are properly qualified (as evidenced by
444 appropriate certification) and experienced in, the operation of the IGS. Owners
445 further undertake that the Vessel shall arrive at the loading port with her cargo tanks
446 fully inerted and that such tanks shall remain so inerted throughout the voyage
447 and the subsequent discharging of the cargo. Any time lost owing to deficient or
448 improper operation of the IGS shall not count as laytime or, if the Vessel is on
449 demurrage, as demurrage.

450 12.2 The Vessel's IGS shall fully comply with Regulation 62, Chapter II-2 of the
451 SOLAS Convention 1974 as modified by its Protocol of 1978 and any subsequent
452 amendments and Owners undertake that the IGS shall be operated by the Master,
453 officers and crew in accordance with the operational procedures as set out in the
454 IMO publication entitled "Inert Gas Systems" (IMO 860E) as amended from time
455 to time.

456 12.3 If Charterers so require. Owners shall arrange for the Vessel's tanks to be de-
457 pressurised to facilitate gauging and sampling or to be de-inerted or gas freed to
458 facilitate inspection, in each case in accordance with the operational procedures
459 referred to in Clause 12.2. Any time taken to de-pressurise, gauge, sample and re-
460 pressurise, or to de-inert or gas free, inspect and re-inert thereafter shall count as
461 laytime or, if the Vessel is on demurrage, as demurrage.

462 **13. CLOSED CARGO OPERATIONS**

463 13.1 Owners undertake that the Vessel complies with, and shall be operated for the
464 duration of this Charter in accordance with, the recommendations regarding closed
465 loading and closed discharging operations as set out in the 1996 Edition of ISGOTT
466 as amended from time to time.

467 13.2 If the Vessel has closed sampling equipment, such equipment shall be used, when
468 appropriate, during this Charter.

469 **14. OILY RESIDUES/CLEAN BALLAST**

470 14.1 The Vessel shall arrive at the loading port with clean ballast as defined in Regulation
471 1 (16) of Regulations for the Prevention of Pollution by Oil in Annex 1 of MARPOL
472 unless otherwise agreed. Owners shall instruct the Master to retain on board all oily
473 residues of a persistent nature remaining in the Vessel from the previous cargo. The
474 Master shall, during tank washing, collect the resultant slops into one cargo tank
475 and after maximum separation of the free water, discharge the water so separated
476 overboard. Upon completion of this operation the Master shall notify Charterers
477 by telex of the origin and estimated tonnage of the slops remaining in the said
478 cargo tank, giving a separate estimated quantity for both oil and water. The Master
479 shall further advise whether during deballasting operations it will be necessary
480 to transfer any quantity of ballast water into the cargo tank containing slops. The
481 Master shall minimise the quantity of water retained which in any event shall not
482 exceed 0.15% of the Vessel's current summer deadweight tonnage. In discharging
483 all water separated as aforesaid the Master shall comply with the requirements of
484 the International Convention for the Prevention of Pollution from Ships 1973, as
485 amended by its Protocol of 1978 (MARPOL 73/78). insofar as these do not conflict
486 with any applicable law.

487 14.2 Upon the Vessel's arrival at the loading port the Master, in conjunction with cargo
488 suppliers, shall arrange for the quantity of all segregated slops to be measured

APPENDIX 17

489		(inclusive of any ballast water) and shall make a note in the Vessel's ullage record of
490		the quantity so measured. The Master shall provide Charterers with a slops certificate
491		countersigned by a Terminal representative.

492   14.3   Without prejudice to the provisions of Clause 3.2 Charterers shall be entitled to
493   instruct Owners to load the cargo on top of slops from previous voyages and to
494   discharge such slops together with the cargo loaded hereunder, in which case
495   freight shall be paid under Clause 31 at 50% of the Freight Rate stated in Section
496   H of PART 1 on the net oil quantity of slops, up to a tonnage equivalent to 1% of
497   the Vessel's summer deadweight; otherwise no freight shall be payable on slops.
498   Notwithstanding the foregoing, if the provision for freight for the voyage is on
499   a lump sum basis then Charterers shall have no liability to pay freight on slops.
500   Irrespective of whether Charterers exercise their right to determine the disposal
501   of slops, nothing herein shall give, or be construed as giving, Owners permission
502   to contravene any applicable laws, conventions or regulations regarding the
503   discharge of slops or oily residues. If Charterers instruct Owners to discharge
504   slops ashore at a loading port where slop reception facilities are available, the
505   time used for discharging slops shall not count against laytime or, if the Vessel
506   is on demurrage, as demurrage and all expenses incurred shall be for Owners'
507   account.

508   If a Terminal representative insists that ballast is discharged ashore and, as a result
509   thereof, a freight differential in Worldscale applies, Charterers shall not be liable to
510   pay the freight differential but, in lieu thereof, shall reimburse Owners in respect
511   of the cost actually incurred by them, upon receipt by Charterers of full supporting
512   documentation from Owners. Charterers shall only be liable to reimburse Owners for
513   quantities of ballast discharged up to a maximum equivalent to 30% of the Vessel's
514   current summer deadweight.

515   14.4   Charterers shall have no liability to pay deadfreight to Owners pursuant to
516   this Clause 14 unless Charterers have initially instructed Owners to load the
517   cargo on top of slops but have subsequently instructed Owners to keep slops
518   segregated.

519   **15. AGENCY**

520   Charterers shall nominate Agents at loading and discharge ports but such Agents shall be
521   employed, instructed and paid by Owners.

522   **16. CANCELLATION**

523   16.1   Time shall be of the essence in relation to the arrival of the Vessel at the first loading
524   port under this Charter. Owners undertake to advise Charterers promptly if at any
525   time Owners or the Master have reason to believe that the Vessel may not arrive at
526   the first loading port by the Cancelling Date stated in Section G of PART 1 or by any
527   new cancelling date determined under this Clause 16.

528   16.2   If the Vessel is not ready to load by the Cancelling Date stated in Section G of
529   PART 1 or by any new cancelling date determined under this Clause 16 Charterers
530   shall have the option of cancelling this Charter which option shall be exercisable
531   within forty-eight (48) hours after the Cancelling Date or any new cancelling date
532   determined under this Clause 16.

533   16.3   If at any time it appears to Charterers that the Vessel's arrival at the first loading
534   port will be delayed beyond the Cancelling Date, or beyond any new cancelling
535   date determined under this Clause 16, Charterers may require Owners to notify
536   Charterers in writing of the date and time that they expect the Vessel to be ready to
537   load. In such case. Owners shall provide such information in writing within twelve
538   (12) hours of Charterers' request.

539
540
541
542
543

If the date and time so notified by Owners falls after the Cancelling Date then Charterers shall have the option of cancelling this Charter which option shall be exercisable within ninety-six (96) hours (Sundays and holidays excepted) of receipt of the said notice from Owners or within forty-eight (48) hours after the Cancelling Date, whichever is earlier

544
545
546
547

If Charterers do not exercise their option to cancel this Charter then the new cancelling date for the purpose of this Clause 16 shall be twelve (12) hours after the date and time notified by Owners, or such other date and time as may be mutually agreed.

548
549
550
551
552

16.4   If Owners fail, or fail timeously, to respond in writing to Charterers when required to do so under Clause 16.3, Charterers shall have the option of cancelling this Charter, which option shall be exerciseable within ninety-six (96) hours (Sundays and holidays excepted) after the period allowed for Owners' response under Clause 16.3.

553
554
555
556

16.5   Whether or not Charterers exercise their option to cancel this Charter shall be entirely without prejudice to any claim for damages which Charterers may have in respect of the Vessel not being ready to load by the Cancelling Date slated in Section G of PART 1 or by any new cancelling date determined under this Clause 16.

557
558
559
560
561
562
563
564

16.6   Where the Vessel arrives after the Cancelling Date, or if the Vessel arrives by or after any new cancelling date determined under this Clause 16, laytime shall commence either when the Vessel commences loading or twenty-four (24) hours after tendering of a valid NOR that has become effective under Clause 6.3, whichever first occurs. However, where the arrival of the Vessel after the Cancelling Date, or after the new cancelling date as the case may be, results solely from Charterers' instructions under Clause 22.1, laytime shall commence in accordance with the provisions of Clauses 7.3.1 and 7.3.2.

17.   HALF LAYTIME/HALF DEMURRAGE/FORCE MAJEURE

565

566
567
568
569
570
571
572
573

Any delay arising from adverse tidal conditions which could not reasonably have been predicted, adverse weather, adverse sea state conditions, blockage of access to a port due to casually or wreck, fire, explosion, breakdown or failure of equipment, plant or machinery in or about any loading or discharge port, Act of God, act of war, labour dispute, strike, riot, civil commotion, or arrest or restraint of princes, rulers or peoples shall count as one half laytime or, if the Vessel is on demurrage, at one half of the demurrage rate provided always that the cause of the delay was not within the reasonable control of Charterers or Owners, as the case may be, or their respective servants or agents.

18.   SUSPENSION OF LAYTIME/DEMURRAGE

574

575
576

18.1   Time shall not count against laytime or, if the Vessel is on demurrage, as demurrage when spent or lost:-

577
578
579
580
581

18.1.1   on an inward passage, including awaiting daylight, tide, opening of locks, pilot or tugs or moving from an anchorage, even if topping off and/or lightening has taken place at that anchorage, until the Vessel is securely moored and the Vessel's gangway, if it is to be used, is in place at the berth or other loading or discharge port as ordered by Charterers;

582
583
584

18.1.2   on an outbound passage to an In-port Transfer Position, which passage shall be deemed to commence upon the disconnection of cargo hoses and end upon the Vessel's arrival at such In-port Transfer position; or

585

18.1.3   as a result of a labour dispute, or strike, involving tugs or pilots.

APPENDIX 17

| 586 | 18.2 | Nor shall time count against laytime or, if the Vessel is on demurrage, as demurrage |
| 587 | | when spent or lost:- |

588	18.2.1	as a result, whether directly or indirectly, of breakdown, defect, deficiency
589		or inefficiency of, or other cause attributable to, the Vessel, Master, officers,
590		crew. Owners or their servants or agents;

| 591 | 18.2.2 | as a result of a labour dispute, or strike, involving the Master, officers or |
| 592 | | crew of the Vessel; |

593	18.2.3	in, or in connection with, the handling of ballast unless this is carried out
594		concurrently with loading or discharging of cargo such that no loss of time
595		is involved;

596	18.2.4	in, or in connection with, the discharging of slops unless the discharging is
597		carried out concurrently with loading or discharging of cargo such that no
598		loss of time is involved; or

| 599 | 18.2.5 | in cleaning tanks, pumps and pipelines under Clause 11 |

| 600 | 18.3 | Nothing contained in this Clause 18 shall be affected by the provisions of |
| 601 | | Clause 38. |

602   19.   PART A. LOADING AND DISCHARGE OF CARGO

| 603 | 19.1 | For the purposes of this Clause 19:- |

604	"full cargo"	shall mean the quantity of cargo stated in Section C of PART
605		1 or the total cargo actually loaded as ascertained by adding
606		together the quantities of cargo loaded under each Bill of Lading
607		issued under this Charter, whichever is the greater;

608	"part cargo"	shall mean either the total cargo actually loaded, if less than
609		the quantity stated in Section C of PART 1, or the quantity of
610		each parcel loaded or discharged separately, as the context may
611		require;

612	"bulk discharge"	shall mean the period of time taken by the Vessel to discharge
613		the full cargo or part cargo, as the case may be, excluding any
614		time during which only tank stripping and/or crude oil washing
615		operations are being performed.

616	19.2	The cargo shall be pumped into the Vessel at the expense and risk of Charterers and
617		pumped out of the Vessel at the expense and risk of Owners, in each case only as far
618		as the Vessel's manifold.

619		Owners shall, if requested, make available the personnel, equipment and facilities on
620		board the Vessel which are required for the connection and disconnection of hoses for
621		loading and discharging. Any delay resulting from the failure by Owners to provide
622		such personnel, equipment and facilities shall not count as laytime or, if the Vessel
623		is on demurrage, as demurrage. The Master may require shore supervision of, and
624		approval for, the connection and disconnection of hoses.

| 625 | 19.3 | Owners undertake that:- |

626	19.3.1	the Vessel shall load cargo at the maximum safe rate and in any event shall
627		load a full cargo within a maximum period of twenty-four (24) hours, or pro-
628		rata in the case of a part cargo, provided always that the cargo is capable of
629		being supplied within such time; and

630
631
632
633
634
635
636
637
638
639
640
641
642

19.3.2 the Vessel shall discharge cargo at the maximum safe rate and in any event shall, in the case of cargoes of one or more segregated grades/ parcels discharged concurrently or consecutively, discharge a full cargo within twenty-four (24) hours, or pro rata in the case of a part cargo, or shall maintain a minimum discharge pressure of seven (7) bar at the Vessel's manifold throughout the bulk discharge provided always that the cargo is capable of being received within such time or at such pressure. If restrictions are imposed by the Terminal during discharge, or if physical attributes of the Terminal restrict the discharge rate or pressure, Owners shall only be relieved of the aforesaid obligation for the period and to the extent such restrictions or attributes impede the discharge rate or pressure. The Terminal shall have the right to gauge discharge pressure at the Vessel's manifold.

643
644
645
646
647
648
649

19.4 Any additional time used as a result of the inability of the Vessel to discharge the full cargo within twenty-four (24) hours, or pro rata in the case of a part cargo, or to maintain a minimum discharge pressure of seven (7) bar at the Vessel's manifold throughout the discharge or failure by the Vessel to meet any lesser performance required pursuant to a restriction imposed by the Terminal, shall be for Owners' account and shall not count as laytime or, if the Vessel is on demurrage, as demurrage.

650
651
652
653
654

19.5 In the case of multiple grades of cargoes where the total time taken to discharge the full cargo is in excess of twenty-four (24) hours (or pro rata in the case of a part cargo) and the Vessel fails to maintain a minimum discharge pressure of seven (7) bar throughout the discharge, each grade carried will be assessed separately as follows:-

655
656
657
658
659
660
661
662
663
664
665

19.5.1 The twenty-four (24) hours' allowance (pro rated in the case of a part cargo) plus the appropriate crude oil washing allowance, if any. calculated in accordance with Clause 19.8, shall be apportioned to each grade, which is discharged consecutively, in the ratio that the quantity of that grade discharged bears to the total quantity of all grades of cargo discharged consecutively. This ratio shall be calculated by dividing the quantity of each grade that is discharged consecutively by the aggregate bill of lading quantities for all grades discharged consecutively. For the purposes of this apportionment, where two (2) or more grades are discharged concurrently, the quantities so discharged shall be aggregated and treated as one grade.

666
667
668
669
670
671
672

19.5.2 The allowance apportioned to each grade pursuant to Clause 19.5.1 shall then be offset against the total time actually taken to discharge that grade. Any excess time will not count against used laytime or, if the Vessel is on demurrage, as demurrage. However, if the Vessel maintains a minimum discharge pressure of seven (7) bar throughout the bulk discharge of a particular grade then the time taken to discharge that grade will count in full against used laytime or, if the Vessel is on demurrage, as demurrage.

673
674
675
676
677
678
679
680
681

19.6 If the full cargo cannot be delivered to the Vessel at the rate requested by the Master or within the time allowed in Clause 19.3.1 or if the Terminal is unable to receive the full cargo within twenty-four (24) hours or at a discharge pressure of seven (7) bar measured at the Vessel's manifold, the Master shall present a Note of Protest ("NOP") to a Terminal representative detailing any Terminal restrictions and/or deficiencies as soon as they are imposed and/or become apparent and shall use all reasonable endeavours to have the NOP signed by the Terminal representative. If the Master is unable to obtain a signature from the Terminal representative he shall present a further NOP recording the failure of the Terminal representative to sign the original NOP. In the case of restrictions

APPENDIX 17

682
683
684

imposed by the Terminal or arising from physical attributes of the Terminal, the Master shall ensure that such restrictions are clearly recorded in the Vessel's Pumping Log.

685

686

19.7 No claim by Owners in respect of additional time used in the cargo operations carried out under this Clause 19 shall be considered by Charterers unless it is accompanied by the following supporting documentation:-

687

688

689

19.7.1 the Vessel's Pumping Log signed by a senior officer of the Vessel and a Terminal representative showing at hourly intervals the pressure maintained at the Vessel's manifold throughout the cargo operations; and

690

691

692

19.7.2 copies of all NOPs issued, or received, by the Master in connection with the cargo operations; and

693

694

19.7.3 copies of all other documentation maintained by those on board the Vessel or by the Terminal in connection with the cargo operations.

695

696

19. PART B. CRUDE OIL WASHING AND STRIPPING

697

19.8 Owners undertake that the Vessel is equipped with a fully functional Crude Oil Washing System and that the officers and crew are properly qualified (as evidenced by appropriate certification) and experienced in the operation of such system. whilst Charterers may instruct Owners to carry out additional crude oil washing in all tanks that contained the cargo the Master shall, in any event, arrange for crude oil washing of the cargo tanks at the discharge port to the MARPOL minimum standard, as set out in the Vessel's Crude Oil Washing Operation and Equipment Manual.

698
699
700
701
702

703

704

When the Vessel carries out crude oil washing to the MARPOL minimum standard, in the absence of instructions from Charterers to carry out additional crude oil washing, there shall be no increase in the time allowed for discharge of the cargo. If Charterers instruct Owners to carry out additional crude oil washing then the period referred to in Clauses 19.32 or 19.5, as the case may be, shall be increased by twenty-five per cent (25%).

705
706
707
708

709

710

Owners shall carry out crude oil washing concurrently with discharge of the cargo and the Master shall provide a crude oil washing log identifying each tank washed, and stating whether such tank has been washed to the MARPOL minimum standard or has been the subject of additional crude oil washing.

711
712

713

714

19.9 Owners shall, provided always that the Vessel maintains a minimum discharge pressure of seven (7) bar during bulk discharge or meets such lesser performance required pursuant to a restriction imposed by the Terminal or arising from physical attributes of the Terminal, be allowed a period of not more than two (2) hours per segregated grade/parcel for final draining and stripping purposes unless such final draining and stripping is carried out concurrently with discharge of another grade/parcel. Any time taken for final draining and stripping purposes in excess of such allowance shall not count as used laytime or, if the Vessel is on demurrage, as demurrage

715
716
717
718
719
720
721

722

723

PUMPING ASSESSMENT-EXAMPLE
3 GRADES

724
725
726

	(1) Fuel Oil	35,000 B/L < 7 BAR
COW	(2) Arab Heavy	40,000 B/L < 7 BAR
COW	(3) Arab Light	45,000 B/L $\geq$ 7 BAR

727

728

DISCHARGE TIME

(1)	00.00 1ST June		11.50 1ST June		
	11.50 1ST June		12.00 1ST June Change Grade		

(2)	12.00 1ST June		04.50 2ND June	
	04.50 2ND June		05.00 2ND June Change Grade	

(3)   05.00 2ND June   20.00 2ND June
Full COW required therefore additional 25% Pumping Time allowed

		Hrs	Mins	
Grade (1) 35,000 MT				
120,000 MT X 24 Hours		07	00	Time Allowed
		11	50	Time Taken
(A) Excess		04	50	< 7 BAR
Grade (2) 40,000 MT				
120,000 MT X 30 Hours		10	00	Time Allowed
		16	50	Time Taken
(B)Excess		06	50	< 7 BAR
Grade (3) 45,000 MT				
120,000 MT X 30 Hours		11	15	Time Allowed
		15	00	Time Taken
(C) Excess		00	00	≥7 BAR

Stripping allowance given for grade (3) pumping in excess of seven (7) bar

	Hrs	**Mins**
Total Excess Pumping Time =		
(A) + (B) + (C)	**11**	**40**

20.   CLAIMS TIME BAR

20.1   Charterers shall be discharged and released from all liability in respect of any claim for demurrage, deviation or detention which Owners may have under this Charter unless a claim in writing has been presented to Charterers, together with all supporting documentation substantiating each and every constituent part of the claim, within ninety (90) days of the completion of discharge of the cargo carried hereunder.

20.2   Any other claim against Charterers for any and all other amounts which are alleged to be for Charterers' account under this Charter shall be extinguished, and Charterers shall be discharged from all liability whatsoever in respect thereof, unless such claim is presented to Charterers, together with full supporting documentation substantiating each and every constituent part of the claim, within one hundred and eighty (180) days of the completion of discharge of the cargo carried hereunder.

21.   SLACK TANKS/EVEN KEEL

21.1   Notwithstanding the provisions of Clause 31, if Charterers are unable to supply the quantity of cargo stated in Section C of PART 1 the Vessel shall not be required to proceed to sea until such of her tanks are filled as will place her in a seaworthy condition, and freight shall be paid as if the Vessel had loaded the quantity of cargo stated in Section C of PART 1.

21.2   If for any reason the Vessel is unable to trim to even keel for arrival at a discharge port Owners shall notify Charterers by telex stating the Vessel's expected arrival draught forward and aft. Such notification shall be given as soon as practicable after Owners have received Charterers' Voyage Orders and no later than the Vessel's departure from the loading port.

APPENDIX 17

774
775

22. REVISED CHARTERERS' VOYAGE ORDERS FOR LOADING OR DISCHARGE PORTS

776
777

22.1 If at any time after the date of this Charter, Charterers, notwithstanding that they may have nominated a loading or discharge port, wish to issue revised Charterers' Voyage Orders and instruct Owners to stop and/or divert the Vessel to an alternative

778
779
780
781
782
783

port within any Ranges stated in Section E or F of PART 1, or cause her to await orders at one or more locations. Owners shall issue such revised instructions to the Master as are necessary to give effect to such revised Charterers' Voyage Orders and the Master shall comply with such revised instructions as soon as the Vessel is free of any previous charter commitments.

784
785

22.2 If:-

786

22.2.1 solely by reason of Owners' compliance with such revised Charterers' Voyage Orders, the Vessel suffers delay causing her to arrive at the nominated port after the Cancelling Date stated in Section G of PART 1 or

787
788
789
790

any new cancelling date determined under Clause 16.1, then the Cancelling Date or the new cancelling date, as the case may be, shall be extended by the period of such delay.

791
792

22.2.2 the Vessel arrives at the nominated port after the Commencement Date stated in Section G of PART 1, then any period during which the Vessel has been awaiting orders prior to her arrival, less any time by which the Vessel's

793
794
795
796

arrival at the nominated port would, but for Charterers' instructions to await orders, have preceded the Commencement Date, shall count as laytime or, if the Vessel is on demurrage, as demurrage.

797
798

22.2.3 the Vessel is, after loading, instructed by Owners to stop and await orders at Charterers' request then all time spent by the Vessel awaiting orders shall count as laytime or, if the Vessel is on demurrage, as demurrage.

799

800
801

22.3 Any additional period by which the steaming time taken to reach the alternative port exceeds the time that should have been taken had the Vessel proceeded to such port directly shall count as laytime or, if the Vessel is on demurrage, as demurrage. Such

802
803
804
805
806
807
808

additional period shall be the time required for the Vessel to steam the additional distance at the average speed actually achieved by the Vessel during the voyage or the Charter Speed as stated in Section B.25 of PART 1, whichever is the higher. Charterers shall pay Owners for additional bunkers consumed for steaming the additional distance at the price paid by Owners, net of all discounts or rebates, for the last bunkers lifted.

809
810

23. VESSEL/CARGO INSPECTIONS/BUNKER SURVEYS

811

23.1 Charterers shall be entitled to cause their representative (which term includes any independent surveyor appointed by Charterers) to carry out inspections of the Vessel and/or observe cargo operations and/or ascertain the quantity and quality of the

812
813
814
815
816
817
818
819
820

cargo, water and residues on board, including the taking of cargo samples, inspection and copying of the Vessel's logs, documents and records (which shall include the personal notes of the crew, the rough log book and computer generated data) at any loading and/or discharge port. Charterers' representative may also conduct any of the aforementioned operations at or off any other port to which Charterers may require the Master to divert the Vessel at any time after leaving any loading port. Charterers shall obtain the consent of the owners of any cargo on board at the time before requiring the Vessel to be diverted.

821
822

Charterers' representative shall be entitled to survey, and take samples from, any or all of the Vessel's cargo tanks, bunker fuel tanks and non-cargo spaces at any place referred to above.

823
824
825

23.2   Charterers' exercise of, or failure to exercise, any of their rights under the foregoing provisions shall be entirely without prejudice to the respective rights and obligations of the parties.

826
827
828

23.3   Any delay arising solely as a result of any inspection, survey or sampling under Clause 23.1 shall count as laytime or, if the Vessel is on demurrage, as demurrage.

829
830

831
832
833

23.4   Any delay arising from instructions from Charterers to Owners to divert the Vessel shall be calculated by reference to the additional period by which the steaming time taken to reach the next loading or discharge port exceeds the time that would have been taken had the Vessel proceeded to such port directly and Owners shall be compensated for such delay and bunkers consumed for steaming during such additional period in accordance with the provisions of Clause 22.3.

834
835
836

23.5   Charterers shall also reimburse Owners in respect of port expenses reasonably incurred solely by reason of Charterers' instructions to divert the Vessel.

837
838

24.   MAINTENANCE OF CARGO TEMPERATURE

839

840
841
842
843
844
845

Charterers shall have the right to instruct Owners to maintain the loaded temperature of the cargo up to a maximum of 60°C. Owners undertake that the Vessel is capable of maintaining the cargo temperature up to 60° throughout the laden voyage and discharge of the cargo and that the Master shall advise Charterers, daily at noon local time, of the temperature of such cargo in each of the Vessel's tanks. If the Vessel fails to maintain the required temperature Owners shall be responsible for any resulting loss, damage, cost or expense incurred by Charterers (including, without limitation, any requirement that the Vessel must vacate the berth) and any time lost thereby shall not count as laytime or, if the Vessel is on demurrage, as demurrage.

846
847

25.   CARGO HEATING

848

849

850
851
852
853
854
855
856

Charterers shall have the right to instruct Owners to raise the temperature of the cargo above the loaded temperature up to a maximum temperature of 60°C in each of the Vessel's cargo tanks provided always that the length of the voyage is such as to permit the temperature rise required. In such case the Master shall advise Charterers daily, at noon local time, of the temperature of the cargo in each of the Vessel's tanks. Charterers shall reimburse Owners for the cost of additional bunkers consumed to raise the temperature of the cargo as aforesaid. The quantity of bunkers so consumed shall be calculated in accordance with the following formulae, as substantiated by copies of the Vessel's cargo ullage and tank temperature records for the entire laden voyage, copies of which are to be provided with Owners' claim for reimbursement.

857
858
859

Single Hulk:-
Bunkers consumed (MT) = Quantity of cargo (MT) subject to temperature increase
X
Increase in cargo temperature (°C) X 0.0001

860
861
862
863

Double Hull:-
Bunkers consumed (MT) = Quantity of cargo (MT) subject to temperature increase
X
Increase in cargo temperature (°C) X 0.00007

864
865
866
867

The price for the additional bunkers consumed shall be the price paid by Owners, net of all discounts or rebates, for the last bunkers lifted. Upon presentation of their claim Owners shall provide Charterers with the invoices for the last bunkers lifted and evidence of payment of same.

868
869

26.   LIBERTY

APPENDIX 17

870 871 872
The Vessel shall have liberty to sail with or without pilots, to tow or go to the assistance of vessels in distress and to deviate for the purpose of saving life and property, or for any other reasonable purpose.

873 874
Unless specifically agreed to the contrary by Charterers, Owners undertake that the Vessel will not stop or deviate for the purpose of replenishing bunkers on a laden passage.

875 **27. TRAFFIC SEPARATION AND ROUTEING**

876 877 878 879
Owners shall instruct the Master to observe regulations and recommendations as to traffic separation and routeing as issued, from time to time, by responsible organisations or regulating authorities including, but not limited to, the IMC), the UK Chamber of Shipping (or equivalent), or as promulgated by the Slate of the flag of the Vessel or the State in which management of the Vessel is exercised.

880 881 **28. ICE ON VOYAGE AND ICE AT LOADING OR DISCHARGE PORTS**

882 883 884 885 886
28.1 If on passage to the loading or discharge port the Master finds that the port is inaccessible owing to ice he shall immediately request Charterers by telex to revise Charterers' Voyage Orders and pending a response from Charterers the Vessel shall remain outside the area of ice-bound water. Any time lost awaiting such revised Charterers' Voyage Orders shall count as laytime or, if the Vessel is on demurrage, as demurrage.

887 888 889 890 891 892 893 894 895 896 897 898 899 900
28.2 Upon receipt of such request Charterers shall instruct Owners to order the Vessel to proceed to an alternative ice-free and accessible port within the Ranges stated in Sections E and F of PART 1 and where there are facilities for loading or discharging the cargo, as the case may be. In this event freight shall be paid at the rate applicable under this Charter to such alternative loading or discharge port. Any additional period by which the steaming time taken to reach the alternative port exceeds the time that should have been taken had the Vessel proceeded to such port directly shall count as laytime or, if the Vessel is on demurrage, as demurrage. Such additional period shall be the time required for the Vessel to steam the additional distance at the average speed actually achieved by the Vessel during the voyage or the Charter Speed as stated in Section B.25 of PART 1, whichever is the higher. Charterers shall pay Owners for additional bunkers consumed for steaming the additional distance at the price paid by Owners, net of all discounts or rebates, for the last bunkers lifted.

901 902 903 904 905 906 907 908 909 910 911 912 913 914 915 916 917 918
28.3 If, on or after the Vessel's arrival at the loading or discharge port, there is a danger of her being frozen in, the Vessel shall proceed to the nearest safe and ice-free position and at the same time the Master shall request Charterers by telex to revise Charterers' Voyage Orders. Upon receipt of such request Charterers shall instruct Owners to order the Vessel either to proceed to an alternative ice-free and accessible port, within the Ranges stated in Sections E and F of PART 1, where there is no danger of the Vessel being frozen in and where there are facilities for loading or discharging cargo, or to return to and load or discharge at the port originally nominated, or to remain at the safe and ice-free position to await orders. If the Vessel is ordered to such an alternative port the sums to be paid by Charterers to Owners in respect of freight, additional steaming time and additional bunkers shall be calculated and compensated in accordance with the provisions of Clause 28.2, but if Charterers instruct Owners to load or discharge the Vessel at the port originally nominated, then, subject to Clauses 7, 8, 17, 18 and 19 the whole of the time from the receipt of NOR to load or discharge on the Vessel's first arrival at the port originally nominated until the cargo hoses have been disconnected after the completion of loading or discharging shall count as laytime or, if the Vessel is on demurrage, as demurrage. Any delay caused by ice at the port originally nominated after the final disconnection of the cargo hoses

919   shall count as laytime or, if the Vessel is on demurrage, as demurrage.
920

921   If Charterers instruct Owners to order the Vessel to remain at the safe and ice-free
922   position and await orders then any time lost awaiting orders shall count as laytime or,
923   if the Vessel is on demurrage, as demurrage
924

29. QUARANTINE

925
926   If Charterers require the Vessel to proceed to any port at which, at the time when the
927   Vessel is ordered to that port, there is quarantine then time spent or lost whilst the
Vessel is detained due to such quarantine shall count as laytime or, if the Vessel is on
928   demurrage, as demurrage. However, if quarantine is subsequently declared whilst the
Vessel is on passage to such port Charterers shall not be liable for any delay caused by
929   such quarantine.
930

931   **30. BILLS OF LADING AND INDEMNITIES**
932

933   30.1   Bills of Lading shall be signed as Charterers direct, without prejudice to this Charter.
934   Charterers hereby indemnify Owners:-

935   30.1.1   against all liabilities that may arise from the signing of Bills of Lading in
               accordance with the directions of Charterers to the extent that the terms of
936   such Bills of Lading impose more onerous liabilities than those assumed by
937   Owners under the terms of this Charter; and

938   30.1.2   against claims brought by holders of Bills of Lading against Owners by
939   reason of any deviation required by Charterers under Clauses 22, 25 or 28.
940

941   30.2   All Bills of Lading issued under this Charter shall be deemed to contain War Risks,
       Both-to-Blame Collision and New Jason clauses.
942

943   30.3   If a Bill of Lading is not available at any discharge port to which the Vessel may be
       ordered by Charterers under this Charter or if Charterers require Owners to deliver
944   cargo to a party and/or at a port other than as set out in the Bills of Lading, then
945   Owners shall nevertheless discharge such cargo in compliance with Charterers'
       instructions, upon presentation by the consignee nominated by Charterers ("the
946   Receiver") of reasonable identification to the Master and in consideration of
947   Charterers undertaking:-
948

949   30.3.1   to indemnify Owners (which term shall, for the purpose of this Clause,
950   include Owners' servants and agents) and to hold Owners harmless in
951   respect of any liability, loss, damage, cost or expense of whatsoever nature
952   which Owners may sustain by reason of delivering the cargo to the Receiver
               in accordance with Charterers' instructions;
953

954   30.3.2   to provide Owners on demand, in the event of any proceedings being
955   commenced against Owners in connection with the delivery of the cargo as
956   aforesaid, from time to time, with sufficient funds to defend the same;
957

       30.3.3   to provide Owners on demand with such bail or other security as may be
958   required if, in connection with the delivery of the cargo as aforesaid, the
959   Vessel, or any other vessel or property belonging to Owners, should be
960   arrested or detained or, if the arrest or detention thereof should be threatened,
               in order to prevent such arrest or detention, or to secure the release of such
961   Vessel or property and to indemnify Owners in respect of any loss, damage,
962   cost or expense caused by such arrest or detention whether or not the same
963   be justified, and
964

965   30.3.4   to produce and deliver to Owners all original Bills of Lading in respect

APPENDIX 17

966 967 968	of the cargo loaded by the Vessel as soon as same shall have arrived and/or come into the possession of Charterers whereupon Charterers' liability hereunder shall cease.
969 970	The provisions of the foregoing undertakings shall be governed by English Law.

31. FREIGHT RATE

971
972

31.1 The Freight Rate shall be that stated in Section H of PART 1. If the cargo quantity stated in Section C of PART 1 is a minimum quantity, then the freight payable for any cargo loaded in excess of the said minimum quantity shall, notwithstanding this Clause 31, be at the Overage rate stated in Section H of PART 1, unless a lump sum freight has been agreed in which case no Overage shall be payable. Where the Freight Rate staled in Section H of PART 1 is expressed as a percentage of Worldscale the Worldscale rate shall be the rate in force at the date of this Charter.

973

974

975
976
977

31.2 If Charterers instruct Owners to order the Vessel to increase speed under Clause 3 the Freight Rate shall be increased as provided in Section H of PART 1 for each knot of increased speed above the Charter Speed and pro rata for fractions of a knot up to the Maximum Speed. Such increase shall be calculated in accordance with the following example:

978
979
980
981
982

Example: The Vessel proceeds at Charter Speed of 10 knots, the rate for which is Worldscale 40. After 10 days the Master is instructed to complete the voyage at 12 knots. The remainder of the voyage takes 20 days. The increased speed option provides for a premium of 0.5 of a Worldscale point per knot of increased speed over Charter Speed.

983
984
985
986
987

The freight rate for the above voyage would be calculated as follows:

$$\text{Voyage freight rate} = \frac{(W40 \times 10 \text{ days}) + W41^* \times 20 \text{ days})}{30 \text{ (total voyage days)}}$$
$$= W40.67$$
(*1 point premium for 12 knots Maximum Speed)

988
989
990
991
992

If the Vessel fails to maintain the speed ordered, due to breakdown or any other reason whatsoever beyond Charterers' control, the freight rate shall be calculated based on the average speed actually achieved by the Vessel using BP Worldwide Marine Distance Tables to assess the length of the voyage between pilot stations at the loading and discharge ports but the freight rate shall not be less than the Freight Rate at Charter Speed.

993
994
995
996
997
998

31.3 If a lump sum freight is agreed for the voyage this shall be in respect of the overall voyage of the Vessel from the first loading port to the final discharge port.

999
1000
1001

Charterers shall be entitled to load and discharge at additional ports within the Ranges stated in Sections E and F of PART 1. If the lump sum freight stated in Section H of PART 1 specifically includes additional loading or discharge ports or if a further lump sum payment is agreed for additional loading or discharge ports then no other payment shall, subject to Clauses 5 and 34, be made by Charterers and laytime or, if the Vessel is on demurrage, demurrage shall count in accordance with the provisions of this Charter.

1002
1003
1004
1005
1006
1007

In the absence of any agreement in respect of lump sum freight for additional loading or discharge ports Charterers shall reimburse Owners for any additional port costs incurred by Owners in complying with Charterers' instructions. Time used at the additional ports, including time which would otherwise be excluded under Clause 18.1 (subject to the exceptions and exclusions of laytime and/or demurrage found elsewhere in this Charter, including but not limited to those

1008
1009
1010
1011
1012

1013   under Clauses 17 and 18) shall count as laytime or, if the Vessel is on demurrage, as
1014   demurrage. Laytime, or, if the Vessel is on demurrage, demurrage shall commence
1015   upon tender of a valid NOR which has become effective as determined under
1016   Clause 6.3 and shall end when cargo hoses have been finally disconnected. The
1017   provisions of Clause 22.3 shall also apply, and reference in Clause 22.3 to the
1018   term "alternative port" shall for the purposes of this Clause 31.3 be deemed to be
1019   a reference to "additional port".

1020

1021   31.4   Freight shall be payable immediately after completion of discharge, on the gross
1022   quantity of cargo loaded by the Vessel as evidenced by the Bills of Lading furnished
1023   by the shippers, less any sum derived from the operation of Clauses 2, 32 and 33
1024   and less any disbursements or advances made to the Master or Agents at loading
1025   and/or discharge ports, any sums payable by Owners under Clause 34, and any
additional cargo insurance premium for Owners' account under Clause 35, provided
1026   that no freight shall be payable on any quantity that submerges, at any stage of the
1027   voyage, the marks appropriate under the International Load Line Convention, 1966,
1028   or any modification or amendment thereof, to the voyage to be performed under this
1029   Charter.

1030

1031   31.5   All payments due to Owners under this Charter shall be remitted by Charterers to the
1032   account stated in Section K of PART 1.

1033

1034   **32.   ADDRESS COMMISSION**

1035

Charterers shall deduct 1.25% address commission from freight (including fixed and variable
1036   freight differentials), and any deadfreight and demurrage payable under this Charter.

1037

   33.   CARGO RETENTION

1038

   33.1   If any quantity of cargo remaining on board the Vessel ("ROB") upon completion
1039   of discharge is judged by an independent surveyor appointed by Charterers to be
1040   liquid, or if Charterers can show that the ROB would have been liquid if Owners
and/or the Master, officers and crew had followed Charterers' instructions for the
1041   management of the cargo, then Charterers shall be entitled to deduct from freight
the value of such quantity of cargo calculated on the basis of the free on board
1042   ("FOB") value at the loading port plus freight thereon calculated in accordance
1043   with Clause 31 hereof.

1044

1045   33.2   For the purpose of this Clause 33, any quantity of ROB shall be regarded as liquid
1046   if sampling and testing, which testing shall be performed as soon as practicable
1047   after sampling, shows the ROB to have had a dynamic viscosity of less than 600
1048   centipoise at its temperature when sampled from the Vessel's tank or, if Charterers'
1049   heating instructions have not been complied with, at the temperature that would have
been applicable in the Vessel's tank if such instructions had been complied with.

1050

1051   Any quantity of ROB which is of insufficient depth to be sampled shall also be
1052   regarded as liquid if the independent surveyor judges it to be liquid after using other
1053   means of testing including, without limitation, a representative number of dips across
1054   each tank.

1055

   33.3   The independent surveyor's findings shall be final and binding upon Owners and
1056   Charterers save for instances of arithmetical error in calculation.

1057

1058   33.4   Charterers hereby agree to indemnify Owners against any liability to a Bill of Lading
1059   holder resulting from non-delivery of any such cargo in respect of which a deduction
from freight is made under this Clause 33 provided always that Charterers shall
1060   under no circumstances be liable to indemnify Owners in an amount greater than the
1061   amount of height so deducted.

APPENDIX 17

1062   33.5   For the purpose of this Clause 33, slops shall not be included in the measured and
1063   reported liquid volume of oil on board the Vessel prior to loading.
1064

1065   33.6   For the avoidance of doubt this Clause 33 refers solely to liquid cargo ROB from
1066   the cargo loaded hereunder and any measured volume of liquid oil on board the
             Vessel prior to loading shall be deducted from any calculation made under this
1067   Clause 33.
1068

34. DUES AND OTHER CHARGES

1069

1070   34.1   If, under Sections 4 and 5 of Part B of the Preamble of Worldscale, a due or charge
1071   is expressly staled to be for the account of Owners or Charterers then such due or
1072   charge shall be payable accordingly. Dues and other charges payable by Charterers
             under Section 5 of Part B of the Preamble of Worldscale shall in the first instance
1073   be paid by Owners and Charterers shall reimburse Owners upon presentation of all
             supporting invoices by Owners.
1074

1075   34.2   If freight for a voyage is not based on Worldscale but is calculated on some other
1076   basis such as, without limitation, an agreed lump sum amount or a per tonne amount,
1077   Charterers shall not be liable for any costs covered by Worldscale, under a fixed
1078   or variable freight differential (Section D of Worldscale), such costs being deemed
1079   to be included in the agreed freight. However Sections 4 and 5 of Part B of the
             Preamble of Worldscale shall still apply.
1080

1081   34.3   If a charge is imposed upon Charterers by the owner of a berth by reason
1082   of prolonged occupation of the berth by the Vessel for reasons beyond the
1083   control of Charterers, their servants or agents then such charge shall be paid
1084   by Owners.
1085

35. CARGO INSURANCE

1086

1087   Any additional premiums which may be charged by cargo underwriters on any cargo
1088   insurance in respect of the cargo carried hereunder by reason of the Vessel's age and/or
1089   condition shall be for Owners' account, and Charterers shall be entitled to deduct the cost
     of any such additional premium from freight payable under Clause 31.
1090

36. CODING OF CARGO DOCUMENTATION – US CUSTOMS REGULATIONS

1091

1092   36.1   If Charterers require the Vessel to discharge at a port within the jurisdiction of the
1093   US Customs Service, the Master shall insert Owners' Unique Identifier on each
1094   Bill of Lading accompanying a shipment of imported cargo in accordance with US
             Customs Regulations (19 CFR Parts 4 and 178). Owners shall provide Charterers
1095   and Agents on request with details of their Unique Identifier in respect of any cargo
             carried hereunder.
1096

1097   36.2   If the Master fails to insert Owners' Unique Identifier under this Clause 36 Owners
1098   shall be liable for any delays resulting therefrom and any time lost thereby shall not
1099   count as laytime or, if the Vessel is on demurrage, as demurrage.
1100

37. UNITED STATES COAST GUARD ("USCG") CERTIFICATE OF FINANCIAL RESPONSIBILITY/UNITED STATES COAST GUARD REGULATIONS

1102

1103   37.1   Owners undertake that the Vessel shall carry on board a valid USCG Certificate of
1104   Financial Responsibility ("COFR") as required under the US Federal Oil Pollution

1105
1106
1107
1108
1109
1110
1111

Act 1990 and that for the duration of this Charter the said COFR shall be maintained in all respects valid for trading to ports in the USA. Owners further undertake that the Vessel shall carry on board copies of the Vessel's Federal Oil Spill Response Plan and any US State specific Response Plan (individually and collectively "Response Plan") that have been approved by the USCG or by the appropriate State Authority respectively and that the Master shall operate the Vessel fully in accordance with the said Response Plan.

1112
1113
1114
1115

37.2 Owners undertake that the Vessel shall for the duration of this Charter either comply with all applicable USCG Regulations or carry on board appropriate waivers from the USCG if in any respect whatsoever the Vessel does not so comply.

38. EXCEPTIONS

1116
1117
1118
1119
1120
1121

38.1 The provisions of Articles III (other than Rule 8), IV, IV bis and VIII of the Schedule to the Carriage of Goods by Sea Act, 1971 of the United Kingdom shall apply to this Charter and shall be deemed to be inserted *in extenso* herein. This Charter shall be deemed to be a contract for the carriage of goods by sea to which the said Articles apply, and Owners shall be entitled to the protection of the said Articles in respect of any claim made hereunder.

1122
1123
1124
1125
1126

38.2 Charterers shall not, unless expressly provided otherwise in this Charter, be responsible for any loss, damage, cost, expense, delay or failure in performance hereunder arising or resulting from Act of God, act of war, hostilities, seizure under legal process, quarantine restrictions, labour disputes or strikes threatened or actual, riots, civil commotions, arrest or restraint of princes, rulers or people.

1127
1128

39. WAR RISKS

1129
1130

39.1 For the purpose of this Clause 39 the words:-

1131
1132

"Owners"   shall include the shipowners, bareboat charterers, disponent owners, managers or other operators who are charged with the management and/or operation of the Vessel, and the Master; and

1133
1134
1135
1136
1137
1138
1139
1140
1141
1142

"War Risks"   shall include any war (whether actual or threatened), act of war, civil war, hostilities, revolutions, rebellion, civil commotion, warlike operations, the laying of mines (whether actual or reported), acts of piracy, acts of terrorists, acts of hostility or malicious damage, blockades (whether imposed against all vessels or imposed selectively against vessels of certain flags or ownership, or against certain cargoes or crews or otherwise howsoever), by any person, body, terrorist or political group, of the Government of any state whatsoever, which, in the reasonable judgment of the Master and/or Owners, may be dangerous or are likely to be or to become dangerous to the Vessel, her cargo, crew or other persons on board the Vessel.

1143
1144
1145
1146
1147
1148
1149
1150
1151
1152

39.2 If at any time before the Vessel commences loading, it appears, in the reasonable judgement of the Master and/or Owners, that performance of the contract of carriage, or any part of it, may expose, or is likely to expose, the Vessel, her cargo, crew or other persons on board the Vessel to War Risks, Owners may give notice to Charterers cancelling this Charter, or may refuse to perform such part of it as may expose, or may be likely to expose, the Vessel. her cargo, crew or other persons on board the Vessel 10 War Risks provided always that if either Section E or F of PART 1 provides for a loading or discharging Range, as the case may be, and the Vessel, her crew, other persons on board, or cargo may be exposed, or may be likely to be exposed, to War Risks, at the port originally nominated by Charterers, then Owners shall first require Charterers to nominate a safe

APPENDIX 17

1153		port which lies within the relevant Range, and may only cancel this Charter if
1154		Charterers shall not have nominated such safe port within forty-eight (48) hours
1155		of receipt of such request.
1156		
1157	39.3	Owners shall not be required to continue to load cargo for any voyage, or to sign
1158		Bills of Lading for any port, or to proceed or continue on any voyage, or on any
1159		part thereof, or to proceed through any canal or waterway, or to proceed to or
1160		remain at any port whatsoever, where it appears, either after the loading of the
		cargo commences, or at any stage of the voyage thereafter before the discharge
1161		of the cargo is completed, that, in the reasonable judgement of the Master and/
1162		or Owners, the Vessel, her cargo (or any part thereof), crew or other persons on
1163		board the Vessel (or any one or more of them) may be, or are likely to be, exposed
1164		to War Risks. If it should so appear, Owners may, by telex, request Charterers
1165		to nominate a safe port for the discharge of the cargo or any part thereof, and if
1166		within forty-eight (48) hours of the receipt of such telex, Charterers shall not have
1167		nominated such a port, Owners may discharge the cargo at any safe port of their
1168		choice (including the loading port) in complete fulfilment of their obligations
1169		under this Charter. Owners shall be entitled to recover from Charterers the extra
1170		expenses of such discharge and, if the discharge takes place at any port other
1171		than the loading port, to receive the lull freight as though the cargo had been
1172		carried to the discharge port originally nominated. Any additional period by
1173		which the steaming time taken to reach the port at which the cargo is discharged
1174		exceeds the time which would have been taken had the Vessel proceeded to the
1175		original discharge port directly, and bunkers consumed for steaming during such
1176		additional period, shall be calculated and compensated in accordance with the
1177		provisions of Clause 22.3.
1178		
1179	39.4	If at any stage of the voyage 'after the loading of the cargo commences, it appears,
1180		in the reasonable judgement of the Master and/or Owners, that the Vessel, her cargo,
1181		crew or other persons on board the Vessel may be, or are likely to be, exposed to War
1182		Risks on any part of the route (including any canal or waterway) which is normally
		and customarily used in a voyage of the nature contracted for, and there is another
1183		longer route to the discharge port, Owners may give notice to Charterers that this
1184		route should be taken. In such case this Charter shall be read in respect of freight
1185		and all other conditions whatsoever as if the voyage performed were that originally
1186		designated.
1187		
1188		However if the Vessel discharges the cargo at a port outside the Ranges stated in
1189		Section F of PART 1, freight shall he paid as for the voyage originally designated
1190		and any additional period by which the steaming time taken to reach the discharge
1191		port exceeds the time which would have been taken to reach the originally designated
		discharge port directly, and bunkers consumed for steaming during such additional
1192		period, shall be calculated and compensated in accordance with the provisions of
1193		Clause 22.3. Any additional port, canal or waterway expenses incurred by Owners as
1194		a result of the Vessel discharging outside the Ranges stated in Section F of PART 1 as
1195		aforesaid shall be for Charterers' account and Charterers shall reimburse to Owners
1196		any amounts due under this Clause 39.4 upon receipt of Owners' invoice together
1197		with full supporting documentation.
1198		
1199	39.5	The Vessel shall have liberty:-
1200		
1201	39.5.1	to comply with all orders, directions, recommendations or advice as
1202		to departure, arrival, routes, sailing in convoy, ports of call, stoppages,
		destinations, discharging of cargo, delivery or in any way whatsoever
1203		which are given by the government of the state under whose flag the Vessel
		sails, or other government to whose laws Owners are subject, or any other
1204		government which so requires, or any body or group acting with the power
1205		to compel compliance with their orders or directions;

1206	39.5.2	to comply with the orders, direction or recommendations of any war risks
1207		underwriters who have the authority to give the same under the terms of the
1208		war risks insurance applicable to the Vessel;
1209		
1210	39.5.3	to comply with the terms of any resolution of the Security Council of the
		United Nations, any directives of the European Community the effective
1211		orders of any other supranational body which has the right to issue and
1212		give the same, and with national laws aimed at enforcing the same to which
1213		Owners are subject, and to obey the orders and directions of those who are
		charged with their enforcement;
1214		
1215	39.5.4	to discharge at any other port any cargo or part thereof which may render the
1216		Vessel liable to confiscation as a contraband carrier;
1217		
1218	39.5.5	to call at any other port to change the crew or any part thereof or other
1219		persons on board the Vessel if there is good reason to believe that they may
		be subject to internment, imprisonment or other sanctions; and
1220		
1221	39.5.6	if cargo has not been loaded or has been discharged by Owners under
		this Clause 39, to load other cargo for Owners' own benefit and carry it
1222		to any other port or ports whatsoever, whether backwards or forwards or
1223		in a contrary direction to the ordinary or customary route.
1224		

1225 39.6 If in compliance with Clauses 39.2 to 39.5 anything is done or not done, such shall
1226 not be deemed to be a deviation, but shall be considered as due fulfilment by the
1227 party concerned of its obligations under this Charter.

40. BOTH-TO-BLAME COLLISION

1229 40.1 If the liability for any collision in which the Vessel is involved while performing this
1230 Charter falls to be determined in accordance with the laws of the USA, or the laws of
1231 any State which applies laws similar to those applied in the USA in the circumstances
envisaged by this Clause 40, the following provision shall apply:-

1232

"If the Vessel comes into collision with another vessel as a result of the negligence
1233 of the other vessel and any act, neglect or default of the Master, mariner, pilot or the
1234 servants of the carrier in the navigation or in the management of the Vessel, the owners
1235 of the goods carried hereunder will indemnify the carrier against all loss or liability
1236 to the other or non-carrying vessel or her owners in so far as such loss or liability
represents loss of, or damage to, or any claim whatsoever of the owners of, said goods,
1237 paid or payable by the other or non-carrying vessel or her owners to the owners of said
1238 goods and set off, recouped or recovered by the other or non-carrying vessel or her
1239 owners as part of their claim against the carrying vessel or carrier.

1241 The foregoing provisions shall also apply where the owner, operators or those in
1242 charge of any vessel or vessels or objects other than, or in addition to, the colliding
1243 vessels or objects are at fault in respect of collision or contact."

1245 40.2 Whilst Charterers shall procure that all Bills of Lading issued under this Charter
shall contain a provision in the foregoing terms, to be applicable where the liability
1246 for any collision in which the Vessel is involved falls to be determined under the
1247 preamble of this Clause 40, Charterers neither warrant nor undertake that such
1248 provision shall be effective. In the event that such provision proves ineffective
Charterers shall, notwithstanding anything to the contrary herein provided, not be
1249 obliged to indemnify Owners.

41. GENERAL AVERAGE

1252

APPENDIX 17

1253
1254
1255

General Average shall be adjusted and settled in London in accordance with the York-Antwerp Rules, 1994 or any modification or re-enactment thereof for the time being in force.

1256 **42. NEW JASON**

1257
1258
1259

If, notwithstanding Clause 41, General Average is adjusted in accordance with the law and practice of the USA, the following provision shall apply:-

1260

"In the event of accident, danger, damage or disaster before or after the commencement of the voyage, resulting from any cause whatsoever, whether due to negligence or not, for which, or for the consequence of which, the carrier is not responsible, by statute, contract or otherwise, the cargo shippers, consignees or owners of the cargo shall contribute with the carrier in general average to the payment of any sacrifices, losses or expenses of a general average nature that may be made or incurred and shall pay salvage and special charges incurred in respect of the cargo.

1261
1262

1263
1264

1265
1266
1267
1268
1269

If a salving ship is owned or operated by the carrier, salvage shall be paid for as fully as if the said salving ship or ships belonged to strangers. Such deposit as the carrier or his agents may deem sufficient to cover the estimated contribution of the cargo and any salvage and special charges thereon shall, if required, be made by the cargo shippers, consignees or owners of the cargo to the carrier before delivery".

1270
1271

43. CLAUSE PARAMOUNT

1272
1273
1274

All Bills of Lading issued under this Charter shall be deemed to contain the following Clause Paramount:-

1275

"CLAUSE PARAMOUNT

(1) This Bill of Lading shall have effect subject to any national law making the International Convention for the unification of certain rules of law relating to bills of lading signed at Brussels on 25th August 1924 (The Hague Rules) or the Hague Rules as amended by the Protocol signed at Brussels on 23rd February 1968 (The Hague/Visby Rules) compulsorily applicable to this Bill of Lading. If any term of this Bill of Lading be repugnant to that legislation to any extent, such term shall be void to that extent but no further. Neither the Hague Rules nor the Hague/Visby Rules shall apply to this Bill of Lading where the goods carried hereunder consist of live animals or cargo which by this Bill of Lading is stated as being carried on deck and is so carried.

1276
1277

1278

1279
1280
1281
1282
1283

1284
1285
1286
1287
1288

(2) Save where the Hague or Hague/Visby Rules apply by reason of (1) above, this Bill of Lading shall take effect subject to any national law in force at the port of shipment or place of issue of the Bill of Lading making the United Nations Convention on the Carriage of Goods by Sea 1978 (the Hamburg Rules) compulsorily applicable to this Bill of Lading in which case this Bill of Lading shall have effect subject to the Hamburg Rules which shall nullify any stipulation derogating therefrom to the detriment of the shipper or consignee.

1289
1290

1291
1292
1293
1294

(3) Where the Hague, Hague/Visby or Hamburg Rules are not compulsorily applicable to this Bill of Lading, the carrier shall be entitled to the benefits of all privileges, rights and immunities contained in Articles I to VIII of the Hague/Visby Rules.

1295

(4) Nothing in this Bill of Lading shall be construed as in any way restricting, excluding or waiving the right of any relevant party or person to limit his liability under any available legislation and/or law".

1296
1297

1298 **44. OIL POLLUTION INSURANCE**

APPENDIX 17

1299
1300
1301

44.1   Owners warrant that they have, and shall maintain in force throughout the period of this Charter, the following oil pollution insurances:-

1302

    44.1.1   the standard oil pollution insurance cover (currently US$500 million) available, from time to time, from their Protection and Indemnity Club; and

1303
1304

    44.1.2   any additional oil pollution insurance cover (currently US$200 million) which is, or becomes, available from market, or other sources provided always that the security of the provider of the cover is acceptable to Charterers.

1305
1306

45.   OIL POLLUTION PREVENTION

1307
1308

45.1   Owners undertake that the Vessel:-

1309
1310

    45.1.1   is a tanker owned by a member of the International Tanker Owners Pollution Federation Limited and will so remain throughout the period of this Charter.

1311

1312

    45.1.2   is entered in the P&I Club stated in Section 9.1 of the BP Shipping Questionnaire last completed by or on behalf of Owners and will so remain unless Owners have given Charterers prior written notice of their intention to change. Owners warrant however, that the Vessel will only be entered in a P&I Club within the International Croup of P&I Clubs.

1313
1314
1315

1316
1317
1318
1319
1320

45.2   When an escape or discharge of Oil occurs from the Vessel and causes or threatens to cause Pollution Damage, or when there is the Threat of an escape or discharge of Oil (i.e. a grave and imminent danger of the escape or discharge of Oil which, if it occurred, would create a serious danger of Pollution Damage, whether or not an escape or discharge in fact subsequently occurs), then upon notice to Owners or Master, Charterers shall have the right (but shall not be obliged) to place onboard the Vessel and/or have in attendance at the incident one or more Charterers' representatives to observe the measures being taken by Owners and/or national or local authorities or their respective servants, agents or contractors to prevent or minimise Pollution Damage and, in Charterers' absolute discretion, to provide advice, equipment or manpower or undertake such other measures, at Charterers' risk and expense, as are permitted under applicable law and as Charterers believe are reasonably necessary to prevent or minimise such Pollution Damage or to remove the Threat of an escape or discharge of Oil.

1321
1322
1323
1324
1325
1326
1327
1328
1329
1330

1331
1332
1333
1334

45.3   The provisions of this Clause 45 shall be without prejudice to any other rights and/or duties of Charterers or Owners whether arising under this Charter or under applicable law or under any International Convention

1335

45.4   In this Clause the terms "Oil", "Threat" and "Pollution Damage" shall have the same meaning as that defined in the Civil Liability Convention 1969 or any Protocol thereto.

1336
1337
1338

46.   LIEN

1339
1340
1341

Owners shall have a lien upon the cargo for all freight, deadfreight, demurrage and the cost of recovery thereof.

47.   SUB-LETTING

1342

Charterers may sub-let the Vessel without prejudice to the respective rights and obligations of either party under this Charter.

1343
1344

APPENDIX 17

1345 **48. ADMINISTRATION**

1346 48.1 Unless otherwise specifically requested by either Owners or Charterers, no
1347 formal charterparty shall be prepared and signed. The terms and conditions of
this Charter shall be evidenced by a recap fixture telex ("Recap Fixture Telex")
1348 issued by Charterers' broker to Owners and Charterers and shall be confirmed
as correct by return telexes from both parties to the said broker who shall
1349 acknowledge receipt of such confirmation telexes to both parties within forty-
1350 eight (48) hours after the lifting of subjects and a charterparty in the format of
1351 this Charter, as modified by the Recap Fixture Telex and bearing the same date
1352 as the Recap Fixture Telex, shall be deemed to have been signed by Owners and
1353 Charterers.
1354

1355 48.2 If either party requires a formal charterparty to be prepared and signed then Owners
1356 shall procure that Owners' broker shall prepare a charterparty in the format of this
1357 Charter, as modified by the Recap Fixture Telex, and bearing the same date as the
1358 Recap Fixture Telex and shall arrange for signature thereof by both Owners and
Charterers.
1359

1360 **49. LAW**
1361

1362 The construction, validity and performance of this Charter shall be governed by English
1363 Law. The High Court in London shall have exclusive jurisdiction over any dispute which
may arise out of this Charter.
1364

In Witness Whereof the parties have caused this Charter to be executed as of the dale first above
1365 written
1366

1367 ....
for and on behalf of
1368

1369 ....
OWNERS
1370

1371 ....
for and on behalf of
1372

1373 ....
CHARTERERS
1374

1375

1376
1377

◆

APPENDIX 1

THE BP SHIPPING QUESTIONNAIRE

APPENDIX 18

RECAP

Sample Recaps

WE ARE PLEASED TO CONFIRM DETAILS OF THE FLWG FIXTURE

CHARTER PARTY: BEEPEEVOY 4   DATED: 2005

SHIP: 'STEAMBOAT WILLIE'

REGISTERED OWNERS: MICKEY AND MINNIE MOUSE

DISPONENT OWNERS: WALT DISNEY

CHARTERERS: DONALD DUCK

BROKER: GOOFY N CO
CO-BROKER: N/A

PRIVATE AND CONFIDENTIAL

VESSEL: STEAMBOAT WILLIE

FLAG: PANAMA
BUILT: 2005
SDWT: 305,261 MT
SDRAUGHT: 22.423 M
LOA: 332.00 M
BEAM: 58.00 M
CAPACITY AT 98PCT EXCL SLOPS: 330,573 CBM (SLOPS 10,068 CBM)
SBT/CBT: SBT
COW: YES
IGS: YES
CLS: YES
VRS: YES
DOUBLE/DOUBLE: YES
TPC: 171.1 T
BCM: 163.50 M
DERRICKS/CRANES: 4 X 20
TONGUE TYPE BOW CHAIN STOPPERS' 2 X 200 TONGUE TYPE
KTM: 63.30 M
COATINGS: PURE EPOXY TOP AND BOTTOM ONLY
CLASS: LLOYDS REGISTER
GRT: 159,016
LADEN SPEED: ABOUT 15.5 KNOTS WSNP
H+M VALUE: USD 138,100,000

LAST 3 CARGOES: N/A, VESSEL IS A NEWBUILDTNG

CARGO

CARGO QUANTITY: MIN 275,000 MTS CHRS OPT FULL CARGO NDFCAPMQS
GRADE: CRUDE OIL
SEGREGATION: MAX 3 GRADES WVNS. IF 3 GRADES LOADED TEXACO
          COMPATIBLE GRADES CLAUSE TO APPLY HEAT: NO
HEAT: NO HEAD REQUIRED

GEOGRAPHICAL

LOADING RANGE: 1/2 PORTS ARABIAN GULF EXCLUDING IRAN/IRAQ BUT INCL
          KHARG, SAROOSH TERMINAL, BASRAH OIL TERMINAL, SIRRI AND
          LAVAN ISLAND

DISCHARGING RANGE: 1 PORT EGYPTIAN RED SEA OR IN CHOPT
          1/2 PORTS UK-CONTINENT (G-H) OR IN CHOPT
          1/2 PORTS EUROMED NEOBIG BUT INCL 1 PORT SIDI KERIR
                    EXCL YUGO, FORMER YUGO AND ALBANIA OR
                    IN CHOPT
          1 PORT EUROMED NEOBIG BUT INCL 1 PORT SIDI KERIR
                    EXCL YUGO, FORMER YUGO AND ALBANIA
                    FOLLOWED BY
          1 PORT UK-CONTINENT (G-H)

CHARTERERS TO DECLARE DISCHARGE PORTS LATEST 1200 LONDON TIME DATE 2005

APPENDIX 18

SUEZ CANAL TRANSIT CLAUSE:

IF THE VESSEL DISCHARGES WITHIN UK/CONT OR MED, CHARTERERS SHALL HAVE THE OPTION TO ROUTE THE VESSEL VIA SUEZ. IF CHARTERERS DECLARE THIS OPTION, THE VESSEL SHALL DISCHARGE AT AIN SUKHNA EITHER ONE OR MORE OF THE PARCELS, OR SUFFICIENT CARGO TO ENABLE THE VESSEL TO TRANSIT THE SUEZ CANAL NORTHBOUND AND RELOAD SAME OR A DIFFERENT GRADE(S) AT SIDI KERIR FOR FINAL DISCHARGE WITHIN UK/CONT OR MED. IF THIS OPTION IS USED THE WORLDSCALE FLAT RATE SHALL BE BASED UPON THE VOYAGE ACTUALLY PERFORMED BASIS SUEZ/SUEZ BUT EXCLUDING ANY ALLOWANCE FOR SIDI KERIR, AIN SUKHNA AND THE SUEZ CANAL DIFFERENTIALS. ANY DEVIATION FOR CALLING AT AIN SUKHNA AND SIDI KERIR OVER AND ABOVE THE DIRECT PASSAGE FROM THE ARABIAN GULF TO THE FIRST DISCHARGE PORT WITHIN UK/CONT OR MED SHALL BE PAID AT THE DEMURRAGE RATE BASED UPON THE C/P BASE SPEED. STEAMING BUNKERS CONSUMED DURING SAID DEVIATION SHALL BE REIMBURSED AT COST AGAINST MASTER'S CALCULATION WITH SUPPORTING DOCUMENTS AND ANY PORT COSTS EXCLUDING ANY OWNERS ITEMS IN AIN SUKHNA AND SIDI KERIR SHALL BE REIMBURSED AT COST. TIME SPENT DISCHARGING IN AIN SUKHNA AND LOADING IN SIDI KERIR SHALL COUNT AS LAYTIME OR DEMURRAGE AS PER MAIN C/P TERMS, EXCLUDING NOTICE TIME ALLOWANCES.

THE SUEZ CANAL TRANSIT COSTS FOR THE LADEN PASSAGE SHALL BE PAID DIRECTLY BY CHARTERERS. CHARTERERS SHALL PAY TO THE OWNERS THE SUEZ CANAL BALLAST TRANSIT DIFFERENTIAL AS PER 2005 WORLDSCALE.

DATES

LAYCAN: 29/30 MONTH 2005

CURRENT POSITION/ETA: SPOT FUJAIPAH

FINANCIAL

FREIGHT RATE: WS AA RED SEA DISCHARGE
            WS BB UKCONT-EUROMED DISCHARGE C/C PLUS WS 2.5 FOR
                SECOND DISPORT N W EUROPE
            WS CC.5 UKCONT-EUROMED-INCL SIDI KERIR DISCHARGE VIA
                SUEZ

DEMURRAGE RATE: USD XXXXX PDPR

OVERAGE: FIFTY PERCENT

FREIGHT PAYMENT DETAILS:

IN USDOLLARS BY TELEGRAPHIC TRANSFER TO:
MICKEY MOUSE BANK
USA
ABA.
SWIFT:

LAYTIME 96 HOURS

TERMS

ADDITIONAL CLAUSES

1. PORT CHARGES AT BASRAH OIL TERMINAL, IF ANY, TO BE FOR
   CHARTERERS ACCOUNT

2. OWNERS OPTION TO BUNKER OUTBOUND AG

3. CHARTERERS WARRANT THAT THE CARGO TO BE LOADED UNDER THIS
   CHARTER, WILL AT ALL TIMES BE LOADED, CARRIED AND DISCHARGED
   IN COMPLIANCE WITH ANY UNITED NATIONS RULES, REGULATIONS,
   POLICIES, RESOLUTIONS, DIRECTIVES OR RECOMMENDATIONS IN
   FORCE WITH REGARDS TO LOADING, CARRIAGE AND/OR DISCHARGE OF
   IRAQI CRUDE OIL, INCLUDING BUT NOT LIMITED TO UN SANCTION 661,
   RESOLUTION 986.

ANY TIME, COST OR CONSEQUENCES IN BREACH OF THE ABOVE, WILL BE FOR CHARTERERS ACCOUNT. CONSISTENT WITH UN DIRECTIVES, ANY AND ALL PORT COSTS IN IRAQ, INCLUDING BUT NOT LIMITED TO AGENCY FEES (IF ANY), WILL BE SETTLED AND PAID BY THE CHARTERERS DIRECTLY INTO THE ACCOUNT ESTABLISHED BY THE SECRETARY GENERAL OF THE UNITED NATIONS PURSUANT TO SECURITY COUNCIL RESOLUTION 986.

THE VESSEL SHALL NOT BE REQUIRED TO TRADE TO ANY PORT OR CARRY ANY CARGO AND THE MASTER SHALL NOT BE REQUIRED TO SIGN ANY BILL OF LADING WHICH WOULD RESULT IN THE VESSEL AND/OR THE OWNER BEING IN VIOLATION OF ANY UNITED NATIONS RULES, REGULATIONS, POLICIES, RESOLUTIONS, DIRECTIVES OR RECOMMENDATIONS.

4. IF FOR ANY REASON THE VESSEL IS DELAYED OR UNABLE TO LOAD AT BASRAH – EXCEPT FOR REASON OF BREAKDOWN OF VESSEL, OR VESSEL'S EQUIPMENT OR FAULT OF MASTER, OFFICERS, CREW – CHARTERER ASSUMES ALL TIME WAITING AT THE DEMURRAGE RATE, WHICH SHALL BE PAID TOGETHER WITH FREIGHT.

5. OWNERS WARRANT THAT THE PERFORMING VESSEL:-
   – WILL BE CERTIFIED ON IOPPC TO CARRY CRUDE OIL
   – HAS A FULLY OPERATIONAL IGS SYSTEM AND THAT THE SAME IS IN USE
   – WILL BE LOAD, CARRY AND DISCHARGED THE CARGO IN A "CLOSED" CONDITION
   – IS SUITABLE FOR S-T-S OPERATIONS AND WILL COMPLY WITH OCIMF S-T-S GUIDE RECOMMENDATIONS

6. BIMCO ISPS CLAUSE – ISPS Clause for Voyage Charter Parties
(A) (i) From the date of coming into force of the International Code for the Security of Ships and of Port Facilities and the relevant amendments to Chapter XI of SOLAS (ISPS Code) in relation to the Vessel, the Owners shall procure that both the Vessel and "the Company" (as defined by the ISPS Code) shall comply with the requirements of the ISPS Code relating to the Vessel and "the Company". Upon request the Owners shall provide a copy of the relevant International Ship Security Certificate (or the Interim International Ship Security Certificate) to the Charterers. The Owners shall provide the Charterers with the full style contact details of the Company Security Officer (CSO).

(ii) Except as otherwise provided in this Charter Party, loss, damage, expense or delay, excluding consequential loss, caused by failure on the part of the Owners or "the Company" to comply with the requirements of the ISPS Code or this Clause shall be for the Owners' account.

(B) (i) The Charterers shall provide the CSO and the Ship Security Officer (SSO)/ Master with their full style contact details and any other information the Owners require to comply with the ISPS Code.

(ii) Except as otherwise provided in this Charter Party, loss, damage, expense, excluding consequential loss, caused by failure on the part of the Charterers to comply with this Clause shall be for the Charterers' account and any delay caused by such failure shall be compensated at the demurrage rate.

(C) Provided that the delay is not caused by the Owners' failure to comply with their obligations under the ISPS Code, the following shall apply:

(i) Notwithstanding anything to the contrary provided in this Charter Party, the Vessel shall be entitled to tender Notice of Readiness even if not cleared due to applicable security regulations or measures imposed by a port facility or any relevant authority under the ISPS Code.

(ii) Any delay resulting from measures imposed by a port facility or by any relevant authority under the ISPS Code shall count as laytime or time on demurrage if the Vessel is on laytime or demurrage. If the delay occurs before laytime has started or after laytime or time on demurrage has ceased to count, it shall be compensated by the Charterers at the demurrage rate.

APPENDIX 18

(D) Notwithstanding anything to the contrary provided in this Charter Party, any additional costs or expenses whatsoever solely arising out of or related to security regulations or measures required by the port facility or any relevant authority in accordance with the ISPS Code including, but not limited to, security guards, launch services, tug escorts, port security fees or taxes and inspections, shall be for the Charterers' account, unless such costs or expenses result solely from the Owners' negligence. All measures required by the Owners to comply with the Ship Security Plan shall be for the Owners' account.

AMENDMENTS/ADDITIONS/DELETIONS TO
BPVOY 4 CHARTER PARTY, 1ST EDITION ISSUED JUNE 1998.

PART 2:
LINE 125 INSERT "SIGNIFICANTLY" AFTER "TO BE"
LINE 176 INSERT "UNEXPECTED ENGINE BREAKDOWN," BEFORE "TO ADVERSE WEATHER"
LINE 219 INSERT "PROCEED THERETO" AFTER "ALWAYS" AND INSERT "AND DEPART" BEFORE "SAFELY AFLOAT"
LINE 234 DELETE "ALL" BEFORE "SUPPORTING"
LINE 254 INSERT AFTER "REPRESENTATIVE", "IF SUCH SIGNATURE IS OBTAINABLE"
LINE 263-4 DELETE "AND HER GANGWAY .... IN PLACE"
LINE 270 INSERT "IF APPLICABLE" AFTER "PRATIQUE"
LINE 275-276 DELETE "FAILING WHICH LAYTIME .. GRANTED"
LINE 279 INSERT "OF INSPECTION" AFTER "CERTIFICATE"
LINE 301 INSERT "50 PER CENT" AFTER "CONSTITUTE"
LINE 312/314/318 CHANGE "(3)" TO "(2)"
LINE 342 INSERT "SUBJECT TO OWNER'S APPROVAL SUCH APPROVAL NOT TO BE UNREASONABLY WITHHELD" AFTER "EN ROUTE THERETO"
LINE 375 AFTER "DEMURRAGE" INSERT "IF, HOWEVER, ADVERSE WEATHER AND/OR ADVERSE SEA STATE CONDITIONS AFFECTS THE IN PORT TRANSFER, BUT DOES NOT AFFECT THE GENERAL PORT, TIME TO COUNT AS LAYTIME OR IF THE VESSEL IS ON DEMURRAGE, AS DEMURRAGE"
LINE 387 AFTER "CLAUSE 18.1" INSERT "AND THE REFERENCE TO ADVERSE WEATHER IN CLAUSE 17"
LINE 416 INSERT "TIME TO COUNT FULL WEATHER PERMITTING OR NOT" AFTER "UNDER CLAUSES", CHANGE "CLAUSES" TO "CLAUSE" AND DELETE "17 AND"
LINE 480 AFTER "DEMURRAGE" INSERT "CHARTERERS SHALL REIMBURSE OWNERS FOR ANY BUNKERS USED IN CONNECTION WITH THIS OPERATION UPON RECEIPT OF OWNERS' INVOICE WITH FULL SUPPORTING DOCUMENTATION"
LINE 489-511 DELETE, REPLACE WITH 'VESSEL TO ARRIVE LOADPORT WITH CLEAN BALLAST ONLY. VESSEL IS FULLY SBT.'
LINE 523 DELETE "CHARTERERS"
LINE 524 DELETE "INSTRUCT" AND "TO" BEFORE AND AFTER "OWNERS" LINE
LINE 528-534 DELETE
LINE 540 INSERT "MUTUALLY AGREED" AFTER "SHALL NOMINATE"
LINE 552 CHANGE "FORTY-EIGHT(48)" TO "TWENTY-FOUR(24)"
LINE 556 DELETE "CHARTERERS MAY REQUIRE"
LINE 558 DELETE FROM "IN SUCH .... CHARTERERS REQUEST"
LINE 560 DELETE "SO" AFTER "AND TIME". INSERT "PURSUANT TO THE PRECEEDING PARAGRAPH OR 16.1" AFTER "NOTIFIED BY OWNERS"
LINE 562 CHANGE "NINETY-SIX (96)" TO "FORTY-EIGHT(48)". INSERT "SATURDAYS" BEFORE "SUNDAYS"
LINE 563 CHANGE "FORTY-EIGHT (48)" TO "TWENTY-FOUR (24)"
LINE 571 CHANGE "NINETY-SIX (96)" TO "FORTY-EIGHT (48)"
LINE 579-586 DELETE
LINE 588 INSERT "AWAITING DAYLIGHT, TIDE," AFTER "ARISING FROM"
LINE 600 DELETE "INCLUDING AWAITING DAYLIGHT, TIDE"
LINE 603-604 DELETE "AND THE VESSEL'S ...IN PLACE"
LINE 613 DELETE "WHETHER DIRECTLY OR INDIRECTLY" BEFORE "RESULT' INSERT "DIRECT"
LINE 652 INSERT "BE CAPABLE OF" AFTER "VESSEL SHALL", CHANGE "LOAD" TO "LOADING" AND INSERT "HOMOGENOUS" AFTER "LOADING"
LINE 720 INSERT "IF POSSIBLE" AFTER "REPRESENTATIVE"

LINE 742 CHANGE "(25 PERCENT)" TO "(50 PERCENT)"
LINE 751 CHANGE "TWO (2)" TO "FOUR (4)"
LINE 789 CHANGE "ALL" TO "REASONABLE"
LINE 792 INSERT "EXCEPT CLAIMS ARISING UNDER A BILL OF LADING" AFTER "ANY
    OTHER CLAIM"
LINE 795 DELETE "FULL"
LINE 878-911 DELETE
LINE 970 INSERT "VESSEL NOT TO TRADE IN ICE OR FOLLOW ICEBREAKERS" AFTER
    "DEMURRAGE"
LINE 990 INSERT "AND PROPER REFERENCE TO CHARTER PARTY" AFTER "NEW JASON
    CLAUSES"
LINE 1051 INSERT "GIVING DUE CREDIT TRAFFIC ROUTINE" AFTER "DISTANCE TABLE"
LINE 1096 AFTER "LIQUID" INSERT "AND PUMPABLE BY VESSELS FIXED PUMPS"
LINE 1097 AFTER "LIQUID" INSERT "AND PUMPABLE BY VESSELS FIXED PUMPS"
LINE 1099 CHANGE "DEDUCT" AFTER "ENTITLED TO" TO "CLAIM"
LINE 1131 INSERT "BE FOR CHARTERERS ACCOUNT AND SETTLED DIRECTLY BY
    THEM UNLESS PROHIBITED BY LAW" AFTER "SHALL" AND DELETE "IN THE
    FIRST INSTANCE BE PAID BY OWNERS" AND INSERT "IMMEDIATELY" AFTER
    "CHARTERERS SHALL"
CLAUSE 34.3 DELETE AND INSERT "EXCESS BERTH OCCUPANCY CLAUSE – IF,
    AFTER DISCONNECTION OF HOSES, THE VESSEL REMAINS AT BERTH FOR
    VESSEL'S PURPOSES (EXCLUDING VESSEL'S BREAKDOWN), OWNERS SHALL
    BE RESPONSIBLE FOR ALL DIRECT COSTS WHETHER ADVISED TO OWNERS
    IN ADVANCE OR NOT, AND INCLUDING CHARGES BY TERMINAL/SUPPLIERS/
    RECEIVERS."
CLAUSE 35 DELETE
LINE 1183 INSERT "NEITHER OWNERS NOR" BEFORE "CHARTERERS" DELETE "NOT
LINE 1188 AT END DELETE "." AND INSERT ", REQUISITION, PERILS OF THE SEA, ACT OF
    PUBLIC ENEMIES OR ASSAILING THIEVES."
LINE 1375 AMEND USD 500 MILLION TO USD 1 BILLON
LINE 1378/9 DELETE "CURRENTLY USD 200 MILLION"
LINE 1419 ADD AT END "SUBJECT TO OWNERS APPROVAL, SUCH APPROVAL NOT TO BE
    UNREASONABLY WITHHELD."

BPAC 5 H2S AND MERCAPTANS CLAUSE – 5.3 FIRST LINE DELETE 'UNDERTAKE' AND
    INSERT "ADVISE THAT ACCORDING TO INFO AVAILABLE FROM CARGO OWNER"
BPAC 8 ISM CLAUSE – ADD AT END 'OWNERS NOT TO BE LIABLE FOR CONSEQUENTIAL
    DAMAGES.'
BPAC 9 JEBEL DHANNA
BPAC 12 RAS TANURA
BPAC 13 ROTTERDAM
BPAC 14 SIDI KERIR

TANKERS INTERNATIONAL WAR RISK CLASUE DATED SEPTEMBER 26, 2001:
ANY ADDITIONAL PREMIUMS PAYABLE BY OWNER IN RESPECT OF WAR RISKS UNDER
THEIR POLICIES OF INSURANCE THAT ARE INCURRED BY REASON OF THE VESSEL
TRADING TO EXCLUDED AREAS NOT COVERED BY OWNER'S BASIC WAR RISK
INSURANCE SHALL BE FOR CHARTERER'S ACCOUNT. ANY BONUSES OR ADDITIONAL
PREMIUMS PAYBLE BY OWNERS IN RESPECT OF THEIR CREW WHICH ARE DUE BY
REASON OF TRADING TO SUCH EXCLUDED AREAS SHALL ALSO BE FOR CHARTERER'S
ACCOUNT.

FOR THE AVOIDANCE OF DOUBT IT IS AGREED THAT IF THE VESSEL IS BOUND TO
ENTER AN EXCLUDED AREA IN ORDER TO ARRIVE AT THE LOADPORT, OR IF THE
VESSEL WILL HAVE TO STEAM AWAY FROM THE DISCHARGE PORT IN ORDER TO LEAVE
AN EXCLUDED AREA THEN THE ADDITIONAL PREMIUMS AND BONUSES PAYABLE BY
CHARTERERS SHALL INCLUDE THOSE PAYABLE FROM THE TIME THE VESSEL PASSES
INTO THE EXCLUDED AREA INWARD BOUND TO THE LOADPORT AND UNTIL THE TIME
THE VESSEL PASSES OUT OF THE EXCLUDED AREA OUTWARD BOUND FROM THE
DISCHARGE PORT CALCULATED AT NORMAL SPEEDS AND PRUDENT NAVIGATION AND
PROVIDED ALWAYS THAT CHARTERERS ARE GIVEN NOTICE OF THE AMOUNT OF SUCH
ADDITIONAL PREMIUM AS SOON AS POSSIBLE AND, IN ANY EVENT, BEFORE SUCH
ADDITIONAL PREMIUM IS PAID.

SUCH ADDITIONAL PREMIUMS AND EXPENSES THAT ARE FOR CHARTERER'S ACCOUNT
ARE PAYABLE BY CHARTERERERS TOGETHER WITH FREIGHT AGAINST OWNER'S'
INVOICE SUPPORTED BY APPROPRIATE DOCUMENTS.

IF SUCH DOCUMENTS ARE NOT AVAILABLE THEN SUCH ADDITIONAL PREMIUMS
AND EXPENSES SHALL BE SETTLED NOT LATER THAN 2 WEEKS AFTER RECEIPT BY
CHARTERER FROM OWNER'S INVOICE AND APPROPRIATE SUPPORTING DOCUMENTS.

APPENDIX 18

ANY DISCOUNT OR REBATE REFUNDED TO OWNER FOR WHATSOEVER REASON SHALL BE PASSED ON TO CHARTERER. ANY PREMIUMS AND INCREASE THERETO ATTRIBUTABLE TO CLOSURE INSURANCE (I.E., BLOCKING AND TRAPPING) SHALL BE FOR OWNER'S ACCOUNT. LOSS OF FREIGHT AND LOSS OF BUNKERS INSURANCE TAKEN OUT BY OWNERS IS RESPECT OF THE VESSEL AND ANY ADDITIONAL PREMIUM RELATING THERETO ARISING FROM CHARTERERS TRADING OF THE VESSEL, SHALL ALSO BE FOR OWNERS ACCOUNT

TECHNICAL

OWNERS WARRANT VESSEL COMPLIES WITH THE FOLLOWING

PORT DETAILS – KHARG ISLAND

MAX BERTHING TRIM 4.00 MTRS BY STERN WITH PROPELLOR FULLY IMMERSED.

BERTH 11
MAX BERTHING DISPLACEMENT 250,000 MT

BERTH 15
MAX BERTHING DISPLACEMENT 250,000 MT

PORT DETAILS – SOROOSH TERMINAL

SUMMER DEADWEIGHT – TERMINAL APPROVAL REQUIRED

V/L'S MUST COMPLY OCIMF FOR MOORING TO SPM'S (ONLY 76 MM CHAIN STOPPERS ACCEPTED)
V/L'S MUST COMPLY OCIMF FOR MANIFOLDS AND ASSOCIATED EQUIPMENT.,
STARBOARD SIDE CONNECTION
DERRICK/CRANE MINIMUM SWL 15 MT REQUIRED
IGS MUST BE OPERATIONAL AND IN USE.
V/L MUST BE CAPABLE OF CLOSED LOADING.
IF REQUIRED TO DEBALLAST ONLY CBT OR SBT VESSELS ARE ACCEPTABLE. V/L MUST HAVE AN OPERATIONAL ODME.
USE OF OBO'S WHEREVER POSSIBLE IS DISCOURAGED. SUCH V/L'S ONLY ACCEPTED IF THE BUYER CAN PROVIDE EVIDENCE OF CREW COMPETENCY IN CRUDE OIL OPERATIONS AND CONFIRM THAT V/L HAS RECENTLY BEEN ENGAGED IN CRUDE OIL OPERATIONS, LAST 2 CARGOES MUST HAVE BEEN CRUDE.
ACCOMMODATION LADDERS MUST BE AFT FACING.

PORT DETAILS – AIN SUKHNA

MUST COMPLY OCIMF FOR MOORING TO SBM'S, MANIFOLDS AND ASSOCIATED EQUIPMENT
10 TON SWL DERRICK/CRANE REQUIRED

COMMISSION 1.25 PCT PAYABLE TO BRAEMAR TANKERS LTD ON FREIGHT, DEADFREIGHT AND DEMURRAGE EARNED UNDER THIS CHARTER PARTY

MANY THANKS YOUR SUPPORT

RGDS-

APPENDIX 19

*Letter of Indemnity wording — <u>CHANGE OF DESTINATION</u>

INTERNATIONAL GROUP WORDING – B

STANDARD FORM LETTER OF INDEMNITY TO BE GIVEN IN RETURN FOR DELIVERING CARGO AT A PORT OTHER THAN THAT STATED IN THE BILL OF LADING

To: [insert name of Owners]
The Owners of the   [insert name of ship]
                      [insert address]
[insert date]

Dear Sirs,
Ship: [insert name of ship]
Voyage: [insert load and discharge ports as stated in the bill of lading]
Cargo: [insert description of cargo]
Bill of lading: [insert identification number, date and place of issue]

The above cargo was shipped on the above ship by [insert name of shipper] and consigned to [insert name of consignee or party to whose order the bill of lading is made out, as appropriate] for delivery at the port of [insert name of discharge port stated in the bill of lading] but we, [insert name of party requesting substituted delivery], hereby request you to order the ship to proceed to and deliver the said cargo at [insert name of substitute port or place of delivery] against production of at least one original bill of lading.

In consideration of your complying with our above request, we hereby agree as follows:

1. To indemnity you, your servants and agents and to hold all of you harmless in respect of any liability, loss, damage or expense of whatsoever nature which you may sustain by reason of the ship proceeding and giving delivery of the cargo against production of at least one original bill lading in accordance with our request.

2. In the event of any proceedings being commenced against you or any of your servants or agents in connection with the ship proceeding and giving delivery of the cargo as aforesaid, to provide you or them on demand with sufficient funds to defend the same.

3. If, in connection with the delivery of the cargo as aforesaid, the ship, or any other ship or property in the same or associated ownership, management or control, should be arrested or detained or should the arrest or detention thereof be threatened, or should there be any interference in the use or trading of the vessel (whether by virtue of a caveat being entered on the ship's registry or otherwise howsoever), to provide on demand such bail or other security as may be required to prevent such arrest or detention or to secure the release of such ship or property or to remove such interference and to indemnify you in respect of any liability loss, damage or expense caused by such arrest or detention or threatened arrest or detention or such interference, whether or not such arrest or detention or threatened arrest or detention or such interference may be justified.

4. The liability of each and every person under this indemnity shall be joint and several and shall not be conditional upon your proceeding first against any person, whether or not such person is party to or liable under this indemnity.

APPENDIX 19

5. This indemnity shall be governed by and construed in accordance with English law and each and every person liable under this indemnity shall at your request submit to the jurisdiction of the High Court of Justice of England.

Yours faithfully
For and on behalf of
[insert name of Requestor]
The Requestor

Signature

Letter of Indemnity wording — CHANGE OF DESTINATION AND NON-PRODUCTION

INTERNATIONAL GROUP WORDING – C

STANDARD FORM LETTER OF INDEMNITY TO BE GIVEN IN RETURN FOR DELIVERING CARGO AT A PORT OTHER THAN THAT STATED IN THE BILL OF LADING AND WITHOUT PRODUCTION OF THE ORIGINAL BILL OF LADING

To: [insert name of Owners]
The Owners of the   [insert name of ship]
                             [insert address]
[insert date]

Dear Sirs,
Ship: [insert name of ship]
Voyage: [insert load and discharge ports as stated in the bill of lading]
Cargo: [insert description of cargo]
Bill of lading: [insert identification number, date and place of issue]

The above cargo was shipped on the above vessel by [insert name of shipper] and consigned to [insert name of consignee or party to whose order the bills of lading are made out, as appropriate] for delivery at the port of [insert name of discharge port stated in the bill of lading] but we, [insert name of party requesting substituted delivery], hereby request you to order the vessel to proceed to

APPENDIX 19

and deliver the said cargo at [insert name of substitute port or place of delivery] to [insert name of party to whom delivery is to be made] without production of the original bill of lading.

In consideration of your complying with our above request, we hereby agree as follows:

1. To indemnify you, your servants and agents and to hold all of you harmless in respect of any liability, loss, damage or expense of whatsoever nature which you may sustain by reason of the ship proceeding and giving delivery of the cargo in accordance with our request.

2. In the event of any proceedings being commenced against you or any of your servants or agents in connection with the ship proceeding and giving delivery of the cargo as aforesaid, to provide you or them on demand with sufficient funds to defend the same.

3. If, in connection with the delivery of the cargo as aforesaid, the ship, or any other ship or property in the same or associated ownership, management or control, should be arrested or detained or should the arrest or detention thereof be threatened, or should there be any interference in the use or trading of the vessel (whether by virtue of a caveat being entered on the ship's registry or otherwise howsoever), to provide on demand such bail or other security as may be required to prevent such arrest or detention or to secure the release of such ship or property or to remove such interference and to indemnify you in respect of any liability, loss, damage or expense caused by such arrest or detention or threatened arrest or detention or such interference, whether or not such arrest or detention or threatened arrest or detention or such interference may be justified.

4. If the place at which we have asked you to make delivery is a bulk liquid or gas terminal or facility, or another ship, lighter or barge, then delivery to such terminal, facility, ship, lighter or barge shall be deemed to be delivery to the party to whom we have requested you to make such delivery

5. As soon as all original bills of lading for the above cargo shall have come into our possession, to deliver the same to you, or otherwise to cause all original bills of lading to be delivered to you.

6. The liability of each and every person under this indemnity shall be joint and several and shall not be conditional upon your proceeding first against any person, whether or not such person is party to or liable under this indemnity.

7. This indemnity shall be governed by and construed in accordance with English law and each and every person liable under this indemnity shall at your request submit to the jurisdiction of the High Court of Justice of England.

Yours faithfully
For and on behalf of
[insert name of Requestor]
The Requestor

Signature

APPENDIX 20

Letter of Indemnity wording — NON-PRODUCTION

INTERNATIONAL GROUP WORDING – A

STANDARD FORM LETTER OF INDEMNITY TO BE GIVEN IN RETURN FOR DELIVERING CARGO WITHOUT PRODUCTION OF THE ORIGINAL BILL OF LADING

To: [insert name of Owners]
The Owners of the   [insert name of ship]
                               [insert address]
[insert date]

Dear Sirs,
Ship: [insert name of ship]
Voyage: [insert load and discharge ports as stated in the bill of lading]
Cargo: [insert description of cargo]
Bill of lading: [insert identification number, date and place of issue]

The above cargo was shipped on the above ship by [insert name of shipper] and consigned to [insert name of consignee or party to whose order the bill of lading is made out, as appropriate] for delivery at the port of [insert name of discharge port stated in the bill of lading] but the bill of lading has not arrived and we, [insert name of party requesting delivery], hereby request you to deliver the said cargo to [insert name of party to whom delivery is to be made] at [insert place where delivery is to be made] without production of the original bill of lading.

In consideration of your complying with our above request, we hereby agree as follows:

1. To indemnify you, your servants and agents and to hold all of you harmless in respect of any liability, loss, damage or expense of whatsoever nature which you may sustain by reason of delivering the cargo in accordance with our request.

2. In the event of any proceedings being commenced against you or any of your servants or agents in connection with the delivery of the cargo as aforesaid, to provide you or them on demand with sufficient funds to defend the same.

3. If, in connection with the delivery of the cargo as aforesaid, the ship, or any other ship or property in the same or associated ownership, management or control, should be arrested or detained or should the arrest or detention thereof be threatened, or should there be any interference in the use or trading of the vessel (whether by virtue of a caveat being entered on the ship's registry or otherwise howsoever), to provide on demand such bail or other security as may be required to prevent such arrest or detention or to secure the release of such ship or property or to remove such interference and to indemnify you in respect of any liability, loss, damage or expense caused by such arrest or detention or threatened arrest or detention or such interference, whether or not such arrest or detention or threatened arrest or detention or such interference may be justified.

4. If the place at which we have asked you to make delivery is a bulk liquid or gas terminal or facility, or another ship, lighter or barge, then delivery to such terminal, facility, ship, lighter or barge shall be deemed to be delivery to the party to whom we have requested you to make such delivery.

APPENDIX 20

5. As soon as all original bills of lading for the above cargo shall have come into our possession, to deliver the same to you, or otherwise to cause all original bills of lading to be delivered to you, whereupon our liability hereunder shall cease.

6. The liability of each and every person under this indemnity shall be joint and several and shall not be conditional upon your proceeding first against any person, whether or not such person is party to or liable under this indemnity.

7. This indemnity shall be governed by and construed in accordance with English law and each and every person liable under this indemnity shall at your request submit to the jurisdiction of the High Court of Justice of England.

Yours faithfully
For and on behalf of
[insert name of Requestor]
The Requestor

Signature

APPENDIX 21

**Code word for this Charter Party
"SHELLTIME4"**

Issued December 1984

Time Charter Party

LONDON,   19

IT IS THIS DAY AGREED between	1

of   (hereinafter referred to as "Owners"), being owners of the   2
good   vessel called   3

(hereinafter referred to as "the vessel") described as per Clause 1 hereof and   4

of   (hereinafter referred to as "Charterers"):   5

**Description and
Condition of
Vessel**

1. At the date of delivery of the vessel under this charter   6
    (a) she shall be classed: 7
    (b) she shall be in every way fit to carry crude petroleum and/or its products;   8

    (c) she shall be tight, staunch, strong, in good order and condition, and in every way fit for the service, with her   9
machinery, boilers, hull and other equipment (including but not limited to hull stress calculator and radar) in a good and   10
efficient state;   11
    (d) her tanks, valves and pipelines shall be oil-tight: 12
    (e) she shall be in every way fitted for burning   13
        at sea – fueloil with a maximum viscosity of   Centistokes at 50 degrees Centigrade any commercial   14
            grade of fueloil ("ACGFO") for main propulsion, marine diesel oil ACGFO for auxiliaries   15
        in port – marine diesel oil/ACGFO for auxiliaries: 16
    (f) she shall comply with the regulations in force so as to enable her to pass through the Suez and Panama Canals   17
by day and night without delay;   18
    (g) she shall have on board all certificates, documents and equipment required from time to time by any applicable   19
law to enable her to perform the charter service without delay;   20
    (h) she shall comply with the description in Form B appended hereto, provided however that if there is any   21
conflict between the provisions of Form B and any other provision, including this Clause 1, of this charter such other   22
provision shall govern.   23

**Shipboard
Personnel
and their Duties**

2. (a) At the date of delivery of the vessel under this charter   24
        (i) she shall have a full and efficient complement of master, officers and crew for a vessel of her tonnage,   25
who shall in any event be not less than the number required by the laws of the flag state and who shall be trained to operate   26
the vessel and her equipment competently and safely;   27
        (ii) all shipboard personnel shall hold valid certificates of competence in accordance with the requirements   28
of the law of the flag state;   29
        (iii) all shipboard personnel shall be trained in accordance with the relevant provisions of the International   30
Convention on Standards of Training. Certification and Watchkeeping for Seafarers, 1978;   31
        (iv) there shall be on board sufficient personnel with a good working knowledge of the English language   32
to enable cargo operations at loading and discharging places to be carried out efficiently and safely and to enable   33
communications between the vessel and those loading the vessel or accepting discharge therefrom to be carried out   34
quickly and efficiently.   35
    (b) Owners guarantee that throughout the charter service the master shall with the vessel's officers and crew,   36
unless otherwise ordered by Charterers,   37
        (i) prosecute all voyages with the utmost despatch: 38
        (ii) render all customary assistance; and   39
        (iii) load and discharge cargo as rapidly as possible when required by Charterers or their agents to do so, by   40
night or by day, but always in accordance with the laws of the place of loading or discharging (as the case may be) and in   41
each case in accordance with any applicable laws of the flag state.   42

**Duty to
Maintain**

3. (i) Throughout the charter service Owners shall, whenever the passage of time, wear and tear or any event   43
(whether or not coming within Clause 27 hereof) requires steps to be taken to maintain or restore the conditions stipulated   44
in Clauses 1 and 2(a), exercise due diligence so to maintain or restore the vessel.   45
    (ii) If at any time whilst the vessel is on hire under this charter the vessel fails to comply with the requirements   46
of Clauses 1.2(a) or 10 then hire shall be reduced to the extent necessary to indemnify Charterers for such failure. If and   47
to the extent that such failure affects the time taken by the vessel to perform any services under this charter, hire shall be   48
reduced by an amount equal to the value, calculated at the rate of hire, of the time so lost.   49
        Any reduction of hire under this sub-Clause (ii) shall be without prejudice to any other remedy available to   50
Charterers, but where such reduction of hire is in respect of time lost, such time shall be excluded from any calculation   51
under Clause 24.   52
    (iii) If Owners are in breach of their obligation under Clause 3(i) Charterers may so notify Owners in writing;   53
and if, after the expiry of 30 days following the receipt by Owners of any such notice. Owners have failed to   54
demonstrate to Charterers' reasonable satisfaction the exercise of due diligence as required in Clause 3(i), the vessel   55
shall be off-hire, and no further hire payments shall be due, until Owners have so demonstrated that they are exercising   56
such due diligence.   57
        Furthermore, at any time while the vessel is off-hire under this Clause 3 Charterers have the option to   58
terminate this charter by giving notice in writing with effect from the date on which such notice of termination is   59
received by Owners or from any later date stated in such notice This sub-Clause (iii) is without prejudice to any rights   60
of Charterers or obligations of Owners under this charter or otherwise (including without limitation Charterers' rights   61
under Clause 21 hereof).   62

2

Period Trading Limit	4. Owners agree to let and Charterers agree to hire the vessel for a period of	63
	commencing from the time and date of delivery of the vessel, for the purpose of carrying all lawful merchandise (subject	64
	always to Clause 28) including in particular	65

in any part of the world, as Charterers shall direct, subject to the limits of the current British Institute Warranties and 66
any subsequent amendments thereof. Notwithstanding the foregoing, but subject to Clause 35. Charterers may order the 67
vessel to ice-bound waters or to any part of the world outside such limits provided that Owners consent thereto (such 68
consent not to be unreasonably withheld) and that Charterers pay for any insurance premium required by the vessel's 69
underwriters as a consequence of such order. 70
    Charterers shall use due diligence to ensure that the vessel is only employed between and at safe places (which 71
expression when used in this charter shall include ports, berths, wharves, docks, anchorages, submarine lines, alongside 72
vessels or lighters, and other locations including locations at sea) where she can safely lie always afloat. Notwithstanding 73
anything contained in this or any other clause of this charter, Charterers do not warrant the safety of any place to which 74
they order the vessel and shall be under no liability in respect thereof except for loss or damage caused by their failure to 75
exercise due diligence as aforesaid. Subject as above, the vessel shall be loaded and discharged at any places as Charterers 76
may direct, provided that Charterers shall exercise due diligence to ensure that any ship-to-ship transfer operations shall 77
conform to standards not less than those set out in the latest published edition of the ICS OCI/OCIMF Ship-to-Ship 78
Transfer Guide. 79
    The vessel shall be delivered by Owners at a port in 80

at Owners' option and redelivered to Owners at a port in 81

at Charterers' option 82

Laydays/ Cancelling	5. The vessel shall not be delivered to Charterers before and Charterers shall have the option of	83
	cancelling this charter if the vessel is not ready and at their disposal on or before	84

Owners to Provide	6. Owners undertake to provide and to pay for all provisions, wages, and shipping and discharging fees and all other	85
	expenses of the master, officers and crew; also, except as provided in Clauses 4 and 34 hereof, for all insurance on the	86

vessel, for all deck, cabin and engine-room stores, and for water; for all drydocking, overhaul, maintenance and repairs 87
to the vessel; and for all fumigation expenses and de-rat certificates. Owners obligations under this Clause 6 extend to 88
all liabilities for customs or import duties arising at any time during the performance of this charter in relation to the 89
personal effects of the master, officers and crew, and in relation to the stores, provisions and other matters aforesaid 90
which Owners are to provide and pay for and Owners shall refund to Charterers any sums Charterers or their agents 91
may have paid or been compelled to pay in respect of any such liability. Any amounts allowable in general average for 92
wages and provisions and stores shall be credited to Charterers insofar as such amounts are in respect of a period when 93
the vessel is on-hire. 94

Charters to Provide	7. Charterers shall provide and pay for all fuel (except fuel used for domestic services), towage and pilotage and shall pay	95
	agency fees, port charges, commissions, expenses of loading and unloading cargoes, canal dues and all charges other	96

than those payable by Owners in accordance with Clause 6 hereof, provided that all charges for the said items shall be 97
for Owners' account when such items are consumed, employed or incurred for Owners' purposes or while the vessel is 98
off-hire (unless such items reasonably relate to any service given or distance made good and taken into account under 99
Clause 21 or 22); and provided further that any fuel used in connection with a general average sacrifice or expenditure 100
shall be paid for by Owners. 101

Rate of Hire	8. Subject as herein provided. Charterers shall pay for the use and hire of the vessel at the rate of per	102
	day, and pro rata for any part of a day, from the time and date of her delivery (local time) until the time and date of her	103
	redelivery (local time) to Owners.	104

Payment of Hire	9. Subject to Clause 3 (iii), payment of hire shall be made in immediately available funds to;	105

        Account 106
in   per calendar month in advance, less: 107
        (i) any hire paid which Charterers reasonably estimate to relate to off-hire periods, and 108
        (ii) any amounts disbursed on Owners" behalf, any advances and commission thereon, and charges 109
which are for Owners' account pursuant to any provision hereof, and 110
        (iii) any amounts due or reasonably estimated to become due to Charterers under Clause 3 (ii) or 111
24 hereof, 112
any such adjustments to be made at the due date for the next monthly payment after the facts have been ascertained. 113
Charterers shall not be responsible for any delay or error by Owners' bank in crediting Owners' account provided that 114
Charterers have made proper and timely payment. 115
    In default of such proper and timely payment. 116
    (a) Owners shall notify Charterers of such default and Charterers shall within seven days of receipt of such notice 117
pay to Owners the amount due including interest, failing which Owners may withdraw the vessel from the service of 118
Charterers without prejudice to any other rights Owners may have under this charter or otherwise; and 119
    (b) Interest on any amount due but not paid on the due date shall accrue from the day after that date up to and 120
including the day when payment is made, at a rate per annum which shall be 1% above the L\S. Prime Interest Rate as 121
published by the Chase Manhattan Bank in New York at 12.00 New York time on the due date, or if no such interest rate 122
is published on that day, the interest rate published on the next preceding day on which such a rate was so published, 123
computed on the basis of a 360 day year of twelve 30-day months, compounded semi-annually. 124

APPENDIX 21

3

Space Available to Charterers	10. The whole reach, burthen and decks of the vessel and any passenger accommodation (including Owners' suite) shall be at Charterers' disposal, reserving only proper and sufficient space for the vessels master, officers, crew, tackle, apparel, furniture, provisions and stores, provided that the weight of stores on hoard shall not, unless specially agreed, exceed tonnes at any time during the charter period.	125 126 127 128
Overtime	11. Overtime pay of the master, officers and crew in accordance with ship's articles shall he for Charterers account when incurred, as a result of complying with the request of Charterers or their agents, for loading, discharging, heating of cargo, bunkering or lank cleaning.	129 130 131
Instructions and Logs	12. Charterers shall from time to time give the master all requisite instructions and sailing directions, and he shall keep a full and correct log of the voyage or voyages, which Charterers or their agents may inspect as required. The master shall when required furnish Charterers or their agents with a true copy of such log and with properly completed loading and discharging port sheets and voyage reports for each voyage and other returns as Charterers may require. Charterers shall be entitled to take copies at Owners' expense of any such documents which are not provided by the master.	132 133 134 135 136
Bills of Lading	13. (a) The master (although appointed by Owners) shall be under the orders and direction of Charterers as regards employment of the vessel, agency and other arrangements, and shall sign bills of lading as Charterers or their agents may direct (subject always to Clauses 35(a) and 40) without prejudice to this charter. Charterers hereby indemnity Owners against all consequences or liabilities that may arise (i) from signing bills of lading in accordance with the directions of Charterers or their agents, to the extent that the terms of such bills of lading fail to conform to the requirements of this charter, or (except as provided in Clause 13(b)) from the master otherwise complying with Charterers' or their agents' orders; (ii) from any irregularities in papers supplied by Charterers or their agents (b) Notwithstanding the foregoing. Owners shall not be obliged to comply with any orders from Charterers to discharge all or part of the cargo (i) at any place other than that show n on the bill of lading and or (ii) without presentation of an original bill of lading unless they have received from Charterers both written confirmation of such orders and an indemnity in a form acceptable to Owners.	137 138 139 140 141 142 143 144 145 146 147 148 149 150
Conduct of Vessel's Personnel	14. If Charterers complain of the conduct of the master or any of the officers or crew. Owners shall immediately investigate the complaint. If the complaint proves to be well founded. Owners shall, without delay, make a change in the appointments and Owners shall in any event communicate the result of their investigations to Charterers as soon as possible.	151 152 153 154
Bunkers at Delivery and Redelivery	15. Charterers shall accept and pay for all bunkers on board at the time of delivery, and Owners shall on redelivery (whether it occurs at the end of the charter period or on the earlier termination of this charter) accept and pay for all bunkers remaining on board, at the then-current market prices at the port of delivery or redelivery, as the case may be. or if such prices are not available payment shall be at the then-current market prices at the nearest port at which such prices are available; provided that if delivery or redelivery does not take place in a port payment shall be at the price paid at the vessel's last port of bunkering before delivery or redelivery, as the case may be Owners shall give Charterers the use and benefit of any fuel contracts they may have in force from time to time, if so required by Charterers, provided suppliers agree.	155 156 157 158 159 160 161 162
Stevedores Pilots. Tugs	16. Stevedores when required shall be employed and paid by Charterers, but this shall not relieve Owners from responsibility at all times for proper stowage, which must be controlled by the master who shall keep a strict account of all cargo loaded and discharged. Owners hereby indemnify Charterers, their servants and agents against all losses, claims, responsibilities and liabilities arising in any way whatsoever from the employment of pilots, tugboats or stevedores, who although employed by Charterers shall be deemed to be the servants of and in the service of Owners and under their instructions (even if such pilots, tugboat personnel or stevedores are in fact the servants of Charterers their agents or any affiliated company); provided, however, that (i) the foregoing indemnity shall not exceed the amount to which Owners would have been entitled to limit their liability if they had themselves employed such pilots, tugboats or stevedores, and (ii) Charterers shall be liable for any damage to the vessel caused by or arising out of the use of stevedores, fair wear and tear excepted, to the extent that Owners are unable by the exercise of due diligence to obtain redress therefor from stevedores.	163 164 165 166 167 168 169 170 171 172 173 174
Supernumeraries	17. Charterers may send representatives in the vessel's available accommodation upon any voyage made under this charter. Owners finding provisions and all requisites as supplied to officers, except liquors. Charterers paying at the rate of per day for each representative while on board the vessel.	175 176 177
Sub-letting	18. Charterers may sub-let the vessel, but shall always remain responsible to Owners for due fulfilment of this charter.	178 179
Final Voyage	19. If when a payment of hire is due hereunder Charterers reasonably expect to redeliver the vessel before the next payment of hire would fall due, the hire to be paid shall be assessed on Charterers' reasonable estimate of the time necessary to complete Charterers' programme up to redelivery. and from which estimate Charterers may deduct amounts due or reasonably expected to become due for (i) disbursements on Owners' behalf or charges for Owners' account pursuant to any provision hereof, and (ii) bunkers on board at redelivery pursuant to Clause 15. Promptly after redelivery any overpayment shall be refunded by Owners or any underpayment made good by Charterers If at the time this charter would otherwise terminate in accordance with Clause 4 the vessel is on a ballast voyage to a port of redelivery or is upon a laden voyage. Charterers shall continue to have the use of the vessel at the same rate and conditions as stand herein for as long as necessary to complete such ballast voyage, or to complete such laden voyage and return to a port of redelivery as provided by this charter, as the case may be	180 181 182 183 184 185 186 187 188 189 190 191

4

| Loss of Vessel | 20. Should the vessel he lost, this charter shall terminate and hire shall cease at noon on the day of her loss; should the vessel he a constructive total loss, this charter shall terminate and hire shall cease at noon on the day on which the vessels underwriters agree that the vessel is a constructive total loss, should the vessel be missing. this charter shall terminate and hire shall cease at noon on the day on which she was last heard of. Any hire paid in advance and not earned shall be returned to Charterers and Owners shall reimburse Charterers for the value of the estimated quantity of bunkers on board at the time of termination, at the price paid by Charterers at the last bunkering port. | 192 193 194 195 196 197 198 |

Off-hire

21. (a) On each and every occasion that there is loss of time (whether by way of interruption in the vessel's service or, from reduction in the vessel's performance, or in any other manner) 199 200

(i) due to deficiency of personnel or stores; repairs; gas-freeing for repairs; time in and waiting to enter dry dock for repairs; breakdown (whether partial or total) of machinery, boilers or other parts of the vessel or her equipment (including without limitation tank coatings): overhaul, maintenance or survey; collision, stranding, accident or damage to the vessel; or any other similar cause preventing the efficient working of the vessel; and such loss continues for more than three consecutive hours (if resulting from interruption in the vessel's service) or cumulates to more than three hours (if resulting from partial loss of service); or 201 202 203 204 205 206

(ii) due to industrial action, refusal to sail, breach of orders or neglect of duty on the part of the master, officers or crew; or 207 208

(iii) for the purpose of obtaining medical advice or treatment for or landing any sick or injured person (other than a Charterers' representative carried under Clause 17 hereof) or for the purpose of landing the body of any person (other than a Charterers' representative), and such loss continues for more than three consecutive hours; or 209 210 211

(iv) due to any delay in quarantine arising from the master, officers or crew having had communication with the shore at any infected area without the written consent or instructions of Charterers or their agents, or to any detention by customs or other authorities caused by smuggling or other infraction of local law on the part of the master, officers, or crew; or 212 213 214 215

(v) due to detention of the vessel by authorities at home or abroad attributable to legal action against or breach of regulations by the vessel, the vessels owners, or Owners (unless brought about by the act or neglect of Charterers); then 216 217 218

without prejudice to Charterers' rights under Clause 3 or to any other rights of Charterers hereunder or otherwise the vessel shall be off-hire from the commencement of such loss of time until she is again ready and in an efficient state to resume her service from a position not less favourable to Charterers than that at which such loss of time commenced; provided, however, that any service given or distance made good by the vessel whilst off-hire shall be taken into account in assessing the amount to be deducted from hire. 219 220 221 222 223

(b) If the vessel fails to proceed at any guaranteed speed pursuant to Clause 24, and such failure arises wholly or partly from any of the causes set out in Clause 21(a) above, then the period for which the vessel shall be off-hire under this Clause 21 shall be the difference between 224 225 226

(i) the time the vessel would have required to perform the relevant service at such guaranteed speed, and 227

(ii) the time actually taken to perform such service (including any loss of time arising from interruption in the performance of such service). 228 229

For the avoidance of doubt, all time included under (ii) above shall be excluded from any computation under Clause 24. 230 231

(c) Further and without prejudice to the foregoing, in the event of the vessel deviating (which expression includes without limitation putting back, or putting into any port other than that to which she is bound under the instructions of Charterers) for any cause or purpose mentioned in Clause 21(a). the vessel shall be off-hire from the commencement of such deviation until the time when she is again ready and in an efficient slate to resume her service from a position not less favourable to Charterers than that at which the deviation commenced, provided, however, that any service given or distance made good by the vessel whilst so off-hire shall be taken into account in assessing the amount to be deducted from hire. If the vessel, for any cause or purpose mentioned in Clause 21 (a), puts into any port other than the port to which she is bound on the instructions of Charterers, the port charges, pilotage and other expenses at such port shall be borne by Owners. Should the vessel be driven into any port or anchorage by stress of weather hire shall continue to be due and payable during any time lost thereby. 232 233 234 235 236 237 238 239 240 241

(d) If the vessel's flag state becomes engaged in hostilities, and Charterers in consequence of such hostilities find it commercially impracticable to employ the vessel and have given Owners written notice thereof then from the date of receipt by Owners of such notice until the termination of such commercial impracticability the vessel shall be off-hire and Owners shall have the right to employ the vessel on their own account, 242 243 244 245

(e) Time during which the vessel is off-hire under this charter shall count as part of the charter period. 246

Periodical Drydocking

22. (a) Owners have the right and obligation to drydock the vessel at regular intervals of On each occasion Owners shall propose to Charterers a date on which they wish to drydock the vessel, not less than before such date, and Charterers shall offer a port for such periodical drydocking and shall take all reasonable steps to make the vessel available as near to such date as practicable. 247 248 249 250

Owners shall put the vessel in drydock at their expense as soon as practicable after Charterers place the vessel at Owners' disposal clear of cargo other than tank washings and residues. Owners shall be responsible for and pay for the disposal into reception facilities of such tank washings and residues and shall have the right to retain any monies received therefor, without prejudice to any claim for loss of cargo under any bill of lading or this charter. 251 252 253 254 255

(b) If a periodical drydocking is carried out in the port offered by Charterers (which must have suitable accommodation for the purpose and reception facilities for tank washings and residues), the vessel shall be off-hire from the time she arrives at such port until drydocking is completed and she is in even way read\ to resume Charterers' service and is at the position at which she went off-hire or a position no less favourable to Charterers, whichever she first attains. However. 256 257 258 259 260

(i) provided that Owners exercise due diligence in gas-freeing, any time lost in gas-freeing to the standard required for entry into drydock for cleaning and painting the hull shall not count as off-hire, whether lost on passage to the drydocking port or after arrival there (notwithstanding Clause 21 K and 261 262 263

APPENDIX 21

5

(ii) any additional time lost in further gas-freeing to meet the standard required for hot work or entry to cargo tanks shall count as off-hire, whether lost on passage to the drydocking port or after arrival there. 264 265

Any time which, but for sub-Clause (i) above, would be off-hire, shall not be included in any calculation under Clause 24. 266 267

The expenses of gas-freeing, including without limitation the cost of bunkers, shall be for Owners account. 268 269

(c) If Owners require the vessel, instead of proceeding to the offered port, to carry out periodical drydocking at a special port selected by them, the vessel shall be off-hire from the time when she is released to proceed to the special port until she next presents for loading in accordance with Charterers' instructions, provided, however, that Charterers shall credit Owners with the time which would have been taken on passage at the service speed had the vessel not proceeded to drydock, All fuel consumed shall be paid for by Owners but Charterers shall credit Owners with the value of the fuel which would have been used on such notional passage calculated at the guaranteed daily consumption for the service speed, and shall further credit Owners with any benefit they may gain in purchasing bunkers at the special port. 270 271 272 273 274 275 276 277

(d) Charterers shall, insofar as cleaning for periodical drydocking may have reduced the amount of tank-cleaning necessary to meet Charterers' requirements, credit Owners with the value of any bunkers which Charterers calculate to have been saved thereby, whether the vessel drydocks at an offered or a special port. 278 279 280

Ship Inspection	23. Charterers shall have the right at any time during the charter period to make such inspection of the vessel as they may consider necessary. This right may be exercised as often and at such intervals as Charterers in their absolute discretion may determine and whether the vessel is in port or on passage. Owners affording all necessary co-operation and accommodation on board provided, however.

281 282 283 284

(i) that neither the exercise nor the non-exercise. nor anything done or not done in the exercise or non-exercise. by Charterers of such right shall in any way reduce the master's or Owners' authority over, or responsibility to Charterers or third parties for. the vessel and every aspect of her operation, nor increase Charterers' responsbilities to Owners or third parties for the same; and 285 286 287 288

(ii) that Charterers shall not be liable for any act. neglect or default by themselves, their servants or agents in the exercise or non-exercise of the aforesaid right. 289 290

Detailed Description and performance	24. (a) Owners guarantee that the speed and consumption of the vessel shall be as follower:-

291

Average speed in knots	Maximum average bunker consumption		
	main propulsion -	auxiliaries	
	fuel oil diesel	oil fuel oil diesel oil	
Laden	tonnes	tonnes	

292 293 294 295

Ballast 296

The foregoing bunker consumptions are for all purposes except cargo heating and tank cleaning and shall be pro-rated between the speeds shown. 297 298

The service speed of the vessel is knots laden and knots in ballast and in the absence of Charterers' orders to the contrary the vessel shall proceed at the service speed. However if more than one laden and one ballast speed are shown in the table above Charterers shall have the right to order the vessel to steam at any speed within the range set out in the table (the "ordered speed"). 299 300 301 302

If the vessel is ordered to proceed at any speed other than the highest speed shown in the table, and the average speed actually attained by the vessel during the currency of such order exceeds such ordered speed plus 0.5 knots (the "maximum recognised speed"), then for the purpose of calculating any increase or decrease of hire under this Clause 24 the maximum recognised speed shall be used in place of the average speed actually attained. 303 304 305 306

For the purposes of this charter the "guaranteed speed" at any time shall be the then-current ordered speed or the service speed, as the case may be 307 308

The average speeds and bunker consumptions shall for the purposes of this Clause 24 be calculated by reference to the observed distance from pilot station to pilot station on all sea passages during each period stipulated in Clause 24 (c). but excluding any time during which the vessel is (or but for Clause 22 (b) (i) would be) off-hire and also excluding "Adverse Weather Periods", being (i) any periods during which reduction of speed is necessary for safety in congested waters or in poor visibility (ii) any days, noon to noon, when winds exceed force 8 on the Beaufort Scale for more than 12 hours. 309 310 311 312 313 314

6

(b) If during any year from the date on which the vessel enters service (anniversary to anniversary) the vessel falls below or exceeds the performance guaranteed in Clause 24(a) then if such shortfall or excess results 315 316

(i) from a reduction or an increase in the average speed of the vessel, compared to the speed guaranteed in Clause 24(a), then an amount equal to the value at the hire rate of the time so lost or gained, as the case may be, shall be deducted from or added to the hire paid; 317 318 319

(ii) from an increase or a decrease in the total bunkers consumed, compared to the total bunkers which would have been consumed had the vessel performed as guaranteed in Clause 24(a), an amount equivalent to the value of the additional bunkers consumed or the bunkers saved, as the case may be, based on the average price paid by Charterers for the vessel's bunkers in such period, shall be deducted from or added to the hire paid. 320 321 322 323

The addition to or deduction from hire so calculated for laden and ballast mileage respectively shall be adjusted to take into account the mileage steamed in each such condition during Adverse Weather Periods, by dividing such addition or deduction by the number of miles over which the performance has been calculated and multiplying by the same number of miles plus the miles steamed during the Adverse Weather Periods, in order to establish the total addition to or deduction from hire to be made for such period. 324 325 326 327 328

Reduction of hire under the foregoing sub-Clause (b) shall be without prejudice to any other remedy available to Charterers. 329 330

(c) Calculations under this Clause 24 shall be made for the yearly periods terminating on each successive anniversary of the date on which the vessel enters service, and for the period between the last such anniversary and the date of termination of this charter if less than a year. Claims in respect of reduction of hire arising under this Clause during the final year or part year of the charter period shall in the first instance be settled in accordance with Charterers* estimate made two months before the end of the charter period. Any necessary adjustment after this charter terminates shall be made by payment by Owners to Charterers or by Charterers to Owners as the case may require. 331 332 333 334 335 336 337

Payments in respect of increase of hire arising under this Clause shall be made promptly after receipt by Charterers of all the information necessary to calculate such increase. 338 339

Salvage	25. Subject to the provisions of Clause 21 hereof, all loss of time and all expenses (excluding any damage to or loss of the vessel or tortious liabilities to third parties) incurred in saving or attempting to save life or in successful or unsuccessful attempts at salvage shall be borne equally by Owners and Charterers provided that Charterers shall not be liable to contribute towards any salvage payable by Owners arising in any way out of services rendered under this Clause 25.	340 341 342 343 344

All salvage and all proceeds from derelicts shall be divided equally between Owners and Charterers after deducting the master's, officers' and crew's share. 345 346

Lien	26. Owners shall have a lien upon all cargoes and all freights. Sub-freights and demurrage for any amounts due under this charter; and Charterers shall have a lien on the vessel for all monies paid in advance and not earned, and for all claims for damages arising from any breach by Owners of this charter.	347 348 349

Exceptions	27. (a) The vessel, her master and Owners shall not, unless otherwise in this charter expressly provided, be liable for any loss or damage or delay or failure arising or resulting from any act, neglect or default of the master, pilots, manners or other servants of Owners in the navigation or management of the vessel; fire, unless caused by the actual fault or privity of Owners; collision or stranding; dangers and accidents of the sea; explosion, bursting of boilers, breakage of shafts or any latent defect in hull, equipment or machinery, provided, however that Clauses 1, 2, 3 and 24 hereof shall be unaffected by the foregoing. Further, neither the vessel, her master or Owners, nor Charterers shall, unless otherwise in this charter expressly provided, be liable for any loss or damage or delay or failure in performance hereunder arising or resulting from act of God, act of war, seizure under legal process, quarantine restrictions, strikes, lock-outs, riots, restraints of labour, civil commotions or arrest or restraint of princes, rulers or people.	350 351 352 353 354 355 356 357 358 359

(b) The vessel shall have liberty to sail with or without pilots, to tow or go to the assistance of vessels in distress and to deviate for the purpose of saving life or property. 360 361

(c) Clause 27(a) shall not apply to or affect any liability of Owners or the vessel or any other relevant person in respect of 362 363

(i) loss or damage caused to any berth, jetty, dock, dolphin, buoy, mooring line, pipe or crane or other works or equipment whatsoever at or near any place to which the vessel may proceed under this charter, whether or not such works or equipment belong to Charterers, or 364 365 366

(ii) any claim (whether brought by Charterers or any other person) arising out of any loss of or damage to or in connection with cargo. All such claims shall be subject to the Hague-Visby Rules or the Hague Rules, as the case may be, which ought pursuant to Clause 38 hereof to have been incorporated in the relevant bill of lading (whether or not such Rules were so incorporated} or, if no such bill of lading is issued, to the Hague-Visby Rules. 367 368 369 370

(d) In particular and without limitation, the foregoing subsections (a) and (b) of this Clause shall not apply to or in any way affect any provision in this charter relating to off-hire or to reduction of hire. 371 372

Injurious Cargoes	28. No acids, explosives or cargoes injurious to the vessel shall be shipped and without prejudice to the foregoing any damage to the vessel caused by the shipment of any such cargo, and the time taken to repair such damage, shall be for Charterers'' account. No voyage shall be undertaken, nor any goods or cargoes loaded, that would expose the vessel to capture or seizure by rulers or governments.	373 374 375 376

Grade of Bunkers	29. Charterers shall supply marine diesel oil/fuel oil with a maximum viscosity of Centistokes at 50 degrees Centigrade ACGFO for main propulsion and diesel oil/ACGFO for the auxiliaries. If Owners require the vessel to be supplied with more expensive bunkers they shall be liable for the extra cost thereof	377 378 379

Charterers warrant that all bunkers provided by them in accordance herewith shall be of a qualm complying with the International Marine Bunker Supply Terms and Conditions of Shell International Trading Company and with its specification for marine fuels as amended from time to time. 380 381 382

Disbursements	30. Should the master require advances for ordinary disbursements at any port. Charterers or their agents shall make such advances to him, in consideration of which Owners shall pay a commission of two and a half per cent, and all such advances and commission shall be deducted from hire.	383 384 385

APPENDIX 21

7

Laying-up	31. Charterers shall have the option, alter consultation with Owners, of requiring Owners to lay up the vessel at a safe place nominated by Charterers, in which ease the hue provided for under this charter shall be adjusted to reflect any net increases in expenditure reasonably incurred or any net saving which should reasonably be made by Owners as a result of such lay-up. Charterers may exercise the said option am number of times during the charter period.	386 387 388 389
Requisition	32. Should the vessel be requisitioned by any government, de facto or de jure, during the period of this charter, the vessel shall be off-hire during the period of such requisition, and any hire paid by such government in respect of such requisition period shall be for Owners' account. Any such requisition period shall count as part of the charter period.	390 391 392 393
Outbreak of War	33. If war or hostilities break out between any two or more of the following countries; U.S.A., U.S.S.R., P.R. C., U.K., Netherlands-both Owners and Charterers shall have the right to cancel this charter.	394 395
Additional War Expenses	34. If the vessel is ordered to trade in areas where there is war (de facto or de jure) or threat of war. Charterers shall reimburse Owners for any additional insurance premia, crew bonuses and other expenses which are reasonably incurred by Owners as a consequence of such orders, provided that Charterers are given notice of such expenses as soon as practicable and in any event before such expenses are incurred, and provided further that Owners obtain from their insurers a waiver of any subrogated rights against Charterers in respect of any claims by Owners under their war risk insurance arising out of compliance with such orders.	396 397 398 399 400 401
War Risks	35. (a) The master shall not be required or bound to sign bills of lading for any place which in his in Owners' reasonable opinion is dangerous or impossible for the vessel to enter or reach owing to any blockade, war, hostilities, warlike operations, civil war, civil commotions or revolutions.	402 403 404
	(b) If in the reasonable opinion of the master or Owners it becomes, for any of the reasons set out in Clause 35(a) or by the operation of international law, dangerous, impossible or prohibited for the vessel to reach or enter, or to load or discharge cargo at, any place to which the vessel has been ordered pursuant to this charter (a "place of peril"), then Charterers or their agents shall be immediately notified by telex or radio messages, and Charterers shall thereupon have the right to order the cargo, or such part of it as may be affected, to be loaded or discharged, as the case may be, al any other place within the trading limits of this charter (provided such other place is not itself a place of peril). If any place of discharge is or becomes a place of peril, and no orders have been received from Charterers or their agents within 48 hours after dispatch of such messages, then Owners shall be at liberty to discharge the cargo or such part of it as may be affected at any place which they or the master may in their or his discretion select within the trading limits of this charter and such discharge shall be deemed to be due fulfilment of Owners' obligations under this charter so far as cargo so discharged is concerned.	405 406 407 408 409 410 411 412 413 414 415
	(c) The vessel shall have liberty to comply with any directions or recommendations as to departure. arrival, routes, ports of call, stoppages, destinations, zones, waters, delivery or in any other wise whatsoever given by the government of the state under whose flag the vessel sails or any other government or local authority or by any person or body acting or purporting to act as or with the authority of any such government or local authority including any dc facto government or local authority or by any person or body acting or purporting to act as or with the authority of any such government or local authority or by any committee or person having under the terms of the war risks insurance on the vessel the right to give any such directions or recommendations. If by reason of or in compliance with any such directions or recommendations anything is done or is not done, such shall not be deemed a deviation.	416 417 418 419 420 421 422 423
	If by reason of or in compliance with any such direction or recommendation the vessel does not proceed to any place of discharge to which she has been ordered pursuant TO this charter, the vessel may proceed to any place which the master or Owners in his or their discretion select and there discharge the cargo or such part of it as may be affected. Such discharge shall he deemed to be due fulfilment of Owners obligations under this charter so far as cargo so discharged is concerned.	424 425 426 427 428
	Charterers shall procure that all bills of lading issued under this charter shall contain the Chamber of Shipping War Risks Clause 1952.	429 430
Both to Blame determined Collision Clause	36. If the liability for any collision in which the vessel is involved while performing this charter falls to be in accordance with the laws of the United States of America, the following provision shall apply:	431 432
	"If the ship comes into collision with another ship as a result of the negligence of the other ship and any act, neglect or default of the master, mariner, pilot or the servants of the carrier in the navigation or in the management of the ship, the owners of the cargo carried hereunder will indemnify the carrier against all loss, or liability to the other or non-carrying ship or her owners in so far as such loss or liability represents loss of, or damage to, or any claim whatsoever of the owners of the said cargo, paid or payable by the other or non-carrying ship or her owners to the owners of the said cargo and set off, recouped or recovered by the other or non-carrying ship or her owners as part of their claim against the carrying ship or carrier."	433 434 435 436 437 438 439
	"The foregoing provisions shall also apply where the owners, operators or those in charge of any ship or ships or objects other than, or in addition to the colliding ships or objects are at fault in respect of a collision or contact."	440 441 442
	Charterers shall procure that all bills of lading issued under this charter shall contain a provision in the foregoing terms to be applicable where the liability for any collision in which the vessel is involved falls to be determined in accordance with the laws of the United States of America.	443 444 445
New Jason Clause	37. General average contributions shall be payable according to the York/Antwerp Rules, 1974, and shall be adjusted in London in accordance with English law and practice but should adjustment be made in accordance with the law and practice of the United States of America, the following provision shall apply:	446 447 448
	"In the event of accident, danger, damage or disaster before or after the commencement of the voyage, resulting from any cause whatsoever, whether due to negligence or not, for which, or for the consequence of which, the carrier is not responsible by statute, contract or otherwise, the cargo, shippers, consignees or owners of the cargo shall contribute with the carrier in general average to the payment of am sacrifices, losses or expenses of a general average nature that may be made or incurred and shall pay salvage and special charges incurred in respect of the cargo."	449 450 451 452 453 454
	"If a salving ship is owned or operated by the carrier, salvage shall he paid for as fully as if the said salving ship or ships belonged to strangers. Such deposit as the carrier or his agents may deem sufficient to cover	455 456

APPENDIX 21

8

the estimated contribution of the cargo and any salvage and special charges thereon shall, if required, be made by the 457
cargo, shippers, consignees or owners of the cargo to the carrier before delivery." 458

Charterers shall procure that all bills of lading issued under this charter shall contain a provision in the foregoing 459
terms, to be applicable where adjustment of general average is made in accordance with the laws and practice of the 460
United States of America. 461

Clause Paramount 38. Charterers shall procure that all bills of lading issued pursuant to this charter shall contain the following 462
clause: 463

"(1) Subject to sub-clause (2) hereof, this bill of lading shall be governed by, and have effect subject to. the 464
rules contained in the International Convention for the Unification of Certain Rules relating to Bills of Lading signed 465
at Brussels on 25th August 1924 (hereafter the "Hague Rules") as amended by the Protocol signed at Brussels on 466
23rd February 1968 (hereafter the "Hague-Visby Rules"). Nothing contained herein shall be deemed to be either a 467
surrender by the carrier of any of his rights or immunities or any increase of any of his responsibilities or liabilities under 468
the Hague-Visby Rules." 469

"(2) If there is governing legislation which applies the Hague Rules compulsorily to this bill of lading. to the 470
exclusion of the Hague-Visby Rules, then this bill of lading shall have effect subject to the Hague Rules Nothing herein 471
contained shall be deemed to be either a surrender by the carrier of any of his rights or immunities or an increase of any 472
of his responsibilities or liabilities under the Hague Rules." 473

"(3) If any term of this bill of lading is repugnant to the Hague-Visby Rules, or Hague Rules if applicable, such 474
term shall be void to that extent but no further." 475

"(4) Nothing in this bill of lading shall be construed as in any way restricting, excluding or waiving the right of 476
any relevant party or person to limit his liability under any available legislation and/or law." 477

TOVALOP 39. Owners warrant that the vessel is: 478
(i) a tanker in TOVALOP and 479
(ii) properly entered in   P&I Club 480

and will so remain during the currency of this charter. 481

When an escape or discharge of Oil occurs from the vessel and causes or threatens to cause Pollution Damage, 482
or when there is the threat of an escape or discharge of Oil (i.e. a grave and imminent danger of the escape or discharge of 483
Oil which, if it occurred, would create a serious danger of Pollution Damage, whether or not an escape or discharge in fact 484
subsequently occurs), then Charterers may, at their option, upon notice to Owners or master, undertake such measures as 485
are reasonably necessary to prevent or minimise such Pollution Damage or to remove the Threat, unless Owners promptly 486
undertake the same. Charterers shall keep Owners advised of the nature and result of any such measures taken by them 487
and, if time permits, the nature of the measures intended to be taken by them. Any of the aforementioned measures taken 488
by Charterers shall be deemed taken on Owners' authority as Owners' agent, and shall be at Owners' expense except to 489
the extent that: 490

(1) any such escape or discharge or Threat was caused or contributed to by Charterers, or 491

(2) by reason of the exceptions set out in Article III, paragraph 2, of the 1969 International Convention on Civil 492
Liability for Oil Pollution Damage. Owners are or, had the said Convention applied to such escape or discharge or to the 493
Threat, would have been exempt from liability for the same, or 494

(3) the cost of such measures together with all other liabilities, costs and expenses of Owners arising out of or 495
in connection with such escape or discharge or Threat exceeds one hundred and sixty United States Dollars (US $160) 496
per ton of the vessel's Tonnage or sixteen million eight hundred thousand United States Dollars (US $16,800,000), 497
whichever is the lesser, save and insofar as Owners shall be entitled to recover such excess under either the 1971 498
International Convention on the Establishment of an International Fund for Compensation for Oil Pollution Damage 499
or under CRISTAL. 500

PROVIDED ALWAYS that if Owners in their absolute discretion consider said measures should be 501
discontinued. Owners shall so notify Charterers and thereafter Charterers shall have no right to continue said 502
measures under the provisions of this Clause 39 and all further liability to Charterers under this Clause 39 shall 503
thereupon cease. 504

The above provisions are not in derogation of such other rights as Charterers or Owners may have under this 505
charter or may otherwise have or acquire by law or any International Convention or TOVALOP. 506

The term "TOVALOP" means the Tanker Owners' Voluntary Agreement Concerning Liability for Oil 507
Pollution dated 7th January 1969, as amended from time to time, and the term "CRISTAL" means the Contract Regarding 508
an Interim Supplement to Tanker Liability for Oil Pollution dated 14th January 1971, as amended from time to time. The 509
terms "Oil", "Pollution Damage", and "Tonnage" shall for the purposes of this Clause 39 have the meanings ascribed 510
to them in TOVALOP. 511

Export Restriction 40. The master shall not be required or bound to sign bills of lading for the carriage of cargo to any place to which 512
export of such cargo is prohibited under the laws, rules or regulations of the country in which the cargo was produced 513
and/or shipped. 514

Charterers shall procure that all bills of lading issued under this charter shall contain the following 515
clause: 516

"If any laws rules or regulations applied by the government of the country in which the cargo was produced 517
and or shipped, or any relevant agency thereof, impose a prohibition on export of the cargo to the place of discharge 518
designated in or ordered under this bill of lading, carriers shall be entitled to require cargo owners forthwith to 519
nominate an alternative discharge place for the discharge of the Cargo, or such part of it as may be affected, which 520
alternative place shall not be subject to the prohibition, and carriers shall be entitled to accept orders from cargo 521
owners to proceed to and discharge at such alternative place. If cargo owners fail to nominate an alternative place 522
within 72 hours after they or their agents have received from carriers notice of such prohibition, carriers shall be 523
at liberty to discharge the cargo or such part of it as may be affected by the prohibition at am safe place on which 524
they or the master may in their or his absolute discretion decide and which is not subject to the prohibition, and 525
such discharge shall constitute due performance of the contract contained in this bill of lading so far as the cargo so 526
discharged is concerned". 527

The foregoing provision shall apply mutatis mutandis to this charter, the references to a bill of lading being 528
deemed to be references to this charter. 529

APPENDIX 21

9

Law and Litigation	41. (a) This charter shall be construed and the relations between the parties determined in accordance with the laws	530
	of England.	531
	(b) Any dispute arising under this charter shall be decided by the English Courts to whose jurisdiction the parties	532
	hereby agree.	533
	(c) Notwithstanding the foregoing, but without prejudice to any party's right to arrest or maintain the arrest of	534
	any maritime properly, either party may, by giving written notice of election to the other party, elect to have any such	535
	dispute referred to the arbitration of a single arbitrator in London in accordance with the provisions of the Arbitration	536
	Act 1950, or any statutory modification or re-enactment thereof for the time being in force.	537
	(i) A party shall lose its right to make such an election only if:	538
	(a) it receives from the other party a written notice of dispute which -	539
	(1) slates expressly that a dispute has arisen out of this charter;	540
	(2) specifies the nature of the dispute; and	541
	(3) refers expressly to this clause 41(c)	542
	and	543
	(b) it fails to give notice of election to have the dispute referred to arbitration not later than 30 days from	544
	the date of receipt of such notice of dispute.	545
	(ii) The parties hereby agree that either party may -	546
	(a) appeal to the High Court on any question of law arising out of an award;	547
	(b) apply to the High Court for an order that the arbitrator state the reasons for his award;	548
	(c) give notice to the arbitrator that a reasoned award is required; and	549
	(d) apply to the High Court to determine any question of law arising in the course of the reference.	550
	(d) It shall be a condition precedent to the right of any party to a stay of any legal proceedings in which maritime	551
	property has been, or may be, arrested in connection with a dispute under this charter, that party furnishes to the other	552
	party security to which that other party would have been entitled in such legal proceedings in the absence of a stay.	553
Construction	42. The side headings have been included in this charter for convenience of reference and shall in no way affect	554
	the construction hereof.	555

APPENDIX 22

1. Agents		STANDARD STATEMENT OF FACTS (OIL AND CHEMICAL TANK VESSELS) (SHORT FORM) RECOMMENDED BY THE BALTIC AND INTERNATIONAL MARITIME CONFERENCE (BIMCO) AND THE FEDERATION OF NATIONAL ASSOCIATIONS OF SHIP BROKERS AND AGENTS (FONASBA)	
2. Vessel's name		3. Port or Place	
4. Owners/Disponent Owners		5. Vessel moorad	
		6. Hoses connected (load.)	7. Loading commenced
8. Cargo (also indicate possible details as to slops)		9. Loading completed	10. Hoses disconnected (load.)
		11. Hoses connected (disch.)	12. Discharging commenced
13. Charter Party *		14. Discharging completed	15. Hoses disconnected (disch.)
16. Bill of Lading quantity	17. Qutturn quantity	18. Cargo documents on board	19. Vessel sailed *
20. Vessel arrived at anchorage	21. Pilot on board	22. Draft on arrival (fore and aft)	23. Draft on sailing (fore and aft)
24. Notice of readiness tendered		25. Vessel arrived from	26. Vessel sailed to *
27. Next tide available	28. Weighed anchor	29.	
30. Free pratique given		31.	
32. Deballasting commenced	33. Deballasting completed	34.	
35. Ballasting commenced	36. Ballasting completed	37.	
38. Tanks inspected	39. Tanks passed	40.	

DETAILS OF DAILY WORKING *

Data	Day	Hours worked		Hours stopped			Quantity load./disch.		Remarks*
		From	to	days	hours	minutes			

General remarks (state reasons and duration of delays, such as slow pumping, axcess back pressure, etc.) *

Place and date	Name and signature (Master)*
Name and signature (Agents)*	Name and signature (for the Charterers/Shippers/Receivers)*

* See Explanatory Notes overleaf for filling in the boxes

Published by The Baltic and International Maritime Conference (BIMCO), Copenhagen

Printed and sold by Fr. G. Knudtzons Bogtrykkeri A/S, 55 Toldbodgade, Dk-1253 Copenhagen K, Telefax +4533931184, by authority of BIMCO

APPENDIX 22

INSTRUCTIONS FOR FILLING IN THE BOXES

General

It is recommended to fill in the boxes with a short text. When it is a matter of figures to be inserted as is the case in most of the boxes, this should be done as follows:

```
7. Loading commenced
1975-03-15-0800
```

the figures being mentioned in the following order: year–month–date–time.

Boxes Calling for Special Attention

Charter Party*:
Insert name and date of charter, for instance, "Intertankvoy" dated 1975-03-01.

Vessel Sailed*:
Insert date and hour of departure.

Vessel Sailed to*:
State destination.

Details of Daily Working*:
Insert day-by-day figures and indicate in the vertical column marked "Remarks*" all relevant details as to reasons for stoppages such as breakdown of pumps, strikes, shortage of cargo, etc. Moreover, in this box should be stated reasons and duration of delays before berthing, during berthing, between moored and commenced loading, during loading, between completed loading and leaving berth and after leaving berth. Same applies to discharging.

General Remarks*:
This box should be used for insertion of such general observations which are not covered in any of the boxes provided for in the first main group of boxes, for instance, delays on account of slow pumping, excess back pressure, or other general observations.

Signatures*:
It is of importance that the boxes provided for signatures are duly signed by the parties concerned.

APPENDIX 23

TIME SHEET

AGENTS: PORT:

VESSEL'S NAME: OWNERS/DISPONENT OWNERS:

VESSEL ARRIVED ROADS: NOR TENDERED:

VESSEL BERTHED:

LOADING COMMENCED: LOADING COMPLETED:

DISCHARGING COMMENCED: DISCHARGING COMPLETED:

VESSEL SAILED:

CARGO COMMODITY/QUANTITY:

LA YTIME COMPUTATION

TIME WORKED				LAYTIME USED	TIME ON DEMURRAGE	
DATE	DAY	FROM	TO	DAYS HRS MIN	DAYS HRS MIN	REMARKS

APPENDIX 24

LAYTIME, WORKED EXAMPLE
WAYFARER

LOAD PORT – BONNY

			LAYTIME USED	
Sat 23 Apr	0300	NOR tendered	(notice time comm)	
	0900	Laytime comm	– – – – – – – –	
	2400		15 h	00 m
Sun 24 Apr	1500	Anchor A.W. proceed to berth (Laytime stops)	15 h	00 m
	1830	ALL FAST Laytime comm		
	1900	Deballasting comm (Laytime stops)	00 h	30 m
	2130	Deballasting comp Laytime comm		
	2400		02 h	30 m
Mon 25Apr	2400		24 h	00 m
Tue 26 Apr	0030	Hoses disconnected (Laytime stops)	00 h	30 m
		Load Port Laytime used	**57 h**	**30 m**

DISCHARGE PORT – FIUMICINO

Wed 11 May	1415	Arr Anchor NOR tendered (notice time comm)		
	2015	Laytime starts		
	2400		03 h	45 m
Thur 12 May	0600	Port closed (Laytime stops)	06 h	00 m
Fri 13 May	1200	Port opens. Laytime comm	–	–
	2400		12 h	00 m
Sat 14 May	0815	Anchor A.W. Proceed to berth (Laytime stops)	08 h	15 m
	0945	All Fast, Laytime starts		
	2400		14 h	15 m
Sun 15 May	0100	Pump failure (Laytime stops)	01 h	00 m
	0500	Pump repaired (Laytime starts		
	1045	Hoses disconnected	05 h	45 m
		Discharge port Laytime used	**51 h**	**00 m**
+		Load Port	57 h	30 m
		Total time used	108 h	30 m
		Laytime allowed	72 h	00 m
		Time on Demurrage	**36 h**	**30 m**

DEMURRAGE EARNED = $12,000 × 36.5 h = **$18,250**

APPENDIX 25

SPECIMEN CLAUSE

Note: Any measured liquid left on board a tanker after completion of discharge is referred to as ROB (Remaining on board) and that same volume when it is retained or board is called OBQ (On board quantity) prior to commencing to load. Both are reflected accordingly in the respective ship's ullage reports which the owner uses to protect himself against cargo claims which may have been caused by events ashore at either end of the voyage.

SHELL CARGO RETENTION CLAUSE

If on completion of discharge any liquid cargo of a pumpable nature remains on board (the presence and quantity of such cargo having been established by application of the wedge formula in respect of any tank the contents of which do not reach the forward bulkhead, by an independent surveyor, appointed by the charterers and paid jointly by the Owners and Charterers), Charterers shall have the right to deduct from freight an amount equal to the FOB loading port value of such cargo, cargo insurance plus freight thereon; provided, however, that any action or lack of action hereunder shall without prejudice to any other rights or obligations of Charterers, under this charter or otherwise, and provided further that if Owners are liable to any third party in respect of any failure to discharge such pumpable cargo, or any part thereof, Charterers shall indemnify Owners against such liability up to the total amount deducted under this clause.

<u>IN-TRANSIT LOSS CLAUSE</u>

In addition to any other rights which Charterers may have, Owners will be responsible for the full amount of any in-transit loss if in-transit loss exceeds 0.3 per cent and Charterers shall have the right to deduct from freight an amount equal to the FOB port of loading value of such cargo plus freight and insurance due with respect thereto. In-transit loss is defined as the difference between nett vessel volume after loading at the loading port and before unloading at the discharge port.

APPENDIX 26

LOADLINES AND TONNAGE

When describing a ship it is usual to start that she is 'so many tons' and leave it at that. In fact in shipping the word 'ton' has many different meanings.

IMP Tonnage

In July 1982 the current international system of measurement for ships came into force, although it was only in 1996 that it applied to all ships. The Gross Tonnage (GT) is roughly the volume of all the enclosed spaces in the ship measured in cubic metres and divided by a factor which varies according to the type of ship. Net Tonnage (NT) is the Gross after certain deductions have been made, mainly the bridge, engine room, radio room crew accommodation etc. leaving only those spaces concerned with the carrying of the cargo.

Gross is a measure of the internal volume of a ship and most safety regulations are based on this figure. Net is a measure of the ship's cargo volume or earning capacity and therefore harbour and canal dues are usually based on this figure.

Suez and Panama Canal Tonnage

Both these authorities have their own rules for the measurement of gross and net tonnage and ships using the canals are charged on these tonnages. Suez tonnage calculations are based on the Danube rules.

Bill of Lading (B/L) Tonnes

This is the tonnage of cargo loaded as stated on the Bill of Lading and it is on this figure that the freight is paid.

Displacement

The displacement of a ship is the weight of the water she displaces at any given draft. It is obtained by calculating the underwater volume of the ship and multiplying it by the density of salt water. It is thus the total weight of the ship at that draft.

Light Displacement

This is the weight of the ship empty of all contents thus the weight of the structure, fittings, engines, auxiliaries and lubricating oils.

Deadweight

This is the difference between the light and loaded displacement and represents the weight that the ship can carry. Tankers and bulk carriers are described in deadweight because this is the basis on which they are chartered.

APPENDIX 26

Loadlines

Before they are allowed to proceed to sea, all ships are required to be surveyed and marked with a loadline. Governments usually delegate the function of surveying and assigning the loadline to an assigning authority such as Lloyd's Register. The assigning authority will calculate the ship's summer freeboard, which is the distance between the deckline and the top of the line through the loadline disc (see diagram).

The tropical and winter lines are placed 1/48th of the ship's summer draft above and below the summer mark respectively.

The fresh water lines are placed above the summer line so that a ship floating to this line in fresh water would rise to her summer or tropical lines when sailing from fresh to salt water.

The Winter North Atlantic mark only appears on ships less than 100 m in length and is placed 50 mm below the winter line.

Immersion Calculations

To calculate the deadweights for a ship the Tonnes per Centimetre Immersion (TPC) (or on some older vessels Tons per Inch Immersion (TPI)) must be obtained from the ship's particulars. This is the additional weight in tonnes required to sink the ship 1 centimetre. The value of 1/48th of the summer draft is obtained and multiplied by the TCP (or TPI) in order to obtain the tonnage difference.

Note: Some ships are measured in both metric and imperial units, it is useful therefore that anyone concerned with ship operations is familiar with both systems.

Example: The mt Becasse has a Summer Deadweight of 307,134 tonnes. At this deadweight her Summer Draft is 22.427 m and her TPC at that draft is 168 tonnes. The consumption is 100 tonnes per day at a speed of 14.0 knots.

To find her tropical and winter deadweights and drafts take 1/48th of the summer draft.
Correction to summer draft is 22.427 m/48 = 0.467 m.

To find the tropical and winter deadweights the draft correction is multiplied by the TPC:
46.7 cm × 168 tonnes = 7,845.6 say 7,846 mt

Therefore Tropical Deadweight = 307,134 + 7,846 = 314,980 mt at a draft of 22.427 m + 0.467 m
= 22.894 m

APPENDIX 26

Similarly Winter Deadweight is = 307,134 − 7,846 = 299,288 mt at a draft of 22.427 m − 0.467 = 21.96 m

Loadline Chart

The chart indicates the different loadline zones, some are permanent and some are seasonal. A ship is required under the International Loadline Rules to be loaded to her correct loadline when she enters a zone at sea as well as when proceeding to sea after loading a cargo.

Boundary Ports these are ports on the boundary between two zones. A ship arriving at a boundary port must be loaded for the zone which she passes through on the way to the port. When leaving port the ship must be loaded for the zone which she will enter after sailing.

The Loading Calculation

It is important that a ship is loaded in such a way that she is not overloaded at any stage of the voyage and is on the correct draft when crossing a zone boundary. One such method of calculating the tonnage is given below.

Example: The mt Becasse is to load a full cargo of crude oil at Ras Tanura for discharge UK Cont, intention Rotterdam via the Cape of Good Hope. She is due to arrive at the loading port at the end of October. In addition the particulars taken from Clarkson's register the following are assumed to apply for the voyage.

Water, stores and 'constants' 1000 tons
Allow 5 days reserve of fuel throughout the voyage.

Note: The ship was built in 2000 and a speed of 14 knots is assumed.

'Constants' can be thought of as the difference between the theoretical cargo that a ship can load and the actual amount of cargo as measured from her draft marks. In practice the constants increase as the ship grows older and represents the unpumpable ballast water/ bunkers, spare parts carried as well as water, stores/paint and rubbish that accumulates on a ship.

Note: As it is not possible to forecast what problems or delay might arise during a voyage it is usual to calculate the amount of fuel required for a voyage and then add an additional amount for a reserve. In this example a reserve of 5 days is used.

By examining the loadline chart it can be seen that it will be winter when the ship reaches Cape Torinana, off northern Spain so the ship will be required to be on her winter marks when she reaches this point. The distance can be taken from any set of distance tables, including the Worldscale book.

APPENDIX 26

Distance from Cape Torinana to Rotterdam = 802 miles.

Remember in addition to cargo the deadweight (dwt) includes the fuel, water, stores and constants; these must therefore be deducted from the deadweight to obtain the deadweight cargo capacity (dwcc). The next step, therefore, is to calculate the fuel required for the voyage, not forgetting any reserves which are considered necessary.

Taken from Worldscale, the round trip distance from Ras Tanura to Rotterdam via the Cape of Good Hope is (748+21,592)/2 = 11,170 miles.

Assuming a speed of 14.0 knots (1 knot is a nautical mile per hour, this is slightly faster than a statute mile per hour) this will take 798 hours or 33.25 days. The fuel required is therefore:

$$33.25 \times 100 + 5 \times 100 \ (reserve) = 3,825 \ mt.$$

From Ras Tanura to Cape Torinana is (11,170 – 802) 10,368 miles and at 14 knots will take say, 31 days, this will require 31 × 100 tons of fuel = 3,100 mt. Therefore the maximum deadweight leaving Ras Tanura can be calculated as follows:

299,288 mt (winter deadweight which she must be at Cape Torinana) + 3,100 (the fuel used on passage from Ras Tanura to Cape Torinana) = 302,388 mt.

You could ask how will anyone in authority know what the ship's draft was at the time when she was out at sea and far from the eagle eyes of any inspector? It is an easy matter for an inspector in Rotterdam to read the draft of the ship on arrival and after allowing for the fuel consumed between Rotterdam and Cape Torinana check whether or not she was overloaded.

To complete the exercise we can calculate the dwcc when leaving Ras Tanura. She will have on board 1,000 tons of constants plus 3,825 mt of fuel, hence she can load 297,562 mt of cargo (302,388 – (1,000 + 3,825).

This calculation has been simplified to show the main points that have to be taken into consideration when calculating the dwcc. In practice the exact quantities of fuel and stores will only be known by the master at the loading terminal, and the speed can only be an estimate.

APPENDIX 27

UKDC Publications: Soundings – Issue 4 2004

Issue 4 2004

ISPS Code – Legal Implications for Charterparties

The International Ship and Port Facility Security (ISPS) Code came into force on 1st July 2004. In the enhanced 'security culture' in which we now live, the ISPS Code is aimed at protecting ships, crews, ports and port facilities from terrorist activities or attacks. It affects all passenger carrying and other ships over 500gt trading internationally. It imposes stringent security measures on those ships and the ports to which they trade.

Much has already been written about the enormous practical challenge the ISPS Code presents to owners and ports alike. The costs of compliance with the ISPS Code have also been highlighted by the media and at key industry conferences. The ISPS Code, however, also has important legal implications for owners and charterers alike to consider

This briefing is intended to serve as an aide memoire for Members on the key ISPS issues they should address when fixing ships.

Owners' obligations

Ships will not be able to trade internationally without the necessary security certificates. A ship that fails to comply with the ISPS Code, for example, in respect of the security management, or competence of the crew, will likely be found unseaworthy. At the very least, lack of ISPS compliance will be evidence of a lack of due diligence to make the ship seaworthy. The owner will be liable for the consequences. A ship without IS certification will also be at the mercy of the governmental authority tasked with enforcement. This could lead to costly delays and ultimately termination of the charterparty.

Additional costs – Who will pay?

Owners of ships that fall within the ISPS Code will already have invested significant sums of money and time to ensure compliance with the ISPS Code. However, the day-to-day operation of these anti-terror safeguards also affects the cost of loading, carriage and discharge Not only will there be additional carriage requirements, but extra time will be needed in port, for example, for getting security checked personnel on board, and where security levels in operation differ on board and ashore

It is therefore essential that Members provide for an allocation of these costs in their fixtures.

APPENDIX 27

A logical way may be for owners to pay the expenses and delays directly related to the ship's compliance with the ISPS Code. Charterers should pay those arising from employment of the ship i.e. additional port and cargo expenses.

Documentation and information

Owners must provide charterers with documentary evidence of their compliance with the ISPS Code, together with full contact details of their Company Security Officer. Owners are also required to maintain a Continuous Synopsis Record, which includes information regarding the ship's employment.

This information can only be exchanged with co-operation of the parties. For avoidance of doubt, it should be written into the charterparty. In addition, owners must not only be clear on the identity of their direct contracting parties, but must be able to identify any sub-charterers. Where the charterparty contains a liberty to sub-let, that clause must provide for this to be on condition that the sub-charterers' full details are obtained by charterers and passed up the contractual chain.

Pattern of trade- Calls at a non-ISPS port

Even when a ship is ISPS compliant, owners may still be penalised when she has visited a non-ISPS compliant port within her last ten port visits, or even has loaded cargo originating from a non-ISPS compliant port. Inspection, detention, removal or expulsion from the port, removal to another area, or denial of entry in the first place will inevitably give rise to delays, additional costs and losses for owners, even though the ship has remained ISPS compliant throughout.

Owners may wish to preserve the right to decline to comply with charterers' instructions where the ship is being asked to call at a port that is non-ISPS compliant, as this may affect not only future calls but also the ship's marketability. Alternatively, if appropriate, owners should agree adequate indemnities for calling at a non-ISPS compliant port, or in the event that a port becomes non-compliant while the ship is there.

Charterers should check the ship's trading history prior to fixing. If she has recently called at a non-ISPS compliant port, they should be guided by that.

Security levels and port safety

The ISPS Code provides that owners must produce a Ship Security Plan which should indicate the operational and physical security measures the ship itself should take to ensure it always operates at security level 1 (low risk). The Plan should also indicate the additional, or intensified, security measures the ship itself can take to move to and operate at security level 2 (medium risk) when instructed to do so. Furthermore, the Plan should indicate the possible preparatory actions the ship could take to allow prompt response to instructions that may be issued to the ship at security level 3 (high risk).

APPENDIX 27

How will these security levels affect the safety of the port? What happens if a vessel ship is ordered to a port which the owner or charter are aware, at the time of nomination, is operating at security level 2 (medium risk) or 3 (high risk)? Is there a specific or imminent threat to render the port unsafe? Can the owner exercise his right to reject the order and insist on fresh orders?

In most charterparties, there will be an express warranty on the part of the charterer as to the safety of the loading or discharging port. If not, it will be implied. The usual interpretation of warranty as to a safe port is that the charterer is warranting that, at the time of the nomination, the port or place is prospectively safe for the period of the ship's likely visit, in the absence of abnormal or unexpected events.

There are usually two different types of obligations relating to unsafe ports: Some charterparties oblige the charterer to send the ship to a port that is safe in fact. Others merely oblige the charterer to show the exercise of due diligence to investigate the safety of the port before directing the ship there. Previous case law provides some guidance on political unsafety. In the SAGA COB, charterers ordered the ship to Assab and Massawa. Eritrean guerrillas subsequently attacked the ship. Was the port was prospectively unsafe in view of the knowledge that there was known guerrilla activity on land? The Court of Appeal stated:

'The port will not be regarded as unsafe unless the political risk is sufficient for a reasonable ship owner or master to decline to send or sail his vessel there.'

The Court of Appeal did not regard that guerrilla activity was foreseeable as sufficient to turn the port into an unsafe port.

A port at security level 3, which is an exceptional risk of a security incident, is likely by definition to be an "unsafe" port, and perhaps also a port at security level 2. However, if adequate precautions are in place it may not necessarily render the port unsafe. Owners will have to examine all the circumstances known at the time of nomination, on a case by case basis, before deciding whether a port is unsafe or not.

In view of the above comments, Members should consider who should bear the extra costs of providing the ship on standby level 2 or 3 when required for any ports she visits.

Drafting ISPS Clauses.

The BIMCO Documentary Committee has produced an ISPS clause dealing with the basic obligations of owners and charterers in compliance with the ISPS Code. This may be used as a starting point but Members should also consider the cost and safety implications of providing the ship on standby level 2 or 3 and the need to balance the right to decline to call at non-ISPS compliant ports and the provision of adequate indemnities from charterers. Members in need of assistance can contact the Managers.

APPENDIX 27

For further information on any matters covered by Soundings, please contact the Managers

The MTSA broadly mirrors the ISPS Code. All ships over 100gt trading to the US must comply with the new US security rules. ISPS compliant foreign flag ships will be accepted by the US Coastguard as having complied with MTSA. However ships to which the ISPS Code does not apply, for example, those between 100gt and 500gt, must submit security plans. US Coastguard approval is required for plans for US flag ships.

Whilst the application and approval process under the ISPS Code and MTSA differ, the observations above on charterparty terms apply equally to ships trading to the USA which fall within the MTSA regime.

MOCK EXAMINATION

Do not turn to the next page until you have followed the suggestions below.

Overleaf is a sample examination paper In your own interest do not look at it yet but instead, do the same revision of the course as you would do for any examination.

On completing your revision, put away your notes, have pen and paper ready and set aside three hours when you will not be interrupted. In other words create as near as possible examination room conditions.

It is very strongly recommended that you hand write this mock examination. You will have to write the actual examination and many students find that it is difficult to write legibly for three hours without practice. If your writing is illegible you will lose marks. Examiners cannot mark what they cannot read.

Carry out the instructions on the question paper and send your answers to your tutor for marking. Make a note your start and finish times on the front of your answer paper.

THE INSTITUTE OF CHARTERED SHIPBROKERS

MOCK EXAM

Time allowed – Three hours

Answer any FIVE questions – All questions carry equal marks

1. Discuss the factors which influence the current tanker market and explain what longer term effects these factors could have on the future supply of tonnage.

2. What is the definition of Demurrage? Describe the essential information required to calculate demurrage, if incurred, by a tanker.

3. Explain, in full, the meaning of the two cargo descriptions given below and discuss how load line zones may affect the quantity described in (A) and how SG may affect the quantity described in (B):

    (a)   80,000 mt/5percent MOLOO 1-2 grades NH Crude and/or DPP WVNS.

    (b)   Part cargo min 40,000 mt CHOPT up to full cargo NDFCAPMQS max 3 grades WVNS CPP unleaded undarker 2.5 NPA average S.G. 0.78.

4. Using a size of your choice, sketch a modern clean product tanker showing the principal dimensions and characteristics. What are the main routes and cargoes for the size of tanker you have selected? What weather conditions and restrictions may be encountered on these routes?

5. In the tanker industry it is frequently impossible to present an original bill of lading at the port of discharge. Explain the problems this could cause for the Owner and how these may be overcome by the presentation of a Letter of Indemnity. What points must the L.o.I. cover?

6. Many tanker charters are now concluded with an agreement that the "Fixture Recap" will form the agreement on terms. Prepare a full "Fixture Recap" for a tanker cargo of your choice, loading in the Middle East Gulf. Fully explain the points that are included.

7. Select **two** of the following organisations, explain their role and what contribution they make to the tanker industry:

    WORLDSCALE   IMO   ITOPF

8. When fixing a tanker for a period time charter, what issues will the Ship Owner have to bear in mind when negotiating cargo and trading restrictions?